WESTERN DRAMA THROUGH THE AGES

WESTERN DRAMA THROUGH THE AGES

A Student Reference Guide

VOLUME 1

Edited by Kimball King

GREENWOOD PRESS

Westport, Connecticut • London

Library of Congress Cataloging-in-Publication Data

Western drama through the ages : a student reference guide / edited by Kimball King.
    p. cm.
Includes bibliographical references and index.
ISBN-13: 978-0-313-32934-0 (set : alk. paper)
ISBN-13: 978-0-313-32935-7 (vol. 1 : alk. paper)
ISBN-13: 978-0-313-32936-4 (vol. 2 : alk. paper)
1. Drama—History and criticism. 2. Theater—History. I. King, Kimball.
PN1721.W47 2007
809.2—dc22   2007010683

British Library Cataloguing in Publication Data is available.

Library of Congress Catalog Card Number: 2007010683
ISBN-10: 0–313–32934–6 (set)   ISBN-13: 978–0–313–32934–0 (set)
          0–313–32935–4 (vol. 1)   978–0–313–32935–7 (vol. 1)
          0–313–32936–2 (vol. 2)   978–0–313–32936–4 (vol. 2)

First published in 2007

Greenwood Press, 88 Post Road West, Westport, CT 06881
An imprint of Greenwood Publishing Group, Inc.
www.greenwood.com

Printed in the United States of America

The paper used in this book complies with the
Permanent Paper Standard issued by the National
Information Standards Organization (Z39.48–1984).

10 9 8 7 6 5 4 3 2 1

Contents

❧

Preface

SCOPE

Western Drama through the Ages: A Student Reference Guide is an overview of drama designed to reveal the density of the theatrical experience, primarily in Western countries from America and Europe to India. An interested reader can follow the trajectory of the theater from its beginnings to the present, understand the contributions of many countries and societies within those countries, and feel prepared to analyze plays in a more knowledgeable, sophisticated way. Drama is one of the most "social" of the arts, in that people generally attend plays with others and discuss the work afterward. Furthermore, it is possible to see a play without advance preparation. One need only to pursue further studies of the works one enjoys the most.

This guide surveys materials from about 500 years before the birth of Christ and attempts to present major theatrical developments up to the present day. It presents forty-five essays by thirty-nine contributors, many who are internationally acknowledged experts in their respective fields.

Certain decisions, which I believe were the correct ones, were made about these volumes. First, I wanted as many theater authorities as possible to write about their specialties. My intention was that each author would express his or her own viewpoint, even prejudices, which may have been gained from years of intense study of a subject. The heartfelt essay has always seemed to me more valuable than the homogenized version that attempts to please readers of all persuasions (and generally fails to do so). Also, too often theatrical techniques are overlooked in drama reference works. Essays by people working in the theater to-day comment effectively on the acting styles, costumes, directing, dramaturgy, stage design, and voice training.

Second, and most of all, I wanted this guide to be readable. I wanted anyone interested in plays to find descriptions of works or authors that were honest and informative. Certainly I hope that college students will find this volume useful, and I also hope to interest fledgling students, say those in high school, who are just beginning to appreciate the appeal of staged materials. I also wish general theatergoers and readers of dramatic literature to use this volume when they want to gain insight into a particular issue or a dramatic movement or concept, or a national or international dramatic contribution.

ARRANGEMENT

Western Drama through the Ages: A Student Reference Guide begins with four categories which the late Professor John Gassner, unquestionably a great theater authority, has called the major eras of dramatic history: Classical Drama, Renaissance Drama, French Neoclassical Drama, and Modern Drama. Two other eras, Medieval Drama and Restoration Drama, are discussed next.

The third section of this volume is to me notable: a selection of essays on national and regional dramas, usually discussing major plays and dramatists over the centuries in these countries. I wish, of course, that it would have been possible to include the theatrical history of every country, but it was necessary to limit the analyses. One notices immediately that neither American nor British drama is listed specifically in the section on national drama. It seemed redundant to create such sections when chapters on African American theater, Pinter's and Albee's plays, biblical drama, gay drama, musical theater, Southern U.S. drama, and out-door drama—among others—mention almost entirely American or British plays. Most of the essays in this section have been researched in depth by some of the world's most distinguished scholars, such as Professor Christoph Schweitzer on German drama, Professor George Woodyard on Latin American Drama, and Pro-fessor Jerry Wasserman on modern Canadian theater. Professors Grabowski on Polish drama, Ambros on Czechoslovakian theater, O'Malley on eighteenth cen-tury Russian drama, Lindheim on Chekhov, and Rao on Italian drama are also known for their expertise.

The fourth section includes an interesting mixture of movements and issues within the theater, including African American drama, biblical drama and contem-porary drama that grapples with spiritual belief in society, gay theater, issues of gender and theater, musical theater, and outdoor drama.

The fifth section, on important genres and styles, primarily of modern drama, ranges from discussions of comedy and tragedy to such types of modern drama as realism; surrealism; "in yer face" theater, which forces playgoers to confront violence and psychological problems of our times; the theater of the absurd; and more. A few modern playwrights, Edward Albee and Harold Pinter, the late Sarah Kane, Neil LaBute, and others, are discussed.

The final section of essays comprises an examination of theater in practice. Experienced professionals who have taught and worked in the areas of their essays have written on directing, acting, voice coaching, dramaturgy, costume design, and stages in theaters and playhouses.

FEATURES

Each essay includes a list of further reading, resources that will provide reading lists for those who wish to pursue a particular topic or national dramatic history. The volume closes with a general bibliography that I and most of the other scholars who contributed to this guide have studied, and a comprehensive index, so that readers may research the many details available to them in the entries.

No book on a field as rich and varied as the drama can cover every issue that might satisfy every reader. However, I believe that *Western Drama through the Ages: A Student Reference Guide* presents the most comprehensive, reader-friendly study of dramatic adventure available today. All the materials herein have been presented sincerely and thoughtfully. I believe the many contributors and I have presented a source of reading pleasure about important dramatic considerations for years to come.

ACKNOWLEDGMENTS

I wish first of all to thank Robert Gross, who has been my muse throughout this project and who offered constant encouragement, suggested formatting, and contributed three articles to the project. I appreciated the gracious permission of Jackson Bryer to draw upon his own research on drama. Milly Barranger, the retired chair of the Dramatic Arts Department at my university, the University of North Carolina at Chapel Hill, contributed a piece to this volume, and she and Mckay Coble, the current chair, pointed me in the right direction. Barranger, Bonnie Raphael, Karen Blansfield, Bobbie Owen and Julie Fishell, all member of UNC's Dramatic Arts department, contributed essays as well. Many thanks to Thomas Fahy and Lois Gordon for their encouragement in what seemed at times a daunting task. George Butler at Greenwood Press and Anne Thompson, also a Greenwood editor, deserve praise for their forbearance and supervision. All of my contributors have my gratitude. Finally, Mrs. Nina Wallace, who has over the years typed countless articles and books for me, provided exemplary aid at every turn.

PART I

Four Great Eras of Western Drama

๛

Classic Greek and Roman Drama

Brett M. Rogers

INTRODUCTION

Classical drama presents us with a terrible paradox. On the one hand, the characters of tragedy—such notables as blind Oedipus, vengeful Medea, defiant
Antigone—are familiar to modern readers of classical mythology, Shakespearean
tragedy, Freudian psychoanalysis, or the poetry of W.B. Yeats and T.S. Eliot.
No less familiar are the basic plots found in many classical tragedies and comedies—tales of the violation of social boundaries, of the rise and fall of individuals
both noble and humble. Nevertheless, despite its near ubiquitous presence in
modern Western culture, classical drama is equally an encounter with the strange,
an engagement with a foreign world whose practices we no longer follow
and whose values we rarely share. A vast gulf separates us from classical
Athens (490–323 B.C.), the Roman Republic (509–30 B.C.), and the Roman Empire
(30 B.C.–476 A.D.), to which time and place virtually all surviving classical drama
belongs. Moreover, in classical antiquity drama was not "theater" in any modern
sense, but a form of religious song offered in festivals lasting several days; in the
case of classical Athens, drama also functioned as a kind of civic performance
wherein poets and actors sought recognition and glory from their audience, their
fellow Athenian citizens. The fact that classical drama is both totally familiar and
utterly foreign leaves us in a paradoxical situation: how might we learn to read
these familiar dramas through new eyes? How might we take hold of what we have
previously learned about classical drama, set it aside temporarily, and instead
imagine ourselves as members of the Athenian or Roman audience immersed in

the ancient dramatic experience? Only when we confront this paradox can we begin to discern the spirit of classical drama, to recognize its stunning complexity and awe-inspiring beauty, and to understand why classical drama has wielded an immeasurable influence on the ensuing 2,300 years of the Western dramatic and literary traditions.

WHAT IS CLASSICAL DRAMA?

Any discussion of classical drama must begin by asking what we mean when we use the word *drama*. We often take for granted the definition of *drama*, but *drama* can mean several quite different things. For example, consider all the various meanings *drama* might have in a video store. First of all, drama refers to a category used to classify movies; in this instance, drama indicates "a serious narrative," as opposed to other categories like comedy (a humorous narrative), action (an exciting narrative), or foreign (a narrative in another language). When a serious narrative takes a turn for the worse, it can mean something even more specific, "a narrative leading to catastrophe," "a tragedy." It comes as no surprise that film adaptations of Shakespeare's tragedies, which often end in murder and death, are found in the drama section of video stores (although we might expect them to show up in the action section instead). Yet even this Shakespearean example reminds us that drama also means "a prose or verse composition that can be adapted for stage performance," as in the title of the very book you are reading now, *Western Drama Through the Ages*. According to this definition, we might say that everything in our video store counts as drama, including comedies, musicals, and independent films, since all of these productions start out as written compositions and are performed on some kind of stage (be it a stage in an official theater, a sound stage in Hollywood, or a scene staged in the middle of park). Yet drama does not necessarily refer to a narrative or an artistic composition, but can even mean "an event that elicits emotional response." If two people in our video store are trying to choose a movie for rental and in the process one of them argues with the other's choice perhaps too hysterically, the other person may accuse the first person of being a "drama queen" for making too much fuss out of an insignificant event. *Drama* thus encompasses a remarkably broad number of distinct, although related, concepts in English.

While ancient Greek and Roman drama touches upon all of these meanings of drama (a tragedy, a composition for the stage, or an emotionally evocative event), the very word *drama*, which comes from the ancient Greek language, means something slightly but significantly different. In Greek *drama* means "deed," "action," and consequently "performance," and derives from the Greek verb *dran*, "to do." The fact that *drama* means "action" reminds us, who usually encounter classical dramas in scripts and books, of the original production context of these tragedies and comedies, performed onstage and in front of an audience. While *drama* emphasizes the action performed onstage in a classical drama, the language used to describe the audience emphasizes the importance of viewing drama. English *audience* derives from Latin *audio* (to hear, to listen) and stresses only the auditory experience, whereas in Greek the audience members are called *theatai* (viewers), which stresses the visual experience of viewing drama. Moreover, *theatai* shares the same root *thea-* (see, view) with the word *theatron* (viewing-place), from which comes English *theater*. In defining *drama* and *theater* in terms of "action" and "viewing," we modern readers of classical drama face the challenge of both imagining away the static words we read on the page and imagining instead the visual experience of viewing action performed onstage.

It is important to note that when we define *drama* as "action" this does not mean *drama* is "an exciting narrative" featuring the violence and murder found in modern action films. Despite their frequently violent plots, Greek dramas never showed such violence to the viewing audience. To choose one prominent example, in Sophocles's famous tragedy *Oedipus Tyrannus* (often known by its Latin title *Oedipus Rex* or the English translation *Oedipus the King*), Oedipus has already killed his father and committed incest with his mother long before the beginning of the drama. Nor does Oedipus blind himself onstage, in front of the eyes of the audience, but he does so offstage, leaving the horror and impiety of his self-blinding to the imagination or "mind's eye" of audiences. The audience never actually views the actions of murder and blinding, but only witnesses the reports of such actions and the suffering that results. To be sure, some forms of classical drama did feature varying degrees of violence (such as Greek and Roman comedy, mime, and Roman pantomime), but the point remains that the term *drama* does not by definition require such excitement and classical Greek drama certainly avoided such violence. The study of classical drama therefore not only requires us to think in terms of what we can see, but also prompts us to consider what we cannot, in fact, see.

WHAT IS ANCIENT GREEK DRAMA?

Ancient Greek drama consists of three kinds of plays: tragedy, satyr-drama, and comedy. The first tragedies are said to have been performed in 534 B.C. at the festival of Dionysus (the City or Great Dionysia) in Athens; satyr-dramas were added in 502 or 501 B.C., and comedies were first officially produced in Athens in 486 B.C. Greek drama flourished in Athens in the fifth century B.C. under such dramatists as the tragic poets Aeschylus, Sophocles, and Euripides, as well as the comic poet Aristophanes. Greek drama remained popular into the fourth and third centuries B.C. in the hands of such dramatists as the comic poet Menander. While Athens appears to have been the primary locus of dramatic activity in classical Greece, comedies were also performed from the beginning of the fifth century B.C. onward in Syracuse (on the island of Sicily, home to numerous Greek colonies), and some tragic poets are known to have travelled and produced dramas in places like Sicily and Macedonia (north of Greece). Only forty-five ancient Greek dramas survive complete today—thirty-two tragedies, one satyr-drama, and twelve comedies—as well as a multitude of fragments of drama, ranging in length from one word to several hundred lines; these fragments have been preserved in various literary sources and on the scraps of papyrus discovered in the last two centuries in the dry sands of Egypt.

The origins of ancient Greek drama generate a problem that resists straight-forward answer, in part due to the paucity of evidence available to us. No source offers a continuous narrative about the development and production of drama until some two centuries after the first tragedies were produced in 534 B.C. Nor is it easy to glean information from the dramatic texts themselves, since the earliest surviving drama to which we can assign a date is Aeschylus's tragedy *Persians*, performed in 472 B.C., sixty-two years after the first tragedies. Some information comes from fragmentary inscriptions found in the theater of Dionysus in Athens; these inscriptions contain records reaching back as far as 502 or 501 B.C. (at which time the City Dionysia was reorganized), but they do nothing more than list the names of the producer (*choregos*) and poet who were victorious in the annual dramatic competitions. Scattered remarks in literary sources dating to the late fifth century B.C. onward also offer information, but these sources too are woefully incomplete.

Much of our knowledge about the origins of drama comes from the philosopher and scholar Aristotle (384–322 B.C.), whose *Poetics* provides the earliest surviving and fullest account of the origins of Greek poetry, including in his discussion tragedy, satyr-drama, and comedy. According to Aristotle, tragedy developed out of a species of choral poetry known as dithyramb. Choral poetry refers to a tradition of songs performed by a dancing collective or *choros* (chorus) of several men, young men, or young women, dating back to the seventh century B.C. (if not much earlier). In the case of dithyramb, a chorus of either fifty men or fifty young boys performed the songs specifically in honor of Dionysus, the Greek god of wine who was associated with such activities as male fertility and ecstatic worship. Aristotle claims that tragedy developed out of the preludes of dithyramb, when the chorus leader who started the dithyramb (called the *exarchon*) became a distinct character, separate from the rest of the chorus and speaking in dialogue with them—a point reflected in the Greek word for actor, *hypokritês*, which literally means answerer (and which only later attained the pejorative meaning found in its English descendant *hypocrite*). Our sources credit several poets with the invention of tragedy, including a dithyrambic poet Arion and the tragic poet Thespis. Thespis is traditionally named as the victor of the first dramatic competition in 534 B.C. and thus the father of drama (hence actors are also referred to as thespians).

The origin of comedy faces far greater obscurity. While Aristotle's account of tragic and epic poetry survives in the first book of the *Poetics,* his account of comic poetry, which Aristotle promises will comprise the second book of the *Poetics,* does not survive today, if it was ever written at all. Aristotle also says in the first book of the *Poetics* that the history of comedy had been forgotten, although he nevertheless proceeds to offer several possible sources for comedy: a Dorian tradition of poetry either from Megara on the Greek mainland or Sicilian Megara (known for one Epicharmus, a composer of comic mimes); mysterious "phallic songs," of which we know nothing; and invective poetry composed in iambic trimeter known as *iambos.*

Aristotle's account suggests that we might think of Greek drama not just as drama but also as poetry, and prompts us to consider Greek drama in relation to other forms of Greek poetry, to dithyramb and choral poetry, as well as to the epic poetry of Homer, the didactic poetry of Hesiod, and the lyric poetry (that is, poetry accompanied by the lyre) of such figures as Archilochus and Sappho. Greek drama's relationship to epic seems especially important, not only because Aristotle claims elsewhere in the *Poetics* that some epic poets were drawn to compose tragic poetry, but because many dramas utilize the same stories and plots—the same *muthoi* (myths)—as does Greek epic poetry. The tragic poet Sophocles is described in one source as "most Homeric," while another source records that Aeschylus himself is said to have referred to his tragedies as "slices of the feast of Homer." The comedy of Aristophanes also draws on the traditional *muthoi* of Greek poetry, although often to comic or satirical effect. In *Peace* (421 B.C.), Aristophanes takes the mythical ascent of the Greek hero Bellerophon, who rode into the heavens on the back of the winged horse Pegasus, and parodies this mythical journey by having his protagonist, Trygaeus, ride up to heaven on the back of a gigantic dung beetle. It is incumbent upon the modern reader of ancient Greek drama, then, to view drama as choral poetry with epic themes, or, more generally, as a manifestation of Greek traditional poetry.

While Aristotle is right to locate the origins of drama in Greek poetry, some scholars have doubted other facets of the account in the *Poetics* and have looked to other sources of evidence. Aristotle passes over the most likely source for the genre of comedy (called *komoidia* in Greek), the scurrilous poetry sung by a *komos* or band of revelers wandering festively through town at night; notably, the *komos* was also part of the festivities surrounding the City Dionysia. As for tragedy, the historian Herodotus alludes to the possible existence of tragic choruses performed by the people of Sicyon in honor of the sufferings of Adrastos, a legendary king of Sicyon; only later were the choruses transferred to honor Dionysus by the tyrant Cleisthenes of Sicyon (c. 575–550 B.C.), well before the first dramatic competition in Athens. The connection between tragic choruses, Dionysian worship, and a tyrant is suggestive, if only because it evokes a similar connection that exists in the Athenian version of the origin of drama. If the alleged date of the first dramatic competition in Athens (534 B.C.) is accurate, this means that drama was first produced during the tyranny of Peisistratus (546–527 B.C.), under whose rule the arts first flourished in Athens.

Some scholars press further a politically charged origin for Greek drama, and claim drama as a civic, even democratic, poetic form. One line of thought holds that drama only began in Athens around 502 or 501 B.C., at which time the City Dionysia was reorganized and to which time period belong the first dramatic victories found on the inscriptions from the theater of Dionysus. These scholars see Athenian drama as a direct response to a specific political event, the transformation of Athens into a radical democracy in 507 B.C., after the Athenians sent the tyrant Hippias (son of Peisistratus, ruled 527–510 B.C.) into exile and rebuffed a Spartan attempt to install a new tyrant. In this view, it is critical that Greek drama was performed at the City Dionysia, a festival honoring of Dionysus Eleuthereus, "Dionysus who brings freedom"—in this case, freedom from political oppression. Even if Greek drama originally did belong to the period of the tyranny of Peisistratos and therefore antedated the rise of the Athenian democracy, it is still possible that citizens of fifth century democratic Athens ignored the origins of Greek drama and re-interpreted these performances as civic, political, and democratic events.

The Performance of Ancient Greek Drama

In classical Athens, Greek dramas were performed primarily at festivals honoring the god Dionysus: the Rural or Lesser Dionysia, held in early January; the Lenaia or festival in honor of Dionysus Lenaios in late January; finally, the aforementioned City or Great Dionysia in honor of Dionysus Eleuthereus in late March. Because the stormy winters in Greece prevented travel and trade by sea, the Rural Dionysia and Lenaia were locals-only festivals for the Athenians, whereas the more moderate spring climate helped make the City Dionysia something of an international occasion, drawing visitors from throughout Greece. The weather conditions surrounding these festivals might actually explain at least one particular feature of comedy in the fifth century B.C. (what is commonly called Old Comedy), its highly topical nature, delighting in *ad hominem* attacks and inside jokes—namely, the kind of humor that only the local Athenian audience would understand. Notably, the Rural Dionysia and Lenaia featured comic performances only (although tragedies without satyr-dramas were eventually added to the Lenaia in the 430s B.C.), while the City Dionysia showcased a wide variety of dithyrambic, comic, and tragic performances as early as 486 B.C. (when comedy was officially added to the festival).

In order to understand the importance of performance context for the interpretation of Greek drama, let us consider the example of the City Dionysia and the various events related to the festival. The City Dionysia was at once a religious, civic, and poetic festival. Two days before the contests began the *proagon* (pre-contest) took place, at which the dramatic poets and performers appeared to announce the names of and offer hints about their productions. The next day, a procession escorted the statue of Dionysus Eleuthereus into Athens, including animal sacrifice, public feasting, and possibly late-night revelry (the *komos*). Five days of poetic competition ensued. The competitions also began with a series of both religious and civic rituals: a purificatory pig sacrifice, libations poured by the Athenian generals, a display of tribute (money received) from the allies of Athens, the reading aloud of the names of those citizens who received crowns of honor from the city, and a presentation of orphans called *epheboi* whose fathers had fallen in war and who were raised at the expense of the polis.

On the first official day of the City Dionysia, audiences watched dithyrambic contests in which ten choruses—one chorus for each of the ten tribes in Athens —competed for first prize before the eyes of the entire polis; the competition featured both a men's and a boys' division. On the second day, five comic poets competed, each producing one comedy. Tragic competitions followed on the last three days of the festival; each day one tragic poet produced three tragedies, followed by one satyr-drama. Sometimes the trilogy and satyr-drama formed a related, coherent narrative (as in the case of our only surviving trilogy, the *Oresteia* of Aeschylus and its now-lost satyr-drama *Proteus*), but this seems to have been left to the prerogative of the tragic poet. After all three tragic trilogies had been performed, the ten Athenian generals voted for the best dithyrambic chorus, comedy, and tragic trilogy. They placed their votes into a jar, from which five votes were selected by lot to declare a winner. The victorious poet and producer or *choregos* (a wealthy citizen selected by the polis to fund the production) were awarded with crowns of laurel or ivy symbolizing their victory, just as victorious athletes in the ancient Olympic games were awarded with crowns (as were the victors in the 2004 Olympic games held in Athens). In addition, votes were cast for the best *protagonistes*, the "first actor" who had performed the leading roles in one set of trilogies. The prestige of such a victory cannot be underestimated, given that these competitions were attended by as many as 14,000 to 17,000 people—the number of people who could fit into the theater of Dionysus.

The theater of Dionysus was an open-air theater located next to the temple of Dionysus on the southeastern slope of the Acropolis, the fortified citadel of Athens; this location offered the audience a view of the city, located below in the plains, while behind the audience the Acropolis and its temples loomed, including the spectacularly imposing Parthenon (constructed 447–432 B.C.). The theater centered on a large circular space known as the *orchestra,* in which the chorus performed. The *skene,* a temporary wooden stage building on the open side of the *orchestra,* served as a space for the actors to perform and as a backdrop for the dramas; the *skene* only became a permanent physical feature of the theater in the 330s B.C., when the first stone theater in Athens was built. A door in the center of the *skene* allowed characters in the dramas to enter and exit into an imagined interior space (for example, a palace, temple, or cave), while passageways to either side of the *skene* known as *parodoi* (singular *parodos*, "side-entrance") both enabled the entrance and exit for the chorus (hence their entrance song is referred to as the *parodos*) and allowed characters to enter from elsewhere within the dramatized polis or from lands foreign to the dramatic setting. (For those curious about the space and acoustics of a Greek theater, performances of many ancient Greek dramas are still produced in the well-preserved theater at Epidaurus.) These conventions do not require dramas to respect the so-called "unity of space"—the *Eumenides* of Aeschylus features three different settings (the temple of Apollo at Delphi, the temple of Athena in Athens, and the Areopagus or "Hill of Ares" in Athens), and Aristophanic comedies change settings at a dizzying pace—but many tragedies of the fifth century B.C. only featured one dramatic setting and comedies of the later fourth century B.C. seem to have made this practice permanent.

The large audience viewed these dramas from the *theatron* (viewing place). In the fifth century B.C., audiences sat either on the ground or on wooden benches; it was not until somewhere between 338 and 330 B.C. that the seats, and the entire theater of Dionysus, were rebuilt in stone. The audience included Athenian male citizens, resident aliens called metics, and foreign visitors. There is no certain evidence whether Athenian women and slaves were permitted to attend the dramatic performances at the City Dionysia. This uncertainty provides a serious interpretive stumbling block to our understanding of Greek drama. For example, in the *Medea* of Euripides (431 B.C.), Medea criticizes men for thinking that women, who were accustomed to live and work within the household, lead a life without danger; she asserts that "three times I'd rather stand in battle than give birth once!" How would such a comment attacking the military ethos central to ancient Greek life, to definitions of manhood and citizenship, have been received by the audience? Were there women amidst the audience able to assent to such an incendiary opinion? Or were women absent from the theater, enabling a space for dissenting males to ignore such remarks? Certainly the events of the tragic stage reached the ears (if not the eyes) of women, as is parodied in Aristophanes's *Thesmophoriazusae* (Women of the Thesmophoria Festival, 411 B.C.), in which comedy the women of Athens hold an assembly in order to plot revenge against Euripides for his representation of women in his tragedies. In a similar vein, the modern reader must consider the numerous representations—sometimes flattering, sometimes parodic—of slaves in Greek drama.

The production of a given Greek drama required a substantial number of individuals. Besides the poet who composed the drama and the *choregos* who produced and paid for it, a drama consisted of chorus (twelve or fifteen members for a tragic chorus, twenty-four for a comic chorus), a limited number of actors (as many as three actors in a tragedy, four to five in a comedy), and a musician to play the reed-pipes or *aulos* (an instrument akin to the oboe). It is unknown who created the costumes and masks used in these productions, or how technical aspects of the performance may have been managed, such as the deployment of either the *ekkyklema*, a small stage set on rollers that could be pushed out to reveal a scene from the interior of the *skene*, or the *mechane*, a crane on top of the *skene* that could be used for the appearances of gods, for Medea's extraordinary escape in a chariot drawn by dragons at the end of *Medea*, or for Trygaeus's ascent into heaven upon the dung beetle in *Peace*. If the same actors were used throughout a given tragic trilogy and its satyr-drama, the City Dionysia would require the participation of no fewer than 1,200 Athenian citizens. And it was in fact a requirement that the performers be Athenian, male citizens.

The modern reader of drama will notice that no extant tragedy features as few as three characters nor does any comedy feature as few as four characters. Yet Aristotle states in his *Poetics* that tragedy initially only featured one *hypokrites* set against the chorus, and Aeschylus added a second actor and Sophocles added a third actor (other evidence suggests that this last addition occurred during the 460s B.C.). How, then, were these dramas performed? This system demands that actors had to play multiple roles within a single performance. When we combine this requirement with the knowledge that the *protagonistes* of each trilogy also competed for a crown (which suggests that the judges and audience would have watched at least their performances quite carefully), some fascinating implications for performance emerge. For instance, in the *Philoctetes* of Sophocles (409 B.C.), the plot revolves around the attempt of Neoptolemus, son of the hero Achilles, to persuade the hero Philoctetes to hand over the bow of Heracles, which is prophesied to be essential to victory in the Trojan War; unfortunately, when the Greeks had originally sailed to Troy, a snake bit Philoctetes' foot and the wound festered, leading the Greeks to abandon Philoctetes alone on the island of Lemnos. The drama begins when Neoptolemus arrives on Lemnos in the company of the trickster-hero Odysseus; Odysseus explains that Neoptolemus must trick Philoctetes into giving him the bow, then return to Troy. Instead, Neoptolemus takes pity on the wounded but noble Philoctetes, and near the end of the drama, the two decide to reject the Greek cause at Troy and to hold their own. Suddenly the god Heracles, original possessor of Philoctetes' bow, appears out of nowhere above the pair (a convention known by the Latin phrase *deus ex machina* or "god from the machine," referring to the *mechane* or "crane" used for many gods' aerial appearances) and commands the pair to fight in Troy. Many critics have taken Heracles' injunction as a Sophoclean assertion of the exigencies of fate or of the nobility of the Trojan War; however, dramatic convention requires that the actor who plays the trickster Odysseus must also play the deified Heracles, and one cannot help but wonder if contemporary audiences, realizing that the same actor plays both characters, suspected Heracles to be the character Odysseus in disguise, tricking the pair to go to Troy. Since we know almost nothing about the actual staging, masks, or costumes of *Philoctetes,* this must remain pure conjecture, but such possibilities in performance can change a tragedy embracing heroic nobility into a disconcerting farce, altering drastically our understanding of a given Greek drama.

Greek Tragedy and Satyr-Drama

Our knowledge of Greek tragedy derives primarily from the tragedies of three tragic poets: Aeschylus, Sophocles, and Euripides. These three dramatists collectively composed a total of almost 300 dramas, but only thirty-two tragedies and one satyr-drama survive, all dating to the period 472–401 B.C., a mere seventy-one years out of more than two centuries of ancient Greek drama. While we also know the names of various other tragic poets, such as Thespis and Agathon (the latter of whom appears as a character in both Aristophanes's *Women of the Thesmophoria* and Plato's *Symposium*), the tragedies of these other poets are almost entirely lost to us. Thus when we discuss the spirit of Greek tragedy, we can only discuss this spirit in terms of the dramas of these lone three individuals who have subsequently become icons of Greek tragedy, in part because they are all that has survived during the last two millennia.

There is one more issue to consider in seeking the spirit of Greek tragedy. We have explored the Greek definition of *drama,* but *tragedy,* called *tragoidia* in ancient Greek, also merits consideration. *Tragoidia* derives from the words *tragos* (goat) and *ode* (song, from which derives English *ode*); thus *tragoidia* means "goat-song." What exactly this goat-song stands for remains unclear. Is this a "song of the goat," a drama performed either by actors dressed as goats, or, according to one radical theory, drama performed by adolescent males (the *epheboi*) colloquially called *goats* for their stinking breath and randy behavior? Or does goat-song mean "song for the goat," meaning that dramatists competed to win the prize of a goat? Or perhaps goat-song means "song at the goat," telling us that tragedies were performed at a goat sacrifice? Several possible interpretations exist for this puzzling goat-song. On the one hand, Dionysus was associated with satyrs, mythical creatures who were half-men and either half-horse or half-goat. Satyrs were known for their drunken and libidinous behavior (what we might identify as "Dionysian behavior"), so perhaps the term *tragoidia* preserves this connection between Dionysus and his followers, the satyrs. The fact that tragedies were always performed with a concluding satyr-drama featuring a chorus of satyrs might reinforce this connection. On the other hand, the festival of Dionysus seems to have included a goat sacrifice, so this might validate the meanings "song for the goat" (as a prize to sacrifice) or "song at the (sacrifice of the) goat." Regard-less of the precise interpretation of goat-song, the word *tragoidia* alludes to the role of ritual and sacrifice surrounding the performance of Greek drama, which in turn emphasizes the importance of ritual in Greek drama; the characters in most Greek dramas concern themselves with the proper performance of rituals, such as sacrificing to the gods, pouring libations to the dead, completing marriage rites, or purifying the community of the pollution incurred from an act of murder. Perhaps most importantly to any readers of Greek tragedy, *tragoidia* does not indicate whether a given drama is *tragic* or *a serious narrative*.

This is not to say that Greek tragedies did not confront serious issues; rather, Greek tragedies confronted some of the most difficult issues of their times, probing questions of race, religion, morality, social justice, and politics. The seven surviv-ing tragedies of Sophocles (c. 496–406 B.C.) have captivated audiences for centu-ries for their bold explorations of human destiny and the nature of free will. *Oedipus Tyrannus* (c. 429–425 B.C.) famously tells the story of Oedipus, the man who solved the riddle of the Sphinx and became king of Thebes, as he seeks to rid his city of a plague resulting from the pollution of the unpunished (and unsolved) murder of the previous king, Laius. What starts out as an inquiry into murder leads to the revelation that Oedipus, in an attempt to avert a prophecy pre-dicting he would kill his father and marry his mother, has unwittingly committed both the murder of his father Laius and incest with his mother Jocasta. In the revelation and grief of such horrors, Oedipus retains his nobility through an act of self-mutilation, gouging out his own eyes, and by expelling himself from Thebes in order to rid the city of the plague. Oedipus's most strange and cruel fate prompts several questions: is this the punishment a king deserves for seeking to protect his city? Or is this the punishment for seeking knowledge? Are all humans incapable of escaping fate, including great kings and clever men like Oedipus? Is this what it means to be human? There are no easy answers to these questions, but, then again, that is precisely the source of the *tragedy* in *Oedipus Tyrannus*; Oedipus has become king through his ability to solve riddles, but destroys his rule by failing to solve the riddle of his own life.

A similarly bloody fate awaits another *tyrannus* who seeks to protect Thebes, Creon (Oedipus's brother-in-law), in Sophocles' *Antigone* (c. 442/1 B.C.). Creon's ruin ensues when he is determined to punish anyone who will bury the corpse of the expelled king Polyneices, Creon's own nephew. Consequently, Creon's niece Antigone attempts to bury the body but is caught. In what follows, Creon and Antigone lay bare the conflicts at the very heart of ancient Greek custom and law, primarily the conflict between religious piety exemplified in custom and civic duty manifest in obedience to the law. It is intriguing that, in the ancient Greek language, the term *nomos* encapsulates both the concept of "custom" and "law," thus part of the conflict in *Antigone* revolves around determining the meaning of *nomos* that is best for the polis. Perhaps the most remarkable aspect of *Antigone*, however, lies in its female protagonist, who defies Athenian stereotypes about the role of women in society and voices powerful opposition to Creon's regime. In subsequent centuries Antigone has become an icon of familial loyalty and female determination in the face of tyrannical (male) adversity.

We started our discussion of ancient Greek drama with an injunction to see how Greek drama is strange and foreign to our own views. Indeed, this injunction comes from Greek drama itself, which often uses this technique to question its beliefs and values. The earliest surviving Greek drama and the only surviving Greek drama about an actual historical topic, Aeschylus's *Persians* (472 B.C.), was performed only seven years after the Persians had attempted to invade Greece and had ransacked Athens. *Persians* looks at the role of death and grief through the eyes of the enemies themselves, offering an almost sympathetic view of the Persians' failed invasion and the ensuing loss of life. Fifty-seven years later, the Athenians would have their own empire and bring violence against other Greek cities, including the execution of the neutral inhabitants of the island of Melos in 418 B.C. and an invasion of Sicily in the summer of 415 B.C. In the midst of such acts, Euripides would produce *Trojan Women* (415 B.C.), a drama showing the harsh treatment of the women and children who survived the sack of Troy. The former queen Hecuba watches as her family is torn apart, her daughter Cassandra is driven mad, her daughter-in-law Andromache is dragged away as a slave, and her grandson Astyanax (son of Andromache and the famous Trojan warrior Hector) is murdered, thrown from the ruined citadel of Troy. It is hard not to see *Trojan Women* as a criticism about the brutality of war, if not an outright antiwar tragedy (indeed, the play was revived in New York during protests over the American invasion of Iraq in 2003). Neither *Persians* nor *Trojan Women* rejoice in the victories of the Greeks; rather both use the suffering and devastation of an enemy to show the consequences of violence and warfare.

Only one trilogy survives complete from antiquity, the *Oresteia* of Aeschylus (first produced in 458 B.C.). The *Oresteia* provides a unique opportunity to see how the complexities of morality, justice, and law could evolve over the course of a single trilogy. In the opening play, *Agamemnon* the king of Argos (from whom the play takes its title) returns home after a ten-year absence while fighting in the Trojan War. We learn that Agamemnon sacrificed his own daughter Iphigeneia before the war and he has annihilated Troy. Agamemnon's entrance halfway through the tragedy features an awkward welcome by his wife Clytemnestra, who convinces Agamemnon to enter the palace treading upon a crimson carpet. This carpet vividly symbolizes the rivers of blood that will spill throughout this trilogy, most immediately in the murder of Agamemnon (offstage) by Clytemnestra and her secret lover, Aegisthus, an exiled cousin who holds a grudge against Agamemnon (Agamemnon's father Atreus once tricked Aegisthus's father

Thyestes into eating his own children, Aegisthus's brothers). The cycle of violence continues into the second play of the trilogy, *Libation Bearers,* when Agamemnon's son Orestes returns to Argos seven years later and seeks to avenge his father's murder. This play too ends in murder—this time, the double murders of Aegisthus and Clytemnestra by Orestes—but this act does not end the cycle of vengeance, for Orestes is in turn pursued by the *Erinyes* or "Furies," archaic spirits who exact revenge on the behalf of wronged mothers. Thus *Agamemnon* and *Libation Bearers* ask the audience to consider which side has acted with justice: the rightful but brutal king who has killed his own daughter? The mother who has lost her daughter but has taken a lover and thus violated her role as wife and queen? The son who seeks to avenge his father by killing his mother and uncle, even though his father has murdered his sister? Is there any form of justice or law that will end this cycle of bloodshed?

Aeschylus finishes the trilogy with an astounding conclusion in the *Eumenides*. To resolve the conflict between Orestes and the Furies, the goddess Athena invents Greece's first homicide court and selects a jury of Athenians to judge the case on the Areopagus. During the trial, the god Apollo makes a controversial argument that Orestes had to avenge Agamemnon since the father is the only true biological parent, whereas the mother merely carries the offspring, pointing to Athena herself as proof of this (Zeus gave birth to Athena from his own head). The Furies remain unconvinced, as well as half the jury; the trial ends in a tied vote, and Athena, declaring that she will always side with fathers over mothers, pronounces Orestes acquitted of matricide. The Furies threaten to destroy Athens, so Athena offers them a role as protectors of the polis and bribes them with cult worship, transforming the Furies into the Eumenides (hence the play's title). With such a conclusion Aeschylus ends the cycle of blood vengeance with the Athenian homicide court, the violence of archaic vengeance goddesses with the rational justice of the young goddess Athena, and the brutal monarchy of Agamemnon and murderous tyranny of Aegisthus with a declaration of the virtues of democracy in Athens. However other questions arise: does Athena's law court actually replace the old system of vengeance and resolve feuds? What does it mean that Athena's verdict requires the aid of religious cult and good, old-fashioned bribery? Is the *Oresteia* a praise of the virtues of Athenian democracy, or a lament for the days when the elite court of the Areopagos had greater control of Athenian law, control the court had lost just three years before in 461 B.C.? Does Athenian democracy implicitly advocate citizens to deny the importance of mothers? The *Oresteia* thus leaves its audience unsettled and with an array of difficult questions to consider. If we must define "the spirit of Greek tragedy," perhaps it is this unsettled spirit, this epic and often tragic struggle to understand the complexities and limitations of human action and divine injunction.

Greek Comedy: Aristophanes and "Old Comedy"

Where Greek tragedy basks in the failures and limits of humanity, Greek comedy revels in the potential greatness of humankind, or, at least, the potential for happiness. In fact, *komoidia*, the Greek word for the genre of comedy, literally means "song of the revelers" and refers to the *komos*, a ritual in which bands of men wandered around the city singing and drinking in celebration. While our evidence for Greek comedy in the fifth century B.C., what came to be called Old Comedy, is limited to the eleven surviving comedies of Aristophanes (career 427–c. 385 B.C.) and a small collection of various comic fragments, it is clear that comedy functioned as a witty and incisive voice for the polis, decrying the ineptitude of arrogant politicians while exalting the potential greatness of the Athenian citizen.

The comedies of Aristophanes vary wildly in dramatic setting and in theme. Many plays primarily satirize a single target: inept and corrupt politicians (*Knights,* produced in 424 B.C.), the "new education" of the late fifth century B.C. (*Clouds* in 423 B.C.), the law courts (*Wasps* in 422 B.C.), or even the tragic poet Euripides (*Women of the Thesmophoria* in 411 B.C., *Frogs* in 404 B.C.). Of course, no one is safe in the world of Aristophanic comedy, as our poet takes shot at young elite males, foreigners, women, and even the elderly. Aristophanes's biggest target, however, is war itself. He repeatedly offers antiwar comedies, such as *Acharnians* (425 B.C.), *Peace* (421 B.C.), and, most notably, *Lysistrata* (411 B.C.). This reflects the ongoing exhaustion that some Athenians no doubt felt during the protracted Peloponnesian War (431–404 B.C.) that Athens waged against the Spartans and their allies, as well as against an increasing number of Athens's own defecting allies. Indeed, *Lysistrata* captures this frustration in vivid fashion. In the comedy, the women of Greece have grown tired of the Peloponnesian War and the ongoing absence of their husbands, who are always on campaign. The Athenian Lysistrata thus convinces both Athenian and Spartan women to stage a sex strike until their husbands put an end to the war. While *Lysistrata* delights in scenes of both great innuendo and incredibly frank sexualized banter, the play also offers a fantasy about the possibility that the world might just be a better place if the women were in control. In the end, however, the men make peace, everyone makes love, and the natural order of things is restored. On stage, *Lysistrata* ends well for the Athenians; in the real world, the war lasted another seven years.

Drama in the Fourth Century B.C.: Tragic Revivals, Menander, and "New Comedy"

Athens lost the Peloponnesian War to Sparta in 404 B.C. and became an oligarchy ruled by a bloodthirsty group of men we now refer to as the Thirty Tyrants.

Although the Thirty Tyrants were deposed and democracy was restored one year later in 403 B.C., Athens never quite recovered. It may only be mere coincidence, but Greek drama too started to take on a decidedly different character at this same time. The two surviving comedies of Aristophanes from the early fourth century B.C., *Women of the Ecclesia* (c. 393–391 B.C.) and *Wealth* (388 B.C.), show hints of change; while the plots of both plays bear some similarities to Aristophanes' earlier comedies (especially *Women of the Ecclesia*, in which the Athenian women stage a take over of the Athenian government reminiscent of *Lysistrata*), the more fantastic elements found in plays like *Clouds* or *Frogs* are greatly muted. The chorus that had played such a central structural role in fifth century drama has almost completely disappeared in these plays, suggesting that the collective voice of the polis was gradually stepping off the dramatic stage. In a similar vein, the production of Greek tragedies seems to have significantly diminished, and, with the possible exception of the *Rhesus*, dubiously attributed to Euripides, we have no surviving tragedy from the fourth century.

Greek drama, of course, did not come to a complete halt in the fourth century B.C. Interest in fifth century tragedy led to revivals of the plays of Aeschylus, Sophocles, and Euripides throughout the fourth century, and in the 330s B.C. the Athenian statesman Lycurgus successfully passed a motion to collect copies of the scripts of these three tragedians and to place them in the Athenian archives. This legislation thus marked the first step in a long historical process that has led to the survival of Aeschylus, Sophocles, and Euripides into the present day. Lycurgus not only made possible the survival of fifth century tragedy, but also the survival of the theatrical space itself, for he also built the first permanent stone theater in Athens, which can still be seen today on the northeastern slope of the Acropolis.

While tragedy primarily survived in the form of revival in the fourth century B.C., Greek comedy continued to thrive. A variety of later sources inform us that something called "Middle Comedy" gained much popularity in Athens, although no comedy from this period survives today. Nor does much "New Comedy" survive, the direct successor of Middle Comedy and a dramatic form of immense popularity throughout the remainder of antiquity. We know of various comic poets, such as Alexis, Diphilus, and Philemon, but the great popularity of New Comedy was principally due to the success of the comedies of Menander (342/1–292/1 B.C.), whose influence rivals, if not outstrips, the impact of the Greek tragedians. Nevertheless, despite Menander's popularity and influence, only one of his comedies, the *Dyscolos* (variously translated *Old Cantankerous* or *The Miser* and first produced in 316 B.C.), survives wholly intact, recovered as recently as 1957 from an Egyptian papyrus.

The *Dyscolos* of Menander reveals that tastes in comedy had undergone significant changes by the end of the fourth century B.C. The outrageous fantasy and direct political humor of Aristophanic comedy disappear completely in Menander and New Comedy; instead, there are stock characters and situations that could take place in almost any Greek town at any time. Young gentlemen pine for slave girls who turn out to be the long lost daughters of noblemen, face conflict in the form of their own father or the young girl's father, and are surrounded by a host of stereotypical characters—caring friends, clever slaves, social parasites, and the like. While the *Dyscolos* and a small handful of other fragments provide the extent of our evidence for New Comedy, we can observe the powerful influence of Menander at work in the twenty-seven surviving comedies of the Roman dramatists Plautus (c. 254–184 B.C.) and Terence (d. 159 B.C.), who explicitly cite Menander as a source in many of their prologues, in the Greek romance novels of the first through fifth centuries A.D., and later still in the comedies of Shakespeare and the modern "sitcom" or situational comedy.

The Afterlife Of Ancient Greek Drama

In the *Frogs* of Aristophanes (404 B.C.), the god Dionysus visits Hades in order to retrieve Euripides from the realm of the dead. The god soon finds himself judging a poetry contest between Euripides and Aeschylus, and choosing in the end to take not Euripides but Aeschylus back to the realm of the living. Aristophanes thus presents his audience with a twofold vision of Greek drama as something that belongs to the dead, but simultaneously remains important to the present well-being of the living Athenian polis. Regardless of whether he ever intended *Frogs* for later generations of audiences, Aristophanes predicted in *Frogs* the enduring influence and spirit of Greek drama. The tragedies of Aeschylus, Sophocles, and Euripides, as well as the comedies of Aristophanes and Menander had a significant impact on the Romans, who in turn modeled their own dramas on (and sometimes adapted directly from) Greek tragedy and comedy. The comedies of Plautus and Terence explicitly acknowledge their debt to Menander and the poets of New Comedy on many occasions, while the tragedies of Seneca often exhibit some influence from Sophocles and Euripides. (Even the epic poet Virgil shows some signs of influence from Euripidean tragedy in his masterpiece, the *Aeneid*.) In turn, Plautus, Terence, and Seneca all had a direct impact on the evolution of Western drama, carrying the spirit of Greek drama along with them.

Although Greek literature disappeared in Western Europe between the fall of the Roman Empire and the Renaissance, Byzantine scholars preserved Greek drama in the East until the fall of Constantinople led many scholars and booksellers to travel into Western Europe; it is along with them that Greek drama returned to the Western tradition. Greek drama is now visible in many places throughout the world, whether in modern revivals in the pristine theater at Epidaurus or in local productions of *Lysistrata* and *Trojan Women*, two plays often revived by political protesters in times of war. There are frequent productions and adaptations of Aeschylus's *Oresteia*, Sophocles's *Oedipus the King*, and Euripides's *Medea* and *Bacchae* in national theaters, in community playhouses, and on college campuses. At the time of the composition of this volume, a hip-hop adaptation of Aeschylus's *Seven Against Thebes* has just premiered at the New York Theater Workshop, and Aristophanes's *Frogs* has recently seen renewed (after-)life as a musical comedy on Broadway. Even in death, the spirit of Greek drama lives on.

WHAT IS ROMAN DRAMA?

In the broadest terms, *Roman drama* refers to any dramatic form—tragedy, comedy, farce, mime, and pantomime—composed in the Latin language, a language used by the inhabitants of the city of Rome and that eventually became the administrative language of the Roman Republic (509–30 b.c.) and the Roman Empire (30 b.c.–476 a.d.). The diverse nature of Roman drama can be understood by looking at the two different origins of Roman drama. According to one tradition, the Romans witnessed the first dramatic performance in Rome in 364 b.c., when the Etruscans (a race inhabiting the region now known as Tuscany) staged the performance in order to help the Romans avert a plague. The Etruscans seem to have performed some form of dance accompanied by flute music; in turn, young Roman males imitated this dance form, suiting the flute music and their movements to an earlier poetic form known as Fescennine verses, in which males playfully insulted their peers in order to demonstrate their cleverness and wit. Thus it is perhaps better to say that the Etruscans introduced the Romans to the idea of *spectacle* (song and dance), which the Romans themselves modified into something more akin to *drama*. While it is unclear to what extent this Etruscan influence continued to be felt in Roman drama, the Etruscans gave the Romans the Latin word for actor, *histrio* (ancestor of English *histrionic*, a term used to describe someone who is acting in an excessively dramatic manner).

Despite the Etruscan performance, many Romans considered the first official dramatic performance in Rome in 240 b.c. as the birth of Roman drama. At this time, a certain Livius Andronicus was commissioned to stage a tragedy and a comedy at the *ludi Romani* (Roman games), a festival in honor of the god Jupiter Optimus Maximus (Jupiter Best and Greatest) in thanks for the Roman victory over the Carthaginians in the First Punic War (264–241 b.c.). Livius Andronicus was a Greek slave who had been brought to Rome from the town of Tarentum in Southern Italy (a region known in antiquity as *Magna Graecia* or "Great Greece" because it had been colonized by Greeks in the eighth and seventh centuries b.c.). Andronicus's Greek origins are important since he seems to have staged his performances in the style of Greek tragedy and comedy, although it is unclear whether his performances were translations or adaptations of Greek dramas. (It is worth noting that Livius Andronicus is also famous for his translation of

Homer's *Odyssey*, the first epic to appear in the Latin language). Many Romans thus considered the performance of Greek drama in the Latin language—or the translation of Greek drama into "barbarian," as the comic poet Plautus jests—as the birth of Roman drama. Two centuries later the Roman lyric poet Horace would elegantly express this idea that Greek culture dominated over Roman imperial power, writing in his *Epistles* that, "Captive Greece captured her savage captor and brought the arts to rustic Latium [i.e., the Romans]." Greek drama continued to have an impact on the emerging Roman stage, as is evident in the categories the Romans eventually used to describe their dramas.

Originally known as *comoediae* (a Latin transliteration of the Greek word for "comedies"), the *fabulae palliatae* were plays set in Greece, hence they were Roman comedies in Greek dress (literally, "stories wearing a Greek cloak or *pallium*"). These comedies derived from and adapted Greek sources, such as the domestic comedies of the famous Greek dramatist Menander. The *fabulae palliatae* include twenty-one surviving comedies by Plautus and six surviving comedies by Terence, all of which date roughly to the period 206–160 B.C. and which are the sources for much of our knowledge about Roman comedy. In contrast, we do not have any complete *fabulae togatae*, or "stories in Roman dress" (referring to the white *toga* Roman adult males wore), comedies set in Rome or Italy. We do know that *togatae* were composed mainly in the second century B.C. by such authors as Titinius and Afranius, but they are sadly lost to modern audiences.

Most surviving Roman tragedies are also Greek in style, belonging to the category known as the *fabula cothurnata*, a Roman tragedy in Greek dress, referring to the high boots (*cothurni*) tragic actors wore as part of their stage costume. These tragedies were set in Greece, featured Greek characters, and borrowed both from Greek mythology and from Greek tragedians such as Aeschylus, Sophocles, and Euripides. Roman historical dramas set in Rome or Italy were called *fabulae praetextae*, Roman tragedies in Roman dress, referring to the *toga praetexta* worn by the Roman magistrates who would have provided the characters at the center of such dramas. We have several fragments both of *cothurnatae* and *praetextae* dating to the third through first centuries B.C., by such authors as Livius Andronicus, Naevius, Ennius, Pacuvius, and Accius. However, the only dramas surviving in complete form, nine *cothurnatae* and one *praetexta*, are those attributed to the Stoic philosopher Seneca and belong to the period c. 41–65 A.D.

Roman drama consisted of much more than comedy and tragedy. There also existed the *fabulae Atellanae* or Atellan farce, a form of mostly improvised farce derived from the Oscan region of Campania in central Italy. Atellan farce featured actors who used fixed masks to play stock characters in low-life situations and vulgar language. Another largely (but not exclusively) improvised dramatic form was mime, which also originated in the Greek-speaking world, particularly in Magna Graecia and on the Greek-colonized island of Sicily. Although there was a long literary tradition of mime in the Greek-speaking world, our Roman sources treat mime as the lowest form of drama, in part because mimic actors imitated low-life situations in low language, in part because the actors themselves were slaves, freedmen, or (most scandalously) freedwomen, who did not wear masks and who exposed themselves fully to eyes of the public. Similarly considered scandalous was pantomime, in which one actor sang a libretto (*fabula saltica*) while another masked actor acted out the events with gestures and movement. Pantomime was the most popular dramatic form in the first century A.D., only to be rivaled by the popularity of circus games and gladiatorial combat (famous to modern audiences from the Ridley Scott film *Gladiator*). However, despite the immense popularity of Atellan farce, mime, and pantomime, these dramatic forms are mostly lost to us, existing now only in descriptions of particular performances that exhibited spectacular visual effects (like actors vomiting fake blood, onstage crucifixions, and re-enactments of scenes from classical mythology, such as the coupling of Pasiphaë and the bull of Poseidon); we also have titles of individual farces and mimes, a miscellany of literary fragments (that is, quotations in other Roman sources), and visual representations found in the rich archaeological evidence of statuettes, mosaics, and paintings.

The Performance of Roman Drama

Roman comedies and tragedies were performed primarily at festivals known as *ludi* (literally, "games"), temple dedications, triumphal parades celebrating military victories, and even funerals commemorating the death of Roman aristocrats. It is important to recognize that the ancient Romans did not make the modern distinction between religious and civic activity, so that these various religious rituals were also considered civic activities on the behalf of the Roman state. For instance, the *ludi Romani* in 240 B.C.—during which Livius Andronicus staged the first official Roman dramas—were both a form of religious thanks to the god Jupiter Optimus Maximus and a civic celebration of the Roman military victory over the Carthaginians. While the dramatic performances at temple dedications, triumphs, and funerals were one-time events motivated by the success or death of an individual, the *ludi* were state-sponsored events that occurred annually. The late third century B.C. witnessed an increasing number of public *ludi* celebrated in Rome, such that by the late first century B.C., no fewer than forty-three days out of each calendar year were dedicated to *ludi*. Mime and pantomime were also performed at *ludi*, although it is possible that some so-called "popular" mime may have also taken place in public streets, piazzas, and private houses and on no particular occasion.

The Roman nobility played an active role in the organization of dramatic performances. In the case of the *ludi*, civic magistrates, who were ascending the *cursus honorum* (course of magistracies) to political prominence in Rome, were often responsible for funding the *ludi,* for organizing the entertainment, for erecting the temporary wooden stage and audience seating, and so forth; in the case of temple dedications, triumphs, and funerals, the sponsor or the family of the deceased undertook such duties and expenses. In either case, the organizers always belonged to the Roman nobility, with the consequence that most dramatic events would have appeared to the audience as the result of the munificence of the Roman state and the aristocracy—or, at least, of particular aristocrats. Even if the audience did not specifically identify a given performance with the organizer, the organizers likely influenced the choice of the *fabula* or plot of a given dramatic performance, so that a tragedy might be performed to celebrate (directly or indirectly) a particular family's ancestors or the individual himself. This seems to be the case of the *Adelphoe* (*Brothers*) of Terence, which was produced at the funeral games of Lucius Aemilius Paullus in 160 B.C.; some see the theme of clemency as central to the comedy and suggest that the presence of this theme in the comedy is meant to augment Paullus' own reputation as a merciful victor in war. Finally, the very presence of several dramatists in Rome, including Livius Andronicus, Ennius, and Terence, was due to the direct patronage of individual Roman aristocrats. Thus staging a drama in Rome was always, in some sense, a political event, organized for the city, by the city's prominent citizens, and with consequences for the organizers in the eyes of the city.

The Roman stage itself quite literally displays the political nature of Roman drama. Roman theaters were initially temporary wooden structures, built for each festival and taken down afterwards. Both the surviving Roman comedies and South Italian vase-paintings suggest that the stage often looked like a portion of a common city block, wide enough to accommodate the entrances into two or three characters' houses and as tall as two stories in height. Rome had no permanent stone theater until 55 B.C., when the famed Roman general Gnaeus Pompeius Magnus (Pompey the Great) built a magnificent theater with a shrine in honor of the goddess Venus Victrix (Venus the Conqueror) with the likely intent of increasing his political clout and popularity among the Roman populace. While Pompey himself was defeated by Julius Caesar in the Roman civil war and murdered in 48 B.C., Pompey's stone theater set the standard for architecture in the early Roman Empire; later emperors similarly used the construction of theaters and coliseums to host the "bread and circuses"—that is, the food handouts and spectacles of drama, mime, and gladiatorial combat—that appealed to and pacified the Roman masses. Thus the construction of and activities in Roman theaters came to be seen as indicators of an individual's political success.

While the Roman nobility funded Roman dramas, the actors themselves were anything but noble. As opposed to Greek drama in the fifth century B.C., in which actors were adult male citizens of mostly distinguished pedigree, Roman dramas were devoid of aristocrats, for the Roman nobility considered it ignoble to perform in drama. As a result, the actors in Roman dramas were either male slaves or former slaves who had acquired their freedom (known as freedmen). The slaves often belonged to a single owner known as the *dominus gregis* (literally, the "master of the flock"), who served as the director and producer of the drama and who might collaborate with the author or perform as the lead actor. Interestingly, in the performance of mime, women were permitted to act in female roles; consequently, these women sometimes even attained the status of starlets, much like gladiators did in the arena of combat. Of course, like her male counterparts in all forms of Roman drama (as well as gladiators), the female mime-actress was not considered a citizen but considered a low member of society, an indecent counterpart to virtuous Roman *matronae* (wives). Despite their low social status, these actors and actresses must have been well trained in order to perform the highly stylized roles and complicated *cantica* (songs) found in surviving Roman drama. It is an intriguing paradox that the Roman nobility, on the one hand, funded and attended the performance of various forms of Roman drama, but, on the other hand, seem to have disdained the very actors who performed the dramas themselves.

Roman Comedy: Plautus and Terence

Roman comedy is a strange concoction of Greek comedy and Roman sensibility. As Plautus and Terence frequently tell their audiences in the prologues of their plays, the *fabulae palliatae* (comedies in Greek dress) are in large part adaptations of plays from a Greek theatrical movement known as New Comedy, an immensely popular form of comic drama that originated in Athens in the fourth century B.C. at the hands of such renowned dramatists as Alexis, Diphilus, Philemon, and Menander. Yet it is a curious accident of history that Roman comedy in fact provides the majority of our evidence for New Comedy; while only one complete example of Greek New Comedy survives (Menander's *Dyscolos* or *Old Cantankerous*, first performed in 316 B.C.), there exist today twenty-seven complete plays in Latin by Plautus and Terence. Oddly enough, then, the tastes of Roman audiences are primarily responsible for our knowledge of New Comedy.

This accident of history may nevertheless provide one key to our understanding of surviving Roman comedy, for the *fabulae palliatae* are not merely adaptations of Greek comedy, but are also vacations from the city of Rome itself. This is literally true insofar as these comedies were performed at the *ludi* while the Romans were on vacation, during state-sanctioned religious holidays called *feriae* or *dies feriales*. But the *fabulae* or plots of these comedies also took a day off from life in Rome, so that a cavalcade of Greek characters paraded across the stage—in some cases, even other kinds of foreigners appeared, such as the title character in

Plautus's *Poenulus* (*The Little Carthaginian*). Admittedly, these comedies were not altogether foreign to Romans, as many Greek concepts were translated into Roman concepts for the sake of the audience's understanding; thus, Greek characters sometimes bargain with Roman coinage and talk about Roman legislative bodies. Nevertheless, it is important to ask why the Romans found this Greek comedy so pleasurable. Many critics of Roman comedy suppose that this displacement of events from the Roman world to the Greek world made possible the world turned upside down on the Roman stage. Perhaps the Romans enjoyed Greek comedy because the events in the plays happened *over there* in Greece, but *not here* in Italy. It is a sad accident of historical preservation that the *fabulae palliatae* survive from antiquity, but the *fabulae togatae* (the toga-clad stories) did not; it would be a considerable advancement in our knowledge of the history of Western drama if we could see how Roman dramatists handled comedy directly touching on their own home turf. On the other hand, the fact that only the *fabulae palliatae* survive, combined with the distinguished reputations of Plautus and Terence in other ancient sources, might suggest that the Romans themselves found something preferable in keeping their festive play away from Rome and from home.

Interestingly, Plautus and Terence themselves were not of Roman origin (nor, for that matter, were most dramatists during the Roman Republic). Titus Maccius Plautus (c. 254–184 B.C.) seems to have been a slave from Sarsina in the Umbrian region of central Italy. At least, this is part of the *persona* that Plautus may have adopted for himself, as his name suggests: Plautus is a Romanized form of the Umbrian name Plotus, meaning either "big-eared" or "flat-footed," while Maccius likely derives from the name Maccus, a famous stock-character from Atellan farce. (Thus one distinguished critic has recently suggested that Plautus' name is a theatrical pseudonym that would translate into modern American English as something like "Dick Harpo Floppé.") On the other hand, Publius Terentius Afer (Terence the African) seems to have come to Rome as a slave from the city of Carthage. Terence's wit and good looks earned him both his freedom and close relations with various members of the Roman nobility, whose support contributed to his success. Unfortunately, Terence's career was short-lived; ancient sources claim that, when the young dramatist went abroad to Greece in 159 B.C., he died at sea.

Plautus and Terence may not have been native Romans and their *fabulae palliatae* may not have been set in the dramatic location of Rome, but these comedies nevertheless portray and exemplify many fundamental Roman values, even if these values seem somewhat hidden at first. Consider the example of Plautus's *Pseudolus* (first performed in 191 B.C.). Upon first glance, the *Pseudolus* is a wildly extravagant, somewhat un-Roman comedy. The young Athenian gentleman Calidorus has fallen in love with a slave girl Phoenicium, who both lives next door under the control of the villainous pimp Ballio and is about to be sold that very day. In desperation, Calidorus asks his slave Pseudolus for help in procuring Phoenicium. In the process of securing Phoenicium for Calidorus, Pseudolus not only cheats Ballio of his slave girl, but Pseudolus also outwits Calidorus's own father Simo, winning a tidy sum of money in a bet with Simo. By the end of the play, Calidorus has the girl and Pseudolus is both flush with cash and (literally) drunk with success, while father and pimp alike have been hoodwinked. (To make matters worse for Ballio, he has also lost a bet to Simo...on his birthday, no less!) And yet, despite this raucous display of slaves, pimps, and prostitutes, the events in the play reflect traditional Roman values: sons must respect their fathers (Calidorus is still a good son, properly fearful of his father); slaves must respect their masters (Pseudolus may swindle Simo, but he also helps Simo recoup his losses); everyone must respect their place in the order of society (Pseudolus is no less a slave at the end of the play). We might wonder whether every member of a diverse Roman audience would have respected these same moral values, or to what extent a comedy like *Pseudolus* undermines those values by setting them into the midst of crafty slaves and cruel pimps. Nevertheless, in combining wild, comic extravagance with the more traditional moral resolution at the end of his plays, Plautus ensures that all audiences can applaud and go home happy.

The surviving comedies of Plautus and Terence reveal that both dramatists worked with a fairly set stock of characters inherited from New Comedy: the clever slave, the stern father, the lovesick son, the beloved slave girl who turns out to be of noble stock, the greedy pimp, the boastful soldier, the social parasite. Moreover, the dramatists used a relatively fixed number of situations also found in New Comedy: boy loves girl, son resists father, slave tricks father, general misunderstanding and recognition leading to resolution. Nevertheless, Plautus and Terence both applied their own unique touches. As we have already seen in the *Pseudolus*, Plautus delights in eccentric characters and outrageous situations; other Plautine comedies feature such distinctive and enduring characters as miserly old men who bury their savings (*Aulularia* or *The Pot of Gold*) and identical twins separated at birth (*Menaechmi*), or playful elements involving complicated financial swindles (*Trinummus* or *Three Dollar Day*) and even fake haunted houses (*Mostellaria* or *The Ghost*). Indeed, this delight in eccentricity and outrageousness often leaves the characters of the play looking like little more than two-dimensional parodies of humanity, as we see in the learned speech of the profligate youth Philolaches in *Mostellaria*: "I have pondered long and hard, and I have gone through many arguments in heart—if I have something called a heart at all—and I have mulled over and long disputed this matter, and it seems to me that man, of whatever sort he is once he has been born, that he is similar to and has the shape of...now where did I put that example?...that he is like a new house!" Such is the emotional range of Plautine youth.

Terence, in stark contrast to Plautine comedy, does not rely upon outrageous comic elements and purely stock characters, but tends instead toward the subtle exploration and understanding of human character. As a result, the plots of Terence's comedies themselves take on a somewhat different shape that allow for more in-depth character development. In *Adelphoe* (160 B.C.), a strict father Demea gives one of his two sons to his brother Micio so that Micio might raise the boy in a less strict manner and the two "fathers" might compare methods of raising sons—as it turns out, brother knows best. In *Hecyra* (*The Mother-in-Law*) (first performed unsuccessfully in 165 B.C., with two subsequent performances in 160 B.C.), Terence takes the age-old stereotype of the wicked mother-in-law and turns it upside down, showing how the mother-in-law Sostrata helps her daughter and son-in-law find harmony amidst domestic misunderstanding. Perhaps the most iconic representation of the depth and nobility of Terence's characters can be found in the figure of Chremes, the title character of *The Self-Tormenter* (163 B.C.), who famously proclaims, "I am human; I consider nothing that is human alien to me." With such sentiments, Terence moves away from the flat stereotypes of Plautine comedy and refines Roman comedy into a vehicle for a kind of *humanitas* or "humanism" that would go on to deeply influence the classical spirit.

Roman Tragedy and Seneca

The surviving Roman comedies of Plautus and Terence all belong to the late third and early second centuries B.C., at a time when the Romans were gradually expanding the size and influence of their empire. At this same time the Romans also enjoyed performances of tragedy, both the *fabulae cothurnatae* modeled on classical Greek tragedy and (eventually) the *fabulae praetextae* that depicted famous events in the emerging national consciousness of the Roman people. While it is clear that Roman tragedy flourished in the hands of the poets Livius Andronicus and Naevius in the third century B.C., and in the works of Ennius, Pacuvius, and Accius in the second and first centuries B.C., these dramas do not survive today in anything more than fragmentary form, passed down to us in tattered lines and off-handed references in other works of literature. The Roman tragedies that do survive, the ten tragedies attributed to Seneca, belong not to the expanding Roman Republic of the period 240–85 B.C., but rather to the established Roman Empire of the late first century B.C. and the first century A.D.

In some ways, these surviving tragedies of the Roman Empire exhibit features quite similar to what little we know of the tragedy of the Roman Republic. Both phases of Roman tragedy draw heavily and somewhat self-consciously upon the Greek tragedies of Aeschylus, Sophocles, and especially Euripides, the most popular of the Greek tragedians in later antiquity. In the ten Senecan plays, nine are Greek-style *cothurnatae* about famous characters and events from Greek mythology, such as *Thyestes, Medea, Oedipus, Troades* (*Trojan Women*), and *Hercules Furens* (*Hercules Gone Mad*). These tragedies display both basic structural similarities to the older Greek and Roman tragedies (prologues, episodes broken up by Choral interludes) as well as general thematic parallels (intrigue, recognition, and the fall of characters of great social status or power).

The spirit of Senecan tragedy, however, emerges as something more frightening and more philosophically powerful than that of its predecessors. This may derive in some part from Seneca's own biography. Like most Roman dramatists, Lucius Annaeus Seneca (c. 4 B.C.–65 A.D.) was not born on Italian soil but in the city of Cordoba in the Roman province of Spain; quite unlike his tragic ancestors, however, Seneca was one of the wealthiest and most powerful men in the Roman Empire, not only a prominent Stoic philosopher but also the tutor and trusted advisor of the infamous emperor Nero (who reigned from 54–68 A.D.). Seneca's Stoicism has a profound effect on his tragedies, and his characters speak as if they are contemplating the depths and limits of the human soul itself. The hero Hercules in both *Hercules Furens* and *Hercules Oetaeus* (*Hercules on Mt. Oeta*) manifests the idea that, if the human soul should endure great suffering, then an individual may find moral purification. Most Senecan tragedies, however, end with a much bleaker view of humanity. In the *Thyestes*, the character Atreus deliberates at great length whether he will in fact murder the children of his brother and rival for the royal throne of Mycenae, Thyestes; once Atreus has committed himself to the act of murder, he decides to plunge further into the depths of absolute wickedness, feeding the children to Thyestes and reveling in the crime. Although the myth existed for centuries before Seneca (found notably in a lost play by Sophocles in the fifth century B.C. and more recently in a production by the Roman tragedian Lucius Varius Rufus in 29 B.C.), the horror with which Seneca presents the deliberations of Atreus far exceeds anything ever presented on the tragic stage. In fact, Atreus's acts in the tragedy are so wicked that the ghost of his grandfather, the wicked Tantalus, is stirred from his sufferings in the Underworld, while the day has been blotted out, the stars obliterated from the very heavens.

The impossibility of staging events of such cosmic proportions, as well as a general lack of verbal cues for stage directions in the texts, has led some scholars to believe that Seneca did not write his tragedies for production on the Roman stage, but for reading in public recitals. Indeed, tragedies in the early Roman Empire do not seem to have been performed onstage as they had been in classical Athens or during the Roman Republic, but were now the objects of a cultured, literary elite who attended recitals. This likely change in setting for the performance of imperial Roman tragedy, so different from the performance context of Greek and Republican Roman tragedy, may have affected another aspect of the content of Roman tragedy. These tragedies seem to have increasingly appeared to many as veiled forms of criticism of the emperor. It is said that a certain Mamercus Scaurus was forced to commit suicide for allusions to the emperor Tiberius (reign 14–37 A.D.) in his tragedy *Atreus*.

Intriguing in this light is our only surviving *fabula praetexta* (that is, the only tragedy with a dramatic setting in Rome), the pseudo-Senecan *Octavia*. The tragedy depicts the events surrounding the divorce of Nero from his noble wife Octavia, Nero's subsequent marriage to the cruel Poppaea Sabina, and Octavia's subsequent exile and execution. While it is doubtful that Seneca would have written this play during the reign of Nero—and Seneca died three years before Nero, hence the question of the play's authenticity—the tragedy nevertheless belongs to the late first century A.D., just after Nero's death, and thus shows the directness with which tragedy could criticize a recent imperial regime. Or, to put it in different terms, the *Octavia* shows that the Roman cultural elite recognized the preoccupation with the figure of the tyrant so characteristic of classical Greek tragedy, and therefore used tragedy as a vehicle for the exploration and criticism of the imperial tyranny in their own midst.

Roman Drama after the Fall of Rome

With the death of the barren heroine at the end of *Octavia*, Roman drama comes to its own end, insofar as no other comedies or tragedies survive from the Roman Empire. However, just as Hercules endured suffering to bring the seeds of civilization to the frontiers of the Mediterranean world, Roman drama and Roman comedy in particular have endured much to bring forth the seeds of much of the Western dramatic tradition. The comedies of Plautus and Terence have had far-reaching consequences, deeply influencing the stock characters and plots of the Italian tradition of *commedia dell'arte*, which in turn entered into the English language in the form of Shakespeare's comedies, such as the *Comedy of Errors*, an adaptation of Plautus' *Menaechmi*. The historical dramas of Elizabethan theater were also deeply influenced by the tragedies of Seneca. The complex structures of opera derived in some measure from the recitatives and arias of Roman comedy. Even the American musical has seen the resuscitation of Plautus, as in Stephen Sondheim's *A Funny Thing Happened on the Way to the Forum*. Without Plautus and Terence to convey and amplify the conventions of New Comedy, the modern sitcom (situational comedy) simply would not exist today. The spirit of Roman drama is alive and well in the Western tradition.

FURTHER READING

Boyle, A.J. *An Introduction to Roman Tragedy*. London: Routledge, 2006.

Dover, K. *Aristophanic Comedy*. Berkeley: University of California Press, 1972.

Easterling, P.E., ed. *The Cambridge Companion to Greek Tragedy*. Cambridge: Cambridge University Press, 1997.

Hunter, R.L. *The New Comedy of Greece and Rome.* Cambridge: Cambridge University Press, 1985.

Konstan, D. *Roman Comedy.* Ithaca: Cornell University, 1983.

Segal, E. *Roman Laughter: The Comedy of Plautus.* Cambridge: Oxford University Press, 1968.

Storey, I.C. & Allen, A. *A Guide to Ancient Greek Drama.* Malden, Massachusetts: Blackwell Publishing, 2005.

English Renaissance Drama

William Kerwin

The Irish poet William Butler Yeats described the literature of the English Renaissance as possessing "the emotion of multitude." Other critics have spoken of a "confluence," a merging together of classical and native traditions. And the great Russian writer Mikhail Bakhtin, whose work celebrates and explores literature's "polyphony," associated the Renaissance in particular as a period of "carnival." Each of these images aims in its own ways at something similar in the period: a quality of fullness, or even of excess, caused by the meeting of a variety of traditions. But for those living in England at the time, this fullness was not an entirely positive thing: it was, indeed, alternately exhilarating and terrifying. The latter part of that formulation may seem strange to a casual observer now, when the literature of the Renaissance, and especially the works of William Shakespeare, have achieved such iconic associations with tradition and established order. But the period was in fact one of an almost overwhelming instability. Theology, politics, education, economics, gender, and science all saw challenges to older systems of meaning, and the drama, that literary form so suited to the play of dialectic, was the form that best captured those conflicts and turned them into art, mingling idealism and terror. The display of European civilization that the idealistic young Miranda near the close of *The Tempest* calls a "brave new world" is to her seasoned and cynical father Prospero a gathering of sinners, including a "thing of darkness" for which he accepts responsibility.

THE STAGE OF HISTORY

A medieval worldview that emphasized hierarchy and order was being met in England in the sixteenth century by more atomistic, individual, and protean challenges. Indeed Proteus, the Greek mythological character who could change shapes endlessly, might be the best personification of the sixteenth century English world, with its fluid social reality that seemed to many people very close to the world of the theater. "All the world's a stage" says Shakespeare's Jacques in *As You Like It,* and when Shakespeare wrote that line he conveyed a truism of the day: role-playing, or acting, was now the way people got on with life. The history of English Renaissance drama is inseparable from this historical moment, when what role a person played was suddenly a matter of choice and responsibility. Another version of this idea can be seen in Walter Ralegh's poem "What is our life?"

> Our mirth the music of division;
> Our mothers' wombs the tiring-houses be
> Where we are dressed for this short comedy.
> Heaven the judicious sharp spectator is,
> That sits and marks still who doth act amiss;
> Our graves that hide us from the searching sun
> Are like drawn curtains when the play is done.
> Thus march we, playing, to our latest rest,
> Only we die in earnest—that's no jest.
> What is our life? a play of passion...

Ralegh's poem employs two of the great poetic moves of his day: he gives us the metaphor of life-as-theater, and he works through analogy, that trope that suggests parallel systems of order in different spheres of life. Ultimately, those two moves work against each other, as role-playing suggests instability and change, while analogy, with its dependence upon an underlying order or structure, intimates an overarching plan or system. The confrontation between innovation and order faced Englanders in many confusing ways, and one response they seem to have had was to head to the theater: from the founding of the first London public theater in 1567 to the closing of public theaters in 1642, more than fifty million visits were paid, in a city that in 1600 held two hundred thousand people. These audiences were spectators at, and players in, a multitude of dramatic revolutions.

Offstage, the widest-ranging of those changes involved religion. The movements that ultimately led to what we now call the Reformation, accelerated by Martin Luther's bold posting of his ninety-five theses in Wittenberg in 1517, obviously challenged the ways religion was organized, but these movements also challenged the ways thoughts were organized, and helped usher in a different kind of identity. Those who broke with Rome were united in rejecting the papacy and certain Catholic doctrines and practices, as they attempted to purify the faith and return to a more streamlined practice. But this movement soon splintered into numerous forms, which in England were primarily divided between a Catholic-looking Anglican Church, which continued the practice of top-down organization involving bishops, and more radical reformers eventually dubbed "Puritans," who sought a more thorough rejection of Catholic forms. Following the Lutheran motto of "every man his own priest," these more radical Protestants sought to purge the Christian faith of any impediment to an individual's personal relationship to God. Because the Reformation emphasized a Christian's inner experience, it helped foster the patterns of inwardness and individual responsibility that define the Renaissance. The invention of printing presses with moveable type allowed for an explosion in reading and ownership of books, a development that worked in parallel ways with the Reformation: many English homes now owned a bible, allowing private or family reading of scripture, and soon after that other books appeared in homes, fostering an expanding range of private reading experience. That technological shift, from manuscript to print, like all other shifts in the period, was inseparable from the seismic movements created by the Reformation.

The growth of a book culture occurred simultaneously with other aspects of Renaissance intellectual life, including the movement known as humanism. This movement stressed the value of ancient texts and the potential of individuals to achieve an almost divine potential, and it produced a new culture of letters. Italian scholars and artists such as Pico della Mirandola, Leonardo da Vinci, and Michelangelo helped promote the ambitious Pythagorean ideal that "man is the measure of all things," and they saw the human individual as a chameleon-like creature who has the power either to descend to the level of beast or to rise to the status of an angel. Italian life in the fifteenth century was energized by an outpouring of these new ideas and experiments in both visual and literary arts. In the early sixteenth century English court of Henry VIII it was the literary arts that became transformed by Renaissance humanism. The first major landmarks involve the Latin writings of a few well-educated humanists, most notably Thomas More, whose 1516 *Utopia* was part of an exchange of ideas not within England but within a small coterie of humanists living across northern Europe. Interested in reform of all aspects of society, *Utopia* imagines a world governed reasonably and justly, even as it admits that such a world is literally a "no place." These reforming instincts were directed at more attainable goals by later English humanists who created new educational institutions and curricula, and instituted the ways of learning that produced the great English dramatic flowering by expanding what counted as worthy in both subject and form. The use of classical models in schooling helped broaden the educational experience from the study of divinity to the study of the wide range of human experience, represented by authors such as Terence, Plautus, Seneca, Horace, Virgil, Cicero, and above all Ovid. This schooling emphasized learning Latin, and learning it well, but it also stressed a clarity of linguistic use in English, a development essential for the promotion of English as a language worthy of serious literary effort. A 1557 volume entitled *Songs and*

Sonnets helped bring the continent's poetic trends to England and legitimize English-language poetry. The triumph of the vernacular as the language of literature and the great poetry of the sixteenth century fundamentally shaped the dramatic movement beginning at this time.

Transformations in religious and literary realms helped propel political revolutions as well. The Renaissance is often regarded as beginning in England in 1485 and ending in 1660, and each date marks a significant political evolution. The Battle of Bosworth Field began the Tudor dynasty, with its centralization of power and its great regal courts, to be dominated by the epic reigns of Henry VIII (1509–47) and Elizabeth I (1558–1603). The restoration of Charles II in 1660 ended the English Civil War's experiment in republican government, but it also marked the end of untrammeled monarchy. From the consolidation of national power at the period's beginning in 1485 through the overthrow and regicide of Charles I and the Stuart ruling family in 1649 and the return to the throne of his son eleven years later, questions of political rule dominated public life and provided constant subject matter for the stage. And in "real life" these questions were theatrical as well, because kings and their competitors self-consciously thought of them that way, and staged their identities and their power in royal processions, royal pronouncements, and in the case of Charles I even in royal executions. Elizabeth I understood that she herself was playing the role of monarch, saying "we princes...are set on stages in the sight and view of all the world," and objected to the staging of Shakespeare's *Richard II*, with its depiction of a monarch overthrown, saying "know ye not that I am Richard?" Her Stuart successor James I retreated to a more blunt defense of his power based on the alleged divine right of kings as part of a divinely ordained order, seeming to challenge this theatricality of kingship. The deposition and eventual execution of his son, however, demonstrates that the Stuart belief was far from universal, and this political example of the ideology of order dissolved under the pressures of more atomistic and modern forces.

Nowhere were those changes more evident, and more influential, than in London, the center of the theater world and the center of the greatest economic, demographic, gender, and intellectual changes in Renaissance Europe. From a small city of 60,000 people in 1520, London grew to 200,000 in 1600 and 400,000 in 1650. With great shifts in ownership caused by the transfer of church lands to private ownership, and a large influx of rural workers who lost their lands to enclosure, both the number and wealth of London citizens was soaring. The discovery of the "New World" and an increase in foreign trade brought a host of new commodities of London wharves, and London shops and manufacturers boomed. Apprentices and vagrants made up part of the London crowd, and discontent among the former group led to numerous riots and attacks on foreigners. London had a bustling crime life, with thirteen jails or prisons for various categories of debtors or criminals. With so much new growth, wealth, poverty, and desperation joined together, it was almost impossible to maintain older social distinctions, though they were still asserted. William Harrison in 1577 famously outlined the four categories or "degrees" of people: gentlemen; citizens and burgesses; country yeomen; and commoners. But whether one fit the category of "gentlemen" depended not only upon birth but upon appearance: older distinctions governing who was permitted to wear what clothes—sumptuary laws—were reasserted by decrees but ignored on the street. If one could dress and comport oneself like a gentleman, then the category might be claimed, and ultimately, it was playing the role that made the role.

The role-playing involved in gender in the English Renaissance presents a fascinating part of the cultural puzzle. The ideology of order and tradition was both put forth and challenged in the domestic sphere, where a man's authority over his wife was asserted as the analogy to a king's authority over his kingdom. The place of women in English Renaissance culture, the exception of Queen Elizabeth notwithstanding, was officially one of subordination, and when a woman asserted her authority against this hierarchy, she had to do so against a very formidable collection of forces. Whether this element of history actually moves in a different direction from national politics—that is, whether gender roles became more restrictive even as political, economic, and literary roles became more free—has been hotly contested by recent historians. Did women lose authority in the move toward more nuclear households? Or did strong women successfully resist that narrowing of their possible roles? Such women can be found in both history and literature: the number of women writing for publication grew slowly but steadily in the period, and women on the stage often spoke out for their sex. Playwrights in the period—an almost exclusively male group—returned over and over to fictional imaginings of such resistance.

Resistance to centralizing power structures and ancient traditions took on very different—and frankly more successful—forms in the realm of what we would now call science. The period's intellectual changes involved both a new culture of intellectual life and new ideas. At the start of the Tudor monarchy in 1485, England was an intellectual backwater, far behind continental Europe in almost every way; by the Restoration in 1660, the country was leading a broad array of scientific and philosophical disciplines, and the Royal Society, where scientists, or "virtuosi" as they were called, saw new theories debated with a rigorous scientific method. The intervening years had seen challenges to almost every discipline, not just in England but in the scholarly community as a whole, often leading to a complete inversion of received ideas. William Harvey decentered the idea of human physiology by arguing that the heart acts as a pump; new ideas of disease undermined Galenic conceptions of the body that had dominated European life since the Roman Empire; and Galileo inverted ideas of astronomical order by claiming that the sun, not the earth, was at the center of the system of planets.

John Donne provides an encapsulation of how it felt for him to be experiencing the moment of old orders under assault. In a poem called "The Anniversaries," he cries out that new ideas about the world are destroying comforting visions of balance:

> And new philosophy calls all in doubt:
> The element of fire is quite put out;
> The sun is lost, and the earth, and no man's wit
> Can well direct him where to look for it.
> And freely men confess that this world's spent,
> When in the planets and the firmament
> They seek so many new; they see that this
> Is crumbled out again to atomies.
> 'Tis all in pieces, all coherence gone;
> All just supply, and all relation:
> Prince, subject; father, son, are things forgot,
> For every man alone thinks he hath got
> To be a phoenix, and that there can be
> None of that kind of which he is, but he.

This is a vision of the horrors of the new: the heavenly and the political, the physical and the psychic, all are what Hamlet calls "out of joint." And perhaps the greatest fear here is fear of untrammeled individuality, of people thinking there is no "kind" that contains more than one "he." Donne's reaction to the new science condenses others' reactions to the new worlds of church, state, literature, and marketplace—to the whole exciting but fearsome Renaissance world that seemed to take on a new script almost every day.

THE STAGE IN RENAISSANCE ENGLAND

All of these "dramatic" social changes helped produce a more literal dramatic revolution, on the place of the stage itself. Renaissance English theater had a native and ancient tradition upon which to draw, a medieval inheritance that met in the middle of the sixteenth century with all the social changes discussed above, but especially the literary innovations of humanism with its new attention to classical authors and poetic form. The result was theater of a new kind, combining the spiritual energies of English traditions with the aspirations and innovations of the Renaissance. The result was the plays of Shakespeare and his contemporaries or near-contemporaries, including Thomas Kyd, Christopher Marlowe, Ben Jonson, Thomas Middleton, John Webster, John Marston, Thomas Dekker, John Ford, and Philip Massinger.

Medieval legacies included the folk entertainment, the mystery play, and the morality play. Folk entertainment included longstanding traditions of music, dance, carnival parties, and partly submerged ancient rituals, as well as holiday celebrations and public displays of magic, swordsmanship, and juggling not too distant in feel, one might guess, from modern-day buskers. Like our street entertainers, these earlier performers had a dicey relationship with central authority, not because they directly challenged institutions of church or state but because their entertainment came from sources much older than those institutions. Mystery plays, on the other hand, were much more closely connected with the church: they were plays performed by different trade groups, or "mysteries," and they concern themselves with the entire scope of the biblical story, from Creation to the Last Judgment. Generally performed in cycles of separate plays, the mysteries attempted to enact the Christian story of the human race. They were performed annually at the time of a church feast, such as Corpus Christi, and they were enormous public spectacles aimed at an entire city's population. Four such cycles remain available to us, and they provide us with a drama that is both religious and social; the plays retell the biblical story but in local settings and dialects, which sometimes included some rather pointed social criticism. Mysteries lost some favor after the Reformation, as they were associated with Catholic traditions of iconography, but the Chester cycle continued until 1575, leaving open the possibility that a young Shakespeare might have seen such plays, with their grand sense of time and their combination of biblical and local characterization. The "Second Shepherds' Play" from the cycle performed at Wakefield, in Yorkshire, provides a rich example of that mixture of religious instruction and local lyric intensity, in which minor characters such as the shepherds or Noah's wife Gib come across as real—and vibrant—people.

The Reformation promoted another dramatic form, that of the moral play (or the morality play). Moral plays are a different kind of religious drama: they retell not a biblical scene but the story of one imagined moment, cast as a struggle for a single Christian's salvation as he is pulled between allegorical forces. *Mankind* and *Everyman* are two famous and illustrative examples: each has a title character on a path toward salvation who is temporarily drawn to sin. If mystery plays are vehicles of narrative, enacting in a local accent and costume a story that was well-known and considered timeless, moral plays are plays of argument. They provide very little of an aesthetics of realism; their strength is in their ability to present ideas on stage, and to foster a theater of dialectic. Moral plays are preachy and predictable, except for the character known generically as the Vice, a villain who always fails in his quest but who nevertheless gets all of the best lines. Humorous, witty, and seemingly free to mingle with the audience in ways other characters are not, the Vice character lived on in later plays in creations such as Shakespeare's Iago, Richard III, Feste, Falstaff, or Edmund. Part comic and part devil, the moral play's Vice character provided energy and physicality to the drama.

By the middle of the sixteenth century, plays of ideas were beginning to venture further afield than did the traditional moral plays, as they began to build on the culture of dramatic dialectic to consider ideas other than a soul's salvation. In 1562 *Gorboduc*, by Thomas Norton and Thomas Sackville, retells the story of an ancient British king and the bloody struggle between his two sons to succeed him. Norton and Sackville were both involved in the law courts of London, and both were involved in the political debates of mid-century. They turned to the past to stage different approaches to the question of political theory, and the fact that their play was performed at court before Queen Elizabeth demonstrates the seriousness of their ambitions for theater. Like a moral play, *Gorboduc* explores abstract ideas, but the characters are drawn from history, adding an element of realism and social commentary not present in the earlier genre. Sackville and Norton were also innovators of form, introducing unrhymed or blank verse to the stage; they probably borrowed that innovation from the lyric poet Henry Howard, the Earl of Surrey. This is an exemplary instance of the myriad times when playwrights drew upon the works of poets in the Renaissance, making their genre more powerful with the developments of the lyric. Sackville himself contributed lyric characterizations to the 1559 edition of the very popular *A Mirror for Magistrates*, a collection of verse monologues with political lessons. Theater was expanding its sources, incorporating more and more of the Renaissance's innovations.

The First Theaters

The gradual emergence of a new form required new public places. Drama had previously been performed in temporary spaces, or at venues normally for some other purpose, such as churches, markets, courts, homes, or inns. But in 1567 the first public theater, the Red Lion Theatre in Whitechapel, was built; in 1576 three other playhouses were established. Holding audiences of up to three thousand people, these playhouses offered a continuously changing menu of plays at a low price. Funding was lavished on costumes, but not on scenery, and not on scripts either, which were regarded as a much less valuable part of a company's assets than its rich robes and dresses. English theatrical companies had an unusual social position: when sponsored by a member of the nobility, they maintained a great freedom, but without that protection they were legally classified as vagabonds. Plays were often performed at court, but the London public theaters—where the same plays were often staged—were located at the margins of society, in the suburbs and legally distinct "liberties" that also housed the houses of prostitution, the bear-baiting and cockfighting arenas, and other places of ill repute.

Theater in the English Renaissance always had to fight for its legal survival, against London civic authorities who sought to restrict it and Puritans who sought to abolish it altogether. This "antitheatrical" movement had numerous famous examples, including a 1579 pamphlet by Stephen Gosson accusing the theater of promoting almost every vice, from sexual instability to laziness. His diatribe provoked a response by the nobleman Philip Sidney, whose *Defense of Poesy* declared all of the literary arts, including theater, as promoters of an heroic virtue. Sidney brought to the debate over theater's social value all of the elegance and authority of Renaissance humanism, and while playwrights occasionally ran afoul of the law—especially for satire too close to the throne—theaters remained open, except for plague times, until 1642. At that time, at the onset of the great national civil war, the Puritan opposition to the stage finally won the day, deeming that theaters were "spectacles of pleasure, too commonly expressing lascivious mirth and levity." It is more than slightly ironic that English Renaissance drama, now celebrated as the essence of English culture, had to struggle for its right to exist at the very high point of its creativity.

With the establishment of public theaters and permanent acting companies in the 1570s and 1580s, the demand for plays was met by a group of highly educated men known as the "university wits." Deeply educated in classical literature, they brought to their writing a reverence for authors such as Seneca in tragedy and Terrence and Plautus in comedy. Originality was less of an artistic goal than creative imitation, as authors turned to extant plays or stories and retold them in English, proud of rather than embarrassed by their wholesale borrowings. Formally, these early plays often retain a stiffness that shows these borrowings were not yet integrated to the local scene, but two plays in the 1580s, Thomas Kyd's *The Spanish Tragedy* and Christopher Marlowe's *Tamburlaine the Great*, show native tradition and classical learning coming together in powerful and epoch-changing ways.

Combining Classical Learning and Native Tradition: Kyd and Marlowe

The Spanish Tragedy draws on the tradition of the Roman writer Seneca and brings it into early modern Europe. Seneca's genre was the revenge play, in which a victimized good man gradually becomes twisted by his attempts to find justice. The revenge play bears a central place in Renaissance English tragedy, and *The Spanish Tragedy* can be seen as a precursor of *Hamlet*, as well as revenge plays by Middleton, Webster, and Ford. Like many Renaissance plays, this one is difficult to date exactly, but it probably was first performed in the late 1580s and was first published in 1592, and was republished and quoted from so many times in the succeeding decades that its popularity is unquestionable. Kyd's protagonist is the good old man Hieronimo, a Knight Marshall of Spain, who is unable to find justice for the murder of his son, Horatio. In act two he cries out, "in revenge my heart would find relief," but corruption in the political elite makes any direct solution impossible. Driven to a frenzy that looks like madness and may be so, Hieronimo gradually learns to work within the cycles of violence and disguise to strike back, with breathtaking bloodiness, at the cast of characters around him. Kyd creates a character whose soliloquies bring something new to the stage—Hieronimo speaks passionately and at great length about his frustrations, and his thoughts and very identity seems to change during the course of his speeches in ways that no morality play character's ever did. Hieronimo also becomes an actor and a theatrical producer, producing his revenge in the course of putting on a play within the play, an example of the metatheater that Shakespeare incorporated into so many of his plays, with *A Midsummer Night's Dream* and *Hamlet* being just two examples. Finally, *The Spanish Tragedy* creates an ambiguous moral as well as psychic universe, in which the right deed is no longer as clear-cut as in medieval drama—we are now seeing Renaissance skepticism, unsure of how justice or salvation are possible in a world gone astray.

Christopher Marlowe continued that exploration of moral ambiguity, and he brought to the form of tragedy a poetry never seen before in English drama. A translator of Ovid's *Amores* and the author of the short epic "Hero and Leander," Marlowe brought into the theater what Ben Jonson latter dubbed "Marlowe's mighty line." Marlowe opens his first play, *Tamburlaine the Great, Part I,* with a Prologue who announces a new era:

> From jigging veins of rhyming mother wits,
> And such conceits as clownage keeps in pay,
> We'll lead you to the stately tent of war,
> Where you shall hear the Scythian Tamburlaine
> Threatening the world with high astounding terms,
> And scourging kingdoms with his conquering sword.

One can hear in these lines—in their disdain for "jigging veins" and "clownage," and in their full-mouthed pleasure with "high astounding terms"—a dismissal of much of previous attempts at drama in English. Marlowe moves us with poetry, displaying an ambition in verse only paralleled by the ambitions of his characters. His most famous and successful plays focus on a single aspiring central figure, whom critics have referred to as his "over-reachers," but in their aspirations lie a beauty and a power that makes it difficult to respond to them only with moralizing judgments. Tamburlaine glories in military conquest;

Doctor Faustus wants complete knowledge; *Edward II* is a king driven by sensuality; and *The Jew of Malta* is a self-defined "Machiavel," or political villain, who wants "infinite riches in a little room." All these characters teeter on the edge of self-parody, sounding at times heroic, at other times comic, and at other times tragic. The downfall of each echoes the morality play's dismissal of a Vice character, but Marlowe first makes his protagonist noble, uncompromising, and above all passionate in ways that no Vice character ever was. Marlowe's biography is so full of shadowy suggestions and spectacular events that he stands alone as a kind of "bad boy" of the period, embodying in his life much of the anarchic and self-destructive chaos of his protagonists.

Local Settings for English Drama

Not all Renaissance dramatists set their plays in dramatically distant places. The genre of domestic tragedy combined local history with moral precepts and dramatic detail. The anonymous *Arden of Faversham* tells the story of Alice Arden's infidelity, and the murder of her husband, with rich and lively local detail, creating a cast of vivid underworld characters as well as staging the aspirations of the local gentry. Thomas Heywood's *A Woman Killed with Kindness* offers a more moralizing look at a failed marriage, perhaps most interesting for the ways it captures Renaissance England's obsessions with female chastity. *The Witch of Edmonton* by William Rowley, Thomas Dekker, and John Ford, gives us the tragic history of a local witchcraft episode, combining the supernatural, the sociological, and the psychological. The 1590s saw a vogue for the English history play, which drew their material from chronicles that celebrated the English past, but were shaped by playwrights both to celebrate and question the English political system. That these history plays are often almost indistinguishable from tragedy demonstrates they are much more than patriotic celebration of order.

William Shakespeare

Coming to the London stage a few years after Marlowe was William Shakespeare, and no chapter of this length, with an aim of introducing the broad scope of English drama in the Renaissance, can give more than the most cursory glimpse at his work. Perhaps one can begin by noting what Shakespeare did NOT do: he wrote no real city comedy (*The Merry Wives of Windsor* does not quite qualify), and with the exception of that play he did not write any plays set in contemporary London. His early career included work in comedy, tragedy, and especially English history plays—he wrote two groups of four plays each, "tetralogies," exploring the English past and political philosophy. That interest in the limits and duties of central authority also defines Shakespeare's tragedies, which cast a famous eye on psychic disintegration but also examine matters of state; one might find an illustrative example in Hamlet's inwardness combined with the observation that "something is rotten in the state of Denmark." *Macbeth, King Lear, Othello,* and all the other tragedies combine studies of individuals with studies of communal identity. The broad trajectory of Shakespeare's career as an author of comedies moves from light to dark, though even early on, in plays such as *The Taming of the Shrew* and *A Midsummer Night's Dream,* cruelty and caprice seem inseparable from the plots that end in marriage. Later comedies such as *Twelfth Night* and *As You Like It* seem most confidently to integrate the various sides of comic theater, while comedies such as *The Merchant of Venice, Troilus and Cressida,* and *All's Well That Ends Well* barely seem comedies at all, having given over so much to portraying the presence of suffering and violence. Near the end of his career Shakespeare participated in a radical generic experiment— part of a vogue for other dramatists as well—labeled "tragicomedies" or "roman-ces," producing in *The Winter's Tale, Cymbeline, Pericles,* and *The Tempest* plays that suspend some of the more realistic bounds governing the rest of his plays and that combine the staging of the suffering of his tragedies with the reconcilia-tion of his comedies. Through it all, Shakespeare drew on all the social energies and literary experimentation described above: he combined humanistic learning with native forms such as moral play elements (especially the Vice); he partici-pated in a new sense of inward life (even if he did not quite, as Harold Bloom has argued, "create the modern"); he helped in the rigorous English examination of political authority; and he brought beautiful poetry to the stage.

Ben Jonson

A third great poet-playwright who flourished at the end of the Elizabethan era was Ben Jonson. Jonson seemed at times to define himself against his great con-temporary Shakespeare, most forcefully in the ways Jonson asserted the impor-tance of following the theories often labeled "neo-classical," but the two shared many things as well. Each was the son of a working class father, and a possessor of great social ambition; each was a great lyric poet; and each had a mastery over multi-plot structures. But perhaps most of all, each used the stage to revel in the powers of language; as Lovewit says in *The Alchemist,* "I love a teeming wit as I love my nourishment."

While Jonson did write tragedies, it was in comedy that this "teeming wit" really came to life. Jonson began writing "Comedies of Humors," in which characters re-present one human instinct or bodily type, and his comedies did not so much escape that paradigm as perfect it: his great comic characters are always types, but their language becomes so crammed with exuberant and sensual detail that being a type feels like a virtue. Here is *The Alchemist's* Sir Epicure Mammon, describing his desire for wealth to a friend, and his hope that this is the day his for-tune will arrive:

Come on, sir. Now you set your foot on shore
In *Novo Orbe*; here's the rich Peru,
And there within, sir, are the golden mines,
Great Solomon's Ophir! He was sailing to't
Three years, but we have reached it in ten months.
This is the day wherein, to all my friends,
I will pronounce the happy word, "Be rich;
This day you shall be spectatissimi."

This poetry pushes us around and demands a fair bit—it helps to have the geography, book knowledge, and Latin skills to feel its emotional movement, and to arrive at the "exceedingly looked at" of the passage's final word. It is above all extreme, and Jonson's great comedies, like Marlowe's tragedies, revel in extremity. *Volpone; or, the Fox* tells of a man who feigns mortal illness to prey upon the greed of those who would win his inheritance. *Epicoene; or, the Silent Woman* shows a man, Morose, driven by his hatred of noise, and his being beguiled by family who dress up a boy as an allegedly mute woman to be his perfect bride. *The Alchemist* features a trio of criminals who use the promises of alchemy to trick a host of greedy people. And *Bartholomew Fair* gives us a panorama of London types, joined by the festivity of the fair and by their own distinguishing absurdities. These comedies tell of con men and suckers, and usually end in the exposure of vice and greed, which suits Jonson's stated goals of showing vice in order to dissuade us from it. But the joy of the play is in watching these sinners at play. Here we can see some of the conflicts in Jonson's life: he is the poet of praise for ordered country traditions, and for integrity of life, but his plays succeed because he shows the exact opposite in the teeming and ambitious London underworld. Jonson published a folio volume of his writing in 1616 under the title *Works*, a presumptuous thing for a poet and playwright to do centuries before the privileged professional niche of Creative Writing: the term *works* was usually reserved for books in philosophy or theology, subjects acknowledged as weighty. This son of a bricklayer wanted to raise both himself and his craft above their origins.

The City Comedy

The shift from Elizabethan to Jacobean drama saw a number of broad changes on the stage, including a new kind of satire, the city comedy. Renaissance English satire migrated from the page to the stage when church authorities banned the publication of verse satires after the genre became too violent for them to endure. "City comedy" describes a wide range of plays that focus upon London life and manners, especially of its new breed, the middle-class citizen. London, more than any individual person, becomes the main character in these plays. Aside from Jonson, the major figures in city comedy are Thomas Middleton and

Thomas Dekker. While each wrote in other genres as well, their city comedy leaves us with a portrait of London as a venal but vital city. Middleton's greatest contribution is *The Chaste Maid of Cheapside*, a fast-moving multi-plot play of London financial and sexual intrigue. The play opens in the home and shop of a goldsmith, YellowHammer, and people arrive, including the sleazy Sir Walter Whorehound, to court both the son and daughter, with the wealth of the shop the universal motive. A second household, the Touchwoods, is defined by its abundance of children; a third, the Kixes, is marred by childlessness; and a fourth, the Allwits, accepts Sir Walter Whorehound as the sexual father of all their children in exchange for his financial support. In all four plots, marriage and fertility are counters in a financial game, and while sex drives several characters, the real lust is for money. At play's end the worst offenders are exposed and isolated, and the young couple undermines their parents' attempts to stop their marriage, but even that union seems decidedly guided by material concern, with the man calling his love "the choicest spoil." That emphasis on trading of the most intimate human actions can stand for the way city comedy in general sees commerce organizing life. A more festive example is Thomas Dekker's *The Shoemaker's Holiday*, set in the home and shop of an energetic shoemaker, Simon Eyre, who eventually becomes the Mayor of London. Dekker gives us a rich and mostly loving portrait of shop, street, and royal court, with a love story involving an aristocratic man dressing as a shoemaker. The play praises the working class culture of the shop, and the virtue and social value of its workers. Dekker writes with the exuberance that defines so much Renaissance writing. But we see here, as we do in Middleton's play, that any optimistic sense of native virtue is shadowed by the way trading determines all: Simon Eyre's ultimate triumph has as much to do with his sneakiness as with his hearty virtue. A third example of the city comedy is a collaboration between Dekker and Middleton—and collaboration was an increasingly common occurrence in the seventeenth century—entitled *The Roaring Girl, or Moll Cut-Purse*. Based on the historical person Mary Firth, the play places this cross-dressing underworld dynamo within a culture of "roaring boys," or rowdies, and makes her a superhero of virtue in a corrupt city. As in other city comedies, a loving thick description of London scenes makes up one side of the play, and the exposure of lustful and greedy citizens provides us with a second and much more ironic tone.

This double feeling also characterizes the genre of tragicomedy or romance. This genre creates a world remote from the familiar, and depicts dangerous and passionate forces at work, only to solve the looming problems before they become tragic, usually through the intervention of an almost magical outside force. Near death experiences and happy endings—such a combination, and an open reliance upon artifice rather than character to conclude the plot, open up this genre to the charge of being aimed at professional success rather than aesthetic integrity. But at times the plays work very well, as can be seen in Shakespeare's

The Winter's Tale and *The Tempest,* and in some of the work of the prolific Francis Beaumont and John Fletcher, working sometimes in tandem and sometimes independently, especially in *Philaster* and *A King and No King.*

Character in Renaissance Tragedy

If during the seventeenth century comedy gradually lost an interest in character, tragedy retained that focus up until the closing of the theaters in 1642, even as it was shadowed by an increasing obsession with violence and moral decay. Shakespeare's successors in writing great tragedies include John Webster and John Ford, each of whom creates spectacularly transgressive characters, straining to push the boundaries of the lurid, but also conveying emotion in remarkably original and complex poetry. Webster's *The Duchess of Malfi* gives us a world in which the tragic title character suffers independently of any choices she makes; her brothers conspire first to madden her and then to kill her and her family. The play's power comes from its articulation of evil, made more shocking in its contrast to the play's title character. Her brother Ferdinand, making reference to medical treatments for anger, calls out:

> Rhubarb, oh, for rhubarb
> To purge this choler! Here's the cursed day
> To prompt my memory, and here't shall stick
> Till of her bleeding heart I make a sponge
> To wipe it out.

Before that prophesied murder takes place, Ferdinand subjects his sister to torment after torment, to an almost comical excess:

> Damn her! That body of hers,
> While that my blood ran pure in't, was more worth
> Than that which thou wouldst comfort, called a soul.
> I will send her masques of common courtesans,
> Have her meat served up by bawds and ruffians,
> And, 'cause she'll needs be mad, I am resolved
> To remove [from] the common hospital
> All the mad folk, and place them near her lodging:
> There let them practice together, sing, and dance,
> And act their gambols to the full o'th' moon.

Ferdinand's sadistic fantasies here almost describe the theater of Webster and his contemporaries, striving as they do to hit ever higher notes of angry violence. John Ford's tragedies are best represented by *'Tis Pity She's a Whore,* the story of Giovanni and Isabella, a brother and sister who fall in love, and ultimately consummate their love, before a gory murder suicide, punctuated by Giovanni coming on stage with his sister's "heart upon a dagger." Imagine *Romeo and Juliet* on steroids. A similarly amplified feeling comes from what Cyril Tourneur does with the genre of the revenge tragedy: even if Shakespeare and Kyd had created orgies of blood, their Hamlet and Hieronimo were driven by a dream of justice, but in *The Revenger's Tragedy* all moral center seems gone. Characters appear like moral play figures—the Duchess has evil sons named Ambitioso and Supervacuo—but no remnant of the good angel remains.

Women in Renaissance Drama

All of these plays, in their sense of the violated woman as the primal sin, bring up the centrality of women within Renaissance drama. Sadly, there are very few contributions by women authors to English Renaissance drama, certainly no real-life counterpart to Virginia Woolf's marvelous fantasy "Shakespeare's Sister," in which Woolf imagines a creative woman of the period destroyed by the complete absence of any "room of one's one" in which to write. The women writers of the period were mostly aristocrats, and this is especially true in drama, which requires a broad network to actually produce a play. Perhaps that is why the first original (as opposed to translated) play by a woman is an example of "closet drama," or theater written to be read. Elizabeth Cary's *The Tragedy of Mariam, the Fair Queen of Jewry* (published 1613), tells the story of the biblical queen's struggle to assert herself and her opposition to her tyrant husband Herod.

Most importantly in terms of Mariam's connections with other Renaissance plays, her struggle is for speech, to maintain a "public voice," not merely a domestic and subordinate one. If Renaissance drama has few women writers, it has a multitude of women who assert their voices and their wills, often with tragic results. Shakespeare's women, from the tamed shrew of his early comedy to the stage-directing Paulina in *The Winter's Tale*, fight for their right to speak; as *Othello*'s Emilia says to her husband Iago, who has told her to be quiet, "No, I will speak as liberal as the north!" In the comedies the central fear of the male characters is women escaping control, leading to an obsession with cuckholdry. In the tragedies, male control of women is at the center of the symbolic order, as well as of individual male identity, and from *Titus Andronicus* to *The Duchess of Malfi* we see the violent effects upon the lives of women of this symbolic centrality.

The Masque

A final genre to note is the masque, a very different form of play. A courtly entertainment, the masque involved acting, music, and dance, as did traditional plays, but it also involved members of the audience as performers, and it relied on elaborate set and costume designs. One of the most famous is *The Masque of Blackness*, a collaboration between Ben Jonson and the Italian-influenced architect Inigo

Jones, staged at the court of King James in 1605. A very dramatic spectacle, this is allegory even beyond that of the moral plays, meant to drive home the power of the ruling family and the virtue of England. The court members who participated in the masque included Queen Anne and eleven of her female companions, painted in blackface to represent women from Africa searching for a purer home, and they provide a rare instance of female actors on the Renaissance stage. The primary interest of these plays today is their clearly political and ideological lines, staging the court's power and its connections to spectacle, as well as to definitions of race and gender.

Jonson ultimately quarreled with Jones over what he saw as the victory of spectacle over language, and the masque's emphasis upon the visual and the ornate is a foreshadowing of some of the developments in English Renaissance drama in the reign of Charles I, leading up to the closing of the theaters in 1642. The drama becomes increasingly baroque and self-reflexive. Despite contrary examples such as the work of Philip Massinger and James Shirley, it is difficult not to feel that the powers of the English Renaissance stage are fading. But the story of Renaissance drama has continued, in four centuries of performances and readings. No plays in the Western dramatic tradition have been staged as often as these. Shakespeare's plays have been produced in every corner of the world, especially in times of political tumult, and are a Rorschach test of a culture's concerns and sensibilities. The ability of Renaissance drama to capture conflict and aspiration gives it a collection of voices that still speak to us, if we listen.

FURTHER READING

Barker, Simon, and Hilary Hinds, eds. *The Routledge Anthology of Renaissance Drama*. London and New York: Routledge, 2003.

Greenblatt, Stephen, Walter Cohen, Jean E. Howard, and Katherine Maus, eds. *The Norton Shakespeare*. New York: Norton, 1997.

Kinney, Arthur, ed. *Renaissance Drama: An Anthology of Plays and Entertainments*. Oxford: Blackwell, 2005.

ॐ

French Neoclassical Drama

Andrew Ade

THE EARLY FRENCH PROFESSIONAL THEATER AND
THE ASCENDANCY OF CLASSICISM

Until its recent decline, the theater held a place of prominence in France's cultural identity. No segment of French theater history enjoyed more lasting prestige than the seventeenth century enterprise of perfecting plays of classical design—works that have been repertory staples of the subsidized national theaters ever since. What began as an academic ideal became the artistic reflection of a monarchy devoted to the consistent exercise of absolute authority and the proliferation of beauty. As historian Jacques Barzun describes it, the long-reigning Louis XIV stared down rebellious nobles and ambitious powerbrokers by promoting a regulatory system of court etiquette, which transformed court life into a rehearsed spectacle of ritualized ceremony. By repositioning the palace community in a configuration of mutual surveillance, the King kept the nobles and state servants perpetually in his view and, equally important, visible to each other. He diverted them with an endless program of high-toned entertainments, including ballets, masques, and new plays by the country's most accomplished dramatists. Stealing focus in this "fusion of revelry and rivalry" was the King himself, who made the private habits of royal daily life (rising, dressing, eating, retiring) a form of giving audience to a select rotating list of favored courtiers. "Life at the court of Louis XIV was a daily drama in which he played the lead," concludes Barzun, with the resplendent suburban Palace of Versailles as its theater.

The careers and reputations of France's first professional actors, managers, and playwrights depended to a large degree on royal and aristocratic recognition, and by the mid-1600s their work aimed for a standard of execution to match the taste of their most privileged audiences. The epithets "Golden Age" and "Great Century," which rightly identify a high water mark for playwriting of a particular mode, also imply, misleadingly, a uniformity of style, stage convention, and dramatic purpose across the spectrum of coexisting theatrical endeavors. In truth, the history of French drama and performance between 1550 and 1700 is the confluence of numerous theatrical sources, native and foreign, esoteric and popular, occurring within a movement toward an official theater to represent a singular taste—i.e., that of the monarch and, by extension, the nation. Yet this movement met with continual resistance from artists and audiences alike, who had their own preferences for, and investments in, the living, interactive art of the theater. In the end, an approved dramatic canon triumphed, but at the cost of creating a sustained cultural divide of endorsement or disenfranchisement. Understanding the history of one requires an acknowledgement of the other, with a balanced regard for the techniques of poetic composition and the available material conditions of presentation.

THEATERS, CONVENTIONS, AND COMPANIES

Theaters

To some degree, we can attribute the remarkable rise and eventual dominance of French classical drama to policy decisions by sixteenth century authorities to control and protect sacred plays (*mystères*), which served to keep the French people connected to the Catholic Church. In 1518, François I granted a monopoly on all play performances of any kind, in Paris and its suburbs, to a century-old acting society, *la Confrérie de la Passion et Résurrection de Notre-Seigneur,* which, by a 1402 royal charter, had already enjoyed exclusive rights to all *religious* plays in the capital. Headquartered in a hall in the hospital of l'Église de la Trinité, the *Confrérie* also staged their mystery plays on the church steps and in street processions. In time the crowd-pleasing farce material, with which they padded the mysteries, and the profane plays they gave to keep their audiences interested began to worry both church and city officials with the prospect of public disorder.

In late 1548, after moving operations into a newly constructed building just north of the central city market, the *Confrérie* suffered a setback: the judicial assembly known as *le Parlement de Paris* banned it from giving further performances of the sacred mystery plays but allowed it to present "other secular, honest and decent mysteries, provided that there is in them no offence or insult to anyone"; the *Confrérie*, moreover, could keep their monopoly on all theater productions in Paris. Now confined to secular drama, the *Confrérie* struggled to generate a new repertoire, but by the late 1580s it had little choice but to operate its theater as a receiving house for visiting productions and arranged seasons by independent companies. It lost a crucial revenue source when, in 1595, the Parlement ended the *Confrérie's* monopoly on city play performances, thereby releasing theater troupes and open-air performers from their obligation to pay them permit fees. Further weakening the group's autonomy, beginning December, 1629, the royal company *Les Comédiens du Roi* (The King's Players) won first option on the theater space, regardless of other more lucrative bookings. Until an edict dissolved the *Confrérie* in 1676, it existed largely as a hamstrung theater landlord.

The theater building the *Confrérie* operated in between 1548 and 1676 was known as the Hôtel de Bourgogne, whose design, as W. L. Wiley has suggested, stuck closely to the dimensions of their original space in the Hôpital de la Trinité, without regard for comfort or sightlines. A rectangular structure with a raised stage at one end—without scenery, roughly 41 feet wide and 34 feet deep—and featuring a shallow upper stage at the back, the Bourgogne could accommodate over one thousand spectators, either standing or seated on benches in the *parterre*, in stage-level private boxes (*loges*) on either side, or on a raked *amphithéâtre* in the far back, rising to gallery seating in "the gods." Every Parisian theater of the period, including the private court theaters at the Louvre (Petit Bourbon) and Tuileries Palace (Salle des machines), assumed this boxed architectural plan; the more amenable thrust platform stage of the rounded London playhouses was never imitated in France.

At its simplest, the Bourgogne stage consisted of a bare playing area with tapestries hanging along the stage perimeter. Plays of romantic adventure, whose action unfolds in an improbable sequence of different locations, and adaptations of classical stories involving the skyward appearance of a mythological character, required painted drops, compressed compartment sets, and complicated mechanical devices. Surviving sketches by the Bourgogne's master set designer Laurent Mahelot reveal that the moveable mansions of medieval set design (*décor simultané*) persisted into the first decades of the seventeenth century, bringing together a play's multiple locations into a single comprehensive glance. By the 1640s, Italian-influenced design replaced the compartments with backdrops and wing flats to transform the space into a Serlian geometric perspective. Costuming was lavish and ornate, with only sparse attention to the historical period of the play action, and were usually the responsibility and property of the actors themselves. Performances took place in the afternoons, lighted by chandelier candles, and often featured live music by a small group of musicians. In stark contrast to English theater custom, actresses, such as Rachel Trépeau, Marie Venier, and her sister Colombe, were permitted to perform women's roles in the decorous poetic plays (though not in the ribald farces) at the Bourgogne from the first years of the seventeenth century, having already appeared on stage in the 1590s with troupes touring the provinces.

None of the Hôtel de Bourgogne's rival houses during this period originated as public theaters. They were instead converted tennis courts (*jeux de paume*), elongated wooden structures with tile roofs and side entrances from the courtyard leading to the street. The most prominent of these, second only to the Bourgogne in prestige, was the Théâtre du Marais, situated less than a mile west, and which opened in 1634. Many of the most successful playwrights of the age premiered their work at the Marais, beginning with Corneille, Mairet, and Tristan L'Hermite. Theater historians believe the Marais introduced the first stage curtain, perhaps for the hit production of *Le Cid* (1637), which preceded the curtain installed at the private Palais-Cardinal theater (later renamed the Palais-Royal), built by Cardinal de Richelieu in 1641. The upper-class practice of taking seats on the stage itself, in full view of the house, and thus reducing the available playing area for the actors, may also have begun here with this production. When the Marais burned to the ground during a performance in 1644, its proprietors quickly rebuilt it with a enlarged stage and added box seating—business-savvy improvements that prompted the Bourgogne to remodel in kind in 1647. Molière's company, L'Illustre Théâtre, also made their first home in a leased tennis court structure (but on the Left Bank) in 1643. Far from viewing these performance spaces as permanent headquarters, actors and playwrights moved with some regularity among all three theaters in response to artistic and administrative changes.

Italian Theater Companies

No account of the diverse seventeenth century theater world would be complete without acknowledging two other important centers of activity, both of which found their way into the fashionable public theaters mentioned above. The first were the Italian companies that had originally performed at the French court in Blois in 1572 by invitation of Charles IX and later by his brother Henry III, whose powerful Florentine mother Catherine de Médici had already exposed them to productions of translated Italian plays. These troupes, notably *I Gelosi*, played unrivaled in France from 1577 to 1599, whether giving command performances or touring the provinces, where they also worked as street mountebanks. While their repertoire embraced everything from tragedy to farce, their specialty was *commedia dell'arte*, built around a set of stock characters (Arlecchino, Pulcinella, Scaramuccia, Pantalone, Columbine, Scapini), whose predictable behaviors and artful physical expression in countless permutations of the same story made their Italian-language plays delightfully comprehensible. (The influence of these character types on French drama is later evident in comedies by Rotrou, Corneille, and Molière.) Although they enjoyed royal protection, the Italians ran up repeatedly against Paris authorities who considered them purveyors of debauchery. After 1599, the Italian troupes began renting out the Hôtel de Bourgogne for regular shows. The wife of the *Gelosi* leader, Isabella Andreini, made a particularly strong impression there in 1603 before her untimely death on her return trip home later that year. In 1660, Louis XIV permitted troupe leader Fiorilli to establish a Théâtre Italien in Paris, where they performed until 1697.

Public Entertainers

The other major element to insinuate its way into the theaters was the home-grown entertainment found in the city streets, squares, and fairgrounds. France's earliest public entertainers may have been born of urban commercial activity— stall sellers, seasonal fair traders, and open-air vendors, aggressively vying to win customers and outbid their competition through amusing monologues and playful harangues that approached dialogue scenes. Paris's natural venues for aspiring stage performers were the two fairgrounds for the annual city fairs, the Saint Germain (late winter) and Saint Laurent (summer). Acrobats tumbled and actors did satirical routines (*parades*) on temporary platform stages near the market pavilions. There as elsewhere in the city, certain performers entertained in order to prime crowds into buying questionable herbal remedies. The most famous of these *opérateurs*, Antoine Girard, hawked his brother's cure-all medicines on a trestle-stage in the Place Dauphine, a square just off the Pont Neuf, to great success between 1618 and 1626. Appearing in his trademark large pliable hat that could take a number of different shapes, Girard embodied the comic persona of "Tabarin" to deliver a variety of entertainments on humorous subjects, grouped as "Questions," "Preambles," and "Fantasies et Dialogues." Girard varied his medicine show by performing original farces opposite his wife and brother, each masked and acting the fixed three roles of valet, mistress and master.

Although there is no record of Girard performing in the Paris theaters, the *Comédiens du Roi* may have played his short, crudely constructed "farces tabarinesques" at the Hôtel de Bourgogne, where the most popular offering between 1600 and 1630 was the rough, bawdy show at the end of every bill. During those decades, each of their three leading *farceurs*, Robert Guérin (whose acting name was Gros Guillaume), Henri Legrand (Turlupin), and Hugues Guéru (Gaultier-Garguille)—the first with a floured face, the second masked, and the third bearded—incarnated a distinct, fixed character type of his own creation, as the native French equivalents of the *commedia* players who alternated rental of the Hôtel de Bourgogne in this period. Because of their capacity to improvise asides and physical gags, it fell to them during intervals or delays to perform songs or spar with an unruly *parterre* crowd to keep up interest and restore quiet.

Most successful of all in the business of audience management was company member Nicolas Des Lauriers, who had started his career performing on outdoor trestle-stages before joining the *Comédiens du Roi* under the stage name "Bruscambille." From 1609 to 1620, Des Lauriers came to the front of the open set stage to regale the incoming audience with original comic discourses on grand and mundane topics, which included a hymn to spittle, an appreciation of cabbage, and a reflection on gout. These witty pre-show speeches also met with a wide readership from three published collections of "fantasies," "harangues," and "prologues" in 1612 and 1615.

Des Lauriers used this stage pulpit to promote the value of theater itself, reminding the audience of its honored role in ancient cultures, the actor's usefulness to society, the qualitative difference between the noble *comédien* and the trivial *bouffon* or *bâteleur*, the art of stage declamation as essential speech training for lawyers, and the benefits of attending finer comedies over degrading farces. His "Prologue on Impatience," for instance, is a comeuppance for hooligans who goad the audience into riotous protests to force the performances to start early, and "Against Censors" inveighs against suspecting civic watchdogs who monitor the actors' work. Taken together, these prologues amount to an animated defense of theatergoing and the acting profession.

The stage work of Des Lauriers and the Bourgogne troupe as a whole evidences the dual nature of the nascent professional theater in France during the opening decades of the seventeenth century. Performers had to develop the capacity for both playful and reproving intimacy with the spectator in their struggle to maintain the audience's engagement in the play at hand. The financial necessity of performing vulgar farce, however, held the troupe's aspirations toward a higher art of verse plays in check. These conditions had defeated Valleran Le Conte, the leader of the *Comédiens du Roi* and France's first professional actor, after setting up operations at the Bourgogne in 1599. Though greatly respected by his peers, Valleran failed to win Parisian audiences over to the more ambitious tragedies and comedies. His sharp comedic talents may have made him his own worst enemy: Thomas Platter, a Swiss medical student visiting Paris that year, noted the enthusiastic reception Valleran received for his encore performance *after* the dignified tragedy, in which he improvised jokes on the events and gossip of the day, somewhat like the stand-up television talk-show hosts of our own day. Within a year, his audience made clear their preference for the coarser, smuttier joke material, and Valleran, after relinquishing the bill to the *farceurs*, finished out his short, uneven career in minor Paris engagements and provincial tours. Between the charm of the Italian players and the popularity of the Bourgogne comics, Paris's professional theater survived for the first third of the century principally on its ability to generate laughs.

CLASSICAL IMITATIONS AND GENRES

Whereas farce immediately connected with the widest audience, the high-minded verse plays in which Valleran and his troupe desired to specialize gradually drew support from the worlds of academic study, wealth and leisure, and royal and political power. The emerging French classical theater would henceforth bear the official imprimatur and the class values of these elite circles of privilege. In 1549, the year following the construction of the Hôtel de Bourgogne and the *Parlement* order forbidding the *Confrérie* to stage sacred plays, the *Pléiade* poet Joachim du Bellay, in his watershed treatise *La Deffense et illustration de la langue françoyse*, urged future French dramatic poets to turn away from medieval farces and morality plays and to restore comedy and tragedy to their ancient dignity, directing them to take as their "Archetypes" the surviving plays of Greece and Rome. For the next two centuries, French writers would debate the fitness of these models for a new era of dramatic art, struggling all the while to understand and enforce the dictates of classical authority.

Humanist scholars had only recently laid the groundwork for the imitation of recovered ancient play scripts. In the 1540s, George Buchanan and Marc Antoine de Muret wrote both Latin translations of ancient Greek plays and original plays in Latin, while Lazare de Baïf, Charles Estienne, Thomas Sebillet, and Jean de Péruse translated Sophocles, Euripides, and recent Italian dramatists into French. High school and university students read the masters of Roman comedy (Plautus and Terence) and tragedy (Seneca) as part of their Latin curriculum, and on occasion had permission to stage them on the school grounds. One such student, Etienne Jodelle, at the age of twenty-one, composed both the first regular French comedy (*Eugène*) and regular French tragedy (*Cléopâtre captive*) between 1552 and 1553. The former received a courtyard production at the Collège de Boncourt; the latter, a command performance for Henri II at the Hôtel de Reims. *Cléopâtre*, written in alexandrines and decasyllables, exhibited the formal components of Senecan tragedy, including a lengthy opening monologue, dialogue scenes of alternating laments, and a chorus, yet it had little in the way of characterization or dramatized situation. *Eugène*, a verse satire of a corrupt cleric, was similarly limited in its observance of Roman comedy.

Jodelle's work reveals a dutiful, if cursory, regard not only for classical texts but also for the Greek, Latin, and Italian dramatic criticism—and the subsequent French commentary—that was known at the time. Renaissance French critics relied heavily on the Late Classical writers Diomedes and Horace (whose *Ars Poetica* received a French translation by Jacques Peletier du Mans in 1545), and especially on the fourth century Roman grammarians Evanthius and Aelius Donatus, whose descriptive poetics assumed the importance of normative rules. Although Jules-César Scaliger would introduce Aristotle's hitherto unknown *Poetics* in his massive seven-part survey of poetic practice, *Poetices Libri Septem* (posthumously published in Lyon in 1561), Aristotelian ideas scarcely influenced the current of French criticism until the advent of Ludovico Castelvetro's Italian commentary a decade later. (Surprisingly, no French translation of Aristotle's *Poetics* existed before Le Sieur de Norville's *La Poétique d'Aristote, traduite du grec* in 1671; André Dacier's own *La Poétique d'Aristote* followed in 1692.)

Comedy

The French humanists' principal concerns with the ancients centered on their genre criticism—i.e., the analytic means to determine what constitutes a legitimate tragedy or comedy. Playwrights and critics alike looked to the prescriptive requirements stipulated by these experts to know how to construct a play, how to denounce a play, and how to defend a play. Risk-taking playwrights in particular participated in the theater debates in two ways: for comedies, they could provide a witty prologue that explained their innovations and their philosophical stance on the genre; for tragedies, they could attach to the published script a preface that argued seriously their specific beliefs about the aims of dramatic art. The early writers of French comedy, therefore, proceeded from received ideas that the play proper consists of a setup of the fictional plot (*protasis*), a complication of the plot (*epitasis*), and the plot's sudden turn for the best (*catastrophe*), all distributed over five acts; it opens with a prologue speech exterior to the action but has no chorus; comedy depicts the lives of average men and women, who speak in easy metered verse that suggests everyday language, and who exhibit behavior consonant with their "true" (i.e., class-determined) nature. Horace, Donatus, and Scaliger unanimously championed the six Roman plays of Terence as the best models for comedy. French comedies in the wake of Jodelle, like Jacques Grevin's *La Trésorière* (1559) and *Les Esbahis* (1561), and Jean de la Taille's *Les Corrivaux* (1562)—cited as the first original comedy in French prose—sought to reconcile the properties of ancient comedy with the needs of the contemporary stage. Other noteworthy comedies of the period include Odet de Turnebé's *Les Contens* (1580), Francois d'Amboise's *Les Néapolitaines* (1584), Jean Godard's *Les Déguisez* (1594), Pierre Troterel's *Les Corrivaux* (1612) and *Gilette* (1617), Adrien de Montluc's *La Coméedie des proverbes* (1616), and Jean Claveret's *L'Esprit fort* (1629), the first French comedy of manners.

A fascinating variant of French comedy grew out of the Hôtel de Bourgogne's teasing prologue routines on the business of theater and, at the same time, exploited the baroque construct called *le théâtre dans le théâtre* (the play-within-a-play), first introduced in Balthazar Baro's *Celinde* (1629). N. Gougenot's *La Comédie des comédiens* (1632), written expressly for the *Comédiens du Roi*, stretches a false cancellation announcement over two full acts before starting the main three-act play, entitled *La Courtisane*. The troupe manager's opening speech gives over to staged chaos, during which he settles disputes among the entire company of thirteen and even recruits a new actor to play the young lover role, until he can lead them off to start *La Courtisane*. As the backstage crisis gives no hint of its fictive nature, it rises to theatrical *trompe l'oeil*; more ingenious, Gougenot has the actors playing fictionalized versions of themselves, which lends them a heightened stage reality. Some months later, the rival company led by Montdory premiered its own *Comédie des comédiens* at the Théâtre de la Fontaine, a newly outfitted tennis-court theater. Its author, Georges de Scudéry, also predicated it on the troupe's efforts to resolve business and personal matters before performing a short play, *L'Amour caché par l'Amour*, but here Montdory complains that his actors insist on performing as though they were a different troupe altogether, working in Lyon under new stage names, no less. He soon capitulates, and the actors carry out their fanciful impersonation with such skill that Montdory finally joins them out of newfound appreciation for the acting profession. Scudéry's *Comédie des comédiens* has the actors playing at several removes from their audience, as a way to showcase their talent and to celebrate the enchanting paradoxical nature of theater. Unfortunately, these two self-conscious, self-referential plays appeared at a time of increasing support for illusionistic, representational theater. A casualty of classicism, the multi-level, metatheatrical French play would not win popular and critical acceptance until the twentieth century.

Tragedy

The gestation of French tragedy proved even more controversial, insofar as its ontological nature was harder to agree upon, its properties more difficult to ascertain, and its form more stressful to achieve. The late classical critics had delineated tragedy as the essential opposite of comedy: its plot, with a basis in history or mythology, must have a beginning, a middle, and an end; it begins in calm but ends in terrible calamity, with death and/or exile; its characters are high-born, powerful, and speak weighty sentiments in poetic verse; it has no prologue speech but assigns a chorus to deliver solemn moral truths about human existence after each of the five acts. With the late sixteenth-century infusion of Aristotelian ideas, French tragic composition had to negotiate additional principles of complex plotting: peripety (the reversal of a character's fortunes), recognition (a character's change from ignorance to knowledge), and plot resolution, created through the plot itself and not by improbable or external means such as *dei ex machina*. Plot, character, thought, and diction had to blend into an organic whole, so as to elicit pity and fear, only to purge them in a satisfying dramatic conclusion.

It is hardly surprising, then, that efforts to meet these standards led to a variety of offshoot tragic forms and, necessarily, creative defenses for them. The publication of Théodore de Bèze's *Abraham sacrifiant* (1550), subsequent to its student production in Lausanne, Switzerland, inaugurated the subgenre of biblical tragedy in France. This new type of sacred drama, which essentially imposed ancient Greek tragic structure onto Judeo-Christian story material, was almost exclusively the work of Protestant writers who believed in its potential moral power. It enjoyed a late-sixteenth-century vogue, encompassing Louis des Masures's *Tragedies saintes* (1566), André de Rivaudeau's *Aman, tragedie saincte* (1566), Jean de la Taille's *Saül le furieux* (1572) and *La Famine* (1573), Robert Garnier's *Juives* (1583), Antoine de Montchrestien's *Aman* (1601) and *David* (1601), and Pierre de Nancel's trilogy *Dina, Josué, Débora* (1606), and had brief revivals before undergoing Racinian refinement in *Esther* (1689) and *Athalie* (1691).

For *Saül le furieux*, its author provided a landmark theoretical preface on tragedy in general, which drew on his fervor for Greek and Roman critics and for new plays made "in the mold of the ancients." In "De l'art de la Tragédie," La Taille repeats various Horatian dicta, including five-act division, the necessity of keeping violence offstage for purposes of decorum, and of introducing the story *in medias res*. His endorsement of Aristotelian ideas, such as the need to move audiences to pity and fear and to avoid the "cold" subjects of excessively evil or saintly heroes, suggests that he already knew of Scaliger's and perhaps Castelvetro's recent commentaries. Most intriguing is his statement, "The history or play must always be performed within a single day, at a single time and in a single place." La Taille's expansion of Aristotle's unity of action and preferred dramatic time span of a single day, to a tripartite structural ideal, marked French criticism's first step toward the establishment of the three unities (action, time, place) that would epitomize classical theory. Proponents of tragedy were eager to promote its moral didacticism and aesthetic pleasures. Important works include Jacques Grévin's *La Mort de César* (1561), Antoine de Montchrestien's *Hector* (1604), Alexandre Hardy's *Mariamne* (1610), Tristan L'Hermite's *La Mariamne* (1630) and *La Mort de Sénèque* (1644), Jean Mairet's *La Sophonisbe* (1634), and Jean de Rotrou's *Hercule Mourant* (1634) and *Saint Genest* (1645). French tragedies before 1630 were stubbornly Senecan in form and style: rich in imagery and epigram but somewhat lifeless in characterization and obtuse in plot. Their failure to make their choruses integral to the action led to its disappearance during the early 1600s. Virtually every French tragedy, however, took an ancient story as its subject, one notable exception being Montchrestien's *La Reine d'Écosse* (1601) on the death of Mary, Queen of Scots.

Tragicomedy

Playwrights' growing resistance to the generic constraints—and audiences' waning interest in the sober tragic stories—gave momentum to a second variation:

tragicomedy. Ostensibly a hybrid of tragedy and comedy, it was in practice a play of romantic adventure, having a possibly heroic central character, who, after weathering certain distressing incidents, meets with a happy ending. To the extent that Aristotle, Horace, and Donatus had acknowledged that some ancient plays deviate from the parameters of tragic construction, many French dramatists felt justified in exploring tragicomedy as the form best suited to stories that need to transgress the severe limits of a single day's duration and the rigid separation of serious and commonplace events. The first French tragicomedy proved to be enduringly popular: Robert Garnier's *Bradamante* (1582) presents the story of a warrior-maiden who, by Charlemagne's decision, must marry the man who defeats her in arena competition, only to win the man she loves in the end after losing to (she thinks) a stranger. The popular success of *Bradamante* guarantied tragicomedy's place in the theaters, and Garnier's effective metrical pattern in alexandrines (12 syllables) and rhyming couplets became thereafter the standard for all French dramatic composition. Among the most celebrated French tragicomedies are Jean de Schelandre's reworked *Tyr et Sidon* (1628), Scudéry's *L'Amour tyrannique* (1638), Rotrou's *Don Bernard de Cabrère* (1647), and Corneille's *Don Sanche d'Aragon* (1649).

The first type of tragicomedy to win public favor after 1600 was pastoral tragicomedy—a mid-sixteenth-century Italian concoction, perfected by Torquato Tasso and Giovanni Battista Guarini. It conjured a fantasy world of archetypal tender lovers in romantic peril, within a mood of rustic harmony, overseen by divine management. Tasso and Guarini invested the pastoral drama with the classical features of five-act structure, a chorus, and a prologue speech in the manner of Plautus's comedies, i.e., given by a mythical or allegorical character such as "Cupid," "Night," "Dawn," or even an Arcadian river. Guarini, author of the benchmark pastoral tragicomedy *Il Pastor Fido* (1590), wrote a spirited defense of all tragicomedy in *Compendio della poesia tragicomica* (1599), championing it for avoiding the excesses of both tragedy and comedy, and for purging the audience's melancholy with delight. These fussy, fanciful Italian plays, mixing the bucolic with the supernatural, found immediate favor with fashionable French audiences who swooned over the pastoral elements in Théophile de Viau's tragedy *Pyrame et Thisbé* (1621). Pastoral tragicomedy's propensity for supernatural characters, who appear in spectacularly staged vignettes on the theater's upper stage, gave rise to the "machine play," the popular subgenre of special-effects theater.

It fell to a young writer of pastoral tragicomedy, de Viau's protégé Jean Mairet, to ignite serious interest in establishing an authoritative classical paradigm for French theater. In his 1631 "Préface" to *Silvanire, ou la Morte-vive* (1630), Mairet, inspired by his Italian predecessors, resolved to hold to the ancient models so precisely as to bring an original French tragicomedy "to its perfection." (He would later realize this objective in his acclaimed *Sophonisbe* (1634), considered the first regular French classical tragedy.) He calls limiting the duration of dramatic action to a single day "one of the fundamental laws of the theater"; remarkably, he backs this claim with the (incorrect) assertion that the ancient dramatists never failed to do so. Mairet's self-assured manifesto had an immediate effect on French classicism, in that it elevated the two long-standing poetic principles of propriety (*la bienséance*) and verisimilitude (*la vraisemblance*) to the essential watchwords of correct dramatic composition. Fellow classicists like Jean Chapelain shared Mairet's belief that propriety's demand for appropriately rendered speech and action—i.e., suited to the social type—in turn becomes the basis for a play's verisimilitude—i.e., its overall believability as a probable action. Carrying further Mairet's argument, they were now able to posit the three unities of action, time, and place. By 1635, when Cardinal Richelieu, himself a theater and Italian arts enthusiast, founded the forty-member *Académie française* to perfect the French language, charter member Chapelain (among others) had enshrined propriety, verisimilitude, and the three unities as indissociable conditions for manifesting true and regular drama. Although it would not go completely unchallenged, this daunting formulation created a long-lasting "official" view of drama that would both glorify and torment its best practitioners at work in an increasingly politicized literary world.

CORNEILLE, RACINE, MOLIÈRE

Pierre Corneille

The mid-seventeenth century call for regularity shaped the practices of the three giants of the French theater, whose names would variously become identified with neo-classicism. The first was Pierre Corneille (1606–84), a native of Rouen, who had trained in law and administration before undertaking a theater career. At 23, he joined forces with a traveling troupe, run by the up-and-coming actor Montdory, to provide them new plays to offer the growing Parisian audience. Nearly all his plays in the first half of his career premiered with this company at their theatrical base, the Théâtre du Marais. After workmanlike efforts exploring dramatic form in comedy, tragicomedy, and tragedy, he had a notable success in *L'Illusion comique* (1636), an ingeniously convoluted play that boasted "so many irregularities that it is not worth considering it." Designed as a tragedy inside a comedy inside a magical frame story, with a *coup de théâtre* revelation of a play-within-the-play only in the last major speech, *L'Illusion* appears initially to express baroque themes of deception, intrigue, and world instability, through the familiar episodic adventure, love tangle, and onstage violence of tragicomedy. Only at the end do we grasp that Corneille had all along been equating the illusion of life with that of the commercial theater, and that, despite our anxieties, the world has its own sense of order and resolution and inclines toward happiness.

Although Corneille freely confessed that *L'Illusion* was a work "of bizarre and extravagant invention," he declared it to be of value because it was *new*—a statement that in effect heralded the work to come as he transitioned to the tragedy envisioned in the Mairet-Chapelain essays. Corneille created a sensation with his next play, *Le Cid* (1637), a Spanish tale in which an indignant slap between two aging Castilian noblemen leads to the honor killing of the aggressor, which in turn imperils his daughter's engagement to the son of the disgraced man. Sell-out audiences thrilled to Corneille's verse text as it deftly captured the hopeless efforts of the young lovers, Chimène and Rodrigue, to extricate themselves from the ties of filial duty, personal honor, and societal expectations in order to preserve their love. After genuine offers of self-sacrifice and Rodrigue's sudden heroism fighting the Moors, they present their heartbreaking dilemma to their King, whose creative resolution sanctions their marrying only after a period of mourning. With this radical condensation of Guillén de Castro's sprawling *Las Mocedades del Cid* (1621), Corneille had hit on a fresh, though generically ambiguous, conception of French drama that would please the paying audience and, after some fierce debate among critics and admonishment by the *Académie* (led by Chapelain), find acceptance.

Over the next decade, Corneille produced a run of regular tragedies on fabled figures of the ancient Mediterranean world—aptly, the imperial setting of artful oratory and rhetoric, as simulated in his heroic verse. He fashioned an alternative classical dramaturgy that is neither truly Greek nor Roman in the handling of plot. As he would later explain in his major statement on dramatic form and purpose, the three-part *Discours sur le poème dramatique* (1660), he redesigned tragedy's first act "to contain the seeds of all that has to happen, as much for the main action as for the episode." Rather than require the spectators to keep in mind the necessary details of the cursed fates of noble families, as traditionally recounted in an extended opening monologue or tedious expository scene, he plunges them straightaway into a world of apprehension, newly troubled by a dream, an oracle, or a recent shift in the political landscape. The complications and tragic errors that trap the characters in a distressing ethical dilemma do not originate in the back story but arise *before the eyes of the audience,* who are thereafter keen to attend the agonizing process by which the characters make choices and face their particular outcomes. This immediacy of incident, rendered clear, swift, and logical, is the product of Corneille's rational approach to creating a unity of action. In the event, it keeps both audience and action fully present in the theatrical experience, and allows spectators to account for the story's beginning, middle, and end.

We find a similar rational economy at work in his reconception of tragic character, beginning with a general axiom: as the story requires that the individual be subordinate to the state, so the dramaturgy makes character subordinate to tragic situation. Corneille reassigns the choric function to confidants (in the synecdochical form of nurses, friends, freed slaves, ladies in waiting and other royal retinue), and he purifies the heroic leads in thought and feeling so that they may act in certitude of noble beliefs, even if it demands the sacrifice of their own lives for a righteous cause. Corneille's men and women possess uncommon souls, open hearts, and conspicuous moral codes. They utter relentlessly elevated sentiments even in the most emotional circumstances. Words signifying abstract qualities of the imagined national character, such as duty (*devoir*), honor (*honneur*), reputation (*gloire*), and virtue (*vertu*), resonate forcefully as they circulate within the play texts; as a result, the characters approach allegory in their embodiment of particular ideals of family and state. Thus, the title character in *Horace* (1640), chosen by Rome to fight to the death the three brothers of his Alban wife, only to slay afterward his sister Camille (the fiancé of one of the dead) for her curses on Rome, nevertheless receives the Roman emperor's pardon in recognition of his true and natural self: "Your virtue places your glory above your crime."

The actions of the Cornelian tragic hero have the transformative power to edify those who bear witness to them. In *Polyeucte* (1642), the Roman governor, his daughter Pauline, and the war hero who loves her ultimately renounce their pagan beliefs for Christianity after seeing the unbending resolve of her converted husband Polyeucte, whose willing martyrdom signals a decisive show of God's grace. *Cinna* (1640) depicts crises of conscience and betrayal that occur among conspirators to assassinate Emperor Augustus. These disaffected but fundamentally decent people experience a change of heart that stays their plans, but the greater triumph is Augustus's magnanimous response to their confession, as urged by Empress Livia: "clemency is the most beautiful mark / By which the world may know a true monarch." All five Corneille plays previously cited evidence a signature plotting device: the crystallization of the story into a configuration of two (or three) imperiled characters standing before a power figure who tests or judges them. Whether the figure unperturbedly resolves the crisis (*L'Illusion, Le Cid, Horace*) or undergoes a painful enlightenment of his own (*Cinna, Polyeucte*), his theatrical function is to teach Corneille's audience (and his monarch) how best to rule. Almost every one of Corneille's plays, therefore, ends in optimism, as either a lessening of sorrow or a prospect of hope.

Corneille vigorously explicated and defended his plays in the seven editions of his work published in his lifetime, either in short supplementary texts titled "Dedicatory Epistle," "Forward," "To the Reader," and "Examination," or in the longer *Discours,* in which he responded to the state of contemporary criticism. The most prominent of these critics was Cardinal Richelieu's protégé, François Hédelin, the

Abbé d'Aubignac, whose influential study of theater practice, *La Pratique du théâ-tre* (1657), stood as the most extensive discussion of ancient drama to date and served as a handbook on the writing of new regular plays based on the inviolable principles of propriety and verisimilitude. Corneille presented a working drama-tist's rebuttal to the official dramaturgy by questioning the unreasonable interpre-tations of verisimilitude, moral utility, pity and terror, and the three unities. His essays, as Marvin Carlson puts it, constitute "the century's most fully developed statement of disagreement with the prevailing assumptions of French neoclassic theatrical theory." He never overcame the ambivalence in his methods; the author of the solemn, neoclassical *Horace* could not forsake the creator of the delightfully irregular *L'Illusion comique*. Despite his claims to applied classicism, Corneille remained in the camp of François Ogier, André Mareschal, and Georges de Scudéry, who favored a more flexible poetics.

Discouraged by the failure of his 1651 tragedy *Pertharite*, Corneille returned to Rouen for an eight-year hiatus, during which he prepared a new edition of his plays and worked out his three *Discours*. His attempt to reconquer the Paris the-ater started strong with *Oedipe* (1659) and the dazzling machine play *La Toison d'or* (1660), but abated until his definitive retirement in 1674. It is possible to view this respectable—but losing—fifteen-year battle as his slow capitulation to an entrenched classicism he could never fully indulge, for within five years a new-comer on the scene would fascinate the devotees of tragedy with an unmatched ability to conform his dramatic composition to the neoclassical ideal.

Jean Racine

Born more than a generation after Corneille, Jean Racine (1639–99) received a rigorous education in philosophy, rhetoric, and classical languages, and assimi-lated the principles of regularity from an early age. He knew the major classicist commentary by the formidable critics Heinsius and d'Aubignac, and even owned the 1573 edition of Pietro Vettori's 1560 Latin translation of Aristotle's *Poetics* (Racine's margin notes are among the first extant French translations of key passages of the *Poetics*.) Unable to obtain a position in the church, Racine con-centrated on tribute poetry to the King, which brought him monetary awards and admission to the court in 1663. He turned his talents to tragedy, but his first produced plays, *La Thébaïde* (1664) and *Alexandre le Grand* (1665), met with only limited success. It is surprising that Racine turned to playwriting at all, given the anti-theater stance of his pious educators at the Convent of Port-Royal, the Catholic collective that followed the austere doctrine of Jansenism. But Racine, reared by relatives after being orphaned at age three, asserted throughout his life an independence from even the most influential institutions and mentors—from all, that is, but one: Louis XIV.

His theater career took off with his third tragedy, *Andromaque* (1667), the first of eight works for the tragedians at the Hôtel de Bourgogne. The story emerges from the physical and emotional desolation of the Trojan War. Pyrrhus, king of Epirus in northwestern Greece, has returned from the ruins of Troy with dead Hector's wife Andromaque and infant son Astyanax as prisoners. When the Greek envoy Orestes arrives to demand the death of Hector's child, Pyrrhus, who desires Andromaque, uses the threat to force her to reciprocate affection for him. Unable to dishonor her husband's memory in that way, she agrees to marry Pyrrhus only to save her child, with the secret aim of killing herself afterward. Egged on by Hermione, Pyrrhus's spurned fiancée, Orestes and his men slay Pyrrhus at the wedding, just moments after his crowning Andromaque, and the shock of Orestes' subsequent report of it drives Hermione to suicide and Orestes mad. Each living character in the deadlock chain of frustrated love (Orestes-Hermione-Pyrrhus-Andromaque-dead Hector) is torn between sexual desire and a sense of commitment, be it honor, pride or duty, and in the end only the devoted Andromaque, now Queen, survives, as her morally compromised captors crumble around her.

This first great play of Racine's offers a new conception of tragedy for a new age. Unlike Corneille's heroic characters, who find the wherewithal to take action according to their convictions, Racine's wage war with themselves too long to arrive at satisfactory solutions, and break free only in irrational and fatal acts of self-preservation. Love, in its recognizable manifestations of passion, desire, jealousy, cruelty, and self-sacrifice, now becomes an authentic cause—or, at least, agency—for tragedy. Corneille saw this as a wrongheaded approach to classical composition and, more personally, as an encroachment on his dramatic territory. Here, and in subsequent plays, he objected to Racine's brazen rewriting of the known historical and mythological facts of the ancient story material and to the anachronisms that riddled the dialogue. But many in the audience, including the King, found in Racine's exploration of the human heart greater psychological realism than they had known before in the theater. Thus, the five acts divide the story into psychological stages rather than action segments, as in Corneille. In what must have resonated publicly as a symbolic contest of gifted tragic poets—perhaps even redolent of Aristophaneste pitting of Aeschylus and Euripides in the underworld poetry contest in *The Frogs*—both men premiered a version of the love story of Titus and Berenice, a week apart, in November 1670; thirty-year-old Racine's *Bérénice* was judged superior to sixty-four-year-old Corneille's *Tite et Bérénice*. In a valiant last effort to prove his flexibility and vitality as a artist, Corneille gave the public a Racinian love tragedy of his own, *Suréna* (1674). When it failed to attract notice, Corneille left the theater for good.

The decade of plays that followed expanded on the tragic universe Racine had begun to chart in *Andromaque*. He took up political intrigue in his next tragedy, *Britannicus* (1669), which depicts the young emperor Nero's murderous first steps toward despotism. Having fallen in love with Junia, the young woman promised to his step-brother Britannicus, Nero breaks with the counsel of his controlling mother Agrippina and his tutor Burrhus, and he poisons Britannicus, whom he also suspects of vying for the throne. But when the distraught Junia takes refuge in the Temple of Vesta, Nero's compounded losses lead him to early madness. This vision of ancient Rome as a practice yard for deceit and treachery, where spies and assassins lurk, and innocence is toyed with or snuffed out, is far darker than that of the conscience-stricken conspirators in Corneille's *Cinna*. Racine's characters creep cautiously through an atmosphere of paranoia, and must weigh the validity of a string of false reports, hushed warnings, and feigned testimonials. The center-piece of *Britannicus* (2.3-8), for instance, is a suspenseful eavesdropping episode of unnatural silences and disjointed dialogue, in which Nero watches and listens from the shadows as Junia, on his command, discourages Britannicus by denying her feelings for him. Once again (and later in *Iphigénie en Aulide*), Racine orchestrates the climax around a killing at a sacred site (altar, temple) to signify the sacrifice that ancient tragedy required. As in all his plays, no kingly adjudicator steps forward to resolve matters that threaten stability; rather, the ruling figure either shares in tragic suffering or exacts punishment on the sinners in absentia: e.g., in the bloody Turkish seraglio tragedy, *Bajazet* (1672), the sultan Amurat never appears on stage, yet puts an end to the scandal at home by sending his wife's and brother's death warrants from abroad, in the invisible, impersonal manner of fate.

Racine's title characters, when not the central tragic figures (*Bérénice, Mithridate, Phèdre*), are the very objects of desire or hatred that unwittingly incite the emotional disorder of the plots (*Andromaque, Britannicus, Bajazet*). Racinian tragic heroes become enslaved by their passions, experience shame, and consult confidants, who may only make things worse. Hesitant and indecisive, they conceal their feelings, which, if made public, would bring punishment down upon them; failing to avoid the ones they fear, they spin lies. When they finally confess openly to those they love but cannot have, their rejection incites them to behave abominably toward them. Increasingly aware of the world closing in and the clock running down on their lives, they take desperate, frenzied action that only backfires and ends in death. *Phèdre* (1677) is the finest example of this tragic paradigm. Racine preserves the essential schema of Euripides's *Hippolytus*, while softening the contours of the main characters so as to make them pitiable to a modern audience. The play's careful presentation of the oscillations in Phèdre's agonizing struggle to manage her illicit love for her step-son, Hippolytus, adroitly renders the tragic character's futile effort to extricate herself from a destiny in which she is utterly complicit.

Much of the strangeness of Racine's theater is due to its unique dramatic purpose of self-analysis. His characters dissect and explicate their motives, predicaments, and ill-fated ends without cease, and rarely if ever do they learn the plays' implicit lessons of wisdom. Their discourse is clean, intelligible, and concentrated, using a vocabulary of only a few thousand words. Where Corneille's texts ring with grandiloquence and glamorize abstract concepts, Racine's produce a flow of recurring words and images that interconnect the characters and simulate the sweep of mounting doom. Words that signify ordinary, often concrete objects acquire symbolic value, often sexual: e.g., "eye," "monster," "design," "veil," "voyage," fires," "flame." What's more, the texts are virtually free of stage directions. Requisite stage design asks only for an all-purpose palace setting, usually a room of common access, in which characters confess their paralyzing crises between entrances and exits. These characteristics and conditions dovetail easily with the unities of action, time, and place that Racine worked to respect.

It is his interpretation of verisimilitude, however, that best accounts for his ability to achieve the plays' remarkable compression and intensity. In the Prefaces to his plays, he describes verisimilitude as the essential picture of a story that the public has come to believe, rather than the strict historical record of events. This gives the playwright greater license to shape the story to dramaturgical parameters while preserving its credibility with the audience. His *Bérénice* (1670) benefited from such thinking, inasmuch as it departed from standard tragic design to realize extreme classical simplicity: the plot simply marks the end to the fabled love affair between Titus, the new Emperor of Rome, and Bérénice, Queen of Judeah, due to insurmountable political pressure (Rome will not allow Titus to marry a foreigner). Although it does not climax in a death, it lays claim to tragedy for its heroic characters, its ability to excite an audience's passions, and for its "majestic sadness," which alone gives us tragic pleasure. Racine concludes, "The principal rule is to please and to move: all the others are made only to achieve this first one."

Molière

The third career of prominence, that of the most versatile theater practitioner of the age, occurred between—but not wholly independent of—those of the two tragic poets: Jean-Baptiste Poquelin (1622–73), working under the professional name "Molière," first won royal approval performing in a revival of Corneille's *Nicomède* in 1658 (later teaming with him for the spectacle *Psyché*), and he gave Racine his first break by producing his two earliest tragedies. But as playwright, Molière had to stake his territory elsewhere to achieve a level of artistry comparable to these masters. While Corneille and Racine each contributed one exceptional comedy to the neoclassical age, respectively, *Le Menteur* (1642) and *Les Plaideurs* (1668), the comic genre belonged unquestionably to Molière. The son of a royal household valet and upholsterer, Molière at twenty-one abandoned the law career he had trained for to form a troupe called *L'Illustre-Théâtre,* with aspirations to distinguish themselves as interpreters of French tragedy. They soon incurred financial problems, for which Molière served briefly in debtor's prison. For the next twelve years they toured the French provinces until returning to Paris in 1658 as the *Troupe de Monsieur,* under the protection of the King's only brother, Philippe, duc d'Orléans. Little is known about Molière's formative touring years beyond the fact that they provided test audiences for the farces and early comedies he wrote to balance the troupe's repertoire. Shortly upon resettling in Paris, Molière scored his first success with a farcical one-act in prose, *Les Précieuses ridicules* (1659), a broadly funny satire of the affected gentility and erudition of the social-climbing bourgeoisie. Ostensively, it targeted the laughably inadequate imitators of the aristocratic literary salons, where wealthy art lovers cultivated a courtly *préciosité*—i.e., an idiom of overrefined conversation and conduct inspired by the gallantry and sensitivity in heroic romance novels. Yet, a stinging criticism of the absurdities of the actual *salons* themselves could not have been lost on members of the audience.

The significance of *Les Précieuses ridicules* lay in Molière's discovery that pretension and obsessive self-regard were viable sources of levity, as effective (and profitable) as clownish costumes and antic situation. It pointed him toward a comedy of character, whose business it is, he wrote, "to present generally all the defects of men, principally of the men of our century." Such satiric purpose inevitably brought him a host of troubles with jealous rivals, offended courtiers, and factions in the religious community. While we cannot reduce Molière's compositional approach to a fixed template, we may identify several major tendencies in his work that drew on his familiarity with classic Roman comedy. He updated the ancient figures of the irritable father (*senex*) and the wily slave (*servus*) to the modern types of the neurotic bourgeois parent (Sganarelle) and his clever, mischievous servant (Mascarille or Scapin)—roles that Molière himself enjoyed taking. It is the comedic function of the latter to contrive ruses that will either accomplish or thwart the wishes of the former, usually in matters of matrimony, as seen in *L'Étourdi* (1655), *Les Précieuses ridicules* (1659), *L'Amour médecin* (1665), *Le Médecin malgré lui* (1666), and *Les Fourberies de Scapin* (1671). Where Roman plots turned on a father's efforts to marry off his son to best advantage, Molière's capitalized on the modern bourgeois difficulty of marrying off a *daughter* safely and profitably: e.g., *Le Dépit amoureux* (1656), *L'École des maris* (1661), *L'École des femmes* (1662), *La Princesse d'Élide* (1664), *Le Médecin malgré lui* (1666), *Le Sicilien* (1667), *L'Avare* (1668), *Monsieur de Pourceaungac* (1669), *Le Bourgeois gentilhomme* (1670), and *Le Malade imaginaire* (1673). A few of his plays, however, scarcely rise above the dirty tricks, misunderstandings, and "comedies of error" of Plautus, including *Sganarelle* (1660), *Dom Garcie de Navarre* (1661), and *Monsieur de Pourceaungac* (1669).

Molière's most mature works, however, give full focus to the destructive effects of human faults and vices, and provide, moreover, sharp, sometimes dark, psychological insights. Each play becomes a study of a small pathology, which the title often announces: *Le Tartuffe* (1664, rewritten 1667) is a dual portrait of a dissembler of piety and his gullible disciple; *Le Misanthrope* (1666), an exposé of a people-hating egotist who, in pursuit of love with an arch coquette, comes up empty-handed; *L'Avare* (1668), the very picture of miserliness and its capacity to compromise a family's emotional and moral health; *Le Bourgeois gentilhomme* (1670), a tableau of foolish middle-class ambition spurred by delusions of social quality; *Les Femmes savantes* (1672), a depiction of how a mania for pedantic intellectual pursuits blinds one to material truths; and *Le Malade imaginaire* (1673), a testament to the power of hypochondria to incapacitate one's reason. Common to all his plays is an eccentric character of stubborn self-interest, who, being duped by opportunists or by his own illusions, throws a household into chaos until a trickster or an agent of chance restores order. Interestingly, the ever-present issue of matrimony, when interpreted as the fruits of young lovers' courtship, is a desirable, enviable prospect, while the road-tested marriage glimpsed in mid-course is less a pairing off than a squaring-off of contentious, dissatisfied husbands and wives.

In addition to his prose and verse comedies, Molière devised hybrid court entertainments with a view to satisfying the King's interest in music and dancing. These were variously categorized as *comédie galante*, *comédie pastorale héroïque*, or *tragédie-ballet*, and could feature machine play special effects. His most popular creation was the *comédie-ballet*, a five-act comedy with a lengthy interlude of music, singing, and ballet after each act. These include *Les Fâcheux* (1661), *L'Amour médecin* (1665), *Monsieur de Pourceaungac* (1669), *Les Amants magnifiques* (1670), *Le Bourgeois gentilhomme* (1670), and *Le Malade imaginaire* (1673). (Revivals have customarily excised the interludes without doing any architectural harm to the comedy within.) Molière capitalized on his relationship with Louis XIV, who bestowed on him play commissions, performance permissions, royal protection (he renamed the troupe "The King's Company" in 1665), actor pensions, cash, his time and society, and, best of all, his own theater, the Palais-Royal, where the troupe could debut new plays or transfer their well-received court productions. Molière also premiered plays at royal residences and retreats (the Louvre, Versailles, Saint-Germain-en-Laye, Chambord).

The marvelous simplicity of Molière's work, despite its capacity for added spectacle, is that normally it requires no more than a table and chair to stage. The language is expansive, borrowed from the different spheres in which Molière moved (court, urban streets, provinces). It makes comic points through basic patterns of repetition: a character reveals a one-track mind by repeatedly asking or responding in the same way to an interlocutor; another is unable to do other than what he is originally told, regardless of changes in context. That bits of knockabout farce continued to appear in his comedies indicates an inherent resistance to a comedy of speech alone, and is, moreover, symptomatic of his qualified allegiance to classicism. His five-act verse texts betray a tempered regard for the Academic rules; his prefaces, even less. Molière preferred to dramatize the debates over his work in protective comedies of their own. In *La Critique de l'École des femmes* (1663), Molière's polemical afterplay to retaliate against hostile criticisms to his latest hit, *L'École des femmes*, Lycidas, a petty adherent to classicism, claims that the play, in which he finds one hundred defects, "sins against all the rules of art," as anyone familiar with Aristotle and Horace could tell. When he begins to count out the ancient terms for the quantitative parts of a play, the sensible Dorante (Molière's spokesman) wittily asks him to "humanize" his speech with more accessible French expressions in place of pretentious Greek. Holding to the belief that the greatest rule of poetry is to please, he asks plainly "whether a play that has reached its goal hasn't followed the right path." On a more practical level, Uranie, a young lady unversed in classicist issues, amusingly observes that "those who talk about the rules the most and who know them better than others do, write comedies that no one finds attractive." Apart from his published defenses of *Le Tartuffe*, which protest a bit too stridently that "the function of comedy is to correct men's vices," Molière spends no more time arguing the merits of classicism.

The three careers discussed above attest to the peculiarly combative art world of mid-seventeenth-century Paris, where to succeed in the theater was to gain bitter enemies. Whether acting on behalf of institutions, private groups, or exercising self-promotion, critics asserted their "authoritative" assessments of new plays to keep themselves equal if not superior to the artist. Thus, close on the heels of Corneille's runaway hit *Le Cid* came a series of pamphlet attacks on the play's unsuitable subject, improbable plot, and structural irregularity. Corneille and his supporters entered into a public squabble (*querelle*) with his accusers—among them, Georges de Scudéry, who turned to the newly founded *Académie* to appraise the work. After a six-month examination, the *Académie* issued a lengthy opinion, which judged *Le Cid* to be in violation of the rules of verisimilitude and held Corneille accountable for the morally irresponsible resolution of the permitted marriage. (Corneille would argue a defense of the play throughout his long life.) Thereafter, dramatists understood that to write a play was to engage politically with the state position on dramatic art.

After the scuffle over *L'École des femmes* in 1663, Molière had to appeal for royal intervention against a religious group known as *les dévots*, who labeled his *Tartuffe* (1664) an offense to piety and a smear on the clergy's moral work of guiding the laity. Some sought to have Molière burned at the stake and, more damaging, ban public performances. Time was on Molière's side, for when a retooled version of the play finally reached the Palais-Royal public in February 1669, its premiere set a box-office record for the troupe. Finally, Racine endured an especially malicious act of sabotage on New Year's Day, 1677, when the Duchess of Bouillon, a financier of the cabal against him, bought up the Bourgogne's first-row boxes for the first six performances of *Phèdre*. While these boxes sat empty, fashionable first-nighters attended the opening of Jacques Pradon's *Phèdre et Hippolyte* at the Théâtre de la Rue Guénégaud on the Left Bank. As a result, Pradon's negligible version of the Greek myth temporarily triumphed over Racine's masterpiece. Historians have speculated that this ordeal prompted Racine to renounce the theater and accept the uncontroversial appointment of royal historiographer and Reader to the King. Only on the request of the King's consort, Mme de Maintenon, twelve years later, did he compose his final two tragedies for private school productions. Clearly, dramatists of the highest skill and sublimity of expression needed a tough skin to withstand the petty dismissals and destructive assaults on their professional reputations.

NEOCLASSICISM: ENFORCEMENT AND DECLINE

Molière died an actor's death: on February 17, 1673, while playing the hysterical hypochondriac in *Le Malade imaginaire* at the Palais-Royal, he collapsed in a stage chair and was taken home to bed where he expired two hours later. His sudden demise initiated a restructuring of the professional French theater. The King ordered Molière's company to vacate the Palais-Royal, merge with the players of the Théâtre du Marais, and move operations to the Théâtre de la Rue Gué négaud. There the combined troupes would specialize in comedy and machine plays while the Hôtel de Bourgogne continued as leaders of tragedy. On August 18, 1680, the King completed the last phase of consolidation by ordering the Bourgogne troupe to merge with the Guénégaud company, and awarding sole rights to all French theater performances to their new entity, the Théâtre-Français (alternately, the Comédie-Française) to distinguish it from the foreign-language performances at the Théâtre-Italien, now occupying Paris' original purpose-built theater, the Bourgogne. Paranoia narrowed the field further: In May, 1697, on the suspicion that the Italian *commedia* players were preparing a play entitled *The False Prude,* featuring a character meant to be taken as Mme de Maintenon, the King promptly exiled the Italians from France. When they returned by invitation in 1716, a year after Louis's death, they gradually assimilated to French-language plays, and evolved into the Opéra Comique.

The King's decree to centralize French theater in 1680, in what was perhaps the ultimate neoclassical gesture, stated its purpose thus: "to render play performances more perfect." To ensure that plays did not offend on social, political, or decency grounds, the King appointed Paris Police Chief D'Argenson in 1701 as the first theater censor; as the official examiner of plays, he (and his successors) determined which new plays could be staged and subsequently published. But the elimination of competition and the imposition of quality control gradually engendered an insular, self-regarding, and self-satisfied state theater. Despite new works by Jean-Galbert Campistron, Hilaire-Bernard Longepierre, Jean-François Regnard, Florent Dancourt, François Lagrange-Chancel, Prosper Jolyot Crébillon, Bernard-Joseph Saurin, and especially, Voltaire, it struggled to keep the neoclassical genres of comedy and tragedy vital and attractive. Emerging modern forms less concerned with classicism, such as the *commedia*-influenced prose comedies of Pierre de Marivaux, the tearful comedies of Pierre-Claude Nivelle de la Chaussée, and the bourgeois drama of Denis Diderot and Michel-Jean Sedaine, gained increased audience approval.

The Comédie-Française

The restless public, furthermore, rediscovered an exuberant alternative to the neoclassical repertory in an ancient site—the Paris fairgrounds. The Comédie-Française soon took legal action to protect its monopoly on French performances. The booth theaters at the fairs, in which actors found ingenious ways to fabricate short plays through monologues, were regularly razed (and rebuilt). Many of their playlets and *parades* mocked the "Roman" repertoire of the state theaters, leaving officials no choice but to prohibit all French utterance and allow only acrobatics. From 1718 to 1721, in fact, fairground troupes unwilling to perform in a foreign language had to perform in total silence; nevertheless, the more enterprising players managed to communicate through signboards. Classicism itself would run its course before the eighteenth century was out, despite the continued influence of its illustrious late seventeenth century champions. Two famous publications of 1674, René Rapin's *Réflexions sur la poétique d'Aristote* and Nicolas Boileau-Despréaux's didactic poem *L'Art Poétique,* had held that the neoclassical principles of verisimilitude, propriety, and the three unities were supreme requirements for theater art. René Le Bossu's *Traité du poëme épique* (1675), echoed these views in his digressions on tragedy and comedy, and André Dacier's *La Poétique d'Aristote* (1692), a modern French translation of the *Poetics* with extensive line-by-line critical commentary, strengthened the prescriptive neo-classic guidelines for drama with fresh interpretations. Dacier had made a fervent defense of the Ancients in the long-running academic debate known as the "Quarrel of the Ancients and the Moderns." But increasingly, the defenders of classicism could not afford to ignore the rising support for the moderns among, primarily, Jean Desmarets de Saint-Sorlin, the brothers Charles, Claude and Pierre Perrault, Antoine Houdar de la Motte, Saint-Evremond, Pierre Bayle, and Marivaux. The Ancients were becoming history.

Ultimately, it was the working playwrights, responding to their audience's shifting tastes, who left classicism behind. Within the plays themselves, characters had been ridiculing the mania for classicism as early as Georges de Scudéry's *La Comédie des comédiens* (1632). By the era of Pierre-Augustin Caron de Beaumarchais, the author of *Le Barbier de Séville* and *Le Mariage de Figaro*, the theater was leading a withering assault on neo-classicism: In the preface to his first play, the bourgeois drama *Eugénie* (1767), Beaumarchais became the first playwright to use the term *classicist* in a derogatory sense. The exclusivity and privilege of the official theater lasted only as long as the monarchy that guarded it. The Freedom of the Theaters Act of 1791 abolished theater censorship and revoked the monopoly of the Comédie-Française; henceforth, as long as one paid copyrights to authors and agreed to municipal supervision, anyone could run a theater. After the century-long rush to establish a rarefied dramatic art patterned solidly on an ancient one, the simultaneous advent of revolution and romanticism forced French theater to invent egalitarian forms of drama for a citizenry that could never do without its theater.

FURTHER READING

Corneille, Pierre. *The Illusion.* Adapted by Tony Kushner. New York: Broadway Play Publishing, 2003.

————. *Three Masterpieces: The Liar, The Illusion, Le Cid.* London: Oberon Books, 2000.

Howarth, William D. *French Theatre in the Neo-Classical Era, 1550–1789.* Cambridge and New York: Cambridge University Press, 1997.

Muratore, Mary Jo. *Mimesis and Metatextuality in the French Neo-Classical Text.* Geneva: Librarie Droz, 1994.

Racine, Jean. *Racine's Phaedra.* Loughcrew, Old Castle, County Meath, Ireland: Gallery Press, 1996.

Modern Drama

Kimball King

Modern Drama, beginning in the late nineteenth century and continuing to the present day is, perhaps, the fourth greatest era of dramatic achievement in Western Theater. By the late nineteenth century the Industrial Revolution and other economic changes insured that prosperous, educated middle-class people would comprise the majority of theater-goers. Therefore, it is not surprising that Scandinavian countries, marginally more democratic yet more prosperous than many nations, should dominate the theater world.

THE BEGINNINGS OF MODERN DRAMA

Although the Norwegian Henrik Ibsen was born in 1828 and devoted most of his life to acting, directing and writing plays, his early works, like *Brand* (1866) and *Peer Gynt* (1867), were verse dramas, difficult to perform. His first play with worldwide recognition was *A Doll's House* (1879) in which a frustrated banker's wife, Nora Helmer, finds that she must leave her husband and children to fulfill a sense of personal independence and integrity. Within nine years Ibsen had completed the last of his plays that featured prose stories of upper-middle class, professional Scandinavian life. *Hedda Gabler* was his final play in this series. Following the lead of Parisian dramatists Eugene Scribe and Victorien Sardou, Ibsen took a "well-made" plot (one which observed the traditional unities of time, place and action) and urgent social issues (sexism, patriarchy, "classism," venereal diseases among all the classes) and combined them in serious plays, which nevertheless contained interesting characters, plot twists and biting social commentary. Later an elderly Ibsen would go on to write avant-garde symbolic plays, such as *When Dead We Awaken* (1900); but he is identified in the imagination of most people with his social problem plays written during his fifties. *Hedda Gabler* is a fine example of the genre, a fitting finale to his catalogue of dramatizations of Scandinavian life. In the play a twenty-nine-year-old Hedda enters a loveless marriage with a timid professor, George Tesman, for fear of being considered "an old maid" if she does not. Evidently her "heart" still belongs to Gilbert Lovborg, a supposedly "recovering" alcoholic who has written a dazzling academic treatise about the future of Western Civilization. Tesman and Lovborg compete for a university professorship, a distressing and unexpected obstacle for the plodding Tesman. Lovborg meanwhile has taken up with Thea Elvsted, a childhood nemesis of Hedda's who appears docile, but who, in fact, has defied social mores by leaving her husband and living openly with another man. Hedda persuades (without great difficulty) Lovborg to take a drink and he ends up, predictably, losing his futuristic manuscript, supposedly inspired by Mrs. Elvsted. Hedda finds the "lost" manuscript but reveals to her horrified husband that she has burned it to show her love for her husband and their unborn child. Critics are divided as to whether Hedda is pregnant or not. The Swedish film director, Ingmar Bergman, offered a production of *Hedda Gabler* to England's National Theatre, and Maggie Smith, as Hedda, appeared physically to be pregnant. My own feeling is that Hedda repeatedly shows she is capable of lying and that, in fact, she pretends pregnancy only to "justify" the burning of the manuscript. In another development, Judge Brock, a family friend, threatens to blackmail Hedda about her loaning Lovborg one of her father's pistols so that he could kill himself. He suggests a sexual ménage-a-trois which is unthinkable to the apparently "frigid" Hedda. Hedda kills herself at the play's conclusion, the one unconventional act of her brief life. Her selfishness and ineffectiveness leads us to believe Ibsen is less certain of male/female stereotypes by the time he had reached sixty years old. Followed by the Swedish Strindberg, fifteen years his junior, Ibsen led the modern drama movement in Scandinavia and the Western world in general.

ENGLISH MODERN DRAMA

Meanwhile in an England inhibited by theater prohibitions and censorship, Oscar Wilde attempted to restore vitality to the modern stage. One of his most successful plays is *The Importance of Being Earnest* in which he wittily skewered the mores of so-called "high society." Wilde chose Half-Moon Street, a fashionable street in Mayfair, as the initial setting of his comic masterpiece. He borrowed an old classical device, a missing child who is later identified by an object. A young woman named Gwendolyn insists that she can only marry a young man named Earnest. In the conclusion of the play, the baby's nurse, who lost the infant in her charge, successfully identifies him as being Earnest and the older brother of his closest friend. Some say that "Earnest" was a code name for a gay man in Wilde's day; others deny this. Still, it is patently absurd that a young woman would insist on a husband's having a particular name. A fabulous role for an actor is provided in the person of Lady Bracknell, Gwendolyn's mother, a woman known for her witty sayings. Most of her *bon mots* contain elements of a harsh political reality, such as her explaining that a better education would lead to acts of violence by the lower orders. Undoubtedly, Wilde suggests keeping the poor in ignorance is a successful means of protecting privilege for the few. Ultimately all the lovers in the play are properly joined together in what appears to be an improbable but happy ending. The combination of biting satire, which exposes the rich, and the successful fulfillment of their most selfish behaviors, oddly endeared the play not only to social critics but to would-be social arbiters.

A few years later George Bernard Shaw, a self-professed Fabian (a society of British progressive liberal reformers), would use the same combination of acid wit and happy coincidence to create plays admired by both left-wing and right-wing audiences. Working with the director Harley Granville-Barker, ostensibly more radical politically than Shaw himself, Shaw produced a collection of plays at the Royal Court theater in Sloane Square.

Sloane Square was in a fashionable part of town called Chelsea, very near chic Sloane Street and Harrod's Department Store, and Chelsea was a place where well-to-do as well as, often, educated and "enlightened" people chose to live in London. Some in the theater world had hoped that the so-called "West End Theatres" around Shaftesbury Avenue and Piccadilly would lose their popularity and that the Sloane Square of Chelsea would become a new center for art. Such was not the case, however. Shaw indeed successfully wrote plays for the Royal Court, and Granville-Barker's plays, such as *Waste* (which dealt with abortion and political corruption) and the *Voysey Inheritance* (thievery in the respectable upper-middle classes) remained mainly unproduced during his lifetime. A play like Shaw's famous *Pygmalion*, later the musical play and movie *My Fair Lady*, revealed Shaw's odd mixture of charm and subversiveness. A cockney flower girl named Eliza Doolittle becomes the subject of a bet between two educated, upper-class gentlemen who are eager to see if she can "pass" for a duchess when she is presented at a society ball. Socialites were entertained by a wide range of lower-class accents and the behavioral *faux pas* of the flower girl/would-be duchess. They failed to notice that Shaw revealed the superficiality of the elite class system by revealing that it was directly related to accidents of pronunciation and that it supported the continued oppression of the masses.

Interestingly, the same Royal Court theater, decades after the brilliant theatrical era of Shaw, became a source of major revitalization in the art world. Damaged by bombing during World War II and largely silent as a leftist platform for a whole generation, the Royal Court, founded by the Socialistic Arts Council established after World War II, opened its doors again to John Osborne's *Look Back in Anger*

(1956), a dissection of a corrupt post–World War II Britain in which the old class system flourished, new universities designed to enlighten the masses were seen as social liabilities, and privilege and cronyism still reigned. Furthermore, the endurance, stoicism and idealism of World War II appeared to have been lost to financial and social dreams of aggrandizement. The British Empire had seemingly been dealt a death blow by the war and the old colonial empire began to dissolve, bit by bit. In 1956 the Egyptians ordered the Suez Canal to move from British to Russian management. The infusion of American money changed patterns of promotion and hopes for equality. Jimmy Porter, the protagonist of *Look Back in Anger* has attended a "red-brick" university considered socially inferior to the Establishment's preferred universities, Oxford and Cambridge. He refused to express gratitude to a country that he believed had betrayed him. Many people believe that *Look Back in Anger* is primarily responsible for a twentieth century renaissance of British dramatists. For years British drama dominated English-speaking theater, worldwide. About twenty years after Osborne's *Look Back in Anger*, David Hare wrote *Plenty* (1978). *Plenty* featured Susan Traherne as an "angry young woman" who mirrored Jimmy Porter's disgust with post–World War II England. Like Jimmy, Susan was disappointed with the pervasive greed of her kinsmen, their lack of idealism, their complacency about loss of Empire. A central event in Susan's life, as Jimmy's had been, was the loss of the Suez Canal. Ignominiously, Britain was being forced to contain the Empire and bow increasingly to the diplomatic demands of the United States. Her favorite recollection was her heroic wartime effort, landing in France to aid the allied forces. Nothing in her later life matched that experience for patriotism and gallantry. Like Osborne before him, (interestingly, Hare delivered Osborne's funeral elegy), and Shaw years before Osborne, all had early beginnings in the Royal Court theater and took pride in Socialist ideals. It is difficult to find a "right-wing" playwright of the highest caliber in England. Czech-born Tom Stoppard has been the most outspoken anti-communist, but nevertheless he could not be said to champion any conservative reactionary causes.

While the English, under Shaw, took their initiative from Ibsen and Scandinavia and continue to this day to have a vital dramatic scene, other countries intruded on the scene, and momentarily, at least, captured the interest of international audiences. One thinks particularly of Russia at the turn of the nineteenth and twentieth centuries, of Ireland prior to World War I, and of America from the 1920s through the 1950s.

FRENCH MODERN DRAMA

Next the French took center stage with absurdist theater beginning with the success of *Waiting for Godot* in 1952. It was probably not until the 1960s that the full impact of that French movement was felt in other parts of the world. In the early 1960s, many American theater studies were almost entirely preoccupied with absurdist drama and French philosophy. The absurdists believed that life was meaningless, without purpose. Unlike the social realists in Scandinavia, Russia, Ireland, England, and America, who had transformed theater into a means of changing culture, the absurdists appeared to suggest that humankind would never improve, that neither any country nor any person could set an example worth emulation. All was in vain. In Beckett's justly famous *Waiting for Godot* two tramps wait for Mr. Godot to appear.

An Irishman by birth, Beckett emigrated to France where he learned to be fluent in French. His masterwork was *En Attendant Godot*. Interestingly, since the French word for God is "Dieu." Godot is "franglais," which is a mixture of French and English often spoken by tourists. "Ot" at the end of a man's name generally connoted affection or a diminutive size. If Mr. Godot is not God—or if he is a diminished, even "cute" God—why is he important to the two tramps who await his arrival? Named Vladimir and Estragon, suggesting first a Russian, then an Hungarian nationality, they are everyman figures. The audience never discovers their nationality, educational background, social or economic milieu or sexual preferences. Unlike the early characters in Ibsen's or Chekhov's or Shaw's plays, few specific character traits are elucidated and no complications of plot or personal convictions bring conflict to the play. Instead of plot there is rambling conversation and mild horseplay—swapping boots and carrots and such. Two other characters appear, Pozzo and Lucky. One is a sadist and the other his victim. It is difficult to see what they represent, except perhaps the predators and their prey that Beckett had observed during his lifetime.

Although "Mr. Godot" never appears to Vladimir and Estragon, a third party promises he will appear tomorrow. The audience is skeptical, assuming that he probably will not appear. Vladimir and Estragon remain, waiting for him. Why? Does he promise salvation, or more modestly, a job? The two tramps resemble all of humankind waiting for someone or something to change their lives, to give it a purpose.

AMERICAN MODERN DRAMA

American theater has a long, noble tradition, but outside of the United States, Eugene O'Neill was perhaps the first American playwright to gain recognition. Beginning with expressionism, O'Neill's *The Hairy Ape* (1922) suggests that mankind was becoming a slave to the very industries that had brought him supposed good fortune. The successful steel business in particular was seen to have had an atavistic effect on man's development, making him less human, more ape-like. O'Neill also experimented with short nautical plays. *The SS Glencairn* series was one of the first products of a creative writing class, (George Peirce Baker's at Harvard) to become a commercial success. O'Neill also contributed to summer stock shows, particularly under Susan Glaspell's guidance, in Provincetown, Massachusetts, and to off-Broadway theater where the Provincetown, Massachusetts players performed during the winter season. Drawing on Freud and Marx for psychological and political ideas, O'Neill became famous with *Beyond the Horizon* (1920), *Desire Under the Elms* (1924), *Mourning Becomes Electra* (1931), *The Iceman Cometh* (1946), and eventually the famous *Long Day's Journey Into Night* (1956), which autobiographically (after alterations) tells the inside secrets of his own dysfunctional family.

O'Neill had made the world aware of America's onstage contributions. He was followed by Lillian Hellman , Clifford Odets and his group theater, and Paul Green and the outdoor "symphonic" theater. Odets introduced natural speech to the American stage and he was followed in this style by Arthur Miller, whose *Death of a Salesman* (1949), among other plays, became a great statement of yearning for—and failing to achieve—the American Dream. Not far in age from Miller was Tennessee Williams, whom the great modern theater-agent Margaret Ramsey once called the most talented playwright of the twentieth century. Nearly every one of Williams's plays was made into a successful movie, though *A Streetcar Named Desire* (1947) is perhaps more closely associated with his name than any other of his striking achievements—in poetry and in the novel.

RUSSIA, IRELAND, AND SCANDINAVIA

Probably the two most important examples of modern drama in the twentieth century have been provided by England and the United States. However, many other nations have been well represented in the movement. If Ibsen is truly "the father of Modern Drama" as many have claimed, Scandinavia can say that Modern Drama had its origins in that region, particularly Norway. However, as this book has attempted to reveal, nearly every country has amassed a significant number of "modern" plays in their native language. One cannot forget the Russians, especially Chekhov, at the end of the nineteenth century. Surely the Irish in the years preceding World War I captured the world's imagination with works by Synge, O'Casey, Yeats, and others.

MODERN DRAMA STYLES

The pessimism of absurdism from such plays as *Waiting for Godot* in the 1950s is a delicious indulgence, but it could not pervade drama. The atom bomb, the holocaust, and World War II itself all suggested that humans had learned nothing from their past and were destined to destroy themselves and the whole earth someday. Therefore, perhaps as a result, a "can-do" attitude of the plays of the 1960s and 70s brought about a new theater era. Feminist plays that indicated that women deserved freedom and respect, African American plays that suggested raw racism could be defeated, gay plays that insisted that sexual orientation was a choice, not a social or biological handicap, appeared.

Realism, naturalism, expressionism, surrealism, didactism, plus "angry" theater, "symphonic" theater, " agit prop" theater, "in yer face" theater, etc. have all played a role in making the late nineteenth through the early twenty-first century especially rich in theatrical offerings. Several successful and memorable plays of the modern era were primarily realistic. Enduring drama sometimes combined realism with another genre—naturalism, expressionism, modernism, etc. For example, Tennessee Williams's realistic plays employ many expressionistic devices, as do Eugene O'Neill's. Both Nobel Prize winner Harold Pinter and Pulitzer Prize winner Sam Shepard wrote plays that combined realistic elements with absurdist ones. One should always remember that a play is what takes place on the stage, and that placing any play too strictly into a category (i.e., realism, absurdism, etc.) can sometimes bewilder viewers. A number of categories "blur." For example, it is difficult to say where realism ends and naturalism begins. In realistic plays the protagonists may well have a greater responsibility for their destiny than in naturalistic ones. For example, the "realistic" *All My Sons* by Miller, faults Joe Keller, who sold the U.S. government faulty plane engines, whereas the more naturalistic *The Hairy Ape* suggests that society has robbed Yank of the ability to shape his life, that his lack of education, income, etc. have made him more vulnerable than Joe. Some critics describe *Waiting for Godot* as being "expressionist," while others call it "surrealistic." And this archetypical absurdist play, *Waiting for Godot* (and other Beckett works) was said by its author not to be "absurd" at all.

Possibly Russian plays at the turn of the century placed a greater blame on social institutions than on intelligent individuals, making them more naturalistic than realistic. The emergence of Ireland with a viable theater, especially in Dublin prior to World War I, suggests that a kind of romanticism replaced naturalism. O'Neill appeared to draw on the romantic for his early works but to write more "naturalistically" in his final endeavors. Both Tennessee Williams and Arthur Miller drew on realism and expressionism. Edward Albee may have brought European absurdism into mainstream American plays when he wrote *The Zoo Story* in 1958 and an essay, "Which Theatre is the Absurd One," in 1960.

It could be asked, "Why have any categories for drama?" Perhaps one needs to search for some names that evoke a common response in most people. Certain societal changes, such as the emerging importance of the role of women, the acceptance by intelligent open-minded people of gay experiences, and the universal denial of racial stereotyping make contemporary drama more inclusive than ever. What is important, perhaps, is what one "sees" in a dramatic piece. Whether it is revealed self-knowledge, social flaws or social injustice, what is important is the viewer's reaction. What is also significant is that audiences have access to all these writers. Theater is one of the most social forms of art, in that one almost invariably shares it with other people, while it is possible to read a poem or novel or see a painting in solitude.

Despite national origins or dramatic techniques, enduring classics of the modern period will be those that capture basic human concerns that bridge the centuries.

FURTHER READING

King, Kimball. *Modern Dramatists: A Casebook of Major British, Irish, and American Playwrights.* New York: Routledge, 2001.

Taylor, John Russell. *Anger and After: A Guide to New British Drama.* London: Methuen, 1969.

———. *The Second Wave: British Drama of the Sixties.* London: Eyre Methuen, 1978.

PART II

Two Other Major Eras of Western Drama

ॐ

Medieval Drama

Edward Donald Kennedy

THE DEATH OF DRAMA

Although much of the literature of the Middle Ages was indebted to classical antiquity, this was not true of medieval drama. During the early medieval period, from the fall of Rome in the late fifth century until the tenth century, drama was essentially dead. It had been killed by the pagans and Christians of late antiquity.

This was due in part to the Romans' lack of interest in drama. Western classical drama had its origins in religious ceremonies of the ancient Greeks, who began producing plays in the fifth century B.C., and it reached its height with the tragedies of Aeschylus, Sophocles, and Euripides and the comedies of Aristophanes. Although much of Roman civilization was based upon that of its Greek predecessors, drama never had the importance among the Romans that it had among the Greeks. There were, to be sure, a number of dramatists, the best known of whom today are Plautus (254–184 B.C.) and Terence (c. 185–159 B.C.), both of whom wrote comedies, and Seneca (c. 4 B.C.–65 A.D.), who wrote tragedies. The plays of these authors, however, were far more influential when they were rediscovered by European writers of the Renaissance than they were in ancient Rome. The tragedies of Seneca, for example, had probably never been intended to be performed but were written as closet dramas, dramas meant to be read rather than performed. The comedies of Plautus and Terence were performed during the days of the Roman Republic but their popularity waned after the establishment of the Roman Empire, and they were performed only occasionally after the reign of Augustus, who ruled at the time of the birth of Christ.

In the *Poetics* Aristotle had defined drama as the "imitation of an action." The Romans, however, often preferred types of entertainment that involved action without imitation. Their theatrical productions included music and dance, circus acts, such as juggling and acrobatics, gladiatorial combats, animal fights, and during times of persecutions, shows that included feeding Christians and other enemies of the state to lions and other wild animals. Some of the productions that did involve imitation of actions were obscene, often pornographic farces (many of which were improvised with little written dialogue) and pantomimes. Those who participated in productions that could be considered performances were generally drawn from the dregs of society, and in the Roman Republic actors, in those days known for loose morals, could not vote or hold political office and had a social rank comparable to that of slaves and prostitutes. They gained more prestige after the Empire was established, and their status appears to have risen as the Empire degenerated. They became an important part of the emperors' method of holding on to power through giving the people bread and circuses, keeping them fed and entertained. It was a way of drawing attention away from the more serious problems of life (similar to the technique shown in the modern musical *Cabaret*, set in Berlin in 1929–30).

Not surprisingly, early Christians had little use for or appreciation of most of the entertainments that amused the pagans, in part because of the immorality, in part because of the brutality. In 198 A.D. an early Christian writer Tertulian wrote an essay *De spectaculis* in which he admonished Christians to stay away from the circuses and theaters. If they wanted entertainment, he said, they could find it through the music and rituals offered by the church. Religion was to be a substitute for secular entertainment. However, even after the empire became Christian in the fourth century, the theaters remained open; and although clergy were forbidden to attend entertainments, laymen could not attend on Sundays and religious holidays, and no Christian could become an actor, the government continued to finance performances. State-sponsored entertainments continued even after the empire was conquered by Germanic tribes in 476, and there are records of productions as late as the sixth century. They became less frequent, however, not only because of Christian disapproval of them but also because of the poverty of the late empire and the need to use government funds for other purposes. Theatrical productions gradually died out.

There continued to be, throughout Europe, secular entertainments of various sorts: wandering minstrels told and sang stories; people performed pantomimes that acted out folk rituals, such as wooing ceremonies and stories from the pagan past in which a hero is killed but is then reborn and those that portray the death of the old year and the birth of the new. The habit of reading drama written in Latin also continued; the plays of Terence and to a lesser extent Plautus were read, and there is some evidence that at times the plays were read aloud by a reader and actors pantomimed the action. Manuscripts of classical Latin plays continued to be copied, and it has been suggested that Chaucer developed the idea for the

five-book structure of his tragic story *Troilus and Criseyde* by having read the
five-act comedies of Plautus.

Some plays, apparently intended as closet dramas, were written in the tenth
century by Hrothsvita of Gandersheim, the canoness of a Benedictine monastery
in Saxony in the eastern part of what is now Germany. Apparently shocked
by having read Latin plays of Terence, she wrote several plays, modeled upon
Terence, but concerned with the lives of the saints and martyrs. So far as we know,
the plays were never acted but were intended to be read at her monastery.
Although they foreshadow later vernacular plays about saints, they seem to have
had no influence on other writers and were apparently unknown outside of her
small circle of readers.

For years drama that was performed by actors who impersonated characters
was dead.

THE REBIRTH OF DRAMA

Drama was reintroduced into western Europe in the tenth century as a part of
the liturgy for the Easter Mass. Just as drama among the ancient Greeks was a
part of their religious observances, among Christians it too was reborn as a part
of the most joyous and triumphant day of their liturgical year.

The Christian Mass had always included elements that were potentially
dramatic. The Mass itself is seen as a bloodless reenactment of the passion of
Christ. ("This is my body broken for you." "This is my blood.") Festival days in
the church had ceremonies with symbols, such as a crèche at Christmas, a star
at Epiphany, and palms on Palm Sunday. On Good Friday there was a ceremony
known as the deposition of the cross in which the cross was removed from the
front of the church and placed in a "tomb" or container of some sort in the church.
On Easter Sunday the cross was replaced at the front of the church, symbolizing
the resurrection. Much of the singing, divided between a priest and a choir or
between the two parts of the choir in what is known as antiphonal singing, was
similar in form to dialogue in drama, except that the crucial element of drama,
impersonation, was missing.

For centuries churches throughout Europe had added embellishments known
as tropes to their traditional liturgies. For example, the traditional liturgy for the
end of the Mass was *"Ite, missa est"* ("Go, it is dismissed"). Some churches
extended this by ending the Mass with *"Ite nunc in pace, spiritus sanctus super
vos sit, iam missa est"* ("Go now in peace, may the holy spirit be with you, now it
is dismissed"). The additional words constitute a trope.

In the tenth century a new trope involving impersonation was added to the
Easter Mass. Known by its opening Latin words *"Quem Quaeritis?"* ("Whom do
you seek?"), this trope concerns the three Marys who visit Christ's tomb on Easter

morning and find the stone rolled away and an angel there. Members of the clergy impersonated the angel and the three Marys. The simplest (although apparently not the earliest) of these is from the Benedictine Abbey of St. Gall in Switzerland. It consists of the following three lines:

Angel: *Quem quaeritis in sepulchro, Christocolae?*

The Marys: *Jesum Nazarenum crucifixum, O caelicolae.*

Angel: *Non est hic, surrexit sicut praedixerat; ite, nuntiate quia surrexit de sepulchro.*

(*Angel:*   Whom do you seek in the tomb, Christians?

The Marys: Jesus of Nazareth, who was crucified, O heavenly one.

Angel: He is not here, he has arisen as he had foretold; go, announce that he has arisen from the tomb.)

This was the beginning of drama in post-classical western Europe. Other versions of this trope are more elaborate with added lines of dialogue. Some have additional scenes in which the Marys buy spices from a merchant or in which they go to tell the news to Peter and John or in which Christ appears to the apostles. Different scenes were indicated by different platforms grouped around a playing area in the nave of the church.

By the eleventh century other dramatic tropes were written for other important days in the liturgical year. Not surprisingly, one for the Christmas Mass was modeled upon the *quem quaeritis* Easter trope but concerned the shepherds who seek the Christ child: "*Quem quaeritis in praesepe, pastores, cicite?*" ("Whom do you seek in the manger, shepherds, say?"). There is one for Epiphany, which celebrates the visit of the wise men, and one, with a wrathful Herod, depicting the slaughter of the innocents for the feast of the Holy Innocents. Liturgical plays remained a part of the Roman Catholic church's liturgy throughout the medieval period and, in some countries, much later.

Some of the later Latin plays were elaborate and, taking well over an hour to perform, would have dominated any church service of which they were a part and thus appear to have been produced separately from the Mass. Since the parts were sung they very much resembled operatic productions. These include the *Play of Daniel* from Beauvais, north of Paris, which was intended for the Christmas season. (Daniel was seen as one of the Old Testament prophets who foresaw the coming of Christ.) Another was *The Play of Herod*, which originated in Fleury and was intended for the festival of the Holy Innocents. These included elaborate staging and costuming, with, for example, actors dressed up as lions for the *Daniel* play.[1] At the Benedikbeuren abbey in Germany a series of plays for Advent and Christmas were written in the twelfth century, and these must have included some spectacular effects since Herod, after slaughtering the innocents, is, according to the stage directions, gnawed to pieces by worms. A Benedikbeuren Passion play, though primarily written in Latin, has some dialogue in German, which indicates that drama was moving from strictly Latin to languages that the audience could understand.

VERNACULAR DRAMA

While Latin plays continued, throughout the Middle Ages, to be performed in churches as part of the liturgy or as special productions in the church, in the twelfth century vernacular drama began to develop for production outside the church. The subjects of most of the vernacular plays was religious, and the authors would have been clerics, but the plays, written for production outside the church, were not restricted to topics that were suited to the liturgy but could be used to teach essential biblical stories in languages that people could understand.

A good example of early vernacular drama is the twelfth-century *Mystère d'Adam* (*Play of Adam*), which was written in Anglo-Norman, the dialect of French spoken in England after the Norman Conquest. Written to be performed on the outer steps of a church and possibly performed during Advent, it covers the Creation story through Cain's murder of Abel and then concludes with a procession of Old Testament prophets. The manuscript is incomplete, and the *Mystère d'Adam* was possibly part of a much longer play and may have included stories from the New Testament as well. The story of the Fall was essential to the instruction of medieval Christians since it explains the necessity of the incarnation of Christ: Adam corresponds to Christ, the new Adam who did not sin. The play treats the biblical story of the Fall with considerable freedom, having the devil tempt Adam first and then, when he fails, turn to Eve, whom he wins over through the type of flattery found in twelfth-century courtly lyric poetry. Adam, before the Fall, is described as serious and peaceful, but Eve, even then, not sufficiently humble. The play is enlivened by the appearance of devils who mingle with the audience and threaten them, and to show that everyone before the new Adam was damned, they lead the murdered Abel away to Hell, although more gently than they do his wicked brother Cain.

A few other vernacular plays from this period also survive: the Anglo-Norman *La Seinte resurreccion* concerning the resurrection of Christ but with many variations on the biblical account, such as dialogue between Pilate and Joseph of Arimathea and the miraculous curing of the soldier Longinus's blindness by the blood and water that flow from Christ's wounds. Another example is a Spanish play, the *Auto de los Reyes Magos* (*Coming of the Magi*), a vernacular account of the wise men's visit to the Christ child that suggests some skepticism on the part of the wise men.

The Vernacular Plays of the Later Middle Ages

Not much drama has survived between the late twelfth and early thirteenth centuries and the fourteenth century. There is, however, a great deal of dramatic material, most of it religious, from the fourteenth and fifteenth centuries, and scholars generally divide these plays into the following categories:

1. The mystery plays presented the most significant events of biblical tradition from the fall of Satan to Judgment Day. These were essentially history plays intended to teach world history that was important to one's salvation.

2. The morality plays, which were produced in England in the fifteenth century, are allegorical plays and include characters with names like "Mankind," "Death," and "Everyman." In contrast to the mystery plays, these plays illustrate a theme such as one might hear in a sermon, such as preparation to face death or the struggles Mankind might have against the temptations of the world. The pattern in these plays is the popular one of a fall followed by redemption, the same pattern that Charles Dickens would later use in *A Christmas Carol*.

3. The saint play told of the life and suffering and death of a saint. In England, probably because of the Reformation, only two of these have survived, a play about the conversion of St. Paul and a play of Mary Magdalene. There are references, however, to a number of other lost English plays about saints such as Thomas à Becket, St. Swithin, and St. Katherine, and a number of saint plays have survived from the Continent.

4. A minor genre is a miracle play, which is usually a play about some miraculous event. The only known miracle play from England is the *Play of the Sacrament* from the town of Croxton. It is based upon a common medieval legend in which a Jew desecrates the host and then, through the display of its miraculous powers, converts to Christianity.[2]

Of the four types, the mysteries and the moralities are the most important and are the ones emphasized in the rest of this chapter.

THE MYSTERY PLAYS

In England, by far the most numerous plays are the mystery plays. These were civic productions associated with various towns and were often produced on Corpus Christi Day, a festival day instituted by Pope Urban IV in 1264 as a joyous celebration of Christ's sacrifice of his body for the salvation of humankind. It usually occurs in June about eight-and-one-half weeks after Easter. It had become a festival day in England by at least 1318. It had parades associated with it in larger towns and the various guilds (organizations of tradesmen) participated in these. It was natural then for productions of plays to follow. Later some productions were shifted back to Pentecost, seven weeks after Easter.

Four cycles (or series) of plays survive from fifteenth-century England: the N-Town (the extant manuscript dating ca. 1468), the York (1477), the Wakefield (dating from the late fifteenth and early sixteenth centuries, sometimes called Towney after the name of the family that owned the manuscript), and the Chester (compiled between 1467 and 1540). The plays would have been performed earlier than the dates given; there were records, for example, that the Chester plays were performed as early as 1422. The N-Town cycle is not associated with a particular town. The "N" possibly stood for Latin *nomen* (name), and it may have been a series of plays written for a traveling company that went from town to town. In addition to these cycles, we have the list of plays of one cycle no longer extant that was performed at the town of Beverly. There are also several non-cyclic or individual plays surviving, such as a play about Abraham's attempted sacrifice of Isaac, found in the Brome manuscript, or a play about Adam and Eve that had been part of a cycle in the town of Norwich. In recent years scholars have been collecting data from public record offices in various parts of England, and these records, published by the University of Toronto Press in the series Records of Early English Drama, indicate that although most plays have been lost, many towns and districts had considerable dramatic activity in the Middle Ages. (In addition to the ones mentioned, records have so far been published for Bristol, Cambridge, Coventry, Cumberland, Westmorland, Gloucestershire, Devon, Dorset, Cornwall, Herfordshire, Worcestershire, Lancashire, Newcastle-upon-Tyne, Oxfordshire, Shropshire, Somerset, and Sussex.) Chaucer's *Miller's Tale,* for example, which is set in Oxford, relies on its reader's familiarity with the medieval play about Noah's flood, although no cycle of plays survives from either Oxford or London, where Chaucer lived.

Topics of Mystery Plays

Of the four cycles that have survived, many have plays that cover the same topics. These were intended as plays that taught the essential truths of Christianity, based upon the Bible and upon legends (such as the rebellion of Satan against God and the ensuing War in Heaven) that had developed from suggestions in the Bible. The plays were produced for an audience in which a great many people would have been illiterate; and they were a way to educate and supplement the teachings of the church. Plays that were invariably performed were those that told of the fall of Satan and of the Creation and Fall of Adam and Eve, stories that explained the reason for the damnation of humankind and thus the necessity for the incarnation of Christ. The cycles usually included the story of Cain's murder of his brother Abel, since people needed to understand that the Fall was not complete with the act of disobedience represented by Adam and Eve's eating the forbidden fruit and that the human race would sink a lot lower. Some Old Testament stories were chosen because they were thought to foreshadow or correspond to events in the New Testament: thus Abraham's attempted sacrifice of his son Isaac was seen as a "figure" of a later, greater event, God's sacrifice of his son; the story of Noah was understood to foreshadow the final destruction of the world, and the waters of the flood, which destroyed the evil of the world, were also seen to represent the water of baptism which eliminated the effects of original sin; Noah's ark, which carried those on board to salvation, was seen as a representation of the church. In the New Testament, some of the vernacular plays presented the same stories that were also a part of the liturgical dramatic tradition, such as the birth of Christ and the visits of the shepherds and wise men, Herod's slaughter of the innocents, and the resurrection of Christ, as well as other stories, such as the passion and death of Christ, that were generally not presented in liturgical drama. The conclusion to a cycle was inevitably Judgment Day at which time the righteous ascended to Heaven and the wicked descended to Hell.

Productions of Mystery Plays

The anonymous dramatists of these plays, whether trained in the classical tradition that literature was to delight as well as teach or simply having the common sense to know that didactic literature is more effective if it entertains, added a considerable amount of non-biblical material to the content of these plays or at least elaborated considerably upon the stories given them in the Bible. Many of the additions were comic and crude and of a type not likely to be found in religious drama of later periods. The book of Genesis, for example, simply indicates that Noah had a wife; the English dramatists present her as a comic shrew and Noah as a hen-pecked husband, who, after talking to God, is afraid to go home and tell his wife that he is to build the ark; and she naturally does not care for its appearance since she can not distinguish the front from the back; in one of the plays she refuses to get on board because she does not want to leave her friends and a slapstick fight breaks out between Noah and his wife. In the best known of the mystery plays, the Wakefield *Second Shepherd's Play* (so named because the manuscript also includes a different earlier version), there is a plot in which a medieval con-artist named Mak steals a sheep from the shepherds who are watching their flocks by night, and, indeed, the plot does present a comic parallel to the story of the birth of the lamb of God. The dramatists also made the most of the notorious villains like Cain, Pharaoh, Herod, and, in the passion plays, the Jewish priests Caiphas and Annas, the Roman soldiers who crucified Christ, and, sometimes, Pontius Pilate. Herod, in particular, was a blustering tyrant, as was Pilate in the Wakefield cycle, and both would threaten the audience.

When Mel Gibson's controversial film "The Passion of the Christ" opened on Ash Wednesday of 2004, a number of critics condemned it for what they perceived as its anti-Semitism. David van Biema, in an essay on the film in *Time*, March 1, 2004, described it as "theologically in tune with the times—the 1300s."

Certainly some of the Passion plays, in England and on the Continent, had anti-Semitism in them (although in England Jews had been driven out of the country about two hundred years before the vernacular plays began to be produced and it is doubtful anyone in the audience would have ever seen a Jew). However, whether one considers Gibson's film anti-Semitic or not, there were two major differences between his film and the medieval productions. One is that while his film focused on one element in the story, the suffering of Christ, that was but one element of the whole story of the life, death, and resurrection of Christ that the medieval productions presented, and thus the torture of Christ received less emphasis. In this respect, the effect of the medieval productions was more like the effect one gets from reading the whole story in the Bible rather than one episode from it. The other difference is that the realistic brutality of Gibson's film would have exceeded anything that could have been presented on the medieval stage, even though the crucifixion play from the York cycle is, judging from its dialogue, brutal. Medieval productions, however, usually lacked the realism of which modern film is capable.

What is said about realism or lack of it in medieval productions must be qualified because accounts of productions differ, and English plays may have been less realistically presented than some of those staged on the Continent. Evidence of the types of props used, such as several yards of "red sea," indicate minimal realism, and the word used to describe a production (English "play," Latin *ludus*, French *jeu*) suggests a game rather than reality. Some productions of Christ's crucifixion, as well as Continental productions depicting the mutilations of saints, used dummies rather than live actors. Noah's ark in English productions appears to have been a flat pre-fabricated boat with wooden animals on board. Some productions on the Continent, however, must have been fairly graphic; one illustration of a production in France shows a saint's entrails being drawn out of his body, and they knew how to stage, in the saints' plays, gory beheadings. Similarly there are records in Bourges of an arena filled with water for Noah's flood with wine barrels pouring out water from above to represent the rain.

The methods by which some of the civic biblical dramas were staged precluded much realism. In larger towns like York and Chester the productions were performed on pageant wagons that were drawn through the streets from one station to another on the day (or days) of the performance, since in some cases the productions took two or three days to complete. Wagons were also used on the Continent in, for example, Lille and Bologna. Scholars have been uncertain about the size of these wagons and how they could be maneuvered through the narrow streets of medieval towns, and some of the action would probably have had to have taken place in the streets in front of where the wagons came to a stop. In large towns like York the various plays were assigned to guilds of tradesmen with the intention, in some cases, of assigning appropriate plays to each group;

thus in York the shipwrights produced the play of the building of Noah's ark; the goldsmiths, the adoration of the magi; and the bakers, the Last Supper. In Chester, the butchers produced the play about the attempted stoning of the woman taken in adultery; the ironmongers, the crucifixion; and the cooks and innkeepers (presumably because they had access to ovens) Christ's harrowing of hell. In small towns, probably only one group, such as a group at the local church, put on the plays in a fixed location on a platform. Both the wagons and the fixed platforms were equipped with trap doors so that in the play about the fall of the rebel angels, the angels could fall through the floor of the stage and then emerge from underneath as hideous devils. Similarly, there were means to hoist actors aloft. In one of the plays about the ascension of Christ into Heaven, Christ says "Send down a cloud, Father," and after a cloud descends from above, Christ gets on it and ascends to Heaven.

Those producing the plays made little attempt to provide special costuming with the notable exceptions of devils (often with fireworks attached to their tails), angels (sometimes shiny gold wings, sometimes wings made of peacock feathers) and God (usually a white beard, crown, and gold face). Characters like Herod and Pharaoh could be distinguished from others by their crowns and scepters. For the most part, however, characters wore contemporary dress. There was no attempt, as there is in modern plays and films, to reproduce the costumes of an earlier era. This was due, in part, to the fact that many people in the Middle Ages did not have a sense of historical change or would even have been aware that people in an earlier time would have dressed or behaved or talked differently or would have had different concerns or worries. Anachronisms were commonplace. Roman soldiers in the plays would be dressed like medieval knights. The shepherds of the nativity plays would swear in the name of Christ or Pilate, and Herod could swear allegiance to Mohammed. The shepherds complain about high taxes and harsh employers, and the plays contain references to corrupt sheriffs and priests, more suitable to late medieval England than to the times in which the plays were historically set. This makes the stories seem immediate and contemporary just as in medieval art biblical scenes showing people in contemporary dress would have sent a message, lost to modern viewers, that the people in biblical times were not much different from those looking at the art. As in later sixteenth-century English drama, the acting was done primarily by men, and by laymen, not clergy, although there are records of occasional performances by women.

Drama on the Continent was similar to that in England in that much of it consisted of dramatizations of biblical stories. However, while in England the same biblical stories were dramatized in most of the cycles, in France a number of other stories, such those of Job, Daniel, and Esther, were presented on stage in an enormous series of plays based upon the Old Testament. There are also many plays about saints that have survived, as one might expect in a Roman

Catholic country, and a long 61,000 line series of plays about the acts of the apostles. Moreover, while biblical drama in England was free to the public and financed by tradesmen, in France the plays tended to be community projects, staged in outdoor theaters, and those attending had to pay admission. There was also a rich tradition of liturgical drama in Italy, and the oldest known Latin passion play, not usually a part of liturgical drama, was produced in the twelfth century at Montecassino. Close to 600 medieval Dutch plays are extant.

Although only one fragment of a secular farce (*Interludium de clerico et puella* [*Interlude (or play) about the clerk and the maiden]*) survives in England, there was apparently much more secular drama on the Continent. In France, there were farces, like the thirteenth-century *Le Garcon et l'Aveugle*, which consists almost solely of a series of cruel tricks played by a boy upon a blind man. There was also more uplifting secular drama, such as a play about the Patient Griselda, a moral story known to readers in England through Chaucer's *Clerk's Tale*, and there were plays on secular historical subjects, such as Julius Caesar, the destruction of Troy, or the siege of Orléans (a play that included Joan of Arc, long before she became a saint). In Germany there survive almost as many secular plays (155) as religious ones (162).

THE MORALITY PLAY

The other major type of English play, the morality, illustrates the medieval love of allegory and its use to present theological lessons. Three English morality plays have survived in their entirety, as well as a fragment of another one entitled *The Pride of Life*. The best known morality and the most frequently produced today is the late fifteenth or early sixteenth century play *Everyman*, which was translated from a Dutch original. The story concerns a well-to-do Everyman, who is absorbed in things of the world until Death approaches him and tells him that he must take a journey to face eternal judgment and to give God an account of how he has spent his life. Frightened, he offers Death a bribe of £1,000 (a fortune in those days) if he will postpone the journey. Death, however, is honest and has no use for money, but he does give Everyman time to find a companion who will go with him. At first Everyman asks those he had trusted most (Fellowship, Cousin, Kindred, and Goods) to take the journey with him and all come up with excuses. (Cousin has a cramp in her toe, and Goods even laughs in his face and tells him he has been a fool to trust him.) He finally turns to his Good Deeds, who, because of neglect, is too weak to stand up, but she nevertheless agrees to accompany him, and she directs him to other worthwhile companions (such as Knowledge) who accompany him to the grave. Although the play was written to illustrate the doctrine of salvation through good deeds (the only one to descend into the grave with him), in its representation of misplaced values and in its presentation of a situation familiar to most people, that of being let down by those that they had always relied on, it is still effective drama.

The other two complete moralities, *The Castle of Perseverance* and *Mankind* have much broader scope: instead of depicting Everyman's journey toward death, both of these plays begin with the birth of Mankind and follow him through the various pitfalls and temptations until he finally achieves salvation. *The Castle of Perseverance* is a long play (about 3,700 lines) with a cast of 36 characters and a setting that ranges from the world to Heaven. It depicts Mankind being tempted by the World, the Flesh, and the Devil, resisting sin and taking refuge in the Castle of Perseverance where he is besieged by the seven deadly sins but defended by the corresponding virtues. The play *Mankind* has a similar plot covering birth to death and salvation; but this play is much simpler than *The Castle of Perseverance* and has just seven characters and is 914 lines long. It was probably performed by a traveling troop of actors who staged the play in inn yards. It is a lively play with crude comedy from the tempters Mischeff, New Guise, and Nowadays, who at one point lead the audience in a scatological sing-along. Scholars of the early twentieth century labeled it degenerate, but it should play well today.

Some plays were a hybrid of the historical characters of the type found in the mystery plays and abstractions found in the moralities. The N-Town Cycle includes a play intended as a prelude to the New Testament plays: the cycle opens with a debate in Heaven between the four daughters of God: Peace, Justice, Truth, and Mercy. In the same cycle, the play *Death of Herod,* has as characters Death who kills Herod and devils who take him away to Hell. The best illustration of this mix of the mystery and morality plays is in the long fifteenth-century saint play *Mary Magdalene* (2,144 lines). In early church tradition Mary Magdalene was identified with other characters who appear in the Bible: she is thought to have been the sinful woman who anointed Christ's feet with ointment and also with the Mary who is the sister of Lazarus and Martha. Thus the play draws upon these biblical characters as well as other biblical/historical figures like Herod, Pilate, and Tiberius Caesar but also includes a number of abstractions that are drawn from the tradition of the morality plays including the World, the Flesh, the Devil, the seven deadly sins, Satan, a bad angel, and a good angel.

INFLUENCE OF MEDIEVAL PLAYS ON LATER DRAMA

This mixture of abstractions and historical characters carries over into plays of the sixteenth century like *Cambises,* a historical play whose cast includes characters with names like Diligence and Shame, and most notably Christopher Marlowe's *Doctor Faustus,* one of the great tragedies of the late sixteenth century. The latter includes among its characters a good angel, a bad angel, and the seven deadly sins. Moreover, the morality theme of the struggle of the forces of good and evil for a man's soul is the major theme of that play, but instead of ending happily like *The Castle of Perseverance* and *Mankind,* it ends in tragedy. Just as the mystery plays are seen to foreshadow the sixteenth century plays concerned with secular history, like Shakespeare's *Richard II* or *Henry V,* the moralities foreshadow tragedies, like *Dr. Faustus* or *King Lear,* in the latter of which major complex characters (Lear, Gloucester) are torn between characters who are extremes of good (Cordelia, Kent, Edgar, Albany) and evil (Goneril, Regan, Edmund, Cornwall).

Medieval plays continued to influence sixteenth century drama in other ways, such as the tradition of using male actors, the unrealistic techniques of staging, and the practice of traveling companies putting on performances in inn yards. It is important too to remember that the production of mystery and morality plays did not end with the beginning of the sixteenth century but they continued to be performed as other types of drama were developing. The Chester cycle was performed as late as 1575, and the latest record of a production of one of the medieval plays in England was the early seventeenth century. Hamlet's reference to actors who "out-Herod Herod" is a reference to the tyrannical king of the mystery plays, which Shakespeare had probably seen performed. Some have suggested that it was probably Puritan influence late in the century that ended the production of the plays since the plays were frequently boisterous, irreverent, and out-of-keeping with newer religious sentiments that developed when religion became more of a Sunday event than a part of everyday life. The church became in many ways more remote, and religious subjects came to be treated with more reverence, with less tolerance for the mixture of religion and slapstick comedy. However, the plays' disappearance in Protestant England during Elizabeth's reign may be due as much to their evocation of past Roman Catholic traditions, and productions may have ended as much for political as for religious reasons. On the Continent, both Luther and Calvin had approved of the production of plays on biblical subjects, but Protestants generally disapproved of the appearance of God on stage, and this limited the scope of what could be presented. Liturgical dramas, however, continued to be produced in churches in Roman Catholic areas of Germany until the seventeenth century, and in the seventeenth century a new biblical drama was produced there, the passion play of Oberammergau, which was deeply indebted to medieval dramatic traditions. It continues to be produced, with modifications, every ten years. In Italy the Church itself turned against drama, and people became more interested in secular plays, but the tradition of liturgical drama lingered on in Spain where some of the plays continued to be produced into the eighteenth and early nineteenth centuries.

A number of productions of medieval plays have been staged in modern times. In England the city of York has presented them at various times on wagons as they were done in the Middle Ages. The city of Durham in 1990 presented them in Durham cathedral, with the cast drawn, as they were in medieval times, from various tradesmen in town. And there have been modernized productions as well, including a modern dress TV production of *Everyman* that begins in a gambling casino and a six-hour production of the mystery plays, adapted by Tony Harrison and directed by Bill Bryden, that was staged in London and filmed for the BBC in 1985. These productions have attracted large audiences and indicate that even in a secular age in which the church is no longer a dominant part of many people's lives, these plays can still entertain and are still powerful drama.

NOTES

1. Productions of the *Daniel* and *Herod,* with appropriate music, were directed by Noah Greenberg in the 1960s for Pro Musica at the Cloisters at the Metropolitan Museum of Art in New York. They were also recorded and had touring companies that performed at places that could provide appropriate medieval settings, such as the chapel at Duke University.

2. Scholars are not always in agreement about the use of the term *miracle play.* Some scholars, for example, sometimes use the term *miracle play* to refer to the mystery plays based on the Bible, and others sometimes use it to refer to plays about saints.

FURTHER READING

Axton, Richard. *European Drama of the Early Middle Ages.* London: Hutchison, 1974.

Beacham, Richard C. *The Roman Theatre and Its Audience.* London: Routledge, 1991.

Beadle, Richard, ed. *The Cambridge Companion to Medieval English Theatre.* Cambridge: Cambridge University Press, 1994.

Bevington, David, ed. *Medieval Drama.* Boston: Houghton Mifflin, 1975.

Davidson, Clifford, ed. *The Saint Play in Medieval Europe.* Medieval Institute Publications. Kalamazoo: Western Michigan University, 1986.

Frank, Grace. *The Medieval French Drama.* Oxford: Clarendon Press, 1954.

Harris, John Wesley. *Medieval Theatre in Context.* London: Routledge, 1992.

Kolve, V.A. *The Play Called Corpus Christi.* Stanford: Stanford University Press, 1966.

Muir, Lynette R. *The Biblical Drama of Medieval Europe.* Cambridge: Cambridge University Press, 1995.

Ogden, Dunbar H. *The Staging of Drama in the Medieval Church.* Newark: University of Delaware Press, 2002.

Potter, Robert A. *The English Morality Play.* London: Routledge & Kegan Paul, 1975.

Simon, Eckehard, ed. *The Theatre of Medieval Europe: New Research in Early Drama.* Cambridge: Cambridge University Press, 1991.

Tydeman, William. *The Theatre in the Middle Ages: Western European Stage Conditions c. 800–1576.* Cambridge: Cambridge University Press, 1978.

Wickham, Glynne. *The Medieval Theatre.* 3rd ed. Cambridge: Cambridge University Press, 1987.

Woolf, Rosemary. *The English Mystery Plays.* London: Routledge & Kegan Paul, 1972.

Restoration Drama

John M. Ware

THE TERM AND THE TIMES

Although labels for British drama derive from historical periods (medieval), monarchs (Elizabethan, Jacobean, or Caroline), and intellectual movements (Renaissance), Restoration drama draws our attention to its explicit connection with a single political event: the restoration of Charles II, the third Stuart king, to the throne of England in 1660. From 1645 to 1658, England had been ruled by Oliver Cromwell and a variety of Parliamentary and military leaders. Cromwell's son Richard succeeded him in 1658 only to find his authority deteriorating. Notwithstanding complications regarding its own authority, the House of Commons invited Charles II to return to the throne in 1660. Regardless of the celebration of Restoration, Charles II returned to rule a nation irrevocably changed by the strife it had undergone; the England of 1660 could never be the England of 1625, when Charles I had succeeded James I. Parliament restored the king but resisted any exercise of power that implied the crown's authority over Parliament itself. For the most part, Charles II avoided open conflict with Parliament and so avoided testing the limits of his authority and Parliament's tolerance. The same cannot be said for James II, whose brief rule, 1685–88, was marked by the desire to reassert the authority of the crown in defiance of Parliamentary power. Out of fear over James's desire for power, his attempts to recognize Roman Catholicism, and the birth of his son, which meant a Roman Catholic successor to the throne of Protestant England, Parliament forced James into exile in 1688.

Despite the end of Stuart rule in 1688, the term Restoration applies to literature produced until the end of the century. To that extent, the Restoration label masks some of the significant changes that take place during the forty years between

1660 and 1700, most significantly England's conscious commitment to a constitutional monarchy in which the authority of the ruling monarch is bound by both the preexisting system of government and the power of the Parliament. The moment of this commitment is typically referred to as the Glorious Revolution or the Bloodless Revolution and involved the invitation extended William of Orange, a Protestant Dutch prince, and his wife Mary, Protestant daughter of James II, to succeed to the English throne abandoned by James II. While the Stuart line would maintain pretensions to the throne of England by right until 1745, when a last and nearly successful attempt was made to regain the throne by force, the Glorious Revolution marks a settling of numerous issues: the extent of the crown's authority, the freedoms guaranteed by law to all English citizens, and broader tolerance for different forms of religious expression. Despite the return of the king in 1660, the forty years constituting the Restoration see England become a nation rather than a kingdom and the English become citizens rather than subjects.

Just as the term Restoration belies the political changes that Charles II faced upon his return to England in 1660, it also obscures the social changes that had taken place between 1642 and 1660, a period referred to as the Interregnum. One area in which historians emphasize change is in the centrality of the court. Without the court at the epicenter of patronage during the Interregnum, other organizations took an interest in the arts. Although audiences lacked performances to attend after Cromwell's government closed the theaters in 1642, they could still find print versions of plays to read. Moreover, the burst of pamphleteering that took place during this time led printers, booksellers, and authors to take a greater interest in the reading audience, so much so that printers and booksellers began to commission works based on what they determined to be the tastes of their audience. The relationship between dramatic production and audience remained significant throughout the seventeenth century as writers debated the merits and effects of Restoration drama.

But clearly the court did return in 1660 and with it the difficulty of accommodating this court and courtly values in general to changed circumstances. Courtly ideals upheld the social hierarchy, the established church, and the preeminence of the monarch. Of course, all of these ideals were already compromised by the time the court was invited to return to England. Even though Charles II patronized learning in the arts and sciences, the results did not always reinstate the courtly ideals of an earlier age or the ideas he had imbibed while in exile in France. John Dryden, appointed poet laureate in 1670, was conversant with the ideas of Nicolas Boileau, Pierre Corneille, and René Rapin, but was determined to keep the ideas of Roman predecessors and French practitioners as influences upon English drama rather than as ideals to be realized or examples to be imitated. Dryden had a good grasp of English literary history and sought to maintain a distinctly English identity in his dramatic and poetic productions. In fact, even within the narrow selection of dramas we review in this chapter, one can see courtly ideals being questioned, contested, defended, and revised. In his efforts to reinvigorate drama, which had become the preeminent English literary form before the close of the theaters, Charles II issued patents for two theater companies: one to Thomas Killigrew for the King's Company and the other to William Davenant for the Duke's Company. At the time the new patents were issued by Charles, there were very few experienced playwrights or producers; the new companies had to negotiate rights to the stock of existing plays and sought to acquire not only theaters and actors, but playwrights as well.

As Restoration politics is marked to some extent by return, so is Restoration drama. At the most basic level, the Restoration marked the return of public performance. But just as the monarchy was restored in a different fashion, so the Restoration theater differed from its Renaissance predecessor. One immediately noticeable difference was the employment of women to play female roles. Although it took some time before actual theaters were constructed to accommodate the new companies, when finished, the theaters boasted several improvements. Rather than extending into the audience in the manner of the Renaissance stage, the Restoration stage extended further back, allowing for layers of scenery to create a sense of perspective or simply to facilitate changes in scene. This deep stage contained several parallel grooves in which panels of scenery fit and could be slid on or off stage. Other changes included the installation of trap doors and elaborate rigging to create special effects such as appearance, disappearance, or flight. While the size of the theater determined to some extent the seating arrangement, all Restoration theaters included a pit or large open space in front of the stage behind which were galleries and boxes. The pit proved to be a popular place for the more vocal audience members. Productions involved more than the play; they included music, the main piece, an entr'acte, and an afterpiece with all parts usually amounting to roughly three hours of entertainment. Productions were varied, meaning that the company tried to mix the types of plays produced in order to offer their audience a variety. And while Charles was critical to the success of Restoration drama through his patronage and attendance, the audience did not consist solely of aristocratic individuals—it ran the gamut from the aristocratic to the genteel to the professional to those in service. As mentioned before, the audience itself interested writers. Not only did playwrights and managers look to the audience in order to answer their tastes, but playwrights often addressed the audience in their prologues and epilogues, and writers such as the diarist Samuel Pepys recorded the details of the audience in addition to those of the performance—both were subjects worthy of observation and record.

For the purposes of this chapter, we will look at three plays in particular. Although playwrights were at a premium in 1660, they were legion by the end of the Restoration and wrote in a wide variety of forms. The three plays we review are examples of heroic drama, dramatic satire, and the comedy of manners. Restoration playwrights wrote a number of interesting tragedies, but they are not typically celebrated for their efforts in this form. Just as the number of plays we discuss falls well short of those meriting attention, the number of writers is attenuated as well. The plays addressed here were written by John Dryden; George Villiers, the Duke of Buckingham; and William Wycherley. This slice of the talented and successful playwrights of the period excludes many notable dramatists, one in particular is Aphra Behn. While Behn was not the first female playwright of the Restoration era, she was easily the most prolific, successful, and influential. Like Dryden, Behn wrote successfully in forms other than drama, and much of her writing, even that which draws on earlier works for inspiration, demonstrates the way in which writers wove issues of the moment, especially politics, into their art. At the time, Behn represented an especially interesting subject for commentary as she wrote Restoration comedy in the manner of her male peers: witty, ribald, and cynical. Her success prompted discussion of the way in which women should write, a topic relevant to the Restoration drama that so often toyed with the extent to which women were naturally "modest."

We'll discuss the plays chronologically rather than generically: first, an example of heroic drama, John Dryden's *The Conquest of Granada*, first performed in 1670; second, an example of dramatic satire or the critical burlesque, George Villiers's *The Rehearsal*, first performed in 1671; and third, an example of the comedy of manners, William Wycherley's *The Country Wife*, most likely first performed in 1675. The order of discussion is serendipitous in that Restoration comedy certainly had the most lasting impact on the drama that succeeded it and the audience that viewed it. This chapter closes with some consideration of that effect. The Restoration period ends with a scathing attack on the immorality and deleterious effects of Restoration comedies in the form of Jeremy Collier's *A Short View of the Immorality and Profaneness of the English Stage* (1698). While its length and vehemence make it seem the result of a crabbed and prudish intellect, Collier raises interesting points about the relation between drama and society, found a sympathetic audience at the time, and has some relevance to contemporary controversies over media.

JOHN DRYDEN AND HEROIC DRAMA

Heroic drama is a fit form to open this discussion since it demonstrates the links between the early seventeenth century theater and the Restoration theater. Despite the ban on public performances during the Interregnum, William Davenant was permitted to stage operas, and in 1656, he staged *The Siege of Rhodes*, a heroic drama that not only modeled the plot elements for later heroic dramas, such as conflicts between love and honor, martial heroes and virtuous heroines, and exotic settings sprinkled with historical detail, but also included such elements of production as songs, music, elaborate scenery, special effects, and women performing female roles. Davenant's intention through this drama was to impress the audience with grandeur: intense emotions and grand ideas raised to their highest pitch. During the Restoration, Dryden adopted the form. Heroic drama allowed Dryden to stage epic poetry, the highest form of poetry for those who held to the classical hierarchy of poetic forms. Dryden wrote his heroic drama in what became known as the heroic couplet: rhymed, iambic pentameter couplets, a form whose expressive power stemmed both from the ease with which it is read and the numerous opportunities the couplet afforded for making the "sound" underscore the "sense." Heroic dramas included other conventions. The main characters were extraordinary both in terms of their birth (deriving from nobility) and in terms of their character (demonstrating extreme valor, courage, idealism, or virtue). Like the characters, the action of heroic dramas tended toward the extreme by including events that were most improbable and constructing plots that were often complex (including a great variety of action) without being intricate (failing to link the action in a particularly coherent way); that is, the plot of these dramas often accumulates without exhibiting a sophisticated or artful design. At the end of heroic dramas, the virtuous tend to be rewarded and villainous punished, which distinguishes heroic drama from tragedy; this distinction suggests that the function of heroic drama, like epic poetry, is to excite awe and admiration rather than effect an emotional catharsis. People have found heroic drama an odd form to coexist with the witty, bawdy, and sometimes deeply cynical Restoration comedies, but the popularity of heroic drama, which is typically seen as running from 1664–80, can be explained by the excitement with which the reopened theaters were greeted, by the desire on the part of theater managers to present audiences with a variety of forms of drama (from heroic drama to comedy, from the old to the new), and perhaps also by the spectacle that such dramas provided—the foreign worlds conjured in contrast to the more prosaic and familiar worlds of the comedies.

The Conquest of Granada by the Spaniards: Part I (Almanzor and Almahide; or, The Conquest of Granada) (1670) is Dryden's fourth heroic drama, and though in its entirety it consists of two parts and ten acts, parts one and two were performed a year apart. In the play, fifteenth-century Granada is besieged by the Christian armies of Ferdinand, king of Spain. Mahomet Boabdelin, the king of Granada, faces not only the challenge of the Christian armies, but also the challenge of reconciling a populace divided into factions along family lines: the Zegrys and the Abencerrages. Act 1 alone sees the introduction of a mysterious but awe-inspiring stranger, Almanzor, hostilities between the two factions that are subdued only after Almanzor kills a Zegry, the conviction of Almanzor on the grounds of disobeying the king's orders, the pardoning of Almanzor by request of Prince Abdalla, the king's brother, more factional fighting that is subdued not by the king but by Almanzor on the king's behalf, and a threatening visit from the Duke of Arcos, the general to Ferdinand.

Whether or not Dryden intended to comment on the political landscape of Restoration England, one can see in the play cautionary notes regarding the perils of factionalism and the need for a strong central ruler. King Boabdelin explains to the leaders of each faction that their "intestine strife" weakens the state and aids its enemies, yet he lacks the authority by which to overcome the costs already accrued in factional fighting. Rather than forcing his subjects to acknowledge their obligation to the state and their king as representative of that state, Boabdelin finds himself in the awkward and debilitating position of having to accommodate his subjects, even though they rarely accommodate him except by force or in fraud. As Boabdelin announces Almanzor's execution, we find this snatch of dialogue raising issues of sovereignty, law, obligation, and factionalism:

Almanzor:

> No man has more contempt than I, of breath,
> But whence hast thou the right to give me death?
> Obeyed as sovereign by thy subjects be,
> But know, that I alone am king of me.
> I am as free as nature first made man,
> Ere the base laws of servitude began,
> When wild in woods the noble savage ran.

Boabdelin:

> Since, then, no pow'r above your own you know,
> Mankind should use you like a common foe;
> You should be hunted like a beast of prey;
> By your own law I take your life away.

Almanzor:

> My laws are made but only for my sake;
> No king against himself a law can make.
> If thou pretend'st to be a prince like me,
> Blame not an act which should thy pattern be.
> I saw th'opprest and thought it did belong
> To a king's office to redress the wrong:
> I brought that succor which thou ought'st to bring,
> And so, in nature, am thy subjects' king.

Boabdelin:

> I do not want your counsel to direct,
> Or aid to help me punish or protect.

Almanzor:

> Thou wan'st 'em both, or better thou wouldst know,
> Than to let factions in thy kingdom grow.

These lines demonstrate the compass of thought in which heroic drama eagerly indulged. The drift of the dialogue takes in everything from the origin of laws, to the application of laws, to the politics of rule. Almanzor opens by claiming that Boabdelin's laws are state-specific and that Almanzor observes a different, and potentially higher, code. Boabdelin attempts to turn Almanzor's code against him through a state-of-nature argument that seems reminiscent of Thomas Hobbes, but Almanzor counters with a constitutional insight: "No king a law against himself can make"; that is, the king is not subject to but is identical with the law and therefore can never act against the law. In fact, only ministers of the king could be found guilty of infractions of English common law. Extending his insights from constitutional to natural law, Almanzor suggests that he may serve as a pattern by which Boabdelin might fashion his own policy, a suggestion that Boabdelin just as naturally resents. The king's rejection is an example of dramatic irony in that he will time and again rely on Almanzor's aid.

Act 2 furthers two conflicts. First, Almanzor has led the forces of Granada to victory over the Castilians and brought about a cessation of factionalism. In an exchange of taunts with his prisoner, the Duke of Arcos, Almanzor promises to release him in order to gain the honor of defeating him in the next battle. We also find Prince Abdalla courting Lyndaraxa, sister to the Zegry leader Zulema. Lyndaraxa claims that there are two facts harming Abdalla's suit: first, Lyndaraxa is already promised to the leader of the Abencerrages, and second, Abdalla is not the king. The second difficulty leads Abdalla to consider betraying his brother in order to gain the throne and the hand of Lyndaraxa. Abdalla entertains a crisis of conscience, one pitting honor and virtue against passion. In act 3, the plot continues its serpentine way. Baobdelin alienates Almanzor's allegiance by not allowing him to free the Duke of Arcos. Abdalla enlists Almanzor's aid in his attempt to gain the throne, which Almanzor gives not because of any "right" to the crown that Abdalla has contrived but strictly on the basis of his friendship with Abdalla. While Almanzor and Abdalla demonstrate the tangled web of obligation and raise questions as to primacy, Abdalla's conversation with Abdelmelech, an Abencerrago and lover of Lyndaraxa, demonstrates the internal struggle between reason and passion, here put in political terms:

Abdalla:

> Your counsels, noble Abdelmelech, move
> My reason to accept 'em, not my love.
> Ah, why did heav'n leave man so weak of defence,
> To trust frail reason with the rule of sense!
> 'Tis overpoised and kicked up in the air,
> While sense weighs down the scale, and keeps it there;
> Or, like a captive king, 'tis borne away,
> And forced to count'nance its own rebel's sway.

Abdelmelech:

> No, no; our reason was not vainly lent;
> Nor is a slave, but by its own consent:
> If reason on his subject's triumph wait,
> An easy king deserves no better fate.

Abdalla confesses the very lack of control that the drama is leading us to see marks one as unfit for leadership, yet it is this lack of control that is driving Abdalla to assume the throne. Abdelmelech counters Abdalla's sense of helplessness by asserting that reason is complicit in any victory of passion over reason, and that any such victory is a manifest signal of the lack of regal authority. While heroic dramas give scant attention to those who are distinguished through their status, deeds, or aspirations, one can shuffle the lines of the two previous quoted passages and deal a much different hand, one that resonates with the ideas regarding the role of consent in government and in slavery that John Locke expresses in his *Second Treatise on Government* (1690). The point is not that Dryden anticipates Locke's views but rather that the flights of abstraction in heroic drama are both frustrating in that one does not "lose" oneself in them and yet intensely interesting in that they highlight issues that occupy the brilliant minds of the Restoration.

While the love of heroes can sometimes be a tedious affair, *The Conquest of Granada* makes some interesting observations on male/female relations. It may be difficult to admire Lyndaraxa's ambition to be queen and difficult to approve of her manipulation of her contesting lovers, but she does resist submitting to male dominance. In her conversation with Abdelmelech, she refuses to accord him dominance over her behavior and anticipates his stereotypical lament:

Lyndaraxa:

> And when did I my pow'r so far resign,
> That you should regulate each look of mine?

Adelmelech:

> Then, when you gave your love, you gave that pow'r.

Lyndaraxa:

> 'Twas during pleasure, 'tis revoked this hour.
> Now call me false, and rail on womankind—
> 'Tis all the remedy you're like to find.

The act continues with a revolt of the Zegrys led by Abdalla and Almanzor. Boabdelin faces them leaving his betrothed, Almahide, and Lyndaraxa in a tower. Almanzor forces his way into the castle, meets Almahide, falls in love with her, and learns of her vow to Boabdelin. When Abdalla asks Almanzor how he can reward him for his efforts, Almanzor answers that he can free Almahide. Before Abdalla acts, Zulema enters and asks Abdalla to grant Almahide to him. Sensing Abdalla's willingness to accommodate Zulema, Almanzor revokes his friendship with Abdalla and storms off.

Act 4 opens with Almanzor offering his services to Boabdelin, the king he was fighting against in act 3. The bulk of the act is taken up with the love affairs of Lyndaraxa and Almahide, each of whom wrestles with earlier vows and competing lovers. In Lyndaraxa's case, we find her managing her situation with admirable wit but also a growing willingness toward cruelty. As has been the case throughout the play, inconstancy underscores failure of character:

Lyndaraxa:

> O could I read the dark decrees of fate,
> That I might once know whom to love, or hate!
> For I myself scarce my own thoughts can guess,
> So much I find 'em varied by success.
> As in some weather-glass, my love I hold;
> Which falls or rises with the heat or cold.
> I will be constant yet, if fortune can;
> I love the king:—let her but name the man.

In addition to Dryden's witty inversion of Lydaraxa's love (she loves the king but awaits the outcome of the rebellion to know which man that will be), the lines also demonstrate his penchant for choosing odd if intriguing similes. The weather-glass, a combination thermometer-barometer, was a seventeenth century invention. As opposed to Wycherley's comedy with its repeated reference to a few areas of common concern, primarily sex and gambling, Dryden's writing draws from so many aspects of seventeenth century life for its similes and metaphors that some vehicles were deemed inappropriate for the meaning they were to convey or the situations in which they were to be voiced. Act 4 ends with Almanzor's rescue of Almahide, and in response to his confession of love she suggests that he should take his suit to Boabdelin and her father, Abenamar.

Act 5 opens with Abdalla, whose rebellion has failed, entreating Lyndaraxa to shelter him, but she refuses him because he never managed to become king. The persistence of family prejudice continues to mark other lovers and presages both that there will have been few lessons learned over these tumultuous acts and also that there must needs be a sequel. Leaping into the drama's vicious circle, Boabdelin vows to reward Almanzor's aid with whatever he may desire, and Almanzor asks Boabdelin to surrender Almahide to him. This piece of insolence earns Almanzor his second doom of execution from Boabdelin, which Almanzor escapes through the request of Almahide. These two lovers share an extended and topical metaphor at their parting:

Almanzor:

> My joys, indeed, are dreams; but not my pain:
> 'Twas a swift ruin, but the marks remain.
> When some fierce fire lays goodly buildings waste,
> Would you conclude
> There had been none, because the burning's past?

Almahide:

> It was your fault that fire seized all your breast;
> You should have blown up some to save the rest:
> But 'tis, at worst, but so consumed by fire,
> As cities are, that by their falls rise high'r.
> Build love a nobler temple in my place;
> You'll find the fire has but enlarged the space.

Almanzor:

> Love has undone me; I am grown so poor,
> I sadly view the ground I had before,
> But want a stock, and ne'er can build it more.

In September of 1666, fire swept through London destroying much of city and displacing much of its populace. Dryden capitalizes on this event as he did in other works. The passage also demonstrates Dryden's ability to write brisk and witty dialogue in which characters extend each other's thoughts. Almanzor first broaches fire as metaphor, but Almahide continues it in order to make her point. This technique of not only understanding but co-opting another's imagery is a favorite device in Restoration drama. It demonstrates both perceptiveness (the intelligence necessary to understand another's point) and invention (the imagination necessary to continue the metaphor but direct it to one's own ends). Perception and invention were critical elements to Restoration writers' concept of wit.

GEORGE VILLIERS AND DRAMATIC SATIRE

Work on *The Rehearsal* began as early as 1663, at which time George Villiers, Duke of Buckingham, and others began to satirize the heroic dramas of Davenant and Robert Howard. In 1665, London suffered an outbreak of plague, the first of the two devastating events to take place between 1665 and 1666 (the second was the afore-mentioned fire). In response to the plague, the theaters closed and people of means vacated the city. By the time that work on *The Rehearsal* resumed, Dryden had become one of the leading figures in heroic drama, and Villiers accordingly took him and *The Conquest of Granada* as the main targets of his satire. He lampooned Dryden in the character of Bayes, the playwright, and Almanzor, Dryden's protagonist of *The Conquest of Granada*, through the character of Drawcansir. To an extent, *The Rehearsal* became a roman à clef of heroic drama: its characters satirized a variety of playwrights and their creations, its scenery satirized heroic drama's excesses, and its text satirized myriad lines from dramas other than Dryden's. So specific was the satire in some points that a key to the play was published in the early eighteenth century.

The Rehearsal did not end the popularity of heroic drama. Although Dryden made his last contribution in 1671, such dramas remained popular for another decade and continued to be written and performed well into the eighteenth century. Perhaps the more interesting impact of *The Rehearsal* was its critique of drama from within drama—accomplished in two ways. First, *The Rehearsal* is a play about plays and playwrights. Second, *The Rehearsal* is a play within a play. This combination of perspective and technique proved profitable to writers in prose, poetry, and drama during the eighteenth century. In addition to such multi-layered satires as Jonathan Swift's *A Tale of a Tub: Written for the Universal Improvement of Mankind* (1704) and Alexander Pope's *The Dunciad Variorum* (1729), we find two particularly notable dramatic satires in Henry Fielding's *The Tragedy of Tragedies; or, The Life and Death of Tom Thumb the Great* (1731) and Richard Brinsley Sheridan's *The Critic; or, A Tragedy Rehearsed* (1779). Undoubtedly influential, *The Rehearsal* is also amusing in its own right. Its mode of satire is typically seen as burlesque, meaning that within the play we realize a discrepancy between the style and the substance, a discrepancy that typically involves exaggerating the style in relation to the substance. Although more complex definitions of burlesque exist, the important points to keep in mind in connection with *The Rehearsal* are its assumption that heroic drama was in and of itself a burlesque (the bombastic presentation of common and occasionally nonsensical ideas) and the various forms of satire in which it indulged: exaggeration, parody, and the reduction of its target to absurdity.

The prologue to *The Rehearsal* indicates the means of conducting the satire; the play will represent heroic drama in such a light that people can see it for what it is. Heroic drama will, in a sense, be unmasked:

We might as well call this short mock-play of ours
A posy made of weeds instead of flowers;
Yet such have been presented to your noses,
And there are such, I fear, who thought 'em roses.
Would some of 'em were here, to see, this night,
What stuff it is in which they took delight.
Here, brisk, insipid rogues, for wit, let fall
Sometimes dull sense; but oft'ner, none at all.

The imposture of heroic drama will be made sensible, plain, evident; a fit intent for an increasingly empirical age and nation. Satire most often seeks to justify its fury by claiming that knowing is the first step on the way to reformation. The Prologue is no exception to this pattern:

...[I]f by my endeavors, you grow wise,
And what you once so praised shall now despise,
Then I'll cry out, swelled with poetic rage,
'Tis I, John Lacy, have reformed your stage.

The irony lies in the fact that Lacy, who acted the part of Bayes, would trumpet his power in a manner befitting a hero from a heroic drama.

Act 1, scene 1 opens with a conversation, in prose, between two friends, Johnson and Smith, who have just encountered each other in London after Smith's having spent some time in the country. Johnson, an avid theater-goer, notes that he has been so horrified by what he has seen in theaters of late that he is considering going into business, which he despises. Smith claims that "country wits" have approved of the new plays, and Johnson replies that "city wits" also applaud them; however, for Johnson, their approbation indicates that the new wits "scorn to imitate nature" and look only "to elevate and surprise." When Smith asks what the phrase "elevate and surprise" means, Johnson responds, "Nay, by my troth, that's a hard matter: I don't understand that myself. 'Tis a phrase they have got among them, to express their no-meaning by. I'll tell you, as near as I can, what it is. Let me see; 'tis fighting, loving, sleeping, rhyming, dying, dancing, singing, crying; and everything but thinking and sense." In addition to addressing the critical concept of wit and introducing one of Restoration drama's favorite targets for satire, business, the opening dialogue demonstrates the extent to which *The Rehearsal* is invested in dramatic criticism. Before we encounter even the slightest hint of burlesque, we are presented with an appropriate, if ignored, standard for good writing (the imitation of "nature") and the new and as yet ill-defined standard ("elevate and surprise"). Johnson's criticism of the new standard is not only that it has no correspondence to nature but also that it cannot be explained.

The two men encounter an author, Bayes, and Johnson asks him to explain the "meaning" of his last play to Smith, which Bayes says he cannot do; however,

Bayes notes that his new play is in its last rehearsal and invites Johnson and Smith to attend it with him. They agree. As they make their way to the theater, Bayes explains some of his rules for writing a play. One is the rule of tranversion, which not only requires that he find moments of wit in other works but that he "transverse" the form of those moments to a form opposite of the original: for instance, prose he turns into poetry, and poetry he turns into prose. The rule implies both a lack of originality and a degree of duplicity regarding the manner in which one's wit is presented. Bayes not only obscures the source but potentially the wit and meaning of what he in effect plagiarizes. Another rule involves a book that he keeps in his pocket, *Drama Commonplaces;* rather than invent anything, he turns to this book to see what has already been written or said on any given subject. Again, the satire underscores Bayes's lack of originality and his desire to disguise it by altering the original language: "[W]hen I have anything to invent, I never trouble my head about it, as other men do; but presently turn over this book, and there I have at one view, all that Perseus, Montaigne, Seneca's tragedies, Horace, Juvenal, Claudian, Pliny, Plutarch's *Lives,* and the rest, have ever thought upon this subject; and so, in a trice, by leaving out a few words or putting in others of my own, the business is done." In act 1, scene 2, Bayes and company arrive at the rehearsal. The satire of Bayes's self-aggrandizement and the exposure of his ineptness to Johnson and Smith continues. Over and again, we find Bayes discounting the "old plain way" of writing and celebrating the "new way," whose advantages Johnson and Smith labor to discern.

Act 2, scene 1 provides a glimpse of Bayes's new way of writing; in this case, we witness frequent whispering between the actors on stage yet the audience remains ignorant of what is said. When asked about characterization, plot, or staging, Bayes offers a stock reply: "[I]t's new." He adds, "I despise your Jonson and Beaumont, that borrowed all they writ from nature. I am for fetching it purely from my own fancy." As for what Bayes's fancy or imagination supplies, Johnson, who has some acquaintance with Bayes's earlier work, notes to Smith, "[I]t is, as I told thee, very fantastical, most abominably dull, and not one word to the purpose." Of the three characteristics, "fantastical" is no longer as clearly pejorative as "dull" or purposeless, but Johnson is tapping a notion of fantastic that characterizes bad poetry; fantastical poetry traffics in the unreal, illusory, and irrational, and its effect on the reader cannot be anything but deleterious. In act 2, scene 3, Bayes stresses that the new way of writing demands similes to express surprise, especially extended similes. Johnson suggests that the similes often seem gratuitous rather than applicable to the occasion, and one gets the sense that the new way of writing is conspicuous, a demonstration of the poet's imagination with only the thinnest strand of connection to the plot of the play.

This disregard for plot is underscored in act 3 as well. After Bayes draws the men's attention to some witty repartee, Smith observes that the dialogue, while brisk, is not "to the purpose, for the play does not go on."

Bayes: Play does not go on? I don't know what you mean; why is not this part of the play?

Smith: Yes, but the plot stands still.

Bayes: Plot stand still! why, what a devil is the plot good for but to bring in fine things?

Bayes objects that one can't stall the plot since the plot serves merely as the rationale for events, scenes, or dialogue. Bayes ascribes Smith's concerns to his vulgarity—his inability to appreciate the ways in which Bayes exceeds "the common pitch." Over the course of the play, Johnson and Smith respond differently to Bayes's absurdities: Johnson humors Bayes while Smith confronts him. In response, Bayes develops different ideas of the critical judgment of the two men. Bayes's sense that Smith lacks judgment is reinforced when Smith questions the placement of a song. Johnson's mock defense of the song earns him the following commendation: "I know you have wit by the judgment you make of this play, for that's the measure I go by—my play is my touchstone." In effect, Bayes lacks any standard by which his play could be found faulty and rather assumes that his play is the means of determining the quality of other people's judgment. The satire reinforces the notion introduced earlier of a tradition of critical tenets, an inherited understanding of what makes drama (or poetry) successful and underscores the way in which the talented, learned, and witty responded negatively to novelty. While the Restoration is often seen as a time of moral laxity, a characterization based largely on its comedies, here we see courtly writers exercising conservative critical judgments. The two positions are not antithetical, but they make for an interesting paradox in thought that should lead us to be cautious regarding blanket generalizations that we make of the Restoration as a period of unbridled license.

The satire in *The Rehearsal* is both halter and switch, castigating heroic drama for its excesses and leading the audience back to the path of true wit. That wit shows itself in Villiers's ability to ridicule heroic drama's conventions. Within Bayes's play, Prince Volscius is preparing to meet his army encamped outside of town, when he is awed by the beauty of Parthenope. Prince Volscius hesitates as she exits, and, partly dressed, indulges in this soliloquy:

Volscius:

How has my passion made me Cupid's scoff!
This hasty boot is on, the other off,
And sullen lied, with amorous design
To quit loud fame and make that beauty mine.

. . .

My legs, the emblem of my various thought,
Show to what sad distraction I am brought.
Sometimes with stubborn honor, like this boot,
My mind is guarded, and resolved to do't:
Sometimes, again, that very mind, by love
Disarmèd, like this other leg does prove.
Shall I to Honor or to Love give way?
"Go on," cries Honor; tender Love says, "Nay,"
Honor aloud commands, "Pluck both boots on";
But softer Love does whisper, "Put on none."

As opposed to moments of utter absurdity, the wit in such burlesque lies in part in our realization of the writer's control of the form; that is, we realize that Villiers knows how to write effective heroic couplets. The humor then exists not only in Volscius's choice of emblems, a pair of boots and a state of undress, for thinking through a conflict between honor and love, but also in our awareness of a talented writer lending his wit to rendering this scene. More contemporary examples of this blend of talent and ridicule exist in the writing of Christopher Guest and others in mockumentaries such as *This Is Spinal Tap* (1984) and especially *A Mighty Wind* (2003).

Act 4, scene 1 continues witty burlesque and introduces the character Draw-cansir, whose dialogue parodies specific lines of Almanzor in *The Conquest of Granada*. As amusing as the satire of Alamanzor is, one of Bayes's most amusing innovations is to have Prince Pretty-man and Prince Volscius engage in a verse dispute over the fact that each loves a different woman. The dialogue begins as a consideration of how such a state could come to be but quickly devolves into a competition to see whose verse can most successfully represent the superiority of each prince's lover. Instead of raising the objects of the verse higher, the verse tends to sink them lower in the audience's estimation. We pick up at the lip of the descent:

Volscius:

If incense thou wilt offer at the shrine
Of mighty love, burn it to none but mine.
Her rosy lips external sweets exhale;
And her bright flames make all flames else look pale.

Pretty-man:

Perhaps dull incense may thy love suffice;
But mine must be adored with sacrifice.
All hearts turn ashes which her eyes control:
The body they consume as well as soul.

Volscius:

> My love has yet a power more divine;
> Victims her altars burn not, but refine:
> Amidst the flames they ne'er give up the ghost,
> But, with her looks, revive still as they roast.
> In spite of pain and death, they're kept alive:
> Her fiery eyes makes 'em in fire survive.
> . . .
> Let my Parthenope at length prevail.

Pretty-man:

> I'll sooner have a passion for a whale,
> In whose vast bulk, though store of oil doth lie,
> We find more shape, more beauty, in a fly.

In the effort to cap each other's imagery, the imagery itself turns to the grotesque. Parthenope's love is so powerful as to enflame and sustain her lovers so that their reward is to "roast" eternally. Johnson and Smith agree that Bayes has a knack for "writing smooth verse," but Smith adds that Bayes's accomplishment is one of numbers, while his failure is one of sense.

Act 5 includes the climactic scene of Bayes's play, which involves flying kings, obscure lyrics, a character who is interrupted every time she tries to speak, a battle ended by an eclipse, and the representation of said eclipse through a dance of the moon, earth, and sun. The act and the play end with Johnson and Smith sneaking away to dine while Bayes is offstage addressing the players, the players sneaking away while Bayes is offstage looking for the gentlemen, and Bayes leaving in a huff. The epilogue to *The Rehearsal* reiterates the centrality of traditional standards, plot, and sense to its critique of heroic drama:

> The play is at an end, but where's the plot?
> That circumstance our poet Bayes forgot,
> And we can boast, though 'tis a plotting age,
> No place is freer from it than the stage.
> The ancients plotted, though, and strove to please
> With sense that might be understood with ease;
> They every scene with so much wit did store
> That who brought any in, went out with more:
> But this new way of wit does so surprise,
> Men lose their wits in wond'ring where it lies.

The epilogue calls for the application of this ancient standard in order to curtail the "prodigious way of writing" that has become so common over "these ten years." Again, Villiers demonstrates that any attribution of "license" to the

Restoration requires elaboration. The court of Charles II and genteel entertainment involved liberties; yet subscribers to courtly lifestyles and cultured living were clearly concerned with the pretensions exercised by those who influenced public taste. To this extent, *The Rehearsal* is criticism modeled and performed. Although its epilogue is addressed to the audience, it targets writers of Bayes's new way and leaves the audience relatively unscathed. While *The Rehearsal* devolves into absurdity at times, that absurdity is intended to echo the absurdity of the form being satirized. Moreover, *The Rehearsal* is elitist in some respects. It treats a form of drama that resonated with many people over a length of time as a freak or a fancy and implies that people of wit and judgment, such as Johnson and Smith are, should be able to see through heroic drama's alluring spectacle and vapid rhetoric.

WILLIAM WYCHERLEY AND RESTORATION COMEDY

Restoration comedy is most often classified as the "comedy of manners." While the term is associated with the period, it also refers to a comedic approach that extends well past the seventeenth century and into other forms of literature than drama. In its approach, the comedy of manners avoids the highly stylized language of heroic dramas and the elaborate attention to love of earlier romantic comedies, and demonstrates stronger links to early seventeenth century city comedies. Restoration comedies typically focus on the codes and conduct of a particular set of people in society, most often people of property and means though not necessarily those of aristocratic status. While the action that takes place in these comedies may be intricately plotted, the events themselves are of less significance than the behavior of the characters. The characters are predictable in that we are certain to encounter fops (fools whose vanity leads them to affect characteristics they don't possess), wits (men and women of intelligence and spirit), sharpers of various sorts, lovers, cits, and servants. All of these characters engage in intrigues having to do with sex, money, and love.

Restoration comedies engage in the dramatic satire of which *The Rehearsal* is an example, but instead of satirizing a particular form of drama and its authors, the comedy of manners satirizes the characters who people the stage. Yet the satire is not evenly spread; we often encounter characters who are flawed yet attractive. These morally suspect characters are perceptive and imaginative; they demonstrate concern for friends, an aversion to affectation, and a delight in society. Moreover, these wits do not necessarily suffer ill consequences for their actions. In part, because of this lack of overt correction, these comedies were sometimes seen as advocating a kind of moral laxity. At the same time, comic dramatists could defend their satiric productions by arguing that their deliberate disregard of conventional social codes of conduct was intended to underscore the problems of those codes as much as the immorality of the offending characters. To an extent, this argument is legitimate. Restoration comedies model conflicts in values, and the search for advocacy of any single approach to the challenges of living in the late seventeenth century may be futile. Some critics have noted that even the attractive characters err in their judgments and that the satiric net is cast wide. But it is also the case that some aspects of Restoration comedies are disquieting. Compelling characters act in ways that are as predatory and vindictive as they are liberating. Moreover, the comedies also model a social hierarchy in which characters of wit and ability act independently of social conventions. Acting contrary to social conventions is not necessarily a bad thing, but the manipulation of flawed conventions seems a disingenuous form of critique. To some extent, the cynical implications of this revised social hierarchy, one in which wit rather than property or title garnered admiration, were softened through romantic love: witty lovers could avoid the fate that a debased society would impose on them through their application of intelligence to their situation. The Restoration myth of romantic love with a cynical twist celebrates successful if select lovers. One might conclude that while it offered abundant entertainment and reason to laugh, Restoration comedy offered little cheer. But that is, perhaps, the bitter aftertaste of a delightful satire.

The Country Wife (1675) is William Wycherley's third and most popular play. From its initial production, audience members differed regarding the extent to which the play's portrayal of sexuality exceeded the bounds of propriety. While the play remained popular, its bawdiness demanded revision over the course of the eighteenth century in order to be staged, and it continues to be one of the most frequently performed Restoration comedies. With the exception of the prologue, epilogue, and some couplets that conclude particular acts, the play is written entirely in prose. Act 1, scene 1 takes place entirely in the lodgings of Horner, the protagonist of the play, whose name suggests his penchant for making cuckolds of men—giving them horns—by seducing their lovers or wives. Horner is talking with Quack, a physician who, at Horner's request, has spread the rumor that Horner has suffered a venereal disease and been treated in a way that leaves him impotent "as a eunuch." Act 1 consists of a series of visits from people who have heard the rumor with varying degrees of conviction and sympathy. At the opening, however, we learn that Horner deliberately seeks the reputation of eunuch in order to gain access to women that he couldn't have access to before because of his reputation as a notorious rake—defined by Samuel Johnson as "a man addicted to pleasure." One implication of Horner's "new unpracticed trick" is that he is more predatory than proud; he doesn't mind seeing his reputation fall in order to achieve what he considers to be a more worthy goal.

First to enter Horner's lodgings are Sir Jasper Fidget and his wife, Lady Fidget, and his sister, Mrs. Dainty Fidget. Sir Jasper seeks to determine the veracity of the rumor regarding Horner's impotence, delights in his conclusion that it's true, and taunts Horner by forcing him into familiarity with Lady Fidget. After Sir Jasper and the women leave, Horner explains his logic to Quack. By taking on the reputation of impotence, Horner will provide women of society what they truly want: a way to satisfy their desires without cost to their reputations: "[Y]our women of honor, as you call 'em, are only chary of their reputations, not their persons, and 'tis scandal they would avoid, not men." This attitude is typical of Restoration comedy in which reputation functions like credit; credit has a tenuous connection to actual value and is calculated on history, present situation, and prospects. Moreover, credit affords one the ability to pursue one's aims without actually paying for the satisfaction. So long as the women of quality in Restoration comedies can maintain the reputation of honor or virtue, they can act in any way they please. The hazard is in the loss of reputation, which would result in a loss of ability to effect one's ends. Horner's coup is in ensuring women that they can maintain their reputations despite his company. Moreover, the desire to humiliate Horner that we see in men such as Sir Jasper leads them to force Horner into women's company, thereby giving Horner more opportunity to seduce women of reputation.

The next characters to enter Horner's lodgings are his friends Harcourt and Dorilant. Horner maintains the deception with them as well by suggesting that among the benefits of impotency is more time for "lasting, rational, and manly pleasures" such as drinking and socializing. Harcourt disagrees, and we see a staple of Restoration comedy in the elaboration of witty similes or analogies. Harcourt goes first: "[M]istresses are like books. If you pore upon them too much, they doze you and make you unfit for company; but if used discreetly, you are the fitter for conversation by 'em." Dorilant follows: "A mistress should be like a little country retreat near the town, not to dwell in constantly, but only for a night and away, to taste the town the better when a man returns." Horner counters that to be "a good fellow" and "a good friend," one must be neither "a lover of women" nor "a lover of money." He then offers his friends a dichotomy: choose the "joy" of wine or "the grief and torments" of love. To some extent, Horner falls victim to his own dichotomy in that his pursuit of women of honor will keep him from enjoying the company of his friends, but the initial assertion that to be sociable one must be liberal seems an apt ideal for the Restoration rake.

Another visitor, Sparkish, is announced and before he enters, the three men describe him as someone who is full of conceit, who is oblivious to the low opinion that people have of him, who assumes that he is welcome in company when in fact people find him tiresome. Sparkish is objectionable because he pretends to be what he is not. Horner criticizes such men: "A pox on 'em, and all that force nature, and would be still what she forbids 'em! Affectation is her greatest monster." Coming from a man seeking the reputation of eunuch, the line seems ironic;

yet Horner is cunning rather than affected. Horner's observation and the other men's acquiescence to it support an ethic of nature (a critical term in *The Rehearsal* as well). This ethic assumes that people have natures that they ought to recognize and with which they should act in accordance; however, the wits subscribe to a kind of elite cynicism by suggesting that most people act in a way that conceals rather than reveals their nature. The observation is cynical because it sees people as largely hypocritical, elitist because it sees society as a meritocracy of wit. Sparkish enters and immediately rallies Horner on his impotency. Sparkish's attempts at wit are not absurd in the manner of Bayes, but they are often simply not funny. Noting the lack of response by the wits to his raillery, he observes, "Well, I see one had as good go to law without a witness, as break a jest without a laugher on one's side." At times, Sparkish will be witty, but usually in ways that are self-incriminating; whether as here (in which case, he exposes that he would consider keeping someone, a "laugher," nearby to make him appear witty) or in ironic remarks as when he insists on dining with the three gentlemen who are eagerly trying to force him out of the house and so avoid him: "What, d'ye think I'll eat then with gay, shallow fops and silent coxcombs? I think wit as necessary at dinner as a glass of good wine, and that's the reason I never have any stomach when I eat alone." Sparkish inadvertently confesses to having no wit.

Pinchwife, a 40-something former acquaintance of the three men and the brother to Sparkish's fiancée, enters as soon as Sparkish leaves. He has come to town with his 21-year old bride to attend Sparkish's wedding to Alithea. In some respects, Pinchwife is the second most important male character in the play. He's so suspicious of Horner and so determined not to be made a cuckold that he would disguise the fact that he is married. The antagonism between Horner and Pinchwife is palpable in this dialogue, and if the play has heretofore led us to see Horner as grossly predatory, it leads us to see Pinchwife as someone who wants a woman whom he can possess and control. Horner admires women with wit ("I think no young woman ugly that has it, and no handsome woman agreeable without it"), while Pinchwife would rather have an ignorant and pliable wife. Pinchwife demonstrates two character flaws in his initial appearance: an extremely jealous temperament and overweening confidence in his ability to "understand the town" as he puts it. Both aspects of his character lead him to bring about rather than avoid what he fears.

Act 2, scene 1 opens at Pinchwife's house with a conversation between Margery, Pinchwife's "country wife," and Alithea, Pinchwife's sister. Margery is an interesting character because she allows Wycherley to consider character and environment. On the one hand, the country will stand throughout the play, as it does throughout all Restoration comedies, as the source of things "rustic" and unsophisticated. On the other hand, Margery demonstrates an appetite for the attractions of the town and an aptitude for manipulation. Much of the humor surrounding the character of Margery lies in the way that Pinchwife's efforts to "keep her in ignorance" backfire. As Pinchwife encourages Margery to understand that she should love him rather than any other man, he makes it clear that this is not the town way: "Ay, my dear, you must love me only, and not be like the naughty town-women, who only hate their husbands and love every man else, love plays, visits, fine coaches, fine clothes, fiddles, balls, treats, and so lead a wicked town-life." Margery immediately responds by expressing a desire for these things, and Alithea notes, "The fool has forbid me discovering to her the pleasures of the town, and he is now setting her agog upon them himself." Margery confirms this when she tells Pinchwife that his reluctance to allow her to attend a play made her, "as 'twere, desire it."

Sparkish and Harcourt enter Pinchwife's house so that Sparkish can introduce Harcourt to Alithea; Pinchwife, upon seeing them, locks Margery in a separate room. Sparkish introduces Harcourt to Alithea, and Harcourt expresses his admiration of her, which provides the central romantic concern of the plot. After Sparkish, Alithea, and Harcourt exit, Lady Fidget, Mrs. Dainty Fidget, and Mrs. Squeamish all appear at Pinchwife's lodgings in order to meet his wife, and when he can't persuade them to leave, he leaves himself. After noting Pinchwife's intense jealousy, the women discuss the difficulties facing women of "quality." They begin by complaining that married women of "quality" are seldom engaged in extra-marital affairs by men of quality who "use us with the same indifferency and ill-breeding as if we were all married to 'em." Worst still, the women note that men of quality spread rumors about having had affairs with women of quality, rumors all the more awful given that they are not true; that is, women of quality both suffer defamation of character and neglect. *The Country Wife* stands out for the numerous opportunities it takes to satirize the behavior of men through the mouths of its female characters. Although the wits earlier expressed reluctance to marry, the women at this point, and others, express both some dissatisfaction with the married state and also a sense that many men are imposters when it comes to their sexual prowess and intrigues.

Act 2 closes with Horner making Lady Fidget understand that he is in fact not impotent but that he has spread the rumor himself in order to shield those with whom he would have intrigues from suspicion or scandal. Lady Fidget responds, "[C]ould you be so generous, so truly a man of honor, as for the sakes of us women of honor, to cause yourself to be reported no man? No man! And to suffer the greatest shame that could fall upon a man, that none might fall upon us women by your conversation?" The remark indicates just how flexible the concept of honor is when it is applied without reference to any ideals but those of pleasure shielded from the world's prying eyes. After complimenting Horner on his honorable action, Lady Fidget seeks assurance that Horner is in fact not impotent; ever the empiricist, Horner replies, "I scorn you should take my word; I desire to be tried only, madam." The scene ends with a self-satisfied Sir Jasper leaving Horner with the ladies so that he may attend his own business. As liberality rather than jealousy or economy had been central to the Restoration wit's code of behavior, so is pleasure rather than business. After Sir Jasper exits, Lady Fidget delivers the act's closing couplet: "Who for his business from his wife will run, / Takes the best care to have her business done"; that is, husbands who elevate business over their obligations to their wives will bear some responsibility in leading their wives into intrigues with other men.

Much of act 3 is devoted to Harcourt's pursuit of Alithea, which is important not only for offering the only glimpse of affection in the play but also for offering insight into yet another way in which romantic love is debased by a society where one's reputation means everything, and everything affects one's reputation. It becomes increasingly clear that Sparkish lacks passion for Alithea, although the sign of that failure, his lack of jealousy over Harcourt's treatment of his fiancée, is a dubious register given Pinchwife's actions. Sparkish, like Horner and Pinchwife, uses Alithea as an object or accessory fit for a man who fashions himself fashionable. Alithea argues that Sparkish should be angry with Harcourt for *making love* to her, but Sparkish hears this as if she's suggesting that he should be angry with Harcourt for *loving* her: "If he did love you, 'tis but what he can't help; and 'tis your fault, not his, if he admires you. I hate a man for being of my opinion! I'll ne'er do't, by the world." Alithea recognizes that Sparkish relishes a sign of the approval of wits in his choice for wife: "Is it for your honor of mine, to suffer a man to make love to me?" Sparkish's reply is not without reason: "Is it for your honor or mine, to have me jealous? That he makes love to you is a sign you are handsome; and that I am not jealous is a sign that you are virtuous. That, I think, is for your honor." Although Sparkish makes a good point, Alithea has underscored the fact that Sparkish's trust is one thing, his motives something else; in this case, Sparkish is suffering and forcing Alithea to suffer someone else's designs—designs that Sparkish cannot discover because he is blinded by his own vanity. In wooing her, Harcourt draws Alithea's attention to Sparkish's concern for himself and lack of concern for her: "[Y]ou may see how the most estimable and most glorious creature in the world is valued by him," he tells Alithea, who explains the comment's significance to Sparkish: "[H]e means you care not for me, nor who has me." Sparkish reveals his lack of intelligence, his lack of passion, and also his frustration with women: "Gad, I see virtue makes a woman as troublesome as a little reading or learning." While Sparkish's misogyny is less striking because it is neither predatory like Horner's nor violent like Pinchwife's, his is the public face of their desire to possess women in secret: "I love to be envied, and would not marry a wife that I alone could love; loving alone is as dull as eating alone. . . . And to tell you the truth, it may be I love to have rivals in a wife, they make her seem to a man still but as a kept mistress." Sparkish objectifies women in a new way, as objects that excite him solely because they stimulate the interest of others yet belong to him.

Act 4 deals mainly in the plots of Pinchwife and Horner. In scene 2, we find Pinchwife dictating a letter for Margery to send to Horner as if it were written by her. Over the course of the play, Pinchwife and Horner have brought Horner's desire for Margery to her attention, and Pinchwife is now trying to assess Margery's feelings and at the same time curtail any opportunities for Horner to see Margery. When Margery admits that she finds Horner attractive, Pinchwife concludes, "So, 'tis plain she loves him, yet she has not love enough to make her conceal it from me; but the sight of him will increase her aversion for me and love for him, and that love instruct her how to deceive me and satisfy him, all idiot as she is. Love! 'Twas he gave women first their craft, their art of deluding; out of nature's hands they came plain, open, silly, and fit for slaves, as she and Heaven intended 'em." The passage demonstrates Pinchwife's low estimation of women and his conception of wives as slaves by nature. When Margery resists writing the letter as Pinchwife dictates, he reacts violently: "Write as I bid you, or I will write 'whore' with this penknife in your face." When Margery expurgates some words that she contends she should not write since they are "filthy," Pinchwife again threatens her: "I will stab out those eyes that cause my mischief." Despite Pinchwife's threats, Margery does deceive him by writing a second letter in which she divulges her husband's plot; moreover, she gets her husband to deliver that letter to Horner rather than the one he had dictated to her.

Act 4, scene 3 opens in Horner's lodgings as he explains to Quack the success that he has had in gaining access to women of honor, enjoying "particular privileges," and witnessing their lack of honor and hypocrisy. Quack expresses some doubt and hides behind a screen when Lady Fidget enters. The dialogue that ensues demonstrates the way in which Restoration comedies made euphemisms out of concepts:

Lady Fidget: Well, Horner, am not I a woman of honor? You see I'm as good as my word.

Horner: And you shall see, madam, I'll not be behindhand with you in honor; and I'll be as good as my word too, if you please but to withdraw into the next room.

Lady Fidget: But first, my dear sir, you must promise to have a care of my dear honor.

Lady Fidget expresses concern that her behavior, while not being divulged by Horner himself, will be suspected or become the object of rumor from her acquaintances who are jealous of her honor:

Lady Fidget: [Y]ou must have great care of your conduct; for my acquaintances are so censorious (oh, 'it's a wicked, censorious world, Mr. Horner!), I say, are so censorious and detracting that perhaps they'll talk, to the prejudice of my honor, though you should not let them know the dear secret.

Horner: Nay, madam, rather than they shall prejudice your honor, I'll prejudice theirs; and to serve you, I'll lie with 'em all, make the secret their own, and then they'll keep it. I am a Machiavel in love, madam.

Lady Fidget: Oh, no, sir, not that way.

Horner: Nay, the devil take me if censorious women are to be silenced any other way.

Lady Fidget: A secret is better kept, I hope, by a single person than a multitude; therefore pray do not trust anybody else with it, dear, dear, Mr. Horner.

Not only does honor consist in reputation rather than behavior, but honor is best protected by lowering the behavior of others than raising one's own. Horner's means to protect Lady Fidget's honor sparks her jealousy and reveals her desire to possess him. The degree to which Horner is able to orchestrate the intrigue and cuckold the husband is demonstrated through Sir Jasper Fidget's entrance. In this part of the scene, we shift from "honor" as a euphemism for sex to a double entendre involving "china." Lady Fidget claims that she came to get Horner to help her shop for china: "I was fain to come up to fetch him, or go without him, which I was resolved not to do; for he knows china very well, and has himself very good, but will not let me see it lest I should beg some. But I will find it out, and have what I came for yet." With this remark, Lady Fidget locks herself in a different room of the house ostensibly to search Horner's china. More double entendres tumble forth. First, Horner tells Sir Jasper to remain where he is, and that Horner will "get in to her [Lady Fidget] the back way." Sir Jasper warns his wife, "My Lady Fidget! Wife! He is coming in to you the back way." Lady Fidget replies, "Let him come, and welcome, which way he will." Mrs. Squeamish enters and tries desperately to find Horner and Lady Fidget less out of concern for Lady Fidget's welfare and more out of desire to obtain some china herself as we discover when the characters return with Lady Fidget holding a piece of china:

Lady Fidget: And I have been toiling and moiling for the prettiest piece of china, my dear.

Horner: Nay, she has been too hard for me, do what I could.

Mrs. Squeamish: O Lord, I'll have some china too. Good Mr. Horner, don't think to give other people china, and me none; come in with me too.

Horner: Upon my honor, I have none left now.

Mrs. Squeamish: Nay, Nay, I have known you deny your china before now, but you shan't put me off so. Come.

Horner: This lady had the last there.

Lady Fidget: Yes, indeed, madam, to my certain knowledge he has no more left.

Mrs. Squeamish: Oh, but it may be he may have some you could not find.

Lady Fidget: What, d'ye think if he had had any left, I would not have had it too? For we women of quality never think we have china enough.

Sir Jasper is oblivious to the desires of Lady Fidget and Mrs. Squeamish and the ways in which he abets Horner. Moreover, the scene demonstrates that honor is a disguise, cloak, or mask under which women of quality disguise their desires, through which they try to satisfy them, and by which they try to outvie their peers.

Act 5 opens with Pinchwife delivering Margery, disguised as Alithea, to Horner. Margery has deceived Pinchwife into believing that Alithea is in love with Horner and that Margery is Alithea. After leaving his wife in his rival's hands, Pinchwife informs Sparkish that Alithea has jilted him and will be married to Horner. When Alithea appears, Sparkish berates her for her treachery and spitefully resigns his claim to her. Alithea, who has no idea what Sparkish is talking about, can now admit her affection for Harcourt with a clear conscience.

By the time we return to Horner's lodgings in scene 4, he has enjoyed his intrigue with Margery but not managed to sneak her out before the women of quality arrive for a masquerade and banquet. At the masquerade, the women reiterate their resentment toward their husbands and men in general. Upon inquiry, Horner admits to having avoided women of quality because of their concern for their reputations:

Lady Fidget: Our reputation! Lord, why should you not think that we women make use of our reputation, as you men of yours, only to deceive the world with less suspicion? Our virtue is like the statesman's religion, the Quaker's word, the gamester's oath, and the great man's honor—but to cheat those that trust us.

Mrs. Squeamish: And that demureness, coyness, and modesty that you see in our faces in the boxes at plays, is as much a sign of a kind woman as a vizard-mask in the pit.

Mrs. Dainty Fidget: For, I assure you, women are least masked when they have the velvet vizard on.

Lady Fidget: You would have found us modest women in our denials only.

By the time *The Country Wife* was written, "vizard" in the pit of the playhouse had become synonymous with prostitute. The dialogue clearly undercuts any notion of feminine modesty as an inherent value; rather, it's a value worn by those women of quality who can afford it. Horner asks why the elaborate deception and maintenance of honor, and Lady Fidget answers that it is a matter of gaining a kind of liberty that lets women of quality avoid those whom they dislike and "enjoy the better and more privately those you love." One of the interesting aspects of this dialogue is that it portrays some women as sharing in the predatory and possessive impulses that characterize people such as Horner and Pinchwife. Unfortunately for these women, as they continue to drink, they come to confess their lovers, all of which it turns out to be one and the same man—Horner:

Lady Fidget: Well then, there's no remedy; sister sharers, let us not fall out, but have a care of our honor. Though we get no presents, no jewels of him, we are savers of our honor, the jewel of most value and use, which shines yet to the world unsuspected, though it be counterfeit.

Horner: Nay, and is e'en as good as if it were true, provided the world think so; for honor, like beauty now, only depends on the opinion of others.

Horner's consolation reiterates the extent to which concepts depend upon conventions for their reference. Neither honor nor beauty corresponds to anything in particular; rather they depend entirely on what people believe. The beautiful are not beautiful in light of admired features of face or figure, but due to the fact that people regard them as beautiful whatever those people's reasons and whatever that person's appearance may be.

Shortly after the revelation at the banquet, almost all the other characters arrive at Horner's lodgings. Convinced that Alithea wants to marry Horner and that he brought Alithea to Horner earlier, Pinchwife threatens to make Horner to marry Alithea. Harcourt offers to stand in Horner's place, and Horner resigns his right to marry Alithea to Harcourt, but Pinchwife refuses to recognize this act. As Pinchwife grabs his sword, Margery, fearing for Horner and still wearing Alithea's clothes, enters and asks that the parson marry her to Horner. As an irate Pinchwife prepares to kill his wife, Horner steps in, and Pinchwife prepares to kill them both. Ultimately, Horner begs Quack to inform Pinchwife of his condition and to save both his own and the ladies' reputations from the "censorious world." Sir Jasper believes Quack readily, but Pinchwife is reluctant. The women, Margery included, maintain the deception, and the party ends with a warning to husbands not to constrain their wives lest they bring to pass what they most fear by making them desperate. Pinchwife and Horner are the characters given lines at the end of the play. Pinchwife wishes both that he could believe that he had not been cuckolded and also that he had not married a silly woman. Horner notes that while "[v]ain fops" vie for the reputation of ladies' man, the one who would truly be so must lose the esteem of most men, such as Horner has done—the predator's paradox, it seems. If the epilogue of the play is intended to underscore its message, it is interesting to note that little is said of Horner. Instead the epilogue, spoken by Lady Fidget, directs the satire at two types of men: the Sparkish types, who would be taken as rakes but are in fact frightened when they encounter libidinous women, and elderly men who cast themselves as rakes but really support mistresses whose company other men enjoy. The epilogue ends by noting that while men may boast of intrigues and thereby raise their reputations with their fellows, they will be required to prove themselves to women, who will not be deceived by mere reputation. To that extent, the play promotes a kind of libidinous realism that contests with the world of show constructed by and for men.

JEREMY COLLIER AND THE DIRECTION OF DRAMA

Like heroic drama and dramatic satire, Restoration comedies do not realistically depict Restoration society on stage but offer exaggerations of society for the comedy's own satirical ends. Yet, in order to be effective, satire requires an audience that understands it and willingly submits to authorial control. Yet as the seventeenth century wound to a close, comic dramatists, who had found a mixed response to begin with, found a very vocal critic. Jeremy Collier was a nonjuror, meaning that he was an Anglican divine who refused to take the oath of allegiance to King William and Queen Mary after the forced exile of James II in 1688. This position explains some of Collier's conservative views, but it does not explain the extent to which his opinions found sympathetic ears. That might best be explained by the fact that despite his vehemence Collier makes interesting points that remain relevant. He experienced the plays he wrote about as literary texts rather than performances, and his opinions were those of a moral critic rather than a dramatic or literary critic. The distinction rests both on method and on the kinds of observations that one makes. Rather than plumb dramas for subtleties, Collier assumed that what was performed affected the way in which people behaved, and he argued the deleterious effects of libertine playwrights. In that sense, Collier is an appropriate note to close on given that each of the plays we have considered has dealt with the ideals that inform human behavior and the ways in which those ideals or behavior are (mis)represented on stage. In the introduction to his *A Short View of the Immorality and Profaneness of the English Stage,* Collier offered the following definition of drama: "The business of plays is to recommend virtue and discountenance vice; to show the uncertainty of human greatness, the sudden turns of fate, and the unhappy conclusions of violence and injustice; 'tis to expose the singularities of pride and fancy, to make folly and falsehood contemptible, and to bring everything that is ill under infamy and neglect." The most significant aspect of Collier's definition is his insistence that the play be clear in its message. Collier thought that English dramatists were talented, but he claimed that they employed their talents to the detriment of the populace rather than the betterment; he referred to them as "the enemy."

Collier criticizes Wycherley in particular in his chapter on "The Immodesty of the Stage" for Wycherley's characters of Margery Pinchwife, Horner, and Lady Fidget. As the title of the chapter implies, Collier makes some assumptions about the Restoration audience that *The Country Wife* calls into question. He claims that Restoration comedy is only suitable for those who lack a sense of "honor," without considering the questions that the comedies raise about concepts such as honor. Honor is not the only term that explicitly echoes *The Country Wife.* Collier objects that the language in Restoration comedies is offensive: "Obscenity in any company is a rustic, uncreditable talent, but among women 'tis particularly rude. Such talk would be very affrontive in conversation and not endured by any lady of reputation." Collier argues that to imagine that what women would avoid in conversation is fit for them at the theater is "to abuse them." The abuse is not solely a matter of subjecting the female members of the audience to what they might not wish to hear, but it also rests in his conclusion that female characters are made to speak the language and sentiments appropriate to prostitutes rather than women in general, who are characterized by "native modesty."

As noted in connection with his definition for the purpose of a play, Collier focuses on the way in which playwrights treat vice. In his chapter "The Stage-Poets Make Their Principal Persons Vicious and Reward Them at the End of the Play," he claims that the distinction between virtue and vice is clear in nature and argues that dramatists "endeavor to blot the distinctions, to rub out the colors or change the marks." Dramatists present vice to the audience's understanding in such a way that it is appealing rather than appalling: "To put lewdness into a thriving condition, to give it an equipage of quality, and to treat it with ceremony and respect is the way to confound the understanding, to fortify the charm, and to make the mischief invincible." Wycherley's characters of Horner and Harcourt are noted as vicious characters who are rewarded in the end. Collier concludes, "A fine gentleman is a fine whoring, swearing, smutty, atheistical man. These qualifications, it seems, complete the idea of honor. They are the top improvements of fortune and the distinguishing glories of birth and breeding!" Collier argues that the lack of positive examples in Restoration comedies indicates that comic dramatists are so consumed with satirizing their age that they see all in a jaundiced light and leave no ideal untainted: "The stage seldom gives quarter to any thing that's serviceable or significant, but persecutes worth and goodness under every appearance. He that would be safe from their satire must take care to disguise himself in vice and hang out the colors of debauchery." The last remark is particularly interesting as the inverse of the situation faced by Lady Fidget and women of quality in *The Country Wife*. Collier's objections, despite their lack of analytical support, raise interesting questions about the satire in Restoration comedy. He asks, "Is dissolution of manners such a peccadillo?" Later he turns to the means and ends of satire in his castigation of what comedy lacks: "To laugh without reason is the pleasure of fools, and against it, of something worse. The exposing of knavery and making lewdness ridiculous is a much better occasion for laughter. And this I take to be the end of comedy. And therefore it does not differ from tragedy in the end, but in the means. Instruction is the principal design of both. The one works by terror, the other by infamy." The point that Collier raises has to do with the responsibility of the dramatist. His charge seems to be that Restoration dramatists have, like Sparkish, become vain; they seek to entertain through ingenious displays of wit and fashionable satire, but they fail to press the advantage of the stage by making their audience clearly aware of folly and vice.

Collier's attack did not go unchallenged. The late seventeenth and early eighteenth century critic, John Dennis, replied in *The Usefulness of the Stage* (1698) by blaming the lewdness of the Restoration stage on both the suppression of drama during the Interregnum and the influence of the Charles II's court, which had "united the spirit of French whoring to the fury of Dutch drinking" during their exile. Of course, neither argument challenges the contention that Restoration comedies were lewd. Restoration playwright William Congreve also replied to Collier's attack in *Amendments to Mr. Collier's False and Imperfect Citations* (1698). Congreve makes several interesting points. He suggests in Collier's examples of licentious passages tell us more about Collier's mind than the dramas themselves; that is, Congreve accuses Collier of reading his own licentiousness into the plays. He also accuses Collier of duplicity by reading passages in a way that discredits them but not in the way in which they were intended to be read. Taking issue with Collier's conception of comedy's purpose, Congreve argues that comedy is a genre with a particular subject: the follies of people, whether common or quality. Comedy doesn't deal with the horrible but with vices that many might demonstrate, and it attempts to get its audience to laugh at those vices. To argue, as Collier does, that tragedy and comedy have the same ends but different means is to confuse two distinct forms of drama. Lastly, Congreve claims that one cannot impute to the dramatist the views held by his or her characters. Simply because a comic dramatist represents vicious characters, we do not have reason to believe that the poet is him or herself of such character. Although Congreve made good points, Collier's concern over the relationship between artist, art, and audience was not easily settled. Congreve wrote only one more comedy before giving up drama. After 1700, comedies became much more sentimental with clearer distinctions between vice and virtue. Despite their vehemence, Collier's criticisms found support in the "censorious world" of late Restoration England.

FURTHER READING

Canfield, J. Douglas and Maja-Lisa von Sneidern *Broadview Anthology of Restoration and Early Eighteenth-Century Drama.* Toronto, Canada: Broadview Press, 2001.

Fisk, Deborah Payne *Cambridge Companion to English Restoration Theatre.* Cambridge, England: Cambridge University Press, 2000.

Hume, Robert *The Development of English Drama in the Late Seventeenth Century.* Oxford, England: Oxford University Press, 1976.

Owen, Susan *Companion to Restoration Drama.* Malden, Massachusetts: Blackwell Publishing, 2001.

PART III

National and Regional Theater

ॐ

Modern Canadian Theater

Jerry Wasserman

BEGINNINGS

Modern drama in Canada begins around the turn of the twentieth century, although Canada's fascinating theatrical history reaches back beyond the previous millennium in the ritual performances of its aboriginal inhabitants. Ironically, many of those highly developed forms—native dance, the potlatch, and other ceremonials—were banned at the time modern drama took root in Canada, part of an attempt to assimilate the "dying race" of aboriginal peoples. Canadian plays by European settlers date from as early as 1606 when Marc Lescarbot wrote *Le Théâtre de Neptune en la Nouvelle-France* and staged it in Indian canoes to honour the arrival of French dignitaries at Port Royal, Acadia. Playwriting in English Canada goes back to the eighteenth century, and nineteenth century Canadian playhouses sprang up in substantial numbers, mainly to accommodate American and British touring companies. The first half of the twentieth century saw the development of a thriving amateur theater movement and the best radio drama on the continent. But Canadian theater as an indigenous professional institution dates only as far back as the end of World War II. And English-Canadian drama, in the sense of a body of dramatic work by Canadian playwrights written for performance in professional theaters, is an even more recent development.

Modern French drama in Quebec had its inception with Gratien Gélinas's *Tit-Coq* in 1948, a wartime Montreal love story about an alienated young man who desires to belong. For English Canada the key date was 1967: the year of Canada's Centennial and Montreal's Expo '67. As part of the Centennial celebrations, new Canadian plays were given professional productions from coast to coast, including George Ryga's seminal *The Ecstasy of Rita Joe*. This was a new cultural phenomenon for a nation buoyed by national self-consciousness and pride—plays by Canadian playwrights, performed in Canadian theaters or international centers like New York, where Toronto's John Herbert had a major hit with *Fortune and Men's Eyes*.

The subsequent expansion of Canadian drama was the product of a particular historical moment, like the new European theater that appeared in the 1870s or the new American theater of the 1920s. Like those movements, the Canadian theatrical revolution of 1967 was rooted in an evolution of social and cultural forces that had been gathering momentum for many years.

Alan Filewood notes that the Canadian stage at the turn of the century was "a branch-plant extension of the novel American discovery that if theatre was business, then it could be big business....By 1910 almost every playhouse in Canada was owned directly [by] or contractually locked into the American theatrical syndicates." The syndicates offered Canadian playgoers a predictable commercial product delivered by imported talent—American plays with American players. As an alternative to the Americanism with which Canadians attached to the British Empire felt uncomfortable, Canada's theatrical pioneers turned to trans-Atlantic models. In the first decade of the century, inspired by the vogue of European art theaters, Toronto's Arts and Letters Club Players performed contemporary works from the world repertoire. They especially admired the Irish Abbey Theatre which would be cited time and again as a model for Canadians.

In 1919, industrialist and future cultural mandarin Vincent Massey founded Hart House Theatre in Toronto, dedicated to doing plays which would otherwise have gone unproduced there, including plays by Canadians. Enough such plays were written to fill two modest volumes of *Canadian Plays from Hart House Theatre* by 1927. The most interesting of the Hart House playwrights was Merrill Denison. His published collection, *The Unheroic North* (1923), which included the popular satirical comedy *Brothers in Arms*, established him as Canada's first playwright of note. Unable to make a living writing for the stage in Canada, Denison moved to the United States in 1931 to write for American radio.

THE 1920s AND 1930s

Throughout the 1920s and 1930s amateur theater flourished under the umbrella of the Little Theatre movement. In 1932 the Dominion Drama Festival (DDF) was established to consolidate the activities of Canadian Little Theatres and upgrade the quality of Canada's theatrical arts and crafts through competition and cross-fertilization. A nationwide competition chaired by Vincent Massey, the Festival featured an annual series of regional playoffs climaxing in a national final at which awards were given for production and performance. Community theaters, school and university drama groups, and established amateur companies such as Hart House were eligible, with theater professionals adjudicating, providing critiques and determining winners.

From 1933 to 1970, with a hiatus during the war, the DDF helped institutionalize amateur theater in Canada. It provided a proving ground for Canadian talent, and through trophies and cash prizes it encouraged the writing and production of Canadian plays. In 1934 the Festival organizers could come up with just nine Canadian titles for inclusion on a list of suggested plays sent to participating groups; by 1966 the list contained 240 Canadian titles. But the quality and adventurousness of the work the Festival inspired were often questionable. As late as 1967, the DDF refused to allow Michel Tremblay's *Les Belles-Soeurs*—fifteen unhappy women speaking colloquial, Québequois French—to be produced as part of its all-Canadian celebrations.

Earlier, the DDF had frowned on the multi-media expressionism of Herman Voaden's plays. Voaden was an ardent nationalist and theatrical innovator who desired a Canadian dramatic art as distinctive as the paintings of the Group of Seven. To that end he sponsored a playwriting competition in Toronto in 1929 which suggested that each play be set in the Canadian North and its mood be based on the writer's favorite Canadian painting. Voaden's own work combined the Canadian landscape with techniques drawn from modern dance, Wagnerian opera, and symbolist drama to create a form he called "symphonic expressionism" in plays with titles like *Rocks* and *Earth Song*.

Also in Toronto a group of women journalists organized the Playwrights' Studio Group in 1932 and produced more than fifty new plays in the decade, mainly society comedies. At the other end of the spectrum were the Progressive Arts Clubs in Toronto, Montreal, Winnipeg and Vancouver, leftist workers' theater groups that created and performed agitprop social protest plays throughout the Depression years. In Alberta the Banff School of the Theatre was founded in 1933, later evolving into the Banff School of Fine Arts, still an important training center. An alumnus and later instructor at Banff was Gwen Pharis Ringwood, whose stark prairie tragedies *Still Stands the House* and *Dark Harvest* were among the strongest Canadian plays of the era.

THE 1940s AND 1950s

A significant development for Canadian drama was the rise of radio. What came to be known as "The Golden Age" of Canadian radio began when Andrew Allan became Supervisor of Drama for the Canadian Broadcasting Corporation (CBC) and producer of its weekly *Stage* series. From 1944 to 1955 *Stage* and *Wednesday Night* created consistently bold, imaginative, and broadly popular drama that maintained high standards of excellence. The writers and actors that

Allan assembled—and paid for their work—comprised "far and away the most exciting repertory group that can be heard," *The New York Times* suggested in 1946, and it became Canada's equivalent of a national professional theater. Hundreds of original scripts by Allan's house writers such as Lister Sinclair and Len Peterson were produced for broadcast.

In spite of the varied successes of the DDF and the CBC, neither amateur theatricals nor radio drama could satisfy the need for a vibrant, professional stage culture. John Coulter, who became an award-winning DDF playwright and a frequently produced CBC dramatist after emigrating from Ireland in 1936, was a vocal critic of Canadian theater. He proposed Dublin's Abbey as a model for Canadians, a theater "showing the Irish to themselves...Irish mugs in Irish mirrors." Canadians too, he argued, could find dramatic subject matter in indigenous situations. After a series of plays set in Ireland, Coulter himself turned to Canadian history, achieving great success with a series of plays about Métis rebel leader Louis Riel. First produced in 1950, *Riel* would serve as a paradigm for later Canadian history plays: revisionist history with the rebel as hero, presented as a synthesis of documentary and myth.

Riel was produced by the New Play Society, a professional company founded in Toronto by Dora Mavor Moore, the first Canadian actor to attend RADA. From 1946 to 1950, the Society's full seasons of plays in the Royal Ontario Museum Theatre proved to many skeptics the viability of a professional Canadian stage. In 1954 Toronto got a second homegrown professional theater, the Crest, which presented quality work in repertory until 1966. Its major Canadian playwright was Robertson Davies, whose *A Jig for the Gypsy* and *Hunting Stuart* premiered there in 1954 and 1955. Davies had become English Canada's foremost amateur dramatist with plays such as *Eros at Breakfast* and *Fortune, My Foe* in 1948 and 1949, satires of Canadian philistinism and what he considered the national disease, "emotional understimulation." He remained a significant force in Canadian theater until the mid-1960s when his playwriting career gave way to his work as a novelist.

Davies's journalism also contributed to the developing Canadian theater. Under the pseudonym Samuel Marchbanks he protested the conditions under which Canadian theater workers had to labor—what he called in 1952 "the seedy amateurism which has afflicted the arts here for so long." Consequently, he reacted with enthusiasm to the idea of a world-class Shakespearean summer theater in Stratford, Ontario. Along with Dora Mavor Moore and Festival organizer Tom Patterson, he helped arrange for British producer-director Tyrone Guthrie to head the venture, which held its first season of two plays under a tent in 1953. Guthrie imported stars Alec Guinness and Irene Worth to play the leads and fleshed out the company with Canadian actors, a policy that remained standard for Stratford well into the 1980s.

Stratford Festival

The Stratford Festival became an event of international importance and influence, with its new thrust stage designed by Guthrie and Tanya Moiseiwitsch. It raised the profile of theater in Canada and served as a focus of national cultural pride. Stratford also became a training ground for many of the best Canadian actors of the next three decades, making stars of Christopher Plummer, Frances Hyland, and others. But the Festival did little to support the development of Canadian playwriting. Many saw it as a cultural dinosaur, devouring large subsidies at the expense of smaller theaters whose productions of Canadian plays, often on shoestring budgets, were more central to an emerging national drama than was a theater devoted to Shakespeare. Today, Stratford is an economic behemoth, with four stages and multi-million dollar revenues, a Canadian artistic director and a fully Canadian contingent of actors, directors, and designers.

The success of Stratford and the other new professional theaters was augmented by the establishment of the Canada Council in 1957, which changed the nature of theater in Canada more than any other single development, providing a massive influx of government funding for buildings, companies, and individuals engaged in the arts. It was the most concrete manifestation of the Royal Commission on National Development in the Arts, Letters and Sciences appointed by Prime Minister Louis St. Laurent in 1949 with Vincent Massey as chairman. Its mandate was to examine how government could contribute to the development of those areas of endeavour "which express national feeling, promote common understanding and add to the variety and richness of Canadian life." Its 1951 *Report* found that Canadian culture was being stifled by a lack of support and facilities and the omnipresence of American influences. Its major recommendation was the formation of the Canada Council for the Encouragement of the Arts, Letters, Humanities and Social Sciences to fund Canadian culture at home and abroad.

THE 1960s AND 1970s

Regional Theaters

With Canada Council support, a network of regional professional theaters spread across the country. Beginning with Winnipeg's Manitoba Theatre Centre (MTC) in 1958, each was meant to serve as the focus of theatrical activity in its larger community. Vancouver's Playhouse and Halifax's Neptune were established in 1963, Edmonton's Citadel in 1965, and Regina's Globe in 1966. By 1970 Montreal, Calgary, Fredericton, and Toronto also had theaters catering to regional communities. In addition, to train actors the National Theatre School opened in Montreal in 1960 with separate French and English programs.

At Niagara-on-the-Lake, Ontario, the Shaw Festival began operation in 1962, and Prince Edward Island's Charlottetown Festival was inaugurated in 1964, specializing in Canadian musical theater. In 1969 and 1970 the completion of three major Centennial construction projects—Ottawa's National Arts Centre, Toronto's St. Lawrence Centre, and a new building for the MTC—rounded out a decade of extraordinary growth for the Canadian theater.

"New" Drama

With the superstructure intact, where were the plays that might crystallize the new drama in English Canada? One of the first to do so was George Ryga's *The Ecstasy of Rita Joe,* in which a young Native woman and her boyfriend are destroyed by the white city where they have come to try to improve their lives. It premiered at the Vancouver Playhouse in 1967 in a landmark production remounted for the opening of the National Arts Centre in 1969, when it also aired on national television. Critic Jamie Portman explains that *"Rita Joe* happened during Centennial year when Canadians were anxious to look at themselves. But the look that this play provided was an unsettling one. It punctured the euphoria and the smug complacency of Canada's birthday celebrations and declared unequivocally that all was not well with this country and its institutions." Its implications for Canadian playwriting were equally dramatic: "This was an indigenous Canadian drama that surfaced and succeeded at a time when indigenous Canadian drama was generally considered to be an aberration."

Yet the battle for credibility was not so easily won. The struggles of a half-century had resulted in a Canadian theater that by the late 1960s had already largely become entrenched and conservative. The big subsidized theaters mostly tried to emulate Broadway and London's West End. With few exceptions the regionals served up homogenized theater: safe, commercial seasons of British and American hits plus a smattering of world classics.

But the Canadian Centennial happened to coincide with the most radical cultural upheaval of the century in the Western world: sexual and musical revolutions; long hair, peace marches and a Summer of Love. By 1968 in Chicago, Paris, and Prague the revolution would spill over into the streets. Neither Canada nor its theater could remain immune to these forces. That the most significant Canadian plays of the decade appeared in 1967 and 1968 was not coincidental. *The Ecstasy of Rita Joe, Fortune and Men's Eyes,* and *Les Belles-Soeurs* are very much of their age, marked by strong social consciousness and critical anti-establishment perspectives. Herbert and Tremblay were gay, and all three playwrights were outspoken in their social, artistic, and political views. Neither Herbert nor Ryga was initially allowed entry into the United States to see their own plays in production.

Modern Canadian Drama

Modern Canadian drama was born out of an amalgam of the new consciousness of the age—social, political, and aesthetic—with the new Canadian
self-consciousness. Since the larger theaters were generally unsympathetic and
unaccommodating to both these forces, a newer Canadian theater had to be
invented, an alternate theater. One of its prime movers in Toronto was Martin
Kinch, who describes those heady days as having little to do with nationalism:
"The real influences were Fritz Perls and Timothy Leary, Peter Brook and Jerzy
Grotowski, Tom O'Horgan, Café La Mama, Julian Beck, Judith Malina, and the
ensemble of the Living Theatre; in short, a host of European and American artists,
most of them primarily dedicated to the ethic and the aesthetic of 'doing your
own thing.'"

In 1969 Kinch became codirector of Toronto's Theatre Passe Muraille, founded
the previous year by Jim Garrard as a theater without walls: neither the traditional
fourth wall between actors and audience nor necessarily even the walls of a theater building. A milestone for the new movement was Passe Muraille's production
of Rochelle Owen's *Futz* in 1969. In style and content it established the parameters of the alternate theater's self-conscious anti-conventionality. The sex, obscenity, and nudity it featured would become almost obligatory. When the show was
closed by the morality squad and the company charged, the new movement had
its red badge of courage.

By the summer of 1970 alternate theater in Toronto had undergone a shift from
sensationalism to nationalism. Central to the new emphasis were Ken Gass and
his Factory Theatre Lab, and the new artistic director of Theatre Passe Muraille,
Paul Thompson. Gass set out to prove that Canadian playwrights were just waiting to be discovered and encouraged. His theater would be both a factory and a
laboratory, presenting new works, works-in-progress, and staged ideas. Most
importantly it would be "The Home of the Canadian Playwright." His concept
paid off with a string of notable new plays by David Freeman, Herschel Hardin,
George Walker, and others. Gass remained artistic director of the Factory until
1979, then returned again in 1996 to save the company from imminent demise.

Paul Thompson steered Passe Muraille towards a focus on local subject matter
and collective creation, involving his actors in firsthand research and improvisation, utilizing their particular skills as key elements in the play. When Thompson
took over Passe Muraille, Toronto had some precedent for this kind of theater.
George Luscombe had worked with Joan Littlewood's Theatre Workshop in the
mid-1950s and had founded Toronto Workshop Productions in 1959 based on
Littlewood's political and stylistic principles. In the late 1960s and early 1970s
the Toronto Workshop Productions created potent socio-political theater with
agitprop pieces like *Mister Bones* and *Chicago '70* on race and politics in America,

and its bittersweet evocation of the Canadian Depression, *Ten Lost Years*. The partnership of Luscombe and Toronto Workshop Productions lasted for thirty years.

But Passe Muraille under Paul Thompson became the most important theater in Canada in the 1970s. Creations like *The Farm Show* (first performed in a barn) and *The Adventures of an Immigrant* (performed on Toronto streetcars) made stirring theatrical poetry out of material that was sometimes mundane and always local. Docudrama with a high degree of theatricality became the Passe Muraille trademark: a small company of actors using little but their own bodies and voices to create ingenious stage metaphors. They inspired countless imitators across the country, including the highly successful *Paper Wheat*, about the co-op movement on the Saskatchewan prairies. The company specialized in popularizing and often mythicizing Canadian history in collective scripts or in conjunction with a writer. *Buffalo Jump* with Carol Bolt, *1837: The Farmers' Revolt* with Rick Salutin, and *Far as the Eye Can See* with Rudy Wiebe were some of the best collaborations. Later in the decade Passe Muraille alumni John Gray and Eric Peterson would have international success with *Billy Bishop Goes to War*, their pocket musical about Canada's World War I flying ace, as would Linda Griffiths with her solo play about the Trudeaus, *Maggie & Pierre*. Perhaps the most exciting Canadian playwright to emerge in the 1980s, Judith Thompson, also came out of Passe Muraille with her extraordinary first play, *The Crackwalker*. Passe Muraille remains to the present day a primary locus of Canadian theatrical production and development.

Theater Outside of Toronto

Not everything happened in Toronto. A group of Vancouver university graduates formed Tamahnous Theatre in 1971, a collective that would remain the west coast's most original and progressive company for the next decade, producing *Billy Bishop* and premiering Morris Panych with his "post-nuclear cabaret," *Last Call!* Vancouver's New Play Centre came into being in 1970 dedicated to developing new scripts by local writers, and under the direction of Pamela Hawthorn until 1989 it had a hand in most of the drama from the Pacific coast, including the work of Sharon Pollock, Margaret Hollingsworth, Tom Walmsley, John Lazarus, Sheldon Rosen, and Betty Lambert.

Seeded by government grants from Local Initiatives Programs (LIP) and Opportunities for Youth, new companies doing indigenous theater sprouted everywhere in 1971 and 1972: Edmonton's Theatre 3, Calgary's Alberta Theatre Projects, Pier One in Halifax, CODCO, and the Mummers Troupe in St. John's. Festival Lennoxville in Quebec presented all-Canadian summer seasons of plays from 1972 until 1982.

Most of the action was in Toronto, though, and nothing did more to cement its position at the center of the new movement than Tarragon Theatre. Founded in 1971 by Bill Glassco, who had directed *Creeps,* David Freeman's angry play about cerebral palsied young men, at the Factory Lab earlier that year, Tarragon opened with a revised version of *Creeps.* Its first season ended with a new work which was to become the most influential Canadian play of the 1970s, David French's *Leaving Home.* Its story of generational conflict and a singularly Canadian form of immigrant alienation (ex-Newfoundlanders spiritually adrift in Toronto) elicited strong audience identification, and its accessible style had a broad appeal. Tarragon also introduced English Canada to the plays of Michel Tremblay with Glassco as co-translator. And from 1973 to 1975 Tarragon produced James Reaney's *Donnellys* trilogy, highly theatrical plays about a notorious nineteenth century Ontario family and their murder by vigilantes that many people considered the best work created in the Canadian theater to that time. Combining artistic and commercial success, Tarragon succeeded in bringing Canadian drama into the mainstream under both Glassco, until 1985, and his successor, Urjo Kareda, into the next century.

The wave of new alternate theaters in Toronto crested in 1972 with the founding of Toronto Free Theatre by Tom Hendry, Martin Kinch, and John Palmer. Subsidized by LIP grants, its performances were literally free until 1974. Toronto Free's cultivation of excellent ensemble work and a taste for the psychologically bizarre in scripts and production remained constant until its merger with Centrestage in 1988 to create the Canadian Stage Company.

Notwithstanding the dynamism of the alternate theaters, Canadian plays were mostly relegated to small, low-budget theaters that lacked the financial and technical resources available to the heavily subsidized festivals and regionals. To remedy this situation a group of playwrights met in 1971 to recommend a 50 percent Canadian content quota for all theaters receiving government funding. Though no formal quota system was adopted, the controversy led to an informal policy decision by the Canada Council to lean on its client theaters to do more Canadian plays. The results were startling. By the 1972–73 season nearly 50 percent of the plays produced by subsidized theaters in both English and French were Canadian.

Regional theaters began commissioning new plays by local playwrights. Significant new work came from Sharon Pollock for the Vancouver Playhouse and Theatre Calgary, John Murrell and W.O. Mitchell also for Theatre Calgary, Ken Mitchell and Rex Deverell for Regina's Globe, and David Fennario for the Centaur in Montreal. Ontario's Blyth and Kawartha Summer Festivals proved the value of a homegrown product in their cultivation of Anne Chislett. In each of these cases plays written specifically for local audiences made their way into theaters across the country.

The organizational infrastructure of Canadian theater was strengthened in 1976 by the separation of Canadian Actors' Equity Association from American Equity and the formation of the Professional Association of Canadian Theatres (PACT) and the Association for Canadian Theatre History, a national academic organization. Over the next decade companies like Passe Muraille, Tarragon, and Factory Theatre (minus the "Lab") along with the resurgent regionals and successful middle-of-the-road theaters like Vancouver's Arts Club continued to provide a springboard for Canadian plays. Across the country a new generation of neo-alternates arose: Prairie Theatre Exchange in Winnipeg, Rising Tide Theatre in St. John's, and Nova Scotia's Mulgrave Road Co-op and Ship's Company. Nakai Theatre Ensemble in Whitehorse and Tunooniq in the Arctic ensured the exposure of lively theatrical voices in the Canadian North. In Vancouver Touchstone joined the scene along with Green Thumb, which set the pattern for hard-hitting theater for young audiences.

In Edmonton, Theatre Network, Northern Light, Catalyst, Workshop West and Phoenix Theatre all came on stream before 1982, the year the Edmonton Fringe Festival was born. Modelled on Edinburgh's Fringe, Edmonton's festival has become hugely successful with annual attendance in the quarter-million range, a prototype for the many other Canadian Fringes which have sprung up in its wake.

Meanwhile, Toronto continued its theatrical expansion to the point where it could claim to be second city only to New York for theater in North America. Among its important new companies were Necessary Angel, Nightwood (Canada's foremost feminist theater), Buddies in Bad Times (soon the country's most important gay company), Cahoots (multicultural), and Native Earth Performing Arts, which led the renaissance of Native theater in Canada.

Canadian Theater Awards

Canadian theater's growing cultural prominence was also signified by a series of new awards. Joining the prestigious Chalmers, given since 1972 for best new Canadian play produced in Toronto, were the Canadian Authors' Association Award for Drama (est. 1975) and, in 1981, the Governor General's Award in Drama honoring the best new Canadian play in publication in French and in English. The Doras in Toronto (after Dora Mavor Moore), the Jessies in Vancouver (after Jessie Richardson), the Sterlings in Edmonton (after Elizabeth Sterling Haynes) and the Bettys in Calgary (after Betty Mitchell) celebrate the best work done on those cities' stages in the name of a local theatrical pioneer. Add to those the Mecca awards, honoring English-language theater in Montreal, a counterpart to the Masque awards for French-language theater in Quebec. The $50,000 Alcan Arts Award is now given annually to a producing company in British Columbia, and the Siminovitch Prize for a Canadian theater artist in mid-career is worth $100,000. The 1984–85 publication of three anthologies of Canadian drama in English also helped make Canadian plays more accessible and academically reputable.

1980s TO THE PRESENT

Some things notably changed by the mid-1980s. The nationalism that had inspired and helped kick-start the new Canadian theater had mostly gone out of vogue. Free trade and globalism were becoming the new keywords. As economic issues superseded nationalism on the larger political landscape, economics assumed greater political and artistic impact in the theater. Canada's theater was increasingly perceived as a commercial commodity, having to find its niche in a competitive and fragmented cultural marketplace battered by recession and dominated by home videos. A few writers profited as hit plays from small nonprofit stages got remounted in large, long-run commercial venues. *Love and Anger* by George F. Walker, whose *Nothing Sacred* had been a breakthrough hit in American regional theaters in 1988, and the hard-hitting *Unidentified Human Remains and the True Nature of Love* by Brad Fraser, which also had later international success, crossed over into commercial production, along with Tomson Highway's dark comedy about Native life, *Dry Lips Oughta Move to Kapuskasing.*

The Megamusical

The most significant development of the commercialized theater was the appearance of the megamusical. A building and renovation boom accompanied the phenomenon. In 1985, to accommodate Andrew Lloyd Webber's *Cats,* Toronto's old Elgin Theatre/Winter Garden complex was restored to its former glories and *Cats* ran for two years. In 1989 entertainment mogul Garth Drabinsky renovated another magnificent old vaudeville house, the Pantages, for Lloyd Webber's *Phantom of the Opera,* which ran there for ten years, selling over seven million tickets. Producers Ed and David Mirvish opened *Les Miserables* at their Royal Alexandra Theatre and built the Princess of Wales to house *Miss Saigon.* Drabinsky's Livent Inc. became the largest theatrical production company in North America, importing shows and creating its own musicals for export.

The megamusical boom fueled the theatrical economy, creating international stars of Canadian actors like Brent Carver, and spin-off opportunities for a few Canadian nonmusical plays. But on the whole it posed severe challenges for the Canadian nonprofit theater. Rather than benefitting from a trickle-down of new audiences created by the megas, low-budget companies found themselves in difficult competition for the theater-going dollar. The success of these shows also shaped audience expectation and demand, fostering pressures to conform to the megamusical aesthetic—high on spectacle, low on content, lacking in Canadian reference and empty of political challenge.

By 1998, with the novelty of the genre waning, his empire overextended, and Drabinsky himself accused of cooking the books, Livent collapsed, and the smaller, nonprofit theaters where most Canadian plays are born and performed survived the debacle, but at a cost. Many felt that the economic squeeze of the 1990s created a survival mentality whereby artistic directors tended to minimize risk and opt for safe programming. Canada's "poorly funded non-profits embrace facile populism," complained Kate Taylor in *The Globe and Mail*. And what could be safer or more facile than putting pretty pictures on stage?

Entering the Twenty-First Century in Canadian Theater

Yet one of the strengths of the Canadian theater as it entered the twenty-first century was its development of a complex visual vocabulary, from the neo-baroque *mise en scène* favored by many Québécois playwrights and directors to image-based physical theater, clown, mime, movement, dance, and puppetry. Artistic Fraud of Newfoundland, Montreal's Carbone 14, Toronto's Theatre Smith-Gilmour, Calgary's One Yellow Rabbit, and Vancouver's Boca del Lupo are some of the companies that complement the spoken word with sharply detailed, carefully choreographed visual effects. The remarkably sophisticated marionette shows of Calgary's Ronnie Burkett have been seen and honored around the world. The first major success of the new century was Morris Panych's Vancouver Playhouse production and subsequent international tour of Gogol's *The Overcoat,* performed without a single word. Robert Lepage writes, performs, directs, and designs the visually stunning plays that have made him and his Quebec City company an international phenomenon. Canada's greatest economic success on the world stage, and one of its genuine artistic triumphs, is the spectacle theater of Cirque du Soleil. Since its founding in 1984, the Montreal-based company has redefined the circus and established a global empire, including an increasing number of shows permanently running in Las Vegas.

"Canada on the World Stage" headlined *Canadian Theatre Review*'s Winter 2001 issue examining the export of Canadian drama to the United Kingdom, the United States, Italy, Belgium, India, and Australia. Plays by Michel Tremblay, Morris Panych, Daniel MacIvor, and George F. Walker, as well as a new Cirque du Soleil show, were running simultaneously in Washington DC, at that time, leading Lloyd Rose in the *Washington Post* to declare that "Canada is hot." Though Canada remains a net theatrical importer, playwrights like Walker (*Nothing Sacred*), John Krizanc (*Tamara*), Brad Fraser (*Unidentified Human Remains* and *Poor Super Man*), and Morris Panych (*Vigil*, retitled *Auntie and Me* in

London) have had major international hits. The growing interest in postcolonial studies has also brought added attention to Canadian theater at international conferences and in collections of plays and essays published abroad.

Also being crossed more often is the border dividing Quebec's French-language culture from the theater of English Canada. Until recently, few francophone playwrights from Quebec had any impact in English—notably Gratien Gélinas and Michel Tremblay. Now Robert Lepage, Michel Marc Bouchard, and Wajdi Mouwad regularly appear in English. The bridging of the solitudes from the English side has been less dramatic, but Brad Fraser, Judith Thompson, Wendy Lill, Sally Clark, and Colleen Wagner have gotten French-language productions in Montreal. Théâtre de Quat'Sous, the theater most closely associated with Tremblay's Quebec nationalism, produced four of George Walker's *Suburban Motel* plays in French translation in its 1998–99 season, along with Daniel MacIvor's *Monster*, its first play ever in English.

Cultural diversity is another sign of Canadian theater's relative well-being. The last decade has seen the publication of play anthologies from Newfoundland, the Maritimes, the North, and the "new ethnic West," from lesbians and gays, First Nations, and African Canadians, as well as special *Canadian Theatre Review* issues on Native, Black, South Asian, Chinese, and Italian Canadian theater. Women are more fully represented in the playwriting ranks, thanks in part to feminist theater organizations such as Toronto's Nightwood, founded as a collective in 1979, and perhaps best known for Ann-Marie MacDonald's *Good Night Desdemona (Good Morning Juliet)*. Native Earth Performing Arts (est. 1982) developed Tomson Highway's *The Rez Sisters* and *Dry Lips Oughta Move to Kapuskasing*, and has been instrumental in the work of other important Native writers like Drew Hayden Taylor and Marie Clements.

Montreal's Festival de théâtre des Amériques and Toronto's du Maurier World Stage have been important showcases for innovative theater from Canada and around the world. Two important Calgary festivals, Alberta Theatre Projects' New PlayRites and One Yellow Rabbit's experimental High Performance Rodeo, joined established new play development organizations like the Banff Centre, Playwrights' Workshop of Montreal, Vancouver's New Play Centre/Playwrights Theatre Centre and Toronto's Rhubarb! Festival.

Companies devoted to classical work denote an interesting trend in recent Canadian theater. Toronto's acclaimed Soulpepper company (1998) produces only traditional and modern classics, as does Vancouver's Blackbird (2005). And Shakespearean festivals are everywhere: Shakespeare-on-the-Saskatchewan in Saskatoon, Repercussion Theatre in Montreal, Bard on the Beach in Vancouver, Edmonton's Shakespeare-in-the-Park, a Shakespeare-by-the-Sea in Halifax and another in St. John's, and Toronto's Shakespeare in the Rough. Meanwhile, the Stratford and Shaw festivals enjoy unprecedented box office success. That this kind of foundational theater can thrive alongside theaters devoted to new Canadian plays is a sign of stability and maturity. The continued emergence of exciting young companies creating their own new work, like Vancouver's Electric Company, and the rebirth of Ottawa's National Arts Centre as a vital link in the regional system, co-producing new and established Canadian plays, are cause for further optimism that Canadian theater remains on a healthy trajectory.

FURTHER READING

Appleford, Rob, ed. *Aboriginal Drama and Theatre*. Toronto: Playwrights Canada Press, 2005.

Benson, Eugene and L.W. Conolly. *English-Canadian Theatre*. Toronto: Oxford University Press, 1987.

———, eds. *The Oxford Companion to Canadian Theatre*. Toronto: Oxford University Press, 1989.

Bessai, Diane. *Playwrights of Collective Creation*. Toronto: Simon & Pierre, 1992.

Brask, Per, ed. *Contemporary Issues in Canadian Drama*. Winnipeg: Blizzard, 1995.

Brydon, Diana and Irena R. Makaryk, eds. *Shakespeare in Canada: A World Elsewhere?* Toronto: University of Toronto Press, 2002.

Coulter, John. "The Canadian Theatre and the Irish Exemplar." *Theatre Arts Monthly* 22 (July 1938): 503, 508.

Davies, Robertson. *The Well-Tempered Critic: One Man's View of Theatre and Letters in Canada*. Edited by Judith Skelton Grant. Toronto: McClelland and Stewart, 1981.

Donohoe, Joseph I., Jr. and Jonathan M. Weiss, eds. *Essays on Modern Quebec Theatre*. East Lansing: Michigan State University Press, 1995.

Filewod, Alan. *Collective Encounters: Documentary Theatre in English Canada*. Toronto: University of Toronto Press, 1987.

———. "National Theatre/National Obsession." *Canadian Theatre Review* 62 (Spring 1990): 6

———. *Performing Canada: The Nation Enacted in the Imagined Theatre*. Kamloops, British Columbia: Textual Studies in Canada, 2002.

Gould, Jack. "Canada Shows Us How." *New York Times* Sept. 1, 1946, Sec. II: 7.

Grace, Sherrill and Albert-Reiner Glaap, eds. *Performing National Identities: International Perspectives on Contemporary Canadian Theatre*. Vancouver: Talonbooks, 2003.

Johnston, Denis. *Up the Mainstream: The Rise of Toronto's Alternative Theatres*. Toronto: University of Toronto Press, 1991.

Kinch, Martin. "The Canadian Theatre: In for the Long Haul." *This Magazine* 10 (Nov.–Dec. 1976): 4–5.

Knowles, Richard Paul. *The Theatre of Form and the Production of Meaning: Contemporary Canadian Dramaturgies*. Toronto: ECW Press, 1999.

Much, Rita, ed. *Women on the Canadian Stage: The Legacy of Hrotsvit*. Winnipeg: Blizzard, 1992.

Portman, Jamie. "Ecstasy of Rita Joe Still Manages to Shock and Scourge." *Vancouver Province* April 12, 1976: 10.

Report of the Royal Commission on National Development in the Arts, Letters and Sciences. Ottawa: Edmond Cloutier, 1951.

Rose, Lloyd. "Onstage, Works with a Distinct Canadian Accent." *Washington Post* September 10, 2000: G24.

Rubin, Don, ed. *Canadian Theatre History: Selected Readings.* Toronto: Playwrights Canada Press, 2005.

Taylor, Kate. "The Play's the Thing." *Globe and Mail* December 26, 2000: R1.

Walker, Craig Stewart. *The Buried Astrolabe: Canadian Dramatic Imagination and the Western Tradition.* Montreal: McGill-Queen's University Press, 2001.

Wasserman, Jerry, ed. *Modern Canadian Plays.* 4th ed. 2 vols. Vancouver: Talonbooks, 2000/01.

Zimmerman, Cynthia. *Playwriting Women: Female Voices in English Canada.* Toronto: Simon & Pierre, 1994.

ଞ

Czech Drama

Veronika Ambros

"ENGAGED" PLAYWRIGHTS BETWEEN ENLIGHTENMENT AND GENTLE REVOLUTION

The Swiss playwright Friedrich Dürrenmatt (1972) once remarked that it was not necessary for a playwright in Czechoslovakia (during the periods 1918–38 or 1945–93) to be engaged in politics, since the audience "engaged" an author for political purposes and provided a political reading of any play. In fact, in Bohemia (today the Czech Republic) culture in general and theater in particular have a long-standing tradition of being relevant. Since Czech drama and theater have a history of challenging social, artistic, ideological, and even political order, it came as no surprise for many when in 1989 the Gentle Revolution was staged in theaters and Václav Havel, a playwright and dissident, was subsequently elected president of Czechoslovakia (1989–92) and later the Czech Republic (1993–2003).

Although Shakespeare set *The Winter's Tale* in Bohemia, the land has very little to do with his fictional deserts or coasts. Nonetheless, it was the birthplace of the English Queen Anne of Bohemia the daughter of Charles IV, Holy Roman Emperor, King of Bohemia, and the wife of Richard II of England (1366–94). In this period the first play, *Mastičkář* (*Ungentarius*), written in Czech, German, and Latin (and bogus Hebrew) is recorded. This text about a merchant of ointments, his servant and three Marys, mocks the genre of Easter plays by combining secular and liturgical, sacred and profane elements into a "sacred farce" (Veltruský 1985). Thus, Czech drama was firmly ensconced in the European tradition of Passion plays.

In the fifteenth century, however, the Hussites, followers of the church reformer Jan Hus (c. 1369–1415), opposed drama and rejected actors and jesters. Following the Catholic victory at the White Mountain in 1618, many Protestants had to leave the country. Among the exiles was Jan Ámos Komenský (Comenius) (1592–1670), a teacher, scholar, and the last bishop of the Unity of the Brethren. Komenský's work includes several plays in Latin and a dramatization of his tract *Ianua linguarum reserata* (*The Doorway to Languages Is Open*, 1631) called *Schola ludus* (*School through game/play*, 1654), promoting ideas that have influenced pedagogy ever since.

During the counter-reformation, Bohemia was no longer an independent kingdom with Czech as a language of administration but a province of the Habsburg monarchy. Most plays, mainly school plays introduced by the Jesuits in the sixteenth century, were performed in Latin while the folk theater in the countryside maintained Czech as a language of communication. In the eighteenth century, the court stages, such as the one at the castle Český Krumlov, addressed and entertained the noble audience. There an intricate system of murals and mirrors decorated with scenes from *commedia dell'arte* in the Masquerade Hall (1748) exemplified the way in which the stage challenged the viewer's imagination and evoked an illusion of reality. The few dramatic texts in Czech were less complex and often translations from German or Latin. The puppet theater presented among others the Czech version of the ubiquitous jester named Kašpárek as well as various adaptations of the Faust story.

CREATING A NATION

Following the ideas of the Enlightenment the German philosopher Johann Gottfried von Herder (1744–1803) painted a bright future for the Slavs. Eager to make this vision happen, the representatives of the Czech national revival showed a rapidly increasing interest in Czech language, culture, literature, theater, and drama as an expression of national autonomy. As a result, Czech nationalism found its outlet in theater where the emerging "*theatrical* nationhood" manifested itself through rituals and ceremonies that abolished the division into spectators and actors. In fact, these public events produced "a new form of national communication."

Paradoxically, the prevalent cultural model for Prague (at that time a capital of a province in the Austrian empire) was in general the capital of the monarchy, Vienna. Although the texts reflected an urban petit bourgeois milieu their language maintained an idealized concept of theater as a place where a "noble" speech had to be used, the social and local origins of the characters notwithstanding. As Stanley Kimball comments: "[T]he Czechs always thought of their theatre in ideal terms....Their theatre was, apparently, never to be used to portray the baser emotions, or merely to entertain."

The works by Jan Nepomuk Štěpánek (1783–1844) represent the beginnings of modern Czech drama. His comedy *Čech a Němec* (*Czech and German*, 1816) portrayed the peaceful coexistence of the two nations. Comedies by Václav Kliment Klicpera (1792–1859) had been popular because of their humorous situations and use of language, which in some cases prefigures the devices of the theater of the absurd. This is particularly true of *Veselohra na mostě* (*Comedy on the Bridge*, 1828), a story about people who are caught on a bridge neither permitted to continue their journey nor to return. The Czech composer Bohuslav Martinů turned the playlet into an eponymous opera in 1935.

One of the most prominent proponents of the national revival, Josef Kajetán Tyl (1808–56), used the Viennese local farces by Johann Nepomuk Nestroy as a model for his comedies. This applies for instance to *Fidlovačka* (*Shoemakers fair*, 1834), which introduced the present Czech national anthem, the song "Kde domov můj?" ("Where Is My Home?"). For Tyl, who also wrote several historical plays, the primary goal of theater is to educate by showing "not what is, but what should be." Tyl, like numerous other volunteers, supported the idea of the National Theatre in Prague and contributed to the building, which was completed in 1881.

ENTERING THE INTERNATIONAL STAGE

At the turn of the twentieth century, critics (F.X. Šalda, Otakar Fischer, V. Tille, and J. Vodák) were no longer interested in the utilitarian qualities of the reviewed works, but based on their knowledge of contemporary international trends in theater, literature, and culture applied aesthetic criteria while reviewing the literary and theatrical production. Furthermore, theater directors began to experiment with various models of theater and used modern technologies such as film projections on stage as early as 1902. In addition, genres of "mere" entertainment (cabaret, operettas) and popular culture in general questioned the traditional notion of theater.

Simultaneously, due to the new stage both the famous Prague German literature and also a diversified Czech repertoire (Rainer Maria Rilke, Franz Werfel, Franz Kafka, Antonín Dvořák, Bedřich Smetana) emerged. Initially limited to historical or rural topics, it slowly incorporated impulses of symbolist, naturalist, and realistic drama. The increased number of playwrights included women. In fact, the plays by Gabriela Preissová (1862–1946) *Gazdina roba* (*The Farmer's Woman*, 1889) and *Její pastorkyně* (*Her stepdaughter*, 1890), focusing on female heroines in a rural setting have been a part of the Czech dramatic and operatic canon. The Czech composer Leoš Janáček (1854–1928) based his opera *Jenůfa* (1904) on Preissová's drama in which a child's murder reveals the stifling social conventions. Also set in the countryside was *Maryša* (1894) a successful dramatic work by the Mrštík brothers, Alois (1861–1925) and Vilém (1863–1912), about the eponymous hero-ine who tries to escape her unhappy marriage by poisoning her husband. One of the few comedies of that period, *Naši furianti* (*Our Uppish and Defiant Fellows* also translated as *Our Swaggerers,* 1887) by Ladislav Stroupežnický about farmers trying to outwit each other, has also been part of the Czech dramatic canon.

The majority of dramatic works were initially domestic dramas, historical plays, and fairy tales. One of the prolific authors of this period was Jaroslav Vrchlický (1853–1912) whose dramatic texts were often inspired by Renaissance and antique mythology. As an exponent of Czech history, Alois Jirásek (1851–1930), in his plays *Jan Hus* (1911) and *Jan Žižka* (1903), about the military commander of the Hussites, introduced the conflict between an individual and a collective typical of expressionistic drama.

Julius Zeyer (1841–1901) contributed to the repertoire of the newly established National Theatre with fairy tales (*Radúz and Mahulena,* 1896) and plays on topics allegedly from Czech mythology, but based, in fact, on medieval manuscripts forged at the beginning of the nineteenth century. Zeyer's *Stará historie* (*Old his-tory,* 1883) was the first text to introduce *commedia dell'arte* in Czech. However, while Zeyer confirmed the genre, the very first one-act play by the Čapek brothers, Josef (1886–1945) and Karel (1890–1938), *Lásky hra osudná* (*The Fateful Game of Love,* 1910–11), mocked the same convention, by turning comedy into tragedy. Many techniques developed in this text were used in the later dramatic oeuvre of both brothers, who introduced to Czech drama expressionist elements, science fiction, fairy tale, and other genres, as well as topics such as the clash between intuition and intellect, longevity, creation of a new man, along with individual and collective responsibility.

Between the wars, both Čapeks were popular European authors, known for their innovative approach to theater. Josef Čapek was among the well-known modern artists (e.g., Vlastislav Hoffman, František Muzika, and Bedřich Feuer-stein) who worked as set designers. Karel Čapek's translations of French poetry set an example for the Czech avant-garde poets. His drama *R.U.R* (*Rossum's Uni-versal Robots,* 1921) was immediately translated into many languages (the famous *Theater Guild* in New York performed it as early as 1922), and the word robot that Josef derived from the Czech *robota* (drudgery, unpaid work required of a vassal by a feudal lord) entered the international vocabulary. In contrast to the current con-vention, however, Čapek's robots are not mechanical creatures, but biologically produced androids with great memory capacity and no past to remember.

The play depicts the conflict between intellect and intuition and shows the pro-cess by which the people are dehumanized and the robots are humanized. This creation of the human imagination has an impressive literary pedigree (following in the footsteps of the artificial human being Golem of the medieval Jewish tradi-tion, the Homunculus in Goethe's Faust, and Shelley's monster in Frankenstein).

Although the action focuses on the human characters and their clash with their product, in an expressionistic manner both the title and the subtitle announce a collective hero, the robots, who, true products of "Rossum," i.e., reason, lack emotions, have no "soul." Setting the action on an island, Čapek stressed the utopian character of the prologue. By beginning the story in his own time, Čapek made his audience aware of the dystopia, i.e., of the conceivably catastrophic consequences of contemporary trends, and pointed to the dangers of neglecting to learn from the past.

After the success of *R.U.R.*, the two brothers created a mystery play *Ze života hmyzu* (*From the Life of Insects*, 1922), which belongs as a cornerstone of the Czech theater repertoire. The title indicates again a collective hero and stresses the fictional world as a mere slice of life. The action focuses on the journey of a vagrant (*tulák*) who acts as a guide through several stations of the insect world showing a very human-like behavior of the insects with whom he also interacts. Thus akin to the singer in Bertolt Brecht's *Caucasian Chalk Circle* (1948) he defamiliarizes the familiar.

In spite of the author's indication of the genre as mystery play, which is confirmed in several ways (especially in the names of characters denoting different groups of insects), Čapek's work mixes, in fact, several genres. It is a satirical comedy mocking the human vices. It is a fairy tale with an ending at once tragic and optimistic, and finally it is an expressionistic grotesque in which the insects remain people except for having the insect-like features of real people. The Čapeks have famous predecessors in this as well, for instance in Aristophanes's satirical comedies and animal fables. Yet, as Lubomir Doležel comments, the world of the insects is not a "space of exciting, childlike adventure" but much closer to Kafka's "space of existential anxiety."

Karel Čapek's last drama, *Matka* (*The/A Mother*, 1938) is "the most consistently expressionistic of Čapek's dramas" according to William Harkins. The protagonist's Spanish name Dolores connotes the archetypal *mater dolorosa*, the suffering mother, and the civil war in Spain of that period. The heroine is a widowed mother devoted entirely to her family, who over the course of the play loses her four sons to different causes (medical, technological research, a political battle). Eventually, when she learns that children of her country are being killed, she herself gives her last son a gun to defend his homeland. Written in times of acute political conflicts (war in Spain, Hitler's war threat, the spread of Nazist Party in Czechoslovakia) it has often been considered an openly anti-fascist work. The play, however, accomplishes more than the propagation of ideas. The action is presented as an interior monologue or stream of consciousness in which some of the voices of the protagonist's memory materialize. As the characters themselves claim: "She alone can hear us." Incidentally, Thornton Wilder's *Our Town*, written in the same year as *Matka*, uses a similar technique to conjure up the past. In many respects, Čapek's attempt to stage novelistic stream-of-consciousness techniques in the manner of James Joyce or Virginia Woolf predates the contemporary theater of memory such as that of the Polish director Tadeusz Kantor.

Another prominent Czech playwright and a close friend of the Čapek brothers was František Langer whose comedy in three acts *Velbloud uchem jehly* (*Camel through the Needle's Eye*) written in 1924 was presented by the prestigious Theatre Guild in New York 196 times. Langer questions the stereotypes about impoverished people by showing a young girl from a lowly background skillfully acquiring the knowledge necessary for a successful businesswoman. Her affluent lover, in contrast, offers a male version of Pygmalion, of a taciturn young man who is being molded into a useful and diligent member of the industrious, poor, but clean family of his girl friend.

In *Periferie* (*Periphery*, 1925) as Alfred Polgar writes, the outskirts are not a mere backdrop but the central topic of the play "which discovers in the refuse of a city human dignity and value." The famous German director Max Reinhardt brought this story about crime without punishment, about justice and the inadequacy of the traditional legal system to international stages in Berlin, Vienna, and the United States in 1927 and 1928. In the character of a man in front of the curtain, Langer introduces the epic device of a commentator, who akin to the intertitles in silent movies, describes the movement of the hero and his thoughts, but most of all, similar to a lyrical "I," personifies subjective time.

A similar technique became the main attraction in the Liberated theater, the "most popular theater in Czechoslovakia between the wars" in Michael Quinn's opinion. By improvising their dialogues in front of the curtain, the authors and comedians Jiří Voskovec (1905–81) and Jan Werich (1905–80) (known as V+W) partially revived the tradition of cabarets, music-halls and *commedia dell'arte*. In their rarely recorded talks both actors commented on current issues or on the stage action, hence constantly moving between the fictional world of the stage and the real world of the proscenium, and breaking the illusion of an *as if* world.

In 1936, the Russian director Vsevolod Meyerhold declared

> Only tonight, October 30, 1936, I saw the "zanni"...in the persons of the unforgettable duo of Voskovec and Werich, and was once more bewitched by performers rooted in the Italian *commedia improviso*. Long live *commedia dell'arte!* Long live Voskovec and Werich!

Hence, as the German theater semiotician Herta Schmid said, V+W made "a specific contribution to the anti-illusionist theatre of the European avant-garde."

The first play of the duo *Vest Pocket Revue* (1927) is a good example of their technique. The plot offers only a pretext for a variety of expressions that in keeping with the title mock the crazy comedies of American cinema. The scenes present dialogues, dance, and film as separate units, sometimes without any connection to the action of the plot. As a result, the play points to the "metamorphosis of the relationship between the absurdity of art and absurdity of reality," in the words of Vratislav Effenberger. While the Czech theater historian Adolf Scherl speaks about Voskovec and Werich *lyricizing* the theater, the German journalist Friedrich Torberg sums up the wide range of their humor, which had: "to cover everything that is divided up in Germany among six or eight different types of theatre, revue, and cabaret. From Bert Brecht to Paul Nikolaus, from Erich Kästner to Fritz Grünbaum." In fact, their jokes are often akin to the humor in the popular novel by Jaroslav Hašek *The Fortunes of the Good Soldier Švejk during the War,* adapted for stage by Erwin Piscator and Bertolt Brecht in 1928.

Another type of stage experiment was offered by the director E. F. Burian. In his theater (founded in the 1930s) Burian staged historical texts such as the medieval Mastičkář, folk theater, surrealist plays, and dramatizations of prose and poetry. In the performances of the poem "May," by the romantic Czech poet Karel Hynek Mácha, which used extensively projections, movements, and music, the visual means acquired a prominent position, and created a scenic poem similar to the staging practice of contemporary directors such as Robert Wilson or Robert Lepage.

In general, Czech drama and theater flourished during the first Czechoslovak Republic (1918–38) and came close to the ideal expressed by the stage director Karel Hugo Hilar: "A community in which poet fuses with spectator, director with poet, designer with actor, and theater aesthetician with this entire circle that burns with dramatic enthusiasm." In fact, Czech playwrights of that period were engaged in creating the theater community Hilar envisaged. They were supported by the scholars of the Prague linguistic circle (founded in 1926), who laid the ground for the contemporary semiotics of drama and theater. By examining the use of theatrical signs in folklore and contemporary stage, and by discussing categories such as dialogue and monologue based on current practice, they offered a model of a remarkable cooperation between theater practitioners and theorists.

BETWEEN SOCIALIST REALISM AND MODEL THEATER

In the dire period of the forties and fifties, authors were to comply with the demands of the so-called Socialist Realism, which expected literary texts to serve the needs of the communist party. Yet even then, new names emerged (Pavel Kohout, František Hrubín), as well as Burian's pupils the directors Otomar Krejča and Alfréd Radok, and the playwright Josef Topol. By the end of the fifties small studio theaters introduced a new notion of performance—a combination of text, songs and movements. In addition, Alfréd Radok's extremely successful blend of dance, text, and film projection called *Laterna Magika* [*Magic Lantern*] attracted audiences at the world exhibit in Brussels in 1958.

The artistic efforts of the sixties widely contributed to the impression the British Kenneth Tynan had upon his return from Prague when he called the city "the theatre capital of Europe." Among the most significant playwrights was Josef Topol (1935), whose *Konec masopustu* (*End of the Carnival*, 1963) was staged at the National Theatre (1964) while his remarkable one-act play *Kočka na kolejích* (*Cat on the rails*, 1965) marks the beginning of Krejča's famous *Divadlo za branou* (*Theatre beyond the Gate*, 1965–72).

The fifteen scenes in *Konec masopustu* are set in a Czech village in which all farmers but one joined the cooperative under pressure, an act demanded by the new socialist regime. The exception is explained by Eva Stehlíková:

> František Král, Frank King, is truly the king of the village thanks to his moral qualities. But the days of his reign are numbered and, paradoxically, it is not he who will be killed but his son who is destined to be the next king, which means that the future is being destroyed.

The text of the play ends with an announced trial, which might bestow justice and restore a primordial order of the community.

Hence, what appears at first as a master plot of a socialist realist drama about the re-education of an obstinate opponent of the new rule turns into a very complex play, in which fragments of the actual world are intertwined with that of a mystery play. In addition, close to the manner of analytic drama the present tragedy is caused by past events. The masks, which underscore the carnival of the title are used as a chorus both inside and outside the story, and give the text a mythological and lyrical dimension. The Czech theater historian Stehlíková says about Topol's *Konec masopustu* and Milan Kundera's drama *Majitelé klíčů* (*The Owners of the Keys*, 1962):

> In contrast to the bloodless adaptations of Greek drama, both plays belong to the best Czech plays written in the last century and, through them, Czech audiences experienced the true meaning of the expressions such as "classics" and "tragedy."

At first glance, Kundera's play seems to fit the heroic plot of a socialist realist drama. Set during World War II, the protagonist faces the question of responsibility, a decision about the life and death of his wife and her petit-bourgeois family. Visions of the protagonist, however, somewhat reminiscent of *Matka*, interrupt the linearity of the plot, provide an insight into his inner struggle, and underscore the precarious dilemma of the hero. As a result, Kundera similarly to Topol subverts the norms of socialist realism and sets forth the Czech tradition of poetic drama.

Václav Havel (b. 1936) achieved a similar effect with his first play *Zahradní slavnost* (*The Garden Party*, 1963). His point of departure, however, is the tradition of the Liberated theater, and the linguistic games of V+W, for instance, when the protagonist Hugo Pludek resorts to "vacuous verbal balancing acts" such as the following:

> In fact, they were both sort of right and sort of wrong—or rather, on the contrary—both were wrong and both right, weren't they? I mean they were, were they not?"

Hence, Hugo demonstrates what Havel calls "evasive thinking" and "phraseological ritual." He reveals the mechanism of formulaic language by appropriating fragments of overheard conversations, thus creating a discourse consisting of disjointed catch phrases. While Hugo succeeds professionally, he loses himself, his own identity, in the process. Havel's second play *Vyrozumění* (*The Memorandum*, 1965) targets language bared of any meaning. The memorandum of the title is a text written in an artificial language called *ptydepe*, which endorses the attempts of Gross, the director of the office in which the action is set, to liquidate "any attempt to introduce *ptydepe*." The alleged victory of Gross, however, is at the same time his defeat, since the office uses another new language called *chorukor*.

Martin Esslin, for whom Havel is one of the representatives of satirical absurd theater, lists "hard-hitting satire, Schweikian humor and Kafkaesque depth" among the characteristics of Havel's work. Although Esslin uses Franz Kafka and Jaroslav Hašek as clichés associated with Prague, by including Havel in a literary tradition originally attributed to the West he implies that the divide between East and West is merely an imaginary one. In addition, Havel and most of his colleagues of the sixties (Ivan Klíma, Pavel Kohout, Milan Uhde, and Ladislav Smoček) did not present questions about human existence, as did the representatives of the theater of the absurd such as Ionesco and Beckett. The Czech playwrights devised models of a society in which the individual is caught in a vicious circle of rules a collective imposed on him.

Jan Grossman, the director of the Theatre on the Balustrade, where Havel worked as a stagehand and later as dramaturg, commented on Havel's ability to establish a dialogue with his audience. In fact, the playwrights of the sixties continued the tradition of their predecessors who activated and challenged their spectators by showing absurdity on stage, through which they exposed the absurd conditions around them.

The Soviet invasion of August 1968, however, interrupted the flourishing dramatic and theatrical experiments of the sixties, and brought radical changes to Czech society. As Havel explains:

> [It] did not just mean the routine replacement of a more liberal regime with a more conservative one...it was the end of an era; the disintegration of a spiritual and

social climate; a profound mental dislocation....Suddenly, instead of laughing, one felt like shouting.

FORGING A COMMUNITY

In the seventies, most Czech playwrights were left "without a stage," and the stages remained without their playwrights, directors, and even actors. The acclaimed directors were forced to leave Prague, or work abroad; many writers were not allowed to publish. Even the journals *Divadlo* (*Theater*) and *Divadelní noviny* (*Theater News*) were abolished. Neither the so-called *samizdat* (a limited number of privately distributed manuscripts) nor the publishing houses in exile (Toronto, Cologne) could fill the gap. Yet it was often through them that plays by the so-called dissident authors were performed abroad. In fact, the dramatic texts by Havel, Topol, Kundera, Kohout and other prominent writers of the sixties became, as it were, exiled. The contact with their audience was disrupted. Pavel Kohout, who dramatized two novels in the sixties, continued this line of work with *Uboh ý vrah* (*Poor Murderer*, 1976), based on the short story *Thought* by Leonid Andreyev that opened on Broadway in 1976. Kundera's *Jakub a jeho pán* (*Jacques and his Master*, 1975) an adaptation of Denis Diderot's novel *Jacques le fataliste et son maître* (1796) was staged by Susan Sonntag. Especially popular internationally were three one-act texts by Havel originally conceived to entertain his friends: *Audience (1975), Vernisáž (Unveiling,* 1975) and *Protest* (1978). Although they share their protagonist Vaněk, a dissident, in retrospect, Havel says about them that they "...are essentially not about Vaněk, but plays about the world as it reveals itself when confronted with Vaněk." Hence, this character, similar to the vagrant in Čapek's drama, provides a point of view for the spectator that helps him or her to recognize in the fictional world his or her own world.

In 1977, about a thousand people of various convictions and occupations signed a manifesto Charter 77, demanding human rights, and civil liberties. Havel was one of the first spokesmen of the group, an activity that led first to his arrest, then several years of prison, and eventually paradoxically to his presidency. Upon his return from jail, he wrote numerous essays and the play in seven scenes, *Largo Desolato* (1984), dedicated to the British playwright Tom Stoppard. In many respects, the drama is close to a musical composition. Three of the seven scenes are introduced by solemn music contrasted with the pantomime in which Leopold Kopřiva, a philosopher who expects his imminent arrest, enacts his fear by staring at the main entrance. The fifth scene, "extreme in tempo," motivated by an excessive drug consumption in which the characters repeat the imputations of others, appears as an externalized interior monologue (similar to *Matka, or Majitelé*) and shows *Largo Desolato* as a modern tragedy of a man who lost his identity.

Kopřiva's dilemma, however, is just another version of the predicament the medieval French writer Francois Villon faces in *Hodina mezi psem a vlkem*

(*The hour between dog and wolf*, 1979) by Daniela Fischerová (b. 1948). She presents the fear of a poet who is afraid that if he were banished from Paris he would lose his creativity. By using modern props such as a tape recorder and cameras, Fischerová makes this drama topical by counterpointing the historical character with the present of the actors in a modern trial. The dialogues resemble academic disputes full of paradoxes such as: "The cat's heaven and the mouse's hell look exactly the same." Herein Fischerová not only expresses her distrust of any definite statements but also alludes to a device typical for Villon's poetry, the *oxymoron:* "I die of thirst beside the mountain spring" or "I laugh in tears". This is also true of scenes in which torture and labor are presented simultaneously. The authorities who ordered the play off the program indirectly confirmed its topicality.

Another representative of the generation, who entered the Czech stage after 1968, is Arnošt Goldflam (b. 1946). His work presents a good example of the tendency typical of the seventies and eighties when theaters often refrained from language altogether (*Cirkus Alfred,* Bolek Polívka), or the dramatic texts that resembled screenplay-like-pretexts for staged action. Goldflam captures a certain atmosphere, a state of mind of a character or state of affairs of a generation, and implicitly society. His one-act-play *Biletářka* (*The Ticket Girl,* 1984; published 1989) presents a process in which the interior world surfaces in grotesque form. In the initial situation, the ticket girl from the title announces that the movie theater is facing technical difficulties. At the end, the viewers are admonished to retain their tickets for the next show. Hence, the action can be repeated *ad infinitum.* The text consists of a monologue interrupted by an offstage voice. Framed between the two announcements is the soliloquy of a plain girl who gradually assumes the role of a master and demands that the spectators abide by her rules. The play is also typical of the tendency of the eighties when several companies abolished the boundaries between actors and spectators. By creating a new community of audience and performers, they prepared the ground for the turnabout of 1989 staged in theaters, albeit without a script. Hence, the gentle revolution ultimately confirmed Dürrenmatt's claim about the "engaged" playwrights.

FURTHER READING

Brock, Peter, ed. *The Czech Renascence of the Nineteenth Century.* Toronto: University of Toronto, 1970.

Burian, Jarka. *Leading Creators of Twentieth-Century Czech Theatre.* London: Routledge, 2002.

———. *Modern Czech Theatre. Reflector and Conscience of a Nation.* Iowa: University of Iowa Press, 2000.

Doležel, Lubomir. "Karel Čapek—a Modern Storyteller." in *On Karel Čapek:* Ed. Michael Makin and Jindřich Toman. Ann Arbor, Michigan: University of Michigan Press, 1992. 15–28.

Esslin, Martin. *The Theatre of the Absurd.* Garden City, New York: Doubleday, 1969.

French, Alfred. *Czech Writers and Politics 1945–1969.* Canberra: Australian National University Press, 1982.

Goetz-Stankiewicz, Marketa. *The Silenced Theatre: Czech Playwrights Without a Stage.* Toronto: University of Toronto Press, 1979.

———. ed. *The Vaněk Plays. Four Authors, One Character.* Vancouver: University of British Columbia, 1987.

Harkins, William Edward *Karel Čapek.* New York: Columbia University Press, 1962

Havel, Václav. *Protokoly.* Foreword by Jan Grossman. Praha: Mlada fronta, 1966

———. *The Garden Party.* Translated and adapted from the Czech by Vera Blackwell. London: J. Cape, 1969.

———. *Open Letters.* London: Faber and Faber, 1991.

Kimball, Stanley Buchholz. *Czech Nationalism: A Study of the National Theatre Movement, 1845–83.* Illinois Studies in the Social sciences, 54. Urbana, Illinois: University of Illinois Press, 1964.

Kruger, Loren. *The National Stage (Theatre and Cultural Legitimation in England, France, and America).* Chicago: University of Chicago, 1992.

Polgar, Alfred. In Langer, František, *Periferie.* Praha: Československý spisovatel, 1968, pp. 177–78.

Quinn, Michael. "Jakobson and the Liberated Theater." *Stanford Slavic Studies* 1 (1987): 153–55.

Sayer, Derek. *The Coasts of Bohemia. A Czech History.* Princeton: Princeton University Press, 1998.

Stehlíková, Eva. "The Encounter between Greek Tragedy and Two Czech Playwrights in the Sixties" In: *Eirene.* 2003, vol. 44, No. XXXIX: 229–33.

Steiner, Peter. *The Deserts of Bohemia: Czech Fiction and Its Social Context.* Ithaca, New York: Cornell University Press, 2000.

Thomas, Alfred. *Anne's Bohemia.* Foreword "Czech Literature and Society, 1310–1420" by David Wallace. Chicago: University of Minnesota Press, 1998.

Trenský, Pavel. *Czech Drama Since World War II.* Introduction by William E. Harkins. White Plains, New York: M. E. Sharpe, 1978.

ॐ

German Drama

Christoph E. Schweitzer

GERMAN DRAMA TO THE NINETEENTH CENTURY

In the history of German theater, the first dramatist of any note is Hans Sachs (1494–1576), the author of *Schrovetide* and other plays, the best of which are folksy and humorous. Richard Wagner made him famous in the opera *Die Meistersinger von Nurnberg*. The next century produced two very learned dramatists, Andreas Gryphius (1616–64) and Daniel Caspar von Lohenstein (1635–83). The former wrote a tragedy on the execution of Charles I entitled *Carolus Stuardus*, and *Peter Squentz*, a literary satire with a Shakespearean background.

The eighteenth century was to see the rise of drama in an impressive display of quantity and diversity with Gotthold Ephraim Lessing (1729–81) being the pioneer. He wrote the still popular comedy *Minna von Barnhelm* in which the determined protagonist captures the beloved Tellheim, an officer in the Prussian army who is under suspicion of having misappropriated funds but is ultimately rehabilitated by Frederick II. *Emilia Galotti*, a tragedy, ends with Emilia's begging her father to stab her, thus avoiding becoming the Prince's mistress. With *Nathan der Weise* (*Nathan the Wise*) Lessing created a plea for tolerance that is as relevant today as it was then. Its central parable, based on a story from Giovanni Boccaccio's *Decamerone*, tells us that no one knows who has the true ring—there are three, representing Judaism, Mohammedanism, and Christianity—but that we can prove ultimately that we possess the true one by showing that we are loved best by our neighbors.

Goethe and Schiller

Lessing is the epitome of the Enlightenment. The next generation, called Storm and Stress, rebelled against such emphasis on reason and stressed instead individualism and feeling. Jakob Michael Lenz's (1751–92) *Der Hofmeister* (The Tutor) treats the seduction of a girl entrusted to the protagonist leading to his self-emasculation, while in *Die Soldaten* (The Soldiers) an officer seduces a girl who is then avenged by her bourgeois fiancé who poisons the seducer. In both plays scenes and places change with dizzying rapidity, foreshadowing the structure of Johann Wolfgang von Goethe's (1749–1832) *Götz von Berlichingen* and *Faust I*. *Götz* made Goethe famous. The play is a nostalgic recreation of the times when barons celebrated their freedom and an indictment of the devious ways of the court that were to prevail. In *Egmont* the author created a monument to the Dutch national hero and with *Iphigenie auf Tauris* he renewed Euripides' play with the heroine risking her brother's and her own life by telling the King the truth, thus bringing about a more humane world. *Torquato Tasso* is a play about the artist who cannot come to terms with the world around him nor with his desires. Finally, there is *Faust*, the second part of which was not completed until one year before his death. The first part goes back to the Storm and Stress period and is the more accessible of the two. Its troubled protagonist enters into a pact with the devil, named Mephistopheles, who provides the magic potion that makes Faust young again. After scenes in which Faust and Gretchen (Margarete) profess their love to each other, unsurpassed in German drama for lyrical quality, the two meet in prison where she awaits death for having murdered their child, and he tries to make her escape with him. But she has turned to eternal justice. The second part is much longer and much more demanding since it takes in a great amount of Greek mythology. In the fifth act, Faust, after having reclaimed a great stretch of land from the sea, finally dies at a very old age. Love redeems him, "the eternal feminine pulls us up high."

Friedrich Schiller (1759–1805) started with *Die Räuber* (The Robbers), a play that pits brother against brother and abounds with violence and excessive individualism. In *Kabale und Liebe* (Intrigue and Love) differences of class membership lead to the suicide of the two lovers. Then comes *Don Carlos* in which the ambitious Maquis Posa tries to change the protagonist's unfortunate love for his stepmother to his helping the Dutch in their resistance to the Spanish. The play's most famous line is Posa's plea to Philip II, "Sir, grant freedom of thought." Schiller's best tragedy, *Wallenstein*, has a prelude, followed by two parts, thus making it too long for an evening performance. In it, the great imperial general of the Thirty Years War is murdered for trying to come to an agreement with the Swedes, the Emperor's enemy. Within a world of opportunism only the young lovers remain pure and thus have to die. Queen Elizabeth's decision to have her imprisoned rival executed forms the subject matter of the next play, *Maria Stuart.* Queen Elizabeth is seen at the end bereft of every friend and counselor. French history forms the background of *Die Jungfrau von Orleans.* In Schiller's version she dies a heroic but un-historic death on the battlefield. His last play, the only one ending happily, is the story of the Swiss national hero Wilhelm Tell who, having been forced to shoot an apple off his son's head, kills the bad tyrant.

Between Goethe and Schiller, the latter is the theatrically more effective author while Goethe excels in lyrical language.

Form

The plays that have been mentioned so far were written in a variety of forms. In the Baroque tragedies the Alexandrine—the verse form of Jean Racine—was used. It proved unwieldy in German. Lessing used prose except for his last play, *Nathan der Weise,* which is written in the Shakespearean iambic pentameter. Lenz's plays as well as the early plays of Goethe and Schiller were in prose. These last two turned to iambic pentameter with *Iphigenie auf Tauris* and *Don Carlos,* respectively. In the nineteenth century, Heinrich von Kleist used the same metric form while Franz Grillparzer used a variety of meters. After Grillparzer prose was used predominantly in agreement with the authors' intent of staying close to reality.

THE NINETEENTH CENTURY

The romantics did not produce any plays of significance except for the delightful comedy by Ludwig Tieck (1773–1853), *Der gestiefelte Kater* (Puss in Boots), a textbook example of romantic irony with its destruction of every level of illusion. Even the fictive author of the play appears on the stage to defend his creation.

Heinrich von Kleist (1777–1811) is the author of an often performed comedy, *Der zerbrochene Krug* (The Broken Jug). In it we witness Adam's vain attempt to divert suspicion from himself for having broken a jug when almost being caught trying to seduce Eve. At the end he is chased out of the village. *Penthesilea* is based on Greek mythology. The title character, Queen of the Amazons, and Achilles cannot overcome mistaken assumptions so that in a rage she and her dogs set upon him and tear him to pieces, after which she dies, too. Finally, *Prinz Friedrich von Homburg* tells of the Prince's successful but unauthorized attack for which he is sentenced to death. At first he begs for his life, something of course unbecoming to an officer and shocking at the time, but then is made to see the justice of the verdict and ultimately pardoned.

Just as unusual a playwright as Kleist is Franz Büchner, who died at age twenty-four in 1837. *Dantons Tod* (Danton's Death) shows the end of Robespierre's antagonist as a disillusioned revolutionary in a seemingly senseless world. Similar disillusionment and subsequent boredom inform the comedy *Leonce und Lena* in which even love is an illusion and melancholy prevails. The short play *Woyzeck* was left unfinished, with two possible endings and uncertainty as to the sequence of some scenes. The poor, exploited protagonist is betrayed by Marie, the mother of their child. She takes up with the macho Drum Major, while Woyzeck must subsist on a diet of peas as a guinea pig for the Doctor's experiment. At the end Woyzeck kills Marie with a knife. The emphasis on suffering with people not controlling their lives, and the absence of moral authority, make the play stand in stark contrast to the idealism of Goethe and Schiller. Later, among the naturalist playwrights, we see suffering playing a major role in the dramas of Gerhart Hauptmann.

The plays of the Austrian Franz Grillparzer (1791–1872) deal in part with figures from his country's past, as in *König Ottokars Glück und Ende* (*King Ottocar, His Rise and Fall*) and with Greek mythology as in *Das Goldene Vlien*. Also Austrian is the author of many brilliant comedies, Johann Nepomuk Nestroy (1801–62), a master of witticism and situation comedy, who wrote *Einen Jux will er sich machen* (*To Have a Lark*) which formed the basis of Thornton Wilder's *The Merchant of Yonkers*.

Friedrich Hebbel (1813–63) is the author of *Maria Magdalena* in which the protagonist, expecting a child by a man who abandons her, drowns herself so as to avoid bringing dishonor upon her father. In *Herodes und Marianne* Herodes's doubting Marianne's fidelity in case he should die prompts him to have her killed in that eventuality. When he persists in his doubt, she, revolting against the idea of being someone else's property, pretends unfaithfulness so as to be executed. In *Agnes Bernauer* Hebbel pits private bliss—the love between the bourgeois Agnes and Albrecht, son of a duke—against the interest of the state, which wins out.

Naturalism

In Norway it is Henrik Ibsen, in France Emile Zola, and in Germany Gerhart Hauptmann (1862–1946) who is the representative of Naturalism, a movement that tries to reproduce reality, especially heredity, physical drives, and the environment, as closely as possible. *Vor Sonnenaufgang* (Before Dawn) depicts a family ruined by alcoholism. *Die Weber* (The Weavers) shows the utter depravation and exploitation of a group of weavers and their failed uprising. This was the first German drama with a group of people at its center. With the next two plays Hauptmann returned to depicting the suffering individual. In *Fuhrmann Henschel* the protagonist is a drayman who commits suicide, having married after his wife's death the maid, who cheats on him. Rose Bernd, in the play of the same name, is a peasant girl who is pursued by various men and driven to insanity. As did Faust's Gretchen, Rose kills her own child. Hauptmann also wrote a comedy, *Der Biberpelz* (*The Beaver Coat*), in which the clever protagonist outwits Prussian bureaucracy. In the same vein the protagonist of Carl Zuckmayer's

(1896–1977) *Der Hauptmann von Köpenick* (*The Captain of Köpenick*), which is based on a true story, impersonates an officer and lays bare the blind obedience people pay to the state, represented here by a uniform. Faithfulness to the reproduction of the social setting also characterizes Zuckmayer's *Des Teufels General* (*The Devil's General*) which depicts the voluntary death of a celebrated air force general who finally sees how evil the Nazi regime is.

TWENTIETH CENTURY GERMAN DRAMA

Around the turn of the nineteenth to the twentieth century two Austrian authors should be mentioned. Hugo von Hofmannsthal (1874–1929) is steeped in the European tradition, renewing classical and Spanish drama. He also wrote the librettos for some of Richard Strauss's operas (*Elektra, Der Rosenkavalier, Ariadne auf Naxos*) and adapted the English morality play *Everyman* as *Jedermann,* which is performed in Salzburg during the summer in front of the cathedral. Arthur Schnitzler (1862–1931), like Hofmannsthal born in Vienna and like him contemporary of the likewise Viennese Sigmund Freud, excelled in the presentation of subtle psychological give and take in a series of scenes that make up *Anatol.* In *Reigen* (*La Ronde*) only one of the lovers connects the scene to the next in circular fashion. The play, which questions prevailing moral codes, caused a scandal when first performed.

The following playwrights from this time period are usually associated with Expressionism, a movement that distorts reality so as to create images that reflect the author's visions: Frank Wedekind (1864–1918), Georg Kaiser (1878–1945), and Ernst Toller (1893–1939).

Brecht

The most famous and talented German playwright of the twentieth century is Bertolt Brecht (1898–1956). He collaborated with the composer Kurt Weill (1900–50) in the internationally acclaimed *Dreigroschenoper* (Three-Penny Opera), which is based on John Gay's *Beggar's Opera.* "Mackie Messer" ("Mac the Knife") became its most popular melody. As a Marxist, Brecht had to leave Nazi Germany. He wrote his best plays in exile, ending up in the United States before returning to the German Democratic Republic after the war. *Mutter Courage und ihre Kinder* (*Mother Courage and Her Children*) has the strong-willed, crafty mother trying to survive the Thirty Years War with her three children but losing every one of them. At the end she has to pull the sutler's cart by herself. *Herr Puntila und sein Knecht Matti* (*Mister Puntila and his Man Matti*) portrays the wealthy landowner Puntila as a kind and generous man only when he is drunk, which is often, but extremely mean when sober. Matti finally leaves such

a master. *Der kaukasische Kreidekreis* (*The Caucasian Chalk Circle*) has a prelude
in which land use is changed so as to make it more productive. In the play itself
the bad mother, representing capitalism, loses her child when the judge, in a reversal of Solomon's verdict, decides that the child will be better cared for by the
simple maid who has risked her life in saving that of the child. In *Leben des Galilei*
the Renaissance scientist is shown with both his positive and negative sides.
Brecht called his later plays epic theater in which a narrator, songs, and other
nonrealistic features kept the audience from totally identifying with the character.
By such *"Verfremdungseffekt"* (alienation effects) he expected the spectator
not only to enjoy the performance but also to look critically at the actions of the
various characters.

The vacuum created by World War I was filled first by two Swiss authors. Max
Frisch's (1911–92) plays deal with issues relating to National Socialism, often in a
parabolic manner. In *Als der Krieg zu Ende war* (*When the War Was Over*) the relationship between a Soviet colonel and the wife of a participant in the massacre of
Jews in the Warsaw Ghetto is explored. *Biedermann und die Brandstifter* (*The Fire-
bugs*) makes us aware of how we close our eyes, out of cowardice, in the face of
impending disaster. *Andorra* tells of racial prejudices, specifically anti-Semitism,
when people find Jewish traits in a boy and kill him even though he is not Jewish.
Friedrick Dürrenmatt (1921–90), another Swiss author, used the grotesque and
satire in a series of successful plays. Best known and often produced is *Der Besuch
der alten Dame* (*The Visit*). The wealthiest woman of the world, very much
advanced in age, visits her home town to take revenge on her one-time lover
who had betrayed her so as to marry a girl with better prospects. She promises
the townspeople millions if they would bring about justice, i.e., "take care of her
former lover," an offer they cannot resist. We are so shocked by the outcome
because we are all materialists. *Die Physiker* (*The Physists*) deals with the moral
responsibility of the scientist, in this case with attempts to preserve the secrecy
of atomic research.

In Germany Peter Weiss (1916–82), who spent part of the Hitler period in
Sweden, based *Die Ermittlung, Oratorium in 11 Gesängen* (*The Investigation,
Oratorio in 11 Cantos*) on statements made by witnesses at the Auschwitz
concentration camp trial and thus brings into the open the horrors committed.
The most esteemed playwright of the former German Democratic Republic is
Heiner Müller (1929–95) who wrote, in collaboration with his wife, Inge Müller,
Der Lohnd Ücker (*The Wage Cutter*), which is based on an actual incident.
The play delves into the problems of production quotas in a socialist economy.
The Austrian Peter Handke (b. 1942) caused quite a stir with his *Publikumsbe-
schimpfung* (*Offending the Audience*), which is anti-theater at its best in that
it attacks the values of traditional theater and audiences. Handke based
his *Kaspar* on the nineteenth century foundling Kaspar Hauser. The play is

concerned with language and truth, with the protagonist finding out that meaning is arbitrary.

RETROSPECT AND OUTLOOK

In looking at the history of German drama one should not forget that it developed within a European context. Especially noticeable was the influence of classical models, but there were also French, English—Shakespeare being the most influential—and other European dramatists who played a role in what German playwrights wrote and how they shaped the texts. One should also note that while this chapter has focused on the plays of such well-known authors as Lessing, Goethe, and Schiller, two dramatists were actually more popular in their time, not only in Germany but also elsewhere, including the United States: August Wilhelm Iffland (1759–1814) and August Kotzebue (1761–1819).

Music is an international language. Thus, opera lovers got to know, and still do so, plays by Schiller, Goethe, Büchner, and others since their texts provided the basis for the librettos of many operas.

When looking at the subject matter taken up by the various playwrights, one notices the frequency of the topic of the wronged woman, beginning with Lessing's *Emilia Galotti,* and appearing again in Dürrenmatt's *Der Besuch der alten Dame.* In Dürrenmatt's play passivity has clearly changed to the woman's taking control of the action. Another topic is the clash between the individual and his or her rights and the interest of the state. One can also see that the exceptional individual forms the center of the earlier period. Büchner's *Woyzeck* points to the later period since the two unexceptional protagonists no longer have freedom of choice but are subject to forces beyond their control, forces that bring about suffering. Hauptmann's *Die Weber* is an example of the drama without protagonists.

Up to the eighteenth and into the nineteenth century German princes supported the theaters at their courts, a tradition that the larger cities and the states later took over. Thus, there were, and still are, relatively few private theaters. Only recently has the support for the public theaters been cut back. That fact, as well as the apparent dearth of major new playwrights, has made for an uncertain future. It seems that the theater has lost much of its vitality and with it much of the importance it once had in the German cultural scene.

FURTHER READING

Brandt, George W. *German and Dutch Theatre, 1600–1848.* Cambridge: Cambridge University Press, 1993

Harding, James and Christoph Schweitzer, eds. *German Writers in the Age of Goethe, 1789–1832.* Munich: Thompson/Gale, 1989.

Schweitzer, Christoph, *Men Viewing Women as Art Objects.* Ontario: Camden House, 1998.

ೞ

Modern Indian Drama

Sitanshi Talati-Parikh

BACKGROUND

The arts in India are as rich as her cultural heritage, passed down for centuries, since the advent of civilization. Replete with diverse cultures, religions, philosophies, sects, languages, and people, India's diversity is exemplified in her arts. From ancient classical Sanskrit epics and text to modern Indian languages, including English, Indian theater is vibrant with dimensions ranging from religious, didactic, realistic, political, social, the *tamaasha* and particularly the *natya shashtra*, which is a deeply rooted Indian theater form passed down through the ages.

Music and dance have always played an integral role in all forms of the arts in India—from deified gods and goddesses, to sculpture, paintings, and movies, and of course, live in the theater. Kerala (a state in South India) theater distinguished itself by the importance it gave to actual acting and the use of gestures in lieu of the spoken language. This formed the crux of the entertainment value: educational, religious, and aesthetic, following upon the classical belief that dances not only help dramatic action, but also beautify it.

India has a rich tradition of the epics, scriptures, and classical texts, in part life-stories of the gods and in-part a treatise on the "right" way of life, conforming to ethical, moral, social, religious and spiritual obligations of man. Many modern-day plays still draw upon the rich material of the classics and epics. It shows a continuity of tradition, through time, following upon the fact that Indian society, though increasingly modern, is still deeply rooted in tradition, especially in the rural areas.

Though parts of modern India have given recognition to their playwrights, many dramatists often lapsed into obscurity. Some indigenous playwrights were idolized at home, and others like Satyajit Ray, were ignored until successful in the West. Ray gained true recognition at home only after *The World of Apu* did well in London and New York. Rabindranath Tagore was one of the playwrights who was considered "prophetic" both at home and overseas.

Indian drama is a collection of themes and ideas, often reaching to the classical myths and legends for inspiration and often drawing from sordid reality and realistic situations. Religion, politics, social and cultural issues, marriage, and history all play integral parts in the thematic substance of these plays. Issues of women and their role in society are seen in most plays either directly or in the background. With the advent of modernization and urban development also came the ensuing discontentment, angst, and existential dilemmas.

Most of the writers discussed below write in their local or regional language, all of which have been translated into English. Mahesh Dattani, Gurcharan Das, Manjula Padmanabhan, Asif Currimbhoy, Partap Sharma, Shiv Subramaniam, Rahul da Cunha, and Tanika Gupta are among the Indian playwrights writing in English. Most of these writers are prolific, with many works to their credit. It would not be possible in the scope of this essay to cover all the writers and all their works, so a selection has been made to choose some of the dominant themes, and the writers following up on them.

STYLES OF INDIAN DRAMA

The selection of Indian dramatists shows a wide range of styles and themes from realistic, "man-made" plays, to plays based on myth, legend and history. There have been distinct influences of European dramatists such as Shakespeare, Ibsen, Chekhov, Brecht, and classical Greek and Restoration drama among others.

Contemporary Indian drama such as the plays of Badal Sircar (*Evam Indrajit*), Chandrasekhar Kambar (*Siri Sampige*), Shanta Gokhale (*Avinash*), Manjula Padmanabhan (*Lights Out*) and Satish Alekar (*Mahapoor*) show some absurdist elements and often ask existential questions.

The concept of time and place is greatly challenged by various dramatists, with openness for experimentation like Mahesh Dattani's multi-sets and layered scenes. Experimenting with multi-level staging, moving back and forth in time to create a kaleidoscopic montage effect in drama all work exceedingly well for Dattani. He also shows a great liking for dance and music, whether in the background or directly linked to the setting. With the multi-level staging, often with each stage depicting a different time and place—playing with the concepts of past, present, and future, one finds conversations overlapping and flowing into each other, with underlying metaphorical implications.

Badal Sircar's *Evam Indrajit* also moves back and forth in time, with a blending stream of consciousness that has implied meaning, while Datta Bhagat's *Whirlpool* depicts a cyclical and stagnant nature of time and society, through generations.

Many playwrights, such as Badal Sircar (in *Evam Indrajit*), Girish Karnad (*Hayavadana*) and Arun Mukherjee (*Mareech, The Legend*), have explored the concept of a play-within-a-play. Often the audience's presence is acknowledged by the characters or narrator, in plays such as Panikkar's *The Lone Tusker* and Karnad's *Hayavadana*.

The narrator or the *sutra-dhar* plays an important role in Indian drama. In fact, traditionally (especially in South Indian theater) a performer could spend hours illuminating lines of text, through analogies, associations, and background information. One play performance could last for days, with this form of elaboration on the original script. Often plays carried historical, mythical, and legendary meaning and references, and the stories were often familiar to the audience; therefore the significance of the performance was to elaborate and explore the familiar in greater depth. The narrator could also be a character in the play, and one can note instances when the narrator steps in and out of character in many contemporary plays. Playwrights like Gurcharan Das (*Mira* and *9 Jhakhoo Hill*), Badal Sircar (*Evam Indrajit*), Girish Karnad "*Hayavadana*), K.N. Panikkar (*Aramba Chekkan* and *The Lone Tusker*), and Chandrasekhar Kambar (*Siri Sampige*), G.P Deshpande (*Roads*) among others, have followed upon the traditional role of the narrator, and some of them in experimental forms.

In Badal Sircar's *Evam Indrajit*, the writer is the narrator-cum-philosopher, and is involved in the play, attempting to create a plot as the play goes along. At times, the writer is all the male characters: Amal, Vimal, Kamal, and Indrajit. They all blend into one another signifying imitative and indistinctive characters given birth by society's quelling of the individual.

Girish Karnad's play *Hayavadana* is based on myths and gods, and the people on the "outside" look upon everything with skepticism steeped in reality. The narrator becomes the bridge between the two worlds: myth and reality. In Kambar's *Siri Sampige* the narrator takes on the role of the soothsayer, while in Mukherjee's *Mareech, the Legend*, the characters refuse to let the play come to its ordained conclusion, by arguing with the narrator.

Gurcharan Das's *Mira* draws deeply upon the original legend or story of Mira, the *Bhakti* saint as an inspiration. Song and dance form an integral part of the performance of this one-act play, with a unique style of narration. The onlookers talk about the scene on stage in a stream-of-consciousness fashion. The scene and the discussion of the scene all blend into one continuous dialogue, which is quick, flippant and with a fluid motion of its own. Das's *9 Jhakhoo Hill* also bears a narrator who is a part of the story and is also a prominent character. Here the narrator, Karan, at times talks about his own character as if looking at himself from the outside.

All major contemporary dramatists have used song, dance, poetry, and music liberally, some showing distinct Western influences. The use of Western music in the background is one such example. Examples of plays that incorporate song and dance are *Mareech, the Legend, Mira, The Lone Tusker* and *Aramba Chekkan*. Partap Sharma's *A Touch of Brightness* starts of with poetry, which could be a sardonic take on Frost's "Road Not Taken." Many other playwrights like Mahesh Dattani employ some sort of music in the background, to set the mood and plot.

Influenced in part by classical Sanskrit drama, Rabindranath Tagore had been proclaimed the pathfinder of modern Indian drama. Tagore, disillusioned by the restrictions of the spoken word, was fascinated with song and dance in drama. In fact he even reworked dances into some of his older plays. His later music dramas began to show a greater focus on dances. From verse dramas and prose plays to farce and "riddle plays," from lyrical plays to "symbolical" plays, and from dance-drama to season plays, Tagore has attempted a variety of styles. His use of symbolism in his later plays and invention of genres such as the dance-drama and season-drama created a new phase in Indian drama, without giving up on the traditionality of Indian theater. Tagore was a great experimenter with stagecraft. Interplay of color to denote mood is just one example of his theater, which is considered a work of art. His later plays began to have simpler, more minimalistic settings as opposed to his earlier realistic and naturalistic settings.

EPICS, CLASSICS, MYTHS, LEGENDS, AND HISTORY

The Indian classical texts, ancient legends and myths, historical figures, and revered epics have influenced many playwrights. They have used these texts and legends as a mode of inspiration, allegory, metaphors, classical values, and characterization. Story telling is an old Indian art form. The playwrights take up on the concept, while creating specific identities and themes for the stories. Tagore is an example of a prolific and renowned writer who was also influenced by Indian and Hindu mythology, as seen in his plays like *Formless Jewel*.

Eminent Hindi writer Mohan Rakesh's *One Day in Ashadha* takes up the story of Kalidasa, the great Indian poet, whose love and inspiration withers in his absence and quest for fame. The humility of a small rural town is contrasted to the ostentatiousness and pretensions of a princely court. Malayalam playwright K.N. Panikkar considers theater to be visual poetry, and was influenced by Sanskrit drama and Kerala mythology. The characters in his plays are personifications of themes and ideas such as death, life, nature, love, and destruction, and he creates deep metaphorical meaning in the dialogue.

Girish Karnad, writing in Kannada, also takes up on myth and folk themes. In *Hayavadana,* one of the first modern Indian plays using traditional performance to receive national attention, Karnad blends Indian folk elements with classical performance, showing elements of myth, religion, and ritualism. In *The Fire and the Rain,* he uses the ritualistic practices of the Brahmins to depict the mythical implications on the cosmos.

Chandrasekhar Kambar, a leading playwright in Kannada, also uses myth and superstition, deities, and ritualistic sacrifices in his *Siri Sampige,* which takes the form of a Shakespearean-style tragedy, with a soothsayer, a prophecy and its fulfillment, court jesters, the tragedy of the prince, and villains plotting in the background. The lives of princes and commoners are often alike, both fighting over a woman. Reminiscent of Macbeth's prophecies, the prophecy in this play also eventually comes true, signing off on a note of finality about fate and destiny.

Bengali playwright Arun Mukherjee in *Mareech, the Legend* has also based his play on myth, legend, and the famous Indian epic, *Ramayana.* He stylistically he uses the same basic story and shows different times, places and characters, depicting the relevance of the story even today. He uses scenes from modern times contrasted with similar scenes from the epic and legend. He even uses a scene based in American politics and with American characters. In conclusion he brings in all the characters from different times and even brings in the writer of the *Ramayana,* Valmiki, as a character, where reality and myth all combine into one argumentative scene about the ending, with the characters attempting to change the "pre-ordained" ending.

In *Aurangzeb,* Indira Parthasarathi, a Tamil writer, takes up the true historical story of a Mughal ruler, Aurangzeb, and uses it to draw out the religious tensions that existed and festered since the time of the Mughal conquest of India. It brings to life the stories of his father and king, Shah Jahan, the builder of the Taj Mahal; and Shah Jahan's obsessive need to build expensive and beautiful monuments, at the cost of an impoverished nation. He is contrasted to Aurangzeb, the son who never got a father's love, who despised his father's weaknesses and excesses, and who felt that India should be ruled with a firm hand. The contrasting characters of his two sisters, and the decisions of his brother have all been described with a moving and skillful hand. Parthasarathi has developed lifelike characters from historical figures. His characterization is multi-dimensional, where the audience simultaneously empathizes with and disapproves of, likes and dislikes a character. Once more, one finds hints of Shakespearean tragedy, with the red stain on the hands that refuses to wash off, suggestive of Macbeth. The herd mentality of the masses is discussed, just as in Shakespeare's *Julius Caesar.* The ubiquitous question of religion in politics is as relevant in today's political arena as it was before.

COLONIAL ISSUES

It is noteworthy that the first "modern" play in India was enacted in Calcutta towards the end of the eighteenth century. The play was in English and was directed by a European. The new theater was written and staged in the shadow and wake of the British rule in India. In fact, after independence in 1947, modern Indian drama had a deep sense of the West and its ensuing modernity in drama, while reminiscing about the classics, tradition, and the ethnic. Toward the 1960s came the audience's real awareness of the role of the director and production. The director's auteur came into play since plays were written in the local language, and then translated and performed in English and other local Indian languages. This enabled the writers to reach out to wider audiences, and foster greater experimentation in theater.

The last century of Indian theater is a blend of the ancient (Indian) and the modern (European). Post-colonial India and a multi-cultural West have both displayed a need for a contemporary cultural expression, where the cultural mingling of the East and the West can take place on a common ground. Writing in English, Mahesh Dattani, Gurcharan Das, and Tanika Gupta, among others, have taken this aspect of Indian drama up to give a voice to a new cultural expression and collaboration.

Gurcharan Das provides a fascinating range and style of work, while writing in English. He believes that the play is primarily for the audience (as opposed to the readers). There is a distinct influence of myth, history, the epics, and legend in his work, yet his handling of these themes is not heavy-handed but has a natural sense of continuity and flow. He also shows an influence of traditional Greek drama. *Larins Sahib,* staged at the time the British East India Company was colonizing India, is actually written from a pseudo-British perspective, where the Indians are "natives." The play also surveys the British cavalier attitude toward India, and the roots of colonialism. Das uses the art of witty parlance: back and forth dialogue where wit, philosophy, and intelligence uncover deeper aspects of each character and situation, with every exchange.

9 Jhakhoo Hill goes back in reference to the partition of independent India and of the ensuing disruption of families, where the partition of India is likened to a partition of the mind. Moving ahead in time, it brings out the rise of the middle class in India, one that is "new money," professionals that are crass, street-smart, and racing to get ahead, as opposed to the withering generation of the old rich families that have stature and class, but not the street-smart grit required to push ahead; where the past is being taken over by the future, and the people living in the past are struggling to hold on. The younger generation is at times weak and stifled by an elitist bourgeoisie society, at other times striving to ride to the top with independence and drive. The internal turmoil of the family serves as a metaphor for the Indo-Chinese war raging in the political arena of the time. Gurcharan Das's plays describe the consequences of political decisions at the social level, and the changing aspects of Indian society over time, with the rooted influences of colonialism.

REGIONAL ISSUES

Regional issues play as important a role (if not more) as national issues in modern Indian drama. Marathi playwrights, for instance, writing from and about the state of Maharashtra, whose capital is Bombay (or Mumbai), are seen to concentrate on regional issues that affect their society and people. Most choose to write in their regional language as opposed to Hindi or English, though their works have, in most cases, been translated to English. They look to address the people directly in their social milieu in order to effect social change.

Regional writers like Maharashtrians and Bengalis (among others) have been fighting for social justice, especially for the lower castes, against the rigid caste system prevalent in Hindu society. Dr. B. R. Ambedkar was the social revolutionary idolized by most Maharashtrians for his work in bringing about a change in society. From there arose what was called *Dalit Sahitya*, Marathi writing taking a social stand against injustices, especially towards the lower class (and castes) and the untouchables, and striving to create awareness among others. Marathi dramatists have been prolific, and notable among them are Vijay Tendulkar, G. P. Deshpande, Mahesh Elkunchwar, Satish Alekar, Datta Bhagat, Shanta Gokhale, Rajiv Naik, and Achyut Vaze. Many of these dramatists had a strong socio-political agenda.

POLITICAL ISSUES

G. P. Deshpande was a leading Marxist intellectual, whose plays are notable for their deep political themes, exploring the threat to ideology, impact on people (and their relationships), the collapse of the communist ideal, and the angst and emptiness associated with this loss of belief. *Past One O'clock* brings out the communist politics in India, with patriarchy in politics, and a confrontation between generations and ideological positions, cultures and temperaments. It discusses the history of the Marxist-communist movement in India (India is a socialist democracy, with a smaller socialist-communist political party contesting in a multi-party political arena). In *Roads* he gives contemporary reality the status of an epic, and brings out his customary questions on political standing and the status of society with all its ills. He contrasts the democracy and life of the West, which he finds imperialistic and materialistic, against the communism of the Soviet Union and the religious fundamentalism that pervades the Subcontinent. There is a deep sense of loss, of faith, religion, and belief in society and government that pervades Deshpande's works. His is a call for reform, for a better way of life, freedom from the hackles of society and government, and the ability to choose your own road in life. Whether historical or political, Deshpande's plays analyze the individual entangled and struggling in dark times, the dilemma and connection between the personal and the political. He has been said to have created the genre of the play of ideas or the intellectual play in Marathi.

Mother of 1084 is a heartrending play by eminent Bengali writer Mahasweta Devi, tackling the issues of *Dalit* political uprising, the revolutionary spirit, and the death of a son at the hands of a government that cracks down on uprisings. The mother's pain and need for answers is contrasted against the rest of the family's lack of involvement and the need to move on. The concept of the living who are dead in spirit and the dead who live on in spirit is very strong throughout the play.

Datta Bhagat's *Routes and Escape Routes* and *Whirlpool* follow upon the *Dalit Sahitya* movement in Marathi Drama. The former, while describing three generations involved in the movement, and each generation's take on it, from non-violence to extremist and revolutionary, brings out the ideas of social change, unity and living with conflicting points of view. *Whirlpool* is a play within a play, with scenes resembling Beckett's *Waiting for Godot*, where there is a sort of meta-phorical time travel, alternating as a comment on the present situation and the cyclical nature of society. From one generation to another there is no change—father, son, grandson all are "victims" of society. It also takes up the concurrent themes of casteism and social revolution.

Asif Currimbhoy's *Inquilab* (*Revolution*) deals with the *Naxalite* revolution, where agrarian communists choose violent methods to solve their problems. There are people set against the revolution, all of them with their own personal dilemmas: the dilemma of the poor peasant, the local government, the professor and the husband and wife. Currimbhoy considered this play to be the nightmare and redemption of today's Calcutta. His other plays also take up on political themes; for example, *The Captives* talks about the Indo-China conflict of 1962 and *The Refugee* is about entering into Bangladesh in 1971.

RELIGIOUS ISSUES

Religion in India is at once a divisive and unifying force. With a myriad of religions coexisting in a secular nation, there are bound to be conflicts and issues, often incited by the militant factions of the religions and by political manipulations. It is therefore inevitable that literature and drama would carry deep reverberations of these themes. Religious issues are not a new theme in India, as Indira Parthasarathi's *Aurangzeb* tells us about the religious tensions existing since historical times with the advent of the Mughal invasion of India, and the coming of Islam, which brought about religious tensions between the Hindus and Muslims.

Rabindranath Tagore's plays like *Natir Puja* show his interest in Buddhism's equality as opposed to the inequalities and rigidities of Hinduism. Datta Bhagat (in *Routes and Escape Routes*) and Deshpande talk about the differences between the elitist Hindu Brahmins, and the adopted Buddhist faith of the Dalits. In Deshpande's *Roads,* different characters adopt representative ideas on religion. Kachubhai discusses the impact of Islamic fundamentalism on Hindus, and in turn, their fundamentalist reactions; and he believes that extremism in any form leads to destruction. His is a call for a positive attitude towards all faiths, rather than a critique of others. Gokhale is proud of his country's roots and traditions and talks about *Hindutva* (the Hindu faith) while Gangadhar takes a communist stance.

Mahesh Dattani's *Final Solutions* talks about communal hatred, a pervasive aspect of Indian society, where multiple religious beliefs strive to coexist in mutual harmony, but militant factions create constant threats to peace. The mob or the herd reminds one of Shakespeare's mindless mob, and it is symbolic here of each individual's own simmering sentiments that translate into religious hatred and hysteria. The mob is described as attempting to have a voice of its own, and yet getting clamped down and swayed by the strongest opinion. From an individual it becomes one incensed and destructive mass. It depicts the reality of politicians in India using the vulnerability of the masses and playing on their fears and sentiments.

Interracial or interreligious marriage has traditionally been frowned upon by society, and writers such as Tanika Gupta in *Hobson's Choice* and Vijay Tendulkar in *Kamala* touch upon this topic.

SOCIAL ISSUES

Originally writing in Bengali, Rabindranath Tagore was driven by an intense social motivation in his later works, with a desire to liberate Indian society from the evils of the caste system and other rigidities imposed by Hinduism. His plays like *Guru* and *Rath-yatra* parody the unorthodox beliefs of Hinduism and argue the inequalities of the Hindu caste system. *Bansari* is another example of his preoccupation with society: witty conversation replacing warmth and sentiments in upper class Calcutta society.

Marathi writer, Satish Alekar's *Mahapoor* (*The Deluge*) is a dark, absurdist tale of a young man running the thin line between sanity and insanity, a tale of murder and the questioning of reality amidst the societal setting of sectarianism and the familial setting of rigidly ingrained patriotism against a bloody revolution.

In *The Wooden Cart,* which was originally written in Hindi, Tripurari Sharma discusses the social stigma of being "diseased" in society, where leprosy is used as a metaphor for all other kinds of social stigma.

Also writing in Hindi, Surendra Verma takes up the theme of adultery in a royal household in *From Sunset to Sunrise* and its social acceptance when the man is impotent and the woman is publicly given a chance to impregnate herself with another man, to give birth to an heir. The torment of the husband who faces the shame and the pain of watching his wife choose another man is contrasted against the shame of the woman who has to perform this ritual. The twist in the sordid tale comes when the woman starts enjoying her sexual freedom as opposed to living with an impotent husband. The wrenching soliloquy of an impotent man brings out a theme not touched upon often: a man tormented by his wife's actions imposed and condoned by society.

Mahesh Dattani takes up on the topic of the *hijras* (eunuchs) and their place in society in *Seven Steps Around the Fire*. Relegated to begging and accepting alms at weddings and births in return for good wishes, these people are ostracized from society. Uma, a sociologist, chooses to write her research paper on them and uncovers a shocking story of the love between an upper-class man and a *hijra*, which eventually leads to their deaths. The police and the family manage to hush up the story and no arrests are made, which is a lasting reminder of how many unprivileged people in society still have no voice of redress.

Vijay Tendulkar has been heralded as one of the most exemplary Marathi dramatists. He describes social problems, complexity of human relationships entwined with deep questionings of morality, which in turns brings out the reality of the role of women, and a critique of modern society in India. There is a reevaluation of moral values and social injustice associated with middle-class morality. Within the deeply rooted casteism and socio-economic divisions, each social class in turn looks down upon the other. In *Sakharam Binder*, Laxmi, who is thrown out of her own home and ostracized, in turn looks down upon Champa's immorality. Mistreatment, hatred, and even murder take place, all in the name of false morality and misplaced values. In *Vultures*, the only thread of humanity that exists is within an illicit relationship, which also withers away under the pressure of morality and the dearth of humanity around it, portraying the moral and economic disintegration of the family. Tendulkar's characters are victims of society and middle-class morals and values, along with the rigidly pervasive patriarchal society that likens women to slaves and makes them subservient to men.

Casteism

Casteism, class and sectarian differences still play a major role in themes for Indian drama. *The Fire and the Rain* by eminent Kannada playwright Girish Karnad, takes a critical view of the caste system. A young "hunter" girl Nittilai questions everyone's blind beliefs and reverence of the upper class Hindu Brahmins, of the various gods worshipped by Hindus and of the oppressive needs for rites and rituals in religious belief, imposed by the Brahmins. Karnad shows how a "low" hunter girl has more honor, righteousness, and morality than an upper-class Brahmin. Usha Ganguli's *Rudali* also serves to mock the caste system, and describes lower caste women dealing with upper caste injustices and discrimination. Datta Bhagat deals with the conflict between the Dalits and the Hindus, and their differing perspectives and ideologies. The universal phenomenon of the downtrodden in society is taken on through their characters and stories.

In Bengali playwright Utpal Dutt's *Hunting The Sun,* the setting is historical, but the relevance of issues brought up are valid even today. He brings out the caste issues of the *Shudras* (untouchables) and the imposed *Brahminical* code. His questions are haunting: freedom for the "slaves" leads to a breakdown in society, as there would be no one willing or forced to do the menial tasks required. The *Shudras* are not allowed to read, think, or grow. That is not their place in society, as ordained by the Brahmins. This is the quandary that most upper class people are left with—they refuse to create true freedom for the downtrodden, so that they can maintain the selfish status quo of society. Questions of science are also disregarded as heretical to religion, and the people who believe in science above a blind faith in religion are slaughtered. Just as in modern politics, the politics of the rulers in the play brings out their need for lies and force to keep their people in order. The fight here is about faith: in reason or religion, the fight against superstition and blind beliefs that enslave people, and the resilience and strength of a poor *Shudra* woman, who is tortured but refuses to give up her beliefs.

Family Issues

For traditional Indian society, the family is above all else. Drawing upon a tradition of a close-knit, joint family, the themes in a majority of the plays are linked to families and their power over each other. At what point does one draw the line between the welcome warmth of a family and domination and interference in one's life? Dattani's *Tara* had to face the consequences of her family's ruthless decision all her life. In *Dance Like A Man,* Dattani's Jairaj tries to go against the traditional Indian joint-family system. Tendulkar's *The Vultures* describes a family's economic and moral degeneration at their own hands. Hema and Satish in Bhagat's *Routes and Escape Routes* choose to have an inter-caste marriage, and are ostracized by their family. In Tripurari Sharma's *The Wooden Cart,* a leper is abandoned and ostracized by his family and society because no one wants to "deal" with the problem. In Shanta Gokhale's *Avinash,* a family keeps their problematic family member locked inside a room, and attempts to carry on a regular life.

Tanika Gupta in *The Waiting Room* and Mahesh Dattani in *Where There's A Will* both take up the concept of one family member who is dead, but plays a role as a character that the audience can see and hear, and one who looks at his or her family and realizes what they think, how they react, their dilemmas and their true colors. In another perspective, the character is given one more chance to gain a deeper understanding of his or her life and family before he or she moves on.

WOMEN IN INDIAN DRAMA

Women in Indian society have been in turn deified and worshipped, respected and considered the "wealth" of a family, and on the flip side have been considered "below" men, forced into servitude, bought, sold, and murdered by society (female infanticide and *Sati*). Many dramatists have brought out the troubling status of women, their exploitation and their role in society. While urban India has progressed greatly in emancipating women, many rural areas continue to carry on age-old patriarchal practices. Partap Sharma's *A Touch of Brightness* describes the transition of an enlightened temple dancer Prema to a beggar, who is sold against her will to a whore house and becomes Rukhmani, a girl striving to increase her spiritual knowledge amidst her enforced profession of prostitution. Badal Sircar, a Bengali playwright, touches on the subservience of women in *Evam Indrajit*. G. P. Deshpande's Vasundhara in *Passage to Darkness* is trying to find herself. In Verma's *From Sunset to Sunrise*, Sheelvati has to come to terms with society-imposed adultery, because of an impotent husband. Utpal Dutt's *Hunting the Sun* describes the inspiring story of an enlightened *Shudra* woman, Indrani, whose resilience and strength of character condemns her to torturous death, but also manages to convert a ruthless warrior into a changed man.

Mahesh Dattani's Tara, in *Tara,* is a young girl who is loved just a little less than her twin brother and who is unknowingly used as a scapegoat to better her brother's life, by her parents. Yet there is a sense of forgiveness and tolerance in her behavior along with a latent confusion about the discrimination. Dattani in fact sees the play as being about the gendered self, where Tara and Dan (her twin) are metaphorically and symbolically two personalities of the same self. The story is written with her brother as the narrator, a touching tribute to a girl that is a victim of her family's (and through them modern society's) need to continue to empower the male over the female.

Tanika Gupta, writing in English, based out of England, talks about the liberation of women from their traditional roles in her plays. *Inside Out* which was commissioned by Clean Break for women in prison, talks about a better life for women who have the determination to overcome their circumstances. *Hobson's Choice,* an Indian adaptation of the original Harold Brighouse play, portrays determination, grit, independence, and a keen sense of survival in the form of the protagonist Durga (symbolically the name of an Indian goddess that battles evil). In a subversive twist, the conservative male head of the family, Durga's father, is entirely dependent on her to better his life, just like Durga's husband Ali. This play brings out the reliance men have on the women in the house, though they may refuse to acknowledge it. On a similar note, but with a very different story and style, Mahesh Dattani's *Where There's A Will* shows the underlying strength of Hasmukh Mehta's wife and mistress and their ability to understand each other and Mehta's weakness. Mehta dies thinking he was infallible and supreme, and the reality of his weakness comes through the people he attempted to control.

Vijay Tendulkar describes the reality of middle and lower class women. In *Silence! The Court Is In Session* Benare is condemned by society for an illicit relationship, but no one condemns the man for his actions toward her. No man steps up to help her and the biggest irony is that women also do not step up for her; instead, they are equally vicious and quick in pointing fingers. In *Sakharam Binder*, Laxmi, Champa, and many others are all just housekeepers and servants for their men. Tendulkar goes as far as to point out the reality of the status of women, in *Kamla*. A lower-class *adivasi* (tribal) woman, Kamla, and an educated, well-to-do woman Sarita, despite being in largely different economic circumstances, live in the same social atmosphere, where in reality both are just "slaves" of men. In keeping with the expected norm, and the resilience and loyalty of an Indian woman, Sarita, despite her misery and sense of awakening, stays with her man in his time of need. Tendulkar's Sarita is reminiscent of Ibsen's Nora in *A Doll's House*.

Datta Bhagat in *Routes and Escape Routes* sees an educated woman treated condescendingly by an uncle she still shows respect and concern for. Usha Ganguli (writing in Hindi) in *Rudali* (adapted from Mahasweta Devi's book) describes the economic survival of a poor woman without a male in the family, and the solidarity of spirit of a woman amidst abject poverty.

Malini Bhattacharya has depicted the women's movement in India through her Bengali street plays: *Giving Away the Girl* and *The Monkey Dance* that are protesting the dowry system, and *Why All This Bloodshed?* is about a Muslim woman's rights, following upon the Shah Bano case in the mid-1980s.

Gurcharan Das explores the woman as an inspiration, as a legend, as a lover, and as a multi-dimensional person in *Mira*. Mira was originally a *Bhakti* saint, and had many devotees and followers. His play describes her legendary journey into sainthood. Dealing with the "place" of a woman and her "appropriate" behavior in society, his Mira is unconventional and the nontraditional woman, wrapped in a cloak of tradition. Continuing his positive attitude towards women, in *9 Jhakhoo Hill*, Das brings out the strength and resilience in Ansuya, who takes on the difficult task of supporting her family as opposed to following love and independence.

Rabindranath Tagore also had deep faith in the feminine principle. His works depict a deep understanding and observance of and empathy toward women and their role in society. He considered Woman to be nature's beauty, the epitome of hope, harmony, sensitivity, empathy, spirituality, and strength. *Tapati,* for instance, is a proto-feminist play, while his *Chandalika* deals with an untouchable girl, which is a recurrent theme in his work: equality for the downtrodden.

URBAN ISSUES

Shanta Gokhale and Mahesh Elkunchwar pick up on the urban angst, while writing in Marathi. Others like Manjula Padmanabhan and Mahesh Dattani write in English, and continue the existential quest for a semblance of humanity in a contemporary urban lifestyle. They choose a naturalistic mode, with plays set in a city apartment, where the characters are enmeshed in intense human dramas with mounting tensions, eruptive situations, unraveling relationships, and the general feeling of urban claustrophobia.

Shanta Gokhale's *Avinash* is a disturbing and intense drama of a family's struggle to cope with the protagonist, Avinash, who is manic-depressive and an alcoholic. He is ostracized from society, excluded from the family and forced to remain hidden in a room for life, generating levels of oppressive tensions in the family's social setting. Avinash's presence is pervasive and intense, yet he remains invisible to the audience. In Mahesh Elkunchwar's *Party*, the party represents the superficiality and pretentiousness of urban social gatherings. The "party" is a metaphor to fill up an intellectual and ideological void in urban India. The empty space is taken up by the ego of self-absorbed characters. Elkunchwar's personal interest in Chekhov's work is translated to his own style. Once more an invisible presence at the social gathering threatens to disrupt the semblance of normalness. The urban angst described in these plays draws from the subconscious fears, dilemmas, and insecurity associated with the controls society and other people have on individuals.

Manjula Padmanabhan depicts the escapism, silence, and the lack of genuine concern that exists in an urban environment in her play, *Lights Out*. Every person lives simply to ensure his or her own well-being, and anything that threatens to mar that is determinedly ignored. The backdrop of the play has an invisible (to the audience) woman's heartrending screams of anguish that can be heard night after night, and implications of her being gang-raped are discussed in the household, but the people steadfastly ignore her plight and find the whole thing "intrusive." Rather than do something to help, out of a basic sense of decency and humanity, they wonder why the people involved in the crime cannot go somewhere else. There is truly a "light out" not just in the house, but also in humanity.

Well-known Bengali playwright Badal Sircar's *Evam Indrajit* is a depiction of the meaninglessness of life and its subsequent monotony, in an absurdist fashion. Time and life is cyclical to the point that one cannot differentiate between places, events, time, and people. Everything, including the characters, blends into each other, taking up each other's identities, where clearly, being bound by society leads to a breakdown in independent thinking and being distinctive.

Mahesh Dattani has a particularly strong sense of language and characterization. He superimposes strong characters on fundamental social issues and questions pervasive social norms. His characters come alive and are easily identifiable with an urban audience. He uses the dramatic structure to bring to life characters and stories that are real, bold and powerful. His settings are often as fragmented as the families and social scenarios he is depicting. Dattani's plays have been said to blend the physical and spatial awareness of Indian theater with the textual precision of Western models like the theater of Ibsen or Tennessee Williams.

Bravely Fought the Queen demonstrates how in a hypocritical society, acting is as real as reality. Under layers of drama, pretensions, and social masks lies the reality of social life, at the epicenter of which plays out human drama in its most anguished form. Dattani also brings out the concept of the traditional family in his plays—where generations of family members often live together, embrace and suffocate each other in turn. The past, present, and future all live together under one roof.

Dattani picks up on themes like mixed religions and social caste marriage, a questioning of marriage from a gay person's perspective, the issues of being "Indian" and "Indian-ness"—abroad, and in India, finding oneself to be a social misfit, where one can either be gay or be Indian and being victims of society's hypocritical expectations and norms. Dattani uses his characters to nudge society into a deeper questioning and a call for liberation from society-imposed norms. His *On a Muggy Night in Mumbai* is the first Indian play to openly handle themes of gay love and partnership. This cleverly laid out and moving tragic-comedy genuinely questions the hypocrisy of society.

Others like Asif Currimbhoy and Tanika Gupta take on the reality of contemporary urban life with influences from the time spent abroad—Currimbhoy got his start writing in America. In *The Hungry Ones*, Currimbhoy creates some controversy discussing Allen Ginsberg's trip to India—as the Indians saw it! *The Doldrummers* is about the doldrums that settle over a group of young people living in the suburbs of metropolitan Bombay. Tanika Gupta writes from England, and her plays take up on the social themes of the diaspora, and Indians living in a foreign country, having to blend in with a different culture, and the emancipation of women from their traditional roles as subservient to men, of interracial marriages and gay love.

CONCLUSION

India's diversity at regional and national levels in terms of people, beliefs, languages, religions, culture, and history has created a unique kind of drama: multi-flavored and varied. Yet at the most basic level, all the predominant themes are common, all the writers address similar issues: society, culture, emancipation of women, political and economic conditions, historical influences, and the contemporary versus the traditional. At the very core, Indian drama is not that much different from drama in any other part of the world. Names, faces, and places change, but the themes are all the same, as relevant at the grassroots level as at a national or global level. There is unity in its diversity, openness in its conservatism, embracing of the modern and contemporary while fiercely upholding the traditional, a heartfelt call for socio-political change along with a deep sense of belief in the society's resilience. Indian drama is a tribute to a nation that is diverse and able to open its arms to all.

FURTHER READING

Dattani, Mahesh. *City Plays: Party, Avinash, Lights Out.* Calcutta: Seagull Books, 2004.

Deshpande, G. P. *50 Years of India, China: Crossing a Bridge of Dreams.* New Delhi: Tulika, 2001.

Mee, Erin B., ed. *Drama Contemporary: India.* Baltimore, Maryland: Johns Hopkins University Press, 2001.

Irish Drama

Richard Rankin Russell

EARLY IRISH DRAMA: BEGINNINGS TO THE NINETEENTH CENTURY

Largely because of the rural nature of Gaelic culture and polity, there was long thought to be no native tradition of drama in Ireland, a critical commonplace enabled by the lack of Irish language skills by critics working in the field that prevented them from reading Old Irish and Middle Irish works. Drama has traditionally "been a town art supported by fixed patronage," and the Irish had no native towns, as one of the seminal critics of the early Irish theater, William S. Clark, has argued. Because of the founding of towns and cities in Ireland by successive waves of invaders such as the Danes, Normans, and English, "the history of the stage in Ireland," Clark holds, "is the account of alien forces slowly molding and developing the natural theatrical instincts in the Irish genius". The early Irish great fairs may have included embryonic elements of drama, which became more developed in the acting that sprang up around Irish wakes.

More recently, however, Alan J. Fletcher has argued that there was a native tradition of drama in the Gaelic performing arts that were performed in the context of feasts. Fletcher's study of the seating etiquette in the medieval banqueting hall of Tara, first copied around the mid-twelfth century in the Book of Leinster, has shown that approximately ten of the social orders depicted are "members of the entertainer class most likely to create a festive context conducive to dramatic activity." Based upon his extensive analysis of the function of these entertainers, coupled with his reading of various contemporary Gaelic texts, including Old Irish law tracts, Fletcher concludes that the presence of shouting jesters, acrobats, conjurers, gesticulating storytellers, jugglers, riddlers, farters, poetry reciters, and dancers, who consistently performed at banquets, constituted the first examples of early Irish drama, loosely defined. Additionally, "some Gaelic performing artists dressed in distinctive sorts of costumes and were organized into bands, some of which were [...] touring troupes." These actors were mostly men, but some women also would perform. Although surviving texts emphasize the actors' role as satirists, they may also have danced. Significantly, Gaelic performing artists were perceived by the English as "seditious" and "oppositional," and functioned as resistors of "the English colonial presence."

Clark points out other examples of early Irish drama, including the spread of miming from wakes to weddings and other joyful occasions, and the growing popularity of mumming, which was brought over by English settlers beginning in the fifteenth century and was performed on such pagan celebrations as May Day and such Christian ones as Christmas in County Cork and Wexford. The start of more formal drama in Ireland, however, began in urban churches with the miracle plays used by clergy for religious instruction, which were first dumb shows incorporated into services, then sung in Latin within the liturgy. Soon, miracle plays performed independently from the churches became popular, with most of them coming from England.

In the second half of the fifteenth century, the city of Dublin had grown sufficiently that its trade guilds and city corporation began celebrating the Corpus Christi festival in late May or early June with an extravagant procession. By the end of this century, the city corporation and the Guild of St. George began staging another dramatic religious celebration, the Pageant of St. George's Day. These processions were only done in dumb show, however, and never developed into the religious plays performed on church holidays as they did in such English cities as Chester and York. Clark suggests that the first "secular performance of regular drama in Dublin" came "during the vice-regency of Sir Henry Sidney" in 1569 with a dramatic production by the Dublin city corporation for the Lord Deputy at a banquet hall. By 1589, traveling dramatic troupes from England began arriving in Dublin and staging productions there and at Youghal in County Cork, southern Ireland. With the founding of Trinity College, Dublin in 1592, the college started performing Christmas plays by at least 1629. Another major dramatic site in addition to Dublin and Youghal was the walled town of Kilkenny, southwest of Dublin, which staged plays beginning in the mid-sixteenth century on both Corpus Christi and Midsummer Day, many of which were part of a Protestant effort to convert local Catholics. All of these early festivals, pageants, and plays were either performed by local amateurs or by traveling professional English players.

Professional drama with local Irish actors in a permanent home began with the opening of the Werburgh Street Theatre in the fall of 1637 by the Scottish dancing master and publisher John Ogilby. Christopher Murray points out that "A plague in London during 1636–37 helped Ogilby's recruiting of personnel, for at such times the London theaters were officially closed and the actors and musicians had to look elsewhere for employment." Ogilby also brought the English playwright James Shirley (1595–1666) to Dublin as a writer-in-residence for the Werburgh Street Theatre. This playhouse staged established plays from the London stage such as those by Jonson, Middleton, and Fletcher, along with some of Shirley's own. Shirley's new play, *Saint Patrick for Ireland* (1639) was the first modern play in English to premiere in Dublin. *Saint Patrick* features the saint's Christian triumph over the dark Druids, implicitly suggesting the superiority of English rationality over Irish paganism and legitimizing the continuing English attempts to colonize the island. The only play known by an Irishman known to have been staged at the Werburgh Street Theatre was Henry Burnell's *Landgartha* (1640), which featured a muddled mixture of a story from Danish history interspersed with Irish dancing.

The major Irish theater to replace the one at Werburgh Street was The Theatre Royal, more commonly called "Smock Alley," which opened in 1662 as the first Restoration theater in either England or Ireland. By the 1740s, Smock Alley rivaled the London playhouses at Drury Lane and Covent Garden for both popularity and excellence of production, and became such a training ground for local actors that soon Irish actors began bringing their talents to London. Unfortunately, the Smock Alley productions were often static performances of such imported drama as low English comedy, pantomime, and French dance, as Helen M. Burke has argued. Burke shows that before and after the tenure of Thomas Sheridan, who managed Smock Alley from 1745–58 and attempted to regulate and police the stage, a variety of unauthorized intruders satirized Smock Alley productions through pamphlets, participated in street "riots," and even ventured onstage to disrupt performances. Sheridan and his supporters viewed such riotous performances as examples of the barbarous behavior of the local Irish, whom they often viewed as uncivilized and unsaved Catholics. These "actors," as Burke suggests, came "from different positions in the social, political, and cultural spectrum of Irish life challenged hegemonic structures with their riotous performances and theatrical oppositions," and transformed Irish theater into an egalitarian space freer from conformity to British dramatic strictures than it had been previously.

Well-known Anglo-Irish playwrights from the period 1690 to 1800 include George Farquhar, whose Protestant planter family lost everything in the 1689 siege of Derry in what is modern-day Northern Ireland. Farquhar left Trinity College, Dublin for Smock Alley and became a professional actor, later leaving for London in 1698, where he wrote a series of comedies including *The Beaux' Stratagem* (1707), drawing on his own life set in rural Ireland. Farquhar's rural settings and penchant for drawing on his own life inspired later Anglo-Irish playwrights such as Sir Richard Steele, whose plays such as *The Conscious Lovers*

(1722) were usually romantic comedies, written in reaction to the realism of Restoration comedies of manners; Oliver Goldsmith, whose most famous work, *She Stoops to Conquer* (1773), typifies his dislike of sentimental comedy; and Richard Brinsley Sheridan, whose plays such as *The Rivals* (1775) and *The School for Sandal* (1777) affirm true love within the context of traditional comedies of manners.

MODERN IRISH DRAMA

For the vast part of the nineteenth century Irish theater was virtually moribund. The melodramas and mannered comedies of Dion Boucicault (1820–90) in the latter half of the century proved popular with audiences, yet Boucicault often recycled and reified the stereotypes associated with the Stage Irishman, a caricature given to a violent temper and hyperbolic speech. While the social satirists Oscar Wilde (1854–1900) and George Bernard Shaw (1854–1950) enjoyed great success on the London stage in the 1890s (and Shaw for many more decades after that), neither playwright treated Irish themes in any depth, save for Shaw in his *John Bull's Other Island* (1904). Modern Irish drama is generally thought to originate with the founding of the Irish Literary Theatre in 1897 by W. B. Yeats, Lady Augusta Gregory, George Moore, and Edward Martyn. Gregory raised funds from around the world that enabled the theater to start productions in 1899. One of the first productions that year, Yeats's *The Countess Cathleen,* drew attacks from both Catholics and nationalists who thought there was an anti-Catholic bias in the work. That same season, Frank J. Fay, theater critic for the *United Irishman,* called for a national theater that would feature a natural acting style and the use of Irish actors in national drama. Frank Fay's brother, W. G. Fay, directed the 1901 Irish Literary Theatre production of Douglas Hyde's play in the Irish language, *The Twisting of the Rope.* After more productions that year, the Irish Literary Theatre disbanded, but a new company was formed in 1903 and termed the Irish National Theatre Society.

In 1904, Annie Horniman gave a subsidy for the Irish National Theatre Society to move into a new building, called the Abbey Theatre. The next year, Yeats led a revolt that transferred administrative authority into the hands of the three Abbey directors: himself, Gregory, and John Millington Synge. Various other Irish theater companies flourished at this time, including the Ulster Literary Theatre in Belfast and various Irish-language groups such as *Inghinidhe na hEireann* (Daughters of Erin), but the funding of the Abbey, the prominence of its directors, and its high dramatic standards ensured its pre-eminence over all other groups. One great irony of the early Abbey productions, which were meant in part to recuperate Ireland's Gaelic language and culture, was that they were almost all written and performed in English.

Yeats, Gregory, and Synge all shared a conviction that speech should be the focus of their plays, thus privileging the written text over all else. When Yeats recalled his dramatic work at the Abbey Theatre in his 1937 essay, "An Introduction for My Plays," he pointed out the "two dominant desires" he had for his dramas: "I wanted to get rid of irrelevant movement, the stage must become still that words might keep all their vividness, and I wanted vivid words." Yeats's condemnation of movement, though this stance would be modified in his later drama, is made clearer by understanding his dislike of the style of acting common in English theaters at the time, a style that privileged action, not speech. In his 1900 essay, "Theatre," Yeats complained that these English actors spoke "as if they were reading something out of the newspaper. They forgot the noble art of oratory, and gave all their thought to the poor art of acting, which is content with the sympathy of the nerves, until at last those who love poetry found it better to read alone in their rooms." Thus the Abbey Theatre used Irish actors as much as possible.

Yeats was much taken with the successful Norwegian theater movement of the 1880s and 1890s, especially that of Henrik Ibsen. Ibsen's theater enabled Norway to escape Denmark's cultural shadow, an exemplary maneuver that Yeats felt Ireland's burgeoning theater movement might also make and thus escape England's cultural dominance. More important than this cultural strategy for Yeats, however, was Ibsen's relative preference for conversation over action in his dramatic work. The moment in Ibsen's *A Doll's House* when Nora and her husband sit and talk inaugurated modern theater with its focus on conversation rather than action. Despite his other problems with Ibsen's theater such as his penchant for realism, Yeats probably saw in this moment something quintessentially Irish—speech—and resolved to make it the basis of his theater.

Through years of tramping around the Irish countryside with Lady Gregory collecting Irish folklore, Yeats came to realize the importance of talk and storytelling in Ireland. He grew to appreciate the figure of the *filidh*, the Irish bard/poet who passed down memories and stories from generation to generation with a great degree of integrity because of his awesome powers of memory. But talk can also move and incite. Thus in Gregory's and Yeats's famous 1902 play, *Kathleen Ni Houlihan*, an old woman lures Michael, a young man who is preparing for a wedding, off to fight for her through her persuasive rhetoric. Her talk proves infectious and the implication is that the young man will die for this woman who represents Ireland. This emphasis on the incantatory power of speech in Yeats's dramatic work remains in his late play, *Purgatory* (1938), in which the character of the Old Man manages to convince both himself and his son, whom he finally murders, that the Old Man's mother is in a purgatorial torment for having married beneath her class.

Yeats engaged in a variety of theatrical experiments, but much of his best work is marked by its poetic language and use of dance, masks, and symbolic action. His fascination with Japanese Noh drama influenced his drama after 1913 and enabled him to emphasize the imaginative and spiritual realities that he found in Irish folklore and the Irish aristocracy. Plays such as the Cuchulain cycle featuring the hero of a body of Irish mythology nonetheless show his careful attention to character development over the life of his protagonist.

The Abbey repertoire soon came to feature two main types of plays: Yeats's poetic dramas, which largely depended upon the intonation, pitch, and modulation of carefully chosen actors and actresses who would rhythmically chant their lines, and the more realistic peasant plays, which strove for authenticity in their setting, props, and costume. Both Lady Gregory and John Synge developed particular Hiberno-English dialects for their dramas that simulated vernacular speech in rural Ireland. Gregory was the only one of the three original directors of the Abbey who knew the Irish language well. Her plays, though still underappreciated, show her careful incorporation of the rural dialect near her home in western Ireland, a speech that came to be known as "Kiltartanese"; her nuanced understanding of human nature; and her real talent at dramatic comedy.

Gregory's fictitious setting for most of her plays is called "Cloon," and it is based on Gort, a fairly drab market town two miles south of her home at Coole Park. Gort lies on the border of Counties Clare and Galway with a Catholic and Protestant Church, two hotels and several businesses. Gort's very ordinariness made it a perfect realistic counterpart to Cloon, whose characters are universal and meant to represent the range of classes and people in a typical Irish village. Gregory's characters are largely types and she subscribed to the Aristotelian view that character is necessary to propel the action of drama. At the end of most of her comedies, there is a restoration of order, a convention common to most comedies. However, plays such as *Spreading the News* (1904) end more uneasily, with questions left unresolved. Hazard Adams has pointed out four traits that Gregory's characters share: a marked resistance to governmental authority, a sense of isolation, a strong capacity for myth-making, and a tendency for believing in illusory or romantic images. Her comedies became standard repertoire for the early Abbey.

John Synge also felt strongly about the importance of focusing on talk onstage in his plays. In the "Preface" to his most famous play, *The Playboy of the Western World* (1904), a play that provoked riots during its production, Synge famously affirmed the richness of vernacular language and the importance of replicating such talk in dramatic speech:

> [I]n countries where the imagination of the people, and the language they use, is rich and living, it is possible for a writer to be rich and copious in his words....In a good play every speech should be as fully flavoured as a nut or apple, and such speeches cannot be written by anyone who works among people who have shut their lips on poetry.

In Synge's *The Shadow of the Glen* (1903) the lead female character, Nora, leaves her husband who has feigned his death in order to see if she is having an affair, to go with a tramp who has come to the house. As she leaves, she tells the tramp, "you've a fine bit of talk, stranger, and it's with yourself I'll go." She had been fearful to leave with him because of the rough life she fears she must live on the road but in a grandiloquent burst of speech, he convinces her otherwise. And in Synge's *Playboy*, his protagonist Christy Mahon literally transforms himself from a timid boy to an athletic man through the power of the story he tells about killing his father. Synge's emphasis on conversation was heightened by his use of an Irish-inflected English.

Synge's meeting with Yeats in Paris in 1896 was crucial in developing his literary career. Having just returned from the Aran Islands off the west coast of Ireland, Yeats urged Synge to go there and immerse himself in the culture. After visiting the islands in 1898, Synge learned to incorporate the Irish and Irish-English he heard there into the Hiberno-English dialogue that peppers his dramas. While on the islands, he found the islanders to evince a syncretistic religious worldview that mingled Catholic beliefs with pagan ones. Much of Synge's drama, as Weldon Thornton has argued, often invokes a stereotype but his purpose is almost always to subvert that stereotype. He continually pitted received ideas against reality in order to recreate the cognitive dissonance he experienced on the Aran Islands. Many dramas thus take a received story and twist it into a surprising shape.

With Synge's premature death in 1909 and the withdrawal of Miss Horniman's annual subsidy in 1910, the Abbey Theatre began a decline that was finally arrested in the 1920s, when it started producing the gritty realistic urban dramas of Sean O'Casey. O'Casey's most acclaimed dramatic work, his Dublin trilogy of *The Shadow of a Gunman* (1923), *Juno and the Paycock* (1924), and *The Plough and the Stars* (1926), explore universal human questions against the backdrop of contemporary Irish politics. O'Casey severed his relations with the Abbey after Yeats and Gregory rejected his 1928 play, *The Silver Tassie*. Other leading playwrights in the 1920s included T. C. Murray (1873–1959), Lennox Robinson (1886–1958), and Brinsley McNamara (1890–1963), whose work collectively established domestic realism as the dominant mode of the Abbey Theatre for decades to come.

What had become a largely monolithic, inward-looking Abbey repertoire by the early 1950s could not compete with the Paris productions of the avant-garde drama written by the Irish expatriate Samuel Beckett (1906–89) and the London, then Dublin (at the Pike Theatre) productions of the work of Brendan Behan (1923–64). Beckett's and Behan's works from this decade such as *Waiting for Godot* (1953) and *The Quare Fellow* (1954), respectively, share an emphasis on the fruitlessness, even absurdity of modern life, even as they ask probing existential questions about the human condition and offer muted hope. Behan's career was meteoric and short-lived, while Beckett wrote his increasingly minimalist plays well into his 80s from his home in Paris. Beckett's debt to the spareness of Yeats's late dramas such as *Purgatory* is profound, yet Beckett's drama finally jettisons most of the rudiments of traditional drama for an even more intense focus on the individual psyche than Yeats's plays obtained.

Brian Friel (b. 1929), Thomas Kilroy (b. 1934), and Tom Murphy (b. 1936) have emerged as the outstanding Irish playwrights in Ireland in the latter half of the century. Friel's early radio plays of the late 1950s and early 1960s are not memorable, but contemporary Irish drama began with the production of his fourth stage play, *Philadelphia, Here I Come!* in 1964 at The Gate Theatre in Dublin, an alternate, more experimental playhouse to the traditionally realistic Abbey. Anthony Roche points out that the play's genius lies in its deployment of "a number of innovative theatrical effects, not for their own stylistic sake, but as a means of breaking open the hidebound Abbey Theatre and exposing what the latter claimed to represent—the inner lives of Irish people." The first of these devices was Friel's idea to split his main character into two roles, Public and Private Gar, which ably psychologized him. Christopher Murray notes another revolutionary aspect of the play, surely influenced by Beckett's drama, "was that, while using traditional materials such as a peasant setting and décor, with familiar characters such as a parish priest and a schoolmaster, it dispensed with plot and concentrated on situation or condition. The condition explored is alienation." Finally, just as John Osborne had proposed a new anti-hero for the British stage in Jimmy Porter some nine years before in *Look Back in Anger,* in this drama Friel advances his own anti-hero, Gar. Murray argues that his "uncertainty and agnosticism define Gar as the new anti-hero in Irish drama." Friel's other outstanding plays include *Faith Healer* (1979), a play that explores the mercurial powers of an itinerant faith healer who functions as an analog for the artist; *Translations* (1980), a work that laments the modernity occurring in County Donegal during the British Ordnance Survey of 1833; and *Dancing at Lughnasa* (1990), a semi-autobiographical play about Friel's mother and her sisters, which has been made into a film featuring Meryl Streep.

After a distinguished teaching and writing career as a scholar of the eighteenth-century Irish theater, Tom Kilroy had his comedy, *The Death and Resurrection of Mr. Roche,* staged in 1968 at the Dublin Theatre Festival, while his history play, *The O'Neill,* was performed at the Peacock Theatre, (upstairs from the Abbey), in 1969. Other landmark works by Kilroy include his 1977 drama *Talbot's Box,* about the Dublin mystic Matt Talbot; *Double Cross,* focusing on the twinned Irish characters of Brendan Bracken, Churchill's Minister of Information in World War II, and William Joyce or Lord Haw Haw, Nazi sympathizer and radio broadcaster (1986), performed by the Field Day Theatre Company; and *The Madame*

MacAdam Travelling Theatre, which explores individual and national identities in the officially neutral Ireland of the 1940s. Kilroy's continual forays into dramatic criticism and innovative theater have resulted in a fertile exploration of the stresses attendant upon modern Ireland's emergence onto the global stage.

Tom Murphy's drama charts the lives of a series of disaffected individuals in and around the rural areas of County Galway where he grew up. His first full-length play, *A Whistle in the Dark* (1961), was rejected by Ernest Blythe, then director of the Abbey Theatre. After the new Abbey Theatre opened in 1966 and Tomas MacAnna became director, many of Murphy's plays have been staged by the Abbey, including *A Crucial Week in the Life of a Grocer's Assistant* (1969) and *The Sanctuary Lamp* (1976). His most memorable and redemptive play is *Baile-gangaire* (1985), in which a monstrous mother named Mommo, memorably played by Siobhan McKenna in her last stage role, finally tells the traumatic story of the death of her grandson by fire, a narrative she has been seeking to finish for years, aided by her granddaughters. Mommo, who speaks a mixture of Irish and English, is a figure of Mother Ireland and her guilt at her grandson's death and those of her children recalls the keening iteration of sons by Synge's Maurya in his naturalistic play *Riders to the Sea* (1904). After Mary, Mommo's granddaughter, helps her complete her story, she envisions this family of loss as blessed and made whole by God. By extension, Murphy seems to be suggesting that contemporary Ireland must come to terms with its unconfessed sins in order for full national healing to begin.

The founding of the traveling Field Day Theatre Company by Friel and the actor Stephen Rea in 1980 stands as the outstanding cultural endeavor in Irish drama toward century's end. Field Day took as its central image the fifth province of Ireland, an imaginary space in which calcified cultural, religious, and political identities might be jettisoned and new, more unifying identities formed. Despite the relative nationalism of Friel, Rea, and most of the other intellectuals who came to join the company's board of directors, Field Day early on was easily the most powerful joint artistic contribution to re-imagining identity in Northern Ireland during one of its darkest periods with the ongoing Maze hunger strikes by Irish Republican Army prisoners. Field Day's productions of Friel's plays such as *Translations* and later *Pentecost* (1987), by Belfast-born playwright Stewart Parker (1941–88), were great artistic successes and succeeded, at least for a time, in creating new corridors of communication among estranged Catholics and Protestants in Northern Ireland.

Modern Irish drama has certainly evolved from its beginnings in the early Abbey Theatre, yet it has continued to emphasize speech, storytelling, and character, while exploring a range of subject matter no longer confined merely to Irish folklore or the Irish peasantry. The emergence of new theater companies such as Charabanc and Rough Magic and new playwrights such as Christina Reid,

Anne Devlin, Marina Carr, Conor McPherson, and Martin McDonagh has ensured the continuing vitality of modern, or, more accurately, contemporary Irish drama. Much as the Irish nation has become more cosmopolitan, so has its theater, even while retaining the best aspects of its dramatic inheritance.

FURTHER READING

Adams, Hazard. *Lady Gregory.* Lewisburg, Pennsylvania: Bucknell University Press, 1973.

Burke, Helen M. *Riotous Performances: The Struggle for Hegemony in the Irish Theater, 1712–1784.* Notre Dame, Indiana: University of Notre Dame Press, 2003.

Clark, William Smith. *The Early Irish Stage: The Beginnings to 1720.* Clarendon Press, 1955. Reprint, Westport, Connecticut: Greenwood Press, 1973.

Fletcher, Alan J. *Drama, Performance, and Polity in Pre-Cromwellian Ireland.* Toronto: University of Toronto Press, 2000.

Murray, Christopher. "Drama 1690–1800." *The Field Day Anthology of Irish Literature.* vol. I., Edited by Seamus Deane. Derry: Field Day Publications, 1991.

———. *Twentieth-Century Irish Drama: Mirror up to Nation.* Manchester: Manchester University Press, 1997.

Roche, Anthony. *Contemporary Irish Drama from Beckett to McGuinness.* Dublin: Gill and MacMillan, 1994.

Synge, John Millington. *The Complete Plays* London: Methuen, 1981.

Thornton, Weldon. *J.M. Synge and the Western Mind.* Gerrards Cross, England: Colin Smythe, 1979.

Yeats, William Butler. "The Theatre." *Essays and Introductions.* New York: Macmillan, 1961.

———. "An Introduction for My Plays." *The Collected Works of W.B. Yeats, Vol. III: The Plays.* Edited by David R. and Rosalind Clark. New York: Scribner's, 2001.

Italian Drama

Ennio Italo Rao

MIDDLE AGES

After the fall of the Roman Empire, theatrical activity in Italy draws its direct origins not from classical theater, but from Christian ritual. In the late eighth century an agreement was reached between Charlemagne and Pope Adrian I to standardize the liturgy. This pact allowed for the introduction of tropes, interludes inserted in the liturgical text during Mass, consisting of brief dialogues between the celebrant and the attending clerks.

An example of a trope is afforded by a manuscript in the Benedictine abbey of Montecassino, known as the *Officium Sepulchri Casinense*. The text reads:

> *"Processione finite, vadat Sacerdos post altarem, et versus ad Chorum dicat alta voce: - Quem quaeritis? - Et duo Alii Clerici, stantes in medio Chori, respondeant: - Jesum Nazarenum. - Et Sacerdos: - Non est hic. - Illi vero converse ad Chorum dicant: - Alleluia!*
> [At the end of the procession, let the Priest go behind the altar and turning towards the Chorus let him say aloud: - Whom do you seek? -And two Other Clerks, standing in the middle of the Chorus, will answer: - Jesus of Nazareth. -Then the Priest: - He is not here. -Let the Clerks say when turned to the Chorus: - Alleluia!]"

The text above is an essential version of the most common trope inserted in the liturgy of the Easter celebration. More lines and more characters were introduced as time went by. Tropes are the beginning of formal drama in post-classical Italy. Their language was originally Latin, but it gradually yielded to the vernaculars. Recited at first inside the church, they later moved to its parvis or its facing public square and could be recited at the end of the liturgy by the congregation. By the eleventh century tropes were added to the liturgy of other feast days and their subjects expanded to comprise scenes of the Bible, the Apocrypha, the lives of saints, and legends concerning the Last Judgment. In the twelfth century, new lay characters were introduced: the merchant, the seller of ointments for Christ's body, the guardians of His tomb.

The thirteenth century saw a vast production of mystical poems called *laude*, or "lauds." They were written in the vernacular and recited by lay confraternities of Umbrian ascetics, popularly known as "The Disciplined Ones" or "The Flagellants," from their practice of public self-flagellation, as part of their condemnation of the pleasures of the flesh and the excessive wealth of the Church. The most famous author of *laude* is Jacopone da Todi (1236?–1306?), a Franciscan monk, and his masterpiece is *Pianto della Madonna* ("The Madonna's Lament"), Mary's moving plaint on the crucified Christ. From Umbria the *laude* quickly spread to Veneto, Tuscany, Marches, and Abruzzi. In a movement opposite to that of the trope, the *lauda* went from the public square to the church's interior.

A third theatrical form is provided by the *sacra rappresentazione* ("sacred play"), elaborate dramatizations of episodes from the Old and New Testament, from hagiography, and from the martyrologies. Perhaps derived from the much simpler *laude*, the *sacra rappresentazione* became very popular in Tuscany and in Rome by the second half of the fifteenth century. First performed inside the church, it was transferred to an elaborate stage erected in the public square. The actors were lay citizens (men only). The stage was divided into sections representing Heaven, Earth, and Hell. The unity of time, place, and action was not observed. Written in *ottave*, popular stanzas consisting of eight rhyming hendecasyllables, the *sacra rappresentazione* featured a prologue spoken by an Angel, who explained the action and returned at the end of the play with a brief epilogue emphasizing the moral lesson to be learned by the audience.

Under the sponsorship of the Medici family, the *sacra rappresentazione* found such worthy practitioners as Castellano de'Castellani, Bernardo Pulci and his wife, Antonia Giannotti, and Lorenzo de'Medici himself. But by far the most prolific author was Feo Belcari (1410–84), a very pious man and author of *Rappresentazione e festa di Abraam e Isaac* ("Play and Festival of Abraham and Isaac"), a minor masterpiece that captures all the ethical, dramatic, and sentimental elements of the biblical tale.

Drawing on the formal conventions of the *sacra rappresentazione*, Angelo Poliziano (1454–94) created a new genre, pastoral drama, by telling the story of Orpheus's doomed attempt to bring back his beloved Eurydice from the Underworld in the *Favola d'Orfeo* (1480). Though following the structure and conventions of sacred drama with the necessary alterations (the Angel, for example, is replaced by Mercury, the messenger of the gods), Poliziano produced a secular drama from such classical sources as Virgil's fourth *Georgic*, Ovid's *Metamorphoses X*, Claudian's *Rape of Proserpina*, and Calpurnius Siculus's third *Eclogue*.

It should be interjected at this point that theater (like music and dance) are a constant in every culture in every age. Alongside religious theater, a comic and profane rudimentary form of drama always existed, particularly in rural areas, stemming from the winter festival that replaced the ancient Roman Saturnalia (*Libertates Decembris*, "December's Licenses") and culminating in the election of the Pope of Fools, and from other festivities tied to the crop cycles. In urban areas, university students created satirical poetry containing dramatic elements celebrating conviviality, contempt for authority, and sexual freedom. In Sicily between 1230 and 1250 Cielo d'Alcamo composed a *contrasto* ("dialogue") between a male lover and a reluctant maiden, harking back to the Provencal troubadours' dialogues between a knight and a lady. And all of Italy was crisscrossed by bands of jongleurs, who improvised on a variety of themes, both heroic and erotic. It is interesting that comic and profane elements from these forms of popular theater crept into the *sacra rappresentazione*, especially in the latter's depiction of devils.

RENAISSANCE

Unlike Dante, who considered his age a direct continuation of the Roman Empire, Francesco Petrarca, or Petrarch (1304–74) was convinced that the barbarian invasions of the fifth century had ushered in a dark age that saw the beacon of Greco-Roman civilization dimmed and almost extinguished. To re-conquer the splendor that was Rome, he devised a program named *studia humanitatis* ("the study of mankind," or "liberal arts"), centered on the study of ancient classical literature and focusing on such subjects as grammar, poetry, rhetoric, ethics, and history. A key part of the program was the recovery of the vast body of classical literature that had been lost or neglected during the Middle Ages. Petrarch's program soon won many adherents, who are known as humanists. They feverishly looked for new manuscripts, edited new and existing texts, commenting, emending, and translating them. Ultimately, humanists composed original works in various genres, imitating their classical models. Their admiration for the Latin language was so strong that for half a century the Italian vernaculars ceased to be considered a viable literary vehicle.

Petrarch himself is the first humanist to compose a comedy in Latin, *Philologia* ("Philology"), modeled on Terence. The comedy is now lost, only one verse having come down to us because Petrarch quoted it in a letter. According to Boccaccio, Petrarch may have authored a second comedy, but nothing of it has survived.

Ironically, despite their professed love for classical literature and culture, many humanists drew their inspiration for their comedies mostly from the medieval *novella* and the goliardic tradition. Pier Paolo Vergerio wrote *Paulus*(1389–90?), a comedy set in the world of university students, aimed at "correcting the behavior of the young." Antonio Beccadelli Panormita authored *Janus sacerdos* (*Janus, the Two-Faced Priest,* 1427), a comedy in which a group of students play a cruel prank at the expense of a lecherous homosexual priest. Other notable writers of Latin comedies are Leonardo Bruni Aretino (*Poliscena,* 1433), Ugolino Pisani (*Philogenia*), Enea Silvio Piccolomini, later Pope Pius II (*Chrysis,* 1444), Antonio Barzizza (*Cauteriaria,* 1469?), and Tito Livio dei Frovolisi, author of seven comedies.

In 1426, the young polymath Leon Battista Alberti published *Philodoxus,* purporting it to be a comedy by the Latin playwright Lepidus. The hoax was discovered much later, when a better knowledge of Roman comic meters enabled scholars to identify the comedy as spurious.

Although classical models did not determine the form and content of many of the humanists' comedies, their untiring zeal for classical literature left a fundamental imprint on the future development of Italian and European theater. When in 1429 the German Nicolaus Cusanus found a manuscript containing fourteen comedies by the Roman comic playwright Plautus, twelve of which were unknown to the Middle Ages, the discovery created an immediate sensation. Scholars pored over the texts to emend them, to comment upon them, and to fill the occasional lacunae. Thus, Poggio Bracciolini added a prologue to the first scene of *Bacchides* ("The Two Bacchises"), while Codrus Urceus added a last scene to *Aulularia* and Ermolao Barbaro filled a lacuna in *Amphitryon.* Plautus was one of the first classical authors to be published in printed form (first edition 1472). His fellow Roman playwright Terence, whose six comedies survived the Middle Ages, was the beneficiary of the discovery by Giovanni Aurispa in 1433 of a commentary on his plays by the grammarian Donatus. The numerous editions of Plautus and Terence prompted numerous performances of their plays, principally in Rome and Florence. In 1484 Plautus's *Aulularia* was performed in the popes' Quirinal palace! Thus Plautus and Terence, the very authors Tertulian, St. Ambrose, and St. Augustine urged Christians to shun for the salvation of their souls during the first centuries of the Church, were now performed in cathedrals and cardinals' palaces before a delighted audience composed of popes, prelates, and potentates.

The comedies of Plautus and Terence are based on the plots and characters of Greek New Comedy, whose best writers were Menander, Diphilus, and Philemon. Typical themes are mistaken identity, young love, deliberate deception, with complicated plots often combining those of two Greek originals. A constant character is the intriguing slave (*servus*), who often plots to bring about a tryst between his young and penniless master (*adulescens*) and a prostitute or closely guarded girl, to the dismay of a strict and thrifty father (*senex*). Sometimes the *senex* is himself in love, thus exposing himself to ridicule. Other characters are the braggart soldier, the merchant, the brothel keeper, and the parasite, always ready to cadge a free meal. The plot always has a happy ending, often brought about by a recognition scene in which deception is revealed and true identity established, resulting in the reestablishment of the social order.

The numerous translations into the Italian vernacular and the frequent productions (both in Latin and Italian) of the comedies of Plautus and Terence created a thirst for new comedies in Italian based on their model. The most fertile humus for this literary activity was provided by Ferrara and Florence. Although chronologically the first Italian comedy to observe the rules of classical composition was Publio Filippo Mantovano's *Formicone*, presented at the Mantuan court of the Gonzagas in 1503, critics regard March 5, 1508, the date of the first performance of *La cassaria* (*The Strong Box*) by Ludovico Ariosto (1474–1533) at Ferrara's Este court, as the real birthday of "regular" erudite Italian comedy. The Este family had long sponsored theatrical productions, which were well attended by courtiers and visiting dignitaries. Ariosto participated in them as actor or producer. The performances featured very elaborate costumes and scenery. The backdrops represented an idealized city and were the work of such notable artists as Raphael.

The success of *La cassaria* was such that Ariosto put himself to work on a second comedy, *I suppositi* (*The Presumed Ones,* 1509). After a lengthy hiatus he returned to the genre in 1520 with *Il negromante* ("The Necromancer"), *La Lena* (1528), and *Gli studenti* ("The Students"), which Ariosto never completed. The first two comedies were written in prose, while for the other three Ariosto used the hendecasyllable line ending in a *sdrucciolo* (lost accent falling on the tenth syllable, followed by two unaccented syllables). In Ariosto's opinion, this meter came closest to Plautus' six-foot iambic verse. So satisfied Ariosto was with this solution that he later recast his first two plays in the same meter.

Following faithfully the typical outlines of Plautine and Terentian theater, Ariosto's comedies portray frustrated lovers, mistaken identities, and *beffe* ("practical jokes") inflicted on deserving fools. They teem with such characters as intriguing servants, covetous old men, brothel madams, and fiery lovers. Yet they show some contemporary features: many are set not in a mythical Athens or Rome, but in the cities of Ferrara and Cremona; many introduce characters drawn from contemporary reality, like the necromancer and the Jew; and they are rich in observations of the manners and customs of Ariosto's day, at times openly criticizing his society. *Il negromante,* though requested by the pope, was not performed at the Vatican because of certain criticisms of the Church.

La Lena is considered Ariosto's theatrical masterpiece. The main character, Lena, is married to Pacifico, but has a lover, the elderly Fazio, father of the beautiful Licinia, with whom the youth Flavio is desperately in love. When a dispute arises between Pacifico and one of his creditors over ownership of a barrel, Lena conspires to hide Flavio in it and to have it transported to Fazio's house, thus enabling Flavio and Licinia to meet and eventually marry. The plot is derived from several classical comedies, as well as a novella in Boccaccio's *Decameron.*

Comedy was also the favorite entertainment for the court elite at Urbino. In 1513 an elaborate production of *La Calandria* took place, a collaboration between the Cardinal Bernardo Dovizi da Bibbiena (1470–1520) and the ideal courtier, Baldassare Castiglione (1478–1529). The extremely intricate plot includes twins of opposite sex, a credulous old man, fiery lovers, and an intriguing servant, while characters cross-dress to add to the confusion and the old fool is convinced to hide in a coffin to be able to meet the young object of his infatuation.

While comedy in Ferrara and Urbino was strictly tied to life at court, in Florence it rose out of the Florentine people's natural predilection for spectacle represented by performances of Plautus and Terence, as well as other forms close to theater: masquerades, pageants, and carnival celebrations. Thus, when comedies were written and performed in Florence, their intended audience was not a court elite, but the Florentine people, who, though ruled off and on by the Medici family, had nonetheless experienced life under a republic. This circumstance allowed Florentine playwrights to be much more critical of contemporary society than their court-employed counterparts.

The best known and greatest Florentine comedy is *La mandragola* (*The Mandrake Root*) by Niccolò Machiavelli (1469–1527). Set in Florence in 1504, the comedy was probably completed in 1518. Though drawn from classical models, it fuses material from medieval legend and from several novellas of Boccaccio. It tells of the successful attempt by the young and rich Callimaco to consummate his passion for the virtuous Lucrezia, who is married to a rich but foolish husband. To achieve his end, Callimaco must secure the collaboration of a wily servant, a toady, Lucrezia's husband, her falsely religious mother, and a cynical and amoral friar, Fra Timoteo. Readers clearly see in this comedy the same cynical pragmatism that characterizes Machiavelli's *The Prince*. Machiavelli wrote two other comedies: *Le maschere* (*The Masks*, 1504), destroyed by his nephew because deemed too offensive to some living Florentines; and *Clizia*, set in 1506 and first produced in 1525.

Of all the major classical genres, comedy was the most unstable and the most susceptible to change. Often produced at carnival time or as part of a public feast before diverse audiences, comedies had to adapt style and language to specific circumstances in order to have an impact on the spectator and to be received favorably. The contexts within which they were performed and the disparate nature of the audiences encouraged playwrights to be uninhibited and daring in their treatment of the material. This process led eventually to the subversion of the rules governing the genre and to a rejection of its classical models.

One of the most subversive authors of comedies was Pietro Aretino (1492–1556). Born into a poor family in Arezzo, after attempting to make a living as a painter in Perugia, he moved to Rome to seek his literary fortune. A firebrand and a born iconoclast, Aretino soon ran afoul of authority for certain satirical verses he wrote critical of the pope and the Roman curia. Forced to leave the city, he returned to it in 1523, but he again became involved in intrigues and polemics. In 1525 he wrote *La cortigiana* (*The Courtesan*), but the play was not performed in Rome because it contained virulent attacks against the Church. Forced to flee from Rome after escaping an assassination attempt, Aretino finally settled in Venice, where he performed a revised *La cortigiana* in 1534. While it observes the classical unities of time and place and the canonic division into five acts, the comedy is a chaotic succession of scenes (144 in all!) putting on parade a motley variety of characters ranging from courtiers to swindlers, go-betweens, pedants, good and bad, young and old servants, a fishmonger, real and presumed policemen, bakers, and clerics; and containing numerous references to various prelates, gluttons, and jesters, past and present, who frequented the papal court.

Aretino wrote four other comedies: *Il marescalco* (*The Captain*), composed in 1527–30 and published in 1533; *La Talanta* (1542), *Lo ipocrito* (*The Hypocrite*, 1542), and *Il filosofo* (*The Philosopher*, 1546). All of them show considerable freedom from classical models and contain characters representing sixteenth century reality.

The other rebel against the rules of comedy writing was Giordano Bruno (1548–1600), the revolutionary believer in heliocentricity and the existence of infinite worlds, who also wrote in 1582 a most unusual comedy entitled *Il candelaio* (*The Candle-Maker*). Its five acts and numerous scenes are preceded by a sonnet, a dedication, a plot outline, an anti-prologue, a "proprologo," and a "Bidello," or "Janitor," who casts ridicule on the "Candle-Maker," a euphemism for homosexual. As he presents the trick played on the old miser Bonifacio by a sorcerer, on the pedant Manfurio by Ottaviano, and on the gullible Bartolomeo by an alchemist, Bruno harshly condemns what he considers the chief ills of his age: pedantry, superstition, and ignorance. The language, ranging from Latin to a hodgepodge of dialects, is stylistically diverse, difficult, and often deformed and grotesque, especially when placed on the lips of the pedant Manfurio. While the reader easily recognizes the classical matrix of the comedy, its overall effect is one of chaos, with plot lines that could go on *ad infinitum* and a rhetorically rich language that fails to communicate.

Although the sixteenth century saw in its first thirty years the birth and golden age of erudite, regular comedy and later, with Aretino and Bruno, its demolition, the genre found many (though mediocre) practitioners throughout the century and beyond. Noteworthy are *I simillimi* (*The Look-alikes*, 1548) by the scholar Giangiorgio Trissino (1478–1550), little more than a translation of Plautus's *Menaechmi*; *Vecchio amoroso* (*The Old Man in Love*, 1533–36) by Donato Giannotti (1492–1573); *Amor costante* (*Steadfast Love*, 1536) and *Gli ingannati* (*The Duped Ones*) by Alessandro Piccolomini (1508–78); and *Gli straccioni* (*The Tramps*, 1544) by the distinguished poet Annibal Caro (1507–66).

Anton Francesco Grazzini, called "Il Lasca" (1503–84) contributed eight comedies, Giovanmaria Cecchi (1518–87) twenty-one, while the Neapolitan Giovan Battista Della Porta (1535–1615) authored fourteen.

Given the reverence that the humanists felt for classical literature, it was inevitable that they would turn their attention to one of its loftiest genres: tragedy. Although there had been some earlier attempts, most notably *Eccerinis* by Albertino Mussato (1261–1329), the real stimulus to write tragedies came after the publication in Venice in 1498 of Giorgio Valla's translation of Aristotle's *Poetics*. Further interest was stirred by the new translation by Alessandro de'Pazzi, published by Aldus Manutius in 1536 and by the commentaries and criticisms of such scholars as Francesco Robortello, Sperone Speroni, Julius Caesar Scaliger, and Lodovico Castelvetro.

Unfortunately, Italian tragedians took a strictly academic approach to their compositions, with the result that creativity was suffocated by rigorous adherence to the rules extracted from Aristotle: unity of action, time, and place; and noble characters. The pace is static, with important action occurring offstage and reported by eyewitnesses or messengers. Furthermore, Italian tragedies were trammeled by overblown rhetoric and bombastic language suited for declamation. They abound in brooding soliloquies and show a pronounced taste for the horrible derived from the Roman playwright Seneca the Younger. Some notable tragedies are *Sofonisba* (1513) by Giangiorgio Trissino (1475–1550), and *Rosmunda* (1515) by Giovanni Rucellai (1475–1525). Giovan Battista Giraldi Cinthio (1504–73) contributed a treatise on composing comedies and tragedies as well as several tragedies, including *Orbecche* (1541), *Didone,* and *Cleopatra*. It is interesting that the last two were published posthumously. Sperone Speroni (1500–88) wrote *Canace* in 1546, while the same year Pietro Aretino contributed *Orazia*. Later in the century the great Torquato Tasso (1544–95) wrote the horrific *Il Re Torrismondo* (1587). These plays were read and seldom performed. Today they are read mostly in the schools. The tragedians' strict adherence to classical rules, especially that which limited them to the portrayal of great and noble characters, made them blind to a wealth of tragic material, which had to be dealt with in other genres, like the *novella*. Ironically, the tragic plot of a *novella* by Giraldi Cinthio inspired Shakespeare's *Othello*, while a *novella* by Matteo Bandello provided the plot for *Romeo and Juliette*.

In addition to the rich production of comedies and tragedies, the sixteenth century saw the creation of a variety of dramatic sub-genres. Giraldi Cinthio began to write tragicomedies—tragedies with a happy ending, where villains get their just punishment. He also wrote *Egle* (performed in 1535), a pastoral drama developed from the Greek and Roman eclogue and related in content to Poliziano's *Favola d'Orfeo* (1480). Born as court entertainment, pastoral drama is a hybrid genre, with comic and tragic elements, written in a lofty language and featuring musical interludes. Its themes are the beauty of nature, the simple life, and the pain of unrequited love. Other writers in this genre are Baldassare Castiglione [*Tirsi*, (*Thyrsis*, 1506] and Alberto Lolio (*Aretusa*, performed in 1563). By far the best known pastoral dramas are Torquato Tasso's *Aminta* (1573) and Battista Guarino's seven-thousand-line long *Pastor fido* (*The Faithful Shepherd*, written between 1583 and 1587, performed 1595). *Aminta* was an instant success from its first performance at the court of Mantua. Under the guise of nymphs and shepherds hide courtiers and literati, whom Tasso praises or exposes to ridicule. *Pastor fido* also had great success, especially abroad, where it became the chief inspiration for the subsequent development of European pastoral drama.

Rustic farces, set in the bucolic world of peasants, also became popular as a parody of the pastoral drama. They were written mostly in dialect and featured characters that could be easily identified with the local peasantry. These farces have much in common with the *commedia popolare o rusticale* (popular or rustic comedy). Farces were popular in the Venetian area, in Tuscany, and in Campania, where they were called *farse cavaiole,* (farces from Cava dei Tirreni). A prolific writer who straddled the two genres was Angelo Beolco, known as *"Il Ruzante"* (The Frisky One), from the name of one of his most famous characters. Among his numerous comedies and farces are *La pastoral* (1517–18), *La Betía* (1524–25), and *La Moscheta* (*The Flirt*, 1529).

The sixteenth century also marked the flowering of the *commedia dell'arte* (professional comedy), a unique kind of comedy whose influence quickly spread throughout Europe. The *commedia dell'arte* was comedy improvised around a standardized situation (*scenario* or *canovaccio*) and featured a variety of stock characters. The *scenario* offered a bare-bones plot, duly divided into acts and scenes. Plots were inspired by the most successful erudite comedies and featured love between young people, love between an older man and a younger woman, clever tricks to procure money or food or to outwit a dullard. The comedies were performed by a professional troupe, each actor having a specialization. The set scenes were interrupted by *lazzi* ("gags"), performed by very athletic actors who specialized in acrobatic feats, pantomime, juggling, and obscene gestures.

The characters of the *commedia dell'arte* wore a conventional dress and a mask that made them immediately recognizable to the audience. These include old men: Pantalone from Venice and the Doctor from Bologna; young lovers with such names as Isabella, Silvia and Flaminia, and Fortunio, Ottavio, and Valerio. The heroine's servant was often called Colombina. Another stock character was the descendant of the braggart soldier of Plautine comedy, Capitan Spaventa, often Spanish—a reminder of the ascendancy of Spain in Italian politics after 1559. But the embodiment of the spirit of the *commedia dell'arte* was the jester, or Zanni, who could also be called Arlecchino ("Harlequin"), Pedrolino, Pulcinella, Scapino, Burattino, among many other names. Zanni hailed from Bergamo, Pulcinella from Naples. Most Italian regions eventually created their own jester or their own stock character. It was the jester who provided the comic entertainment of the paying audience.

Professional companies were created in the major Italian cities. They often went on tour and many performed before the crowned heads of Europe. All roles were first played by men. The first woman to perform on stage was Isabella Andreini in 1550. The characters and the contents of the *commedia dell'arte* became quickly familiar in other countries. For example, Pedrolino became the French Pierrot, while Pulcinella became Punch in England. Traces of the *commedia dell'arte* persist to this day, following a trajectory that spans a spectrum encompassing Shakespeare, Molière, and American slapstick. A revival is under way in Italy.

SEVENTEENTH, EIGHTEENTH, AND NINETEENTH CENTURIES

In the seventeenth century the *commedia dell'arte* continued to thrive, with performances attracting spectators in every court and public square in Italy and winning ever wider audiences abroad. It began to decline after 1650 as a result of excessive specialization among actors. Tragedy continued to be cultivated, but its appeal was limited to the refined elite. Practitioners of the genre were Cardinal Giovanni Delfino (1617–99), author of three tragedies (*Cleopatra*, *Lucrezia*, and *Creso*), all printed posthumously. Carlo de'Dottori (1618–85) wrote *Aristodemo* (1657), heavily drawing on Greek tragedy, while showing a penchant for horror reminiscent of the younger Seneca. Another prolific tragedian was Federico Della Valle (c. 1560–1628), author of the biblically inspired *Iudit* (1627) and *Ester* (1627), and *La reina di Scotia* ("The Queen of Scotland," 1628), dealing with the final hours of Mary Stuart before her execution. Inspired by the program issued from the Council of Trent, seeking edifying drama based on the lives of saints and martyrs, *tragedia sacra* (sacred tragedy) had many practitioners. Two Jesuit authors stand out: Pietro Sforza Pallavicino (1607–67), author of *Ermenegildo martire*(1644), and Emanuele Tesauro (1592–1675), who wrote *Ermenegildo* (1661), both plays exalting the martyr's unfaltering faith.

Pastoral drama continued to be popular and was extended from the idyllic world of shepherds to include the realm of fishermen, sailors, and woodsmen. But the century's greatest contribution to the theater by far was the creation of musical drama, which we know today as opera. Very late in the sixteenth century a group of literati and musicians constituted a club in Florence called the Camerata dei Bardi with the aim of recreating Greek drama, intended as a perfect synthesis of language, music, and dance. They found the most suitable subject for their experiment to be Greek mythology and ancient history. The first musical drama is *Dafne* ("Daphne," 1598) with a libretto by Ottavio Rinuccini

(1562–1621) and music by Jacopo Peri (1561–1633). The recognized masterpiece produced by the Camerata is *Orfeo* ("Orpheus," 1607) by Claudio Monteverdi (1567–1643), still performed and several times recorded. The staging of musical drama led to the creation of elaborate scene painting, set decoration, and stage machinery, thus establishing conventions that endure to this day.

Changing tastes and the emergence in Venice of a refined bourgeoisie as the dominant class created dissatisfaction with the *commedia dell'arte* and a demand for its reform and revitalization. Reform came with Carlo Goldoni (1707–92). A lawyer by profession, he became writer-in-residence for the Teatro Sant'Angelo in his native Venice, a privileged perch that allowed him to enact his agenda. Appalled by the absurdity, vulgarity, and tastelessness into which the *commedia dell'arte* had fallen, Goldoni set about its gradual reform, creating a theater that was true to life and reflected the problems facing Italian society. He began by writing out the dialogues and by reducing the *lazzi*, eventually dropping the masks. Among his numerous comedies are *La vedova scaltra* (*The Cunning Widow*, 1748), *La locandiera* (*The Mistress of the Inn*, 1753), and *La bottega del caffè* (*The Coffee Shop*). A keen observer of customs, Goldoni won admirers in Italy and abroad, but also encountered harsh opposition from a Venetian nobleman, Count Carlo Gozzi (1720–1806). A staunch conservative and enemy of innovations, he strongly criticized Goldoni's realism and set out to prove that the public could be happy to watch even a *fiaba* (fairy tale). Accordingly, he wrote ten fairy tales, the most famous being *L'amore delle tre melarance* (*The Love for Three Oranges*, 1761); *Re cervo* (*King Stag*, 1762); *Turandot* (1762), an exotic play set in a mythical China; and *L'augellin belverde* (*The Beautiful Green Bird*, 1765). They proved to be very popular and two of them inspired music by Puccini and Prokofiev in the twentieth century.

In the first half of the eighteenth century, tragedy was dominated by the French models of Racine and Voltaire. In the second half, however, Vittorio Alfieri (1749–1803) came upon the scene with an original voice. He wrote nineteen tragedies between 1775 and 1789, drawn from biblical, Roman, and Renaissance history. A patriot who decried Italy's condition of servitude, he was obsessed with the subject of tyranny. His plays are characterized by the terseness of their language and the strength of the passions it expresses. Although well crafted and adhering to the classical unities, Alfieri's plays are more suited for reading than for performance. After Italy achieved independence, they were known only in academic circles. The most famous of his tragedies is *Saul* (1782), the story of the guilt-ridden king of the Jews.

Eighteenth century Italy made original contributions in the field of musical drama as well. Chief among the authors of *melodrammi* is Pietro Metastasio (1698–1782), a member of the Arcadia Academy that aimed at restoring simplicity and good taste to Italian poetry as an antidote to the artifice and frivolity of the

Baroque. Metastasio produced exquisitely melodious dramas that were immediately set to music by the greatest composers of his day. His best known plays are *Didone abbandonata* (*Dido Abandoned,* 1724), *Semiramide* (*Semiramis,* 1729), and *La clemenza di Tito* (*The Clemency of Titus,* 1734), the last set to music by Mozart.

The nineteenth century in Italy is the century of opera. It saw the rise of such great composers as Gioacchino Rossini (1792–1868), Gaetano Donizetti (1797–1848), Vincenzo Bellini (1801–35), and Giuseppe Verdi (1813–1901), whose music resonated in every opera house from the Alps to Sicily to delirious applause. Although the aforementioned composed magnificent music, their operas' libretti were of uneven quality, ranging from the chaotic *Il trovatore* (*The Troubadour,* 1853) of Salvatore Cammarano, through the mediocre *Macbeth* (1847) by Francesco Maria Piave, to the sublime poetry and dramatic power of *Otello* (1887) and *Falstaff* (1893) by Arrigo Boito.

Tragedies were written by the great romantic poets Ugo Foscolo (1778–1828) and Alessandro Manzoni (1785–1873). The chorus from the latter's *Adelchi* (1822) are among the most sublime verses in the Italian language and until recently had to be memorized by all Italian schoolchildren. The play, however, is very seldom performed as its lack of dramatic power fails to hold an audience.

Theater in the second half of the century fell under the influence of the French "thesis play" of Alexandre Dumas fils and Émile Augier. Themes explored by Italian playwrights were divorce, marriage between different social classes, and the practice of dueling to defend one's honor. A later influence came from the French naturalist school. Exponents of this movement are Marco Praga (1862–1929), whose plays are critical of the conventions of the bourgeois world of his native Milan; and Giuseppe Giacosa (1847–1906). Though his first theatrical works were dramas set in the Middle Ages, Giacosa changed his course, writing plays with a bourgeois setting. His best-known play is *Come le foglie* (*Like Falling Leaves,* 1900), permeated with a melancholy atmosphere reminiscent of Chekhov. Giacosa is also known as the coauthor with Luigi Illica of several libretti for Giacomo Puccini's operas.

TWENTIETH CENTURY TO THE PRESENT

The last years of the nineteenth and the first of the twentieth century witnessed the last pangs of naturalism and saw two giants of Italian literature at work for the theater. Gabriele D'Annunzio (1863–1938), best known for his novels and poetry, wrote *La figlia di Iorio* (*Iorio's Daughter,* 1904), a "pastoral tragedy" set in an undetermined time among the shepherds of Abruzzi. He also wrote three medieval verse tragedies, the best known of which is *Francesca da Rimini* (1901), inspired by the character in Dante's *Inferno.* The other playwright is Giovanni Verga

(1840–1922), who turned to the theater after achieving great fame as the author of late romantic and veristic novels. In 1884 he made a play out of a successful short story, *Cavalleria rusticana* (*Rustic Chivalry*). Later, it formed the libretto for Pietro Mascagni's famous opera. Verga wrote seven other dramatic works, the most famous of which is *La lupa* (*The She-Wolf*, 1896), but he never matched the success of his first theatrical work.

Opera embraced Verismo, spawned from French Naturalism, and saw the masterpieces of Ruggero Leoncavallo, Pietro Mascagni, and Giacomo Puccini, while in the prose theater Luigi Chiarelli (1884–1947) inaugurated the "theater of the grotesque" with *La maschera e il volto* (*The Mask and the Face*, 1916), a comedy based on the paradoxical situations that everyday life presents.

At last, after hosting a long line of homunculi stretching back a century and a half, the Italian stage saw the rise of a giant, fully the peer of Ibsen and Shaw. Having already earned fame as a poet, novelist, and short-story writer, Luigi Pirandello (1867–1936) made his theatrical debut with a number of plays in his native Sicilian dialect: *La morsa* (*The Vise*) and *Lumíe di Sicilia* (*Sicilian Limes*), both of 1910, followed by *Pensaci, Giacomino!* (*Think About It, Giacomino!*) and *Liolà* in 1917, and *Il berretto a sonagli* (*The Cap with Bells*) in 1918. The protagonists of the last three plays are rugged individualists, who defy social conventions and advocate a rational existence free of social prejudices.

It is with *Così è (se vi pare)* [*Right You Are (If You think So)*] of 1917 that Pirandello began to tackle squarely existential problems. The theme faced in this play is that of the relativity of truth, or of the simultaneous existence and validity of multiple truths. In 1921 Pirandello produced *Sei personaggi in cerca d'autore* (*Six Characters in Search of An Author*), a revolutionary play about the nature of artistic creativity. In it six characters from an unfinished short story interrupt the rehearsal of a play by Pidandello and ask the director to enact their tragic story on the stage in order to be fully realized. The play befuddled both audiences and critics. Undaunted, Pirandello continued on his innovative and provocative path and gained recognition and accolades in France, Germany, and the United States. *Enrico IV* (*Henry IV*, 1922) is a further exploration into the theme of reality and a profound study of schizophrenia. In 1932 Pirandello produced *Questa sera si recita a soggetto* (*Tonight We Improvise*), his most controversial play, with action taking place on stage and among the audience, while a director named Dr. Hinkfuss (German for Oedipus) is attempting to put on a play. Some actors disperse among the audience, heckle the actors on stage, and a fight breaks out, while an actress almost dies on stage, overcome by emotion.

Critics accused Pirandello of "cerebralism" and of playing dialectic games, but audiences continued to flock to his plays, recognizing that Pirandello was tackling the most troubling themes: existential anxiety, the relativity of truth, despairing solitude, and the nature of the creative process. He was awarded the prestigious

Nobel Prize in 1934. He still remains the most performed Italian playwright and is as popular in Italy as Shakespeare is in English-speaking countries. There is no professional or amateur theatrical group in Italy that does not include at least one of his plays on its playbill. His influence on modern theater is far-reaching and he is considered the inspiration for the "theater of the absurd."

After Pirandello the most noteworthy voices are those of Eduardo De Filippo (1900–84), born into a family of actors, who wrote plays set in the Neapolitan middle and lower classes and strongly reminiscent of Italian neorealist cinema; and Dario Fo (b. 1926), who has experimented with the *commedia dell'arte*, with a free cabaret form, and with the tradition of the jongleurs. His work has recently (1997) achieved international recognition by being awarded the Nobel Prize.

FURTHER READING

Andrews, Richard. *Scripts and Scenarios: The Performance of Comedy in Renaissance Italy.* Cambridge-New York: Cambridge University Press, 1993.

Bondanella, Peter and Julia Conaway Bondanella, co-eds. *The Macmillan Dictionary of Italian Literature.* London: Macmillan, 1979.

Brand, Peter and Lino Pertile. *The Cambridge History of Italian Literature.* Cambridge: Cambridge University Press, 1996.

Clubb, Louise George. *Italian Drama in Shakespeare's Time.* New Haven: Yale University Press, c. 1989.

Greg, Walter W. *Pastoral Poetry and Pastoral Drama: A Literary Inquiry.* New York: Russell & Russell, 1959.

Herrick, Marvin T. *Comic Theory in the Sixteenth Century.* Urbana, Illinois: University of Illinois Press, 1950.

———. *Italian Comedy in the Renaissance.* Freeport, New York: Books for Libraries Press, [1970].

———. *Italian Tragedy on the Renaissance.* Urbana: University of Illinois Press, 1965.

———. *Tragicomedy: Its Origin and Development in Italy, France, and England.* Urbana, Illinois: University of Illinois Press, 1955.

Hochman, Stanley, ed. *The McGraw-Hill Encyclopedia of World Drama: An International Reference Work in 5 Volumes.* New York: McGraw-Hill, 1984.

Kerman, Joseph. *Opera as Drama.* Berkeley: University of California Press, 2005.

Muir, Lynette R. *The Biblical Drama of Medieval Europe.* Cambridge: Cambridge University Press, 1995.

Radcliff-Umstead, Douglas. *The Birth of Modern Comedy in Renaissance Italy.* Chicago: University of Chicago Press, 1969.

Ragusa, Olga. *Luigi Pirandello: An Approach to his Theatre.* Edinburgh: Edinburgh University Press, 1980.

Richards, Kenneth and Laura Richards. *The commedia dell'arte: A Documentary History.* Oxford: B. Blackwell for Shakespeare Head Press, 1990.

Sadie, Stanley. *History of Opera.* New York: Norton, 1990.

Sternfeld, Frederick. *The Birth of Opera.* New York: Oxford University Press, 1993.

Latin American Theater

George Woodyard

BACKGROUND

Although there has been theater in the Americas since the time of the Spanish conquest, or even before, the movement came into its own in the 1950s and 1960s, soon after World War II, when a new generation of playwrights and directors launched their careers and became the canonical figures of the late twentieth century. The quantity and quality of this movement is astonishingly high, even though it remains generally ignored or unknown by the majority American public. This brief overview will attempt a broad brush approach to a topic that spans 500 years, 20 some countries and represents a combined population of well over a half billion people at the present time.

Colonial Influences

Before the twentieth century, the theater in Latin America was strongly influenced by the colonial powers, both Spain and Portugal. Both countries used their own developing theater traditions at the time of the early conquest to convert the indigenous populations to the Roman Catholic faith. The conquest was a military-political venture, but the religious factor was of equal importance to the early conquerors, and the Indian populations not decimated by wars and European diseases were quickly instructed in the faith. The conquerors took advantage of indigenous dances, songs, and cultural traditions to ease the transition. Within a few years a secular theater began to emerge in those areas of greatest political importance, such as the Caribbean, Mexico and Peru. As the theater in the mother countries passed from its infancy into more developed forms of Renaissance

theater and eventually the baroque, these styles and traditions were quickly transferred to Latin America. In the sixteenth century Fernández de Eslava in Mexico
wrote short pieces that were performed in churches and public plazas extolling,
sometimes with a tongue-in-cheek attitude, the tenets of the church and doctrine.
In Brazil Padre Anchieta developed a serious theater also with a religious bent.
By the end of the seventeenth century, the baroque traditions were well established, and one of the greatest talents of all in the New World, a young Mexican
nun named Sor Juana Inés de la Cruz, wrote both religious and secular plays, in
verse, that stand beside the masterpieces of Lope de Vega or Calderón de la Barca
in Spain as superb examples of baroque literature.

NINETEENTH CENTURY THEATER

If the eighteenth century represented a decline in Spanish and Portuguese literary fortunes, the theater in Latin America reflected the same tendencies, although
productions were often imported from Europe. By the nineteenth century theater
was generally widespread throughout the colonies, including Argentina and the
southern cone. Following the wars of independence from 1810 to 1825, the influence of the late-blooming romantic period in Spain was noticeable and continued,
with many variations, throughout the rest of the century. Writers such as the
Argentine Luis Ambrosio Morante, the Mexican Fernando Calderón, or the
Cuban-born Gertrudis Gómez de Avellaneda began to establish national standards for theater activity. By the end of the century, while the quality was far from
uniform throughout the Americas (and still is not), there were strong indications of
solid development from Mexico to the southern cone. When Pablo Podestá
adapted the legend of the gaucho *Juan Moreira* to the circus in 1884, the modern
Argentine theater was underway.

TWENTIETH CENTURY THEATER

At the beginning of the twentieth century in Argentina the dominant figure was,
curiously, the Uruguayan-born Florencio Sánchez, whose plays captured the
essence of a country in a process of rapid social change. The massive migrations
from Spain and Italy had quickly doubled the population at the end of the nineteenth century. Sánchez created believable and emotional characters with a quick
and sardonic dialogue that epitomized problems of immigration, adaptation, and
social conflict. His masterpiece, *Barranca abajo,* focused on the problems of an
old gaucho, abandoned by his family and by his protective network, who finds
no recourse except suicide. Sánchez's influence is found in authors from Uruguay,
Cuba, Mexico, and of course in Argentina where a school of successors continued
his traditions. By the 1920s Argentine authors were experimenting with the

metatheatrical techniques of Pirandello, who visited there twice. Armando Discé-polo in *Stéfano* and *Mateo* captured a new idiom by combining creole influences with the grotesque.

By the late 1920s a movement to break old traditions in favor of newer European models became apparent. Known as experimental theater in Mexico and independent theater in Argentina, the focus shifted from the actor/actress to the importance of the director in coordinating all aspects of a production. Smaller, intimate theaters for 100 or 200 replaced the gigantic halls used for the popular music reviews. New electric lighting systems capable of highlighting performers and dramatic nuances replaced antiquated gas or even candle systems. The prompter's box disappeared as actors were expected to memorize lines, unlike during previous periods when hasty (sometimes weekly) productions rendered it impossible. Local accents came into vogue instead of the standard Castilian-based speech from Madrid. The role of the director, following the European models of Gordon Craig or Appia and others, became critical for coordinating all aspects of an aesthetic performance. In Mexico the Teatro Ulises 1928 season featured only foreign plays, but it provided the impetus for other groups to stage national plays in the new style. Rodolfo Usigli, the father of the modern Mexican theater, while not a participant in the experimental theater movement, became active in the 1930s. His *El gesticulador* and *Corona de sombra* (1947) are both canonical works that examine history to reinterpret Mexican core values.

In Argentina the movement was characterized by a sociopolitical tendency as well when Leónidas Barletta opened his Teatro del Pueblo in 1930, thereby launching the independent theater movement that lasted until the mid-1950s. A leftist militant romantic, Barletta was a friend and patron of the underprivileged and his theater offered an artistic alternative to the commercial theater of the time. He promoted national authors while at the same time staging Shakespeare, Gogol, Tolstoy, Cervantes, Lope, and Molière, and in the process laid the ground-work for other independent groups such as Juan B. Justo and La Máscara. Barletta also introduced novelist Roberto Arlt to the theater, an author whose master works include *Saverio el cruel,* a play that deals with a hapless peasant type as a pawn of the idle rich.

Other countries in Latin America also caught the new wave. In Puerto Rico the Ateneo in 1938 sponsored a competition for new plays; in Chile the visits by theater groups fleeing the Spanish Civil War led to a major change that came, curi-ously, via the university theater programs, first at the University of Chile (1941) and then at the Catholic University (1943). Also in 1943 a Polish emigree to Brazil staged an expressionist play by Nelson Rodrigues that fostered new concepts. The prosperity and social change that came to Latin America after World War II began to invoke major adjustments, as authors, directors, and impresarios sought to capture a local or national reality to replace the customary imported theater.

A turning point in Argentina was the production of *El puente* (1949) by Carlos Gorostiza, a play with a dual structure that focuses on the agonies of two families, one rich, one poor, equally affected by the deaths of two co-workers in a bridge accident. This canonical play was the first in Argentina to transcend a move from the independent to the commercial theater. The following year marked the debut of Emilio Carballido in Mexico with *Rosalba y los Llaveros,* thereby launching a career marked by diversity, realism, fantasy, and humor. The prolific Carballido set the theater standards in Mexico throughout the rest of the century by combining realism with satire, farce, and humor. His anthologies and support helped to launch later generations of writers.

The relatively favorable conditions for publishing and staging new plays in the 1950s spawned a new burst of activity. Common themes were social, economic, and political issues, plus psychological and even religious matters. Realism is the dominant mode, although experimental styles emerge by the 1960s. In Mexico, Luisa Josefina Hernández, Rafael Solana, Federico S. Inclán and others characterized Mexican society in its new environment. Puerto Rico's René Marqués wrote *Los soles truncos,* a masterpiece describing Puerto Rico's ambivalent status as a commonwealth with a divided heritage. The Colombian Enrique Buenaventura with his Teatro Experimental de Cali adopted a leftist ideology, as did Osvaldo Dragún in Argentina when he wrote the first of his *Historias para ser contadas,* brief but pithy plays that challenged a complacent public.

During the 1950s theater was at best moribund in Cuba under Batista, but the new communist regime of Fidel Castro that came to power in 1959 recognized the power of theater and the arts as a medium for political ideology. Theater was promoted throughout the island, while international festivals and competitions sprang up in order to provide new venues. Exiled Cubans such as José Triana returned to participate in the Revolution. Triana's multi-layered *La noche de los asesinos* was a huge success both at home and abroad, but soon Triana, along with two other writers, Heberto Padilla and Antón Arrufat, was accused of being unfaithful to Revolutionary goals. Groups such as Escambray and Cubana de Acero focused on Revolutionary ideals.

In the 1960s many new trends and issues emerged. In Chile Jorge Díaz began writing an absurdist style of theater, previously unknown in the Americas. His *El cepillo de dientes* played with language in a two-character play that broke traditional rules, and set a pattern of socio-political interest within an absurdist vein. In Argentina the Arthur Miller-inspired, neo-realist theater of Ricardo Halac and the ever-popular Roberto Cossa launched a direction the two authors would continue to pursue throughout the century. At about the same time, a neovanguardist, more experimental, theater developed, more attuned toward a new language of the stage with elements of the Argentine grotesque. Griselda Gambaro and Eduardo Pavlovsky both started writing in the 1960s in an experimental style with resonances of the absurd. Pavlovsky soon moved to more overt political expression and his *El señor presidente* anticipated the horrors of Argentina during its "Dirty War." Gambaro is a master craftsman whose focused plays, both short and full-length, have fascinated an Argentine and international public for the past 30 years.

Across the Americas, theater became increasingly strident and impassioned, both reflecting and anticipating massive social changes sweeping across the hemisphere. By the end of the 1960s two new tendencies were developing: one was to look more deeply into local and national traditions to find expression for social concerns, instead of looking for models in European or North American theater, although Artaud, Brecht and Williams continued to inspire. A series of national and international theater festivals provided a forum for exchanging ideas, for seeing styles and patterns of other groups, especially from neighboring countries, and for discussing with other playwrights, directors, actors, and theater personnel their objectives and their dreams. The theater festival of Manizales, Colombia, first held in October of 1968, marks a turning point because of the interaction of groups from many countries and the participation of such notable personalities as Pablo Neruda and Miguel Angel Asturias, both Nobel laureates. The Manizales festival was not the first international theater festival in the Americas, but it became a landmark for celebrating these traditions.

The second new tendency was the development of the *creación colectiva* (the collective creation), a movement that swept Latin America in the late 1960s and continues to the present, although now greatly reduced in scope. In Colombia Enrique Buenaventura with the TEC (Teatro Experimental de Cali) and Santiago García with La Candelaria were pioneers in this movement which inverted the traditional hierarchy of author, producer, director and actor, and replaced it with a system in which all roles, from author to actor, could be assumed by any and all members of the group. Performances were normally highly politicized, and written texts were minimized with the result that the period is marked by a relative paucity of canonical texts. The pendulum starts to swing back in the mid 1980s with renewed emphasis on the text author, but several groups have maintained a high profile, such as ICTUS in Chile, Yuyachkani and Cuatrotablas in Peru, and Teatro de los Andes in Bolivia, to name only a few.

Recent Developments in Latin American Drama

The past twenty years have been a particularly fertile period, one that coincides with the postmodernist, postcolonial period. Prominent new authors emerge, such as Marco Antonio de la Parra in Chile, Sabina Berman and Víctor Hugo Rascón Banda in Mexico, Roberto Ramos-Perea in Puerto Rico, Eduardo Rovner in Argentina, and a host of others. Their plays provide new ways of looking at history, gender issues, and even theater itself. Sabina Berman, author of some 20 plays, scored a tremendous hit with *Entre Villa y una mujer desnuda* (both on stage and screen) which folds together in witty and entertaining ways issues of traditional Mexican machismo, as seen through Pancho Villa, and contemporary gender questions and sexual mores. In later plays she continues her assaults on problems deeply imbedded in the fabric of Mexican culture as she challenges her reader or public to take a fresh look at Trotsky, Freud, Molière, homosexuality, Judaism, and a plethora of other issues. Her compatriot, Víctor Hugo Rascón Banda, has captured the public imagination through documentary plays, often inspired by actual news events, which focus on issues of vital interest such as death and dying, La Malinche, Tina Modotti, the Juárez murders, and other women's issues.

In the southern cone, the level of dramatic activity has been exceptionally high, even during the periods of brutal dictatorships in both Chile and Argentina. In Chile, earlier writers such as Egon Wolff and Juan Radrigán have been joined by Benjamín Galemiri, Ramón Griffero and Marco Antonio de la Parra. The last, whose success and career have paralleled that of Sabina Berman in the north, challenged the system during the Pinochet years with such remarkable plays as *La secreta obscenidad de cada día*, and has continued to do so with later plays that provide extraordinary insights into Chilean politics, social structures, and values.

While it seems inherently unfair to mention only one or two writers from principal countries, the lists are so long there are no good alternatives. A younger generation has brought new life and new tendencies (Daniel Veronese, Rafael Spregelburd, Alejandro Tantanian, for example) to the Argentine stage, in addition to numerous women writers. A staple has been the work of Eduardo Rovner whose lighter works capture with good humor the foibles of the human condition, especially in Argentina.

The volume of activity in other countries does not match that of Argentina and Mexico, but it is equally important in representing the effort to find a dramatic voice for national and social concerns. Uruguayan theater, closely associated with Buenos Aires, has astonishingly talented women writers such as Maria Ferreira and Marita Fornaro; in Paraguay the indomitable Edda de los Ríos promotes performance and activity. In Venezuela Rodolfo Santana and Gustavo Ott have mesmerized audiences after the sacrosanct years of the "holy trinity" (Isaac Chocrón, José Ignacio Cabrujas, Román Chalbaud). Throughout Central America there is a constant level of activity, notably higher in Costa Rica and Panama. Puerto Rico has shown increasing activity through veteran writers such as Myrna Casas as well as Roberto Ramos-Perea, whose political activism reflects the island's constant identity crisis. Following the collapse of the Soviet system, the situation in Cuba has evolved into greater openness and even frank criticism of the government, a position that would have been unthinkable during the earlier hard-line ideological years.

The cultural interplay with the islands has had a major impact on mainland U.S. Hispanic theater, especially along the eastern seaboard from New York to Florida. The Puerto Rican population in New York has been active for many years (for example, Miriam Colón's Puerto Rican Traveling Theatre), although many other groups promote Hispanic themes and values, such as the Spanish Repertory Theatre and INTAR. In Washington DC the Gala Theatre and Teatro de la Luna have maintained active programs, and naturally in Florida, the Cuban population has taken a lead in sponsoring Hispanic theater, especially the Teatro Avante, directed by Mario Ernesto Sánchez, with its annual festival. The other major component of Hispanic theater in the United States comes from the Chicano influence which emerged in the mid-1960s under the leadership of Luis Valdes in California and has since mushroomed, not just in the four or five states with traditionally large Mexican American populations, but to many cities across the country. With the United States now ranked as the fourth largest Spanish speaking country in the world, it is not surprising to find a wealth of theater activity to reflect these cultural influences.

These comments address the traditional theater but do not attempt to describe the myriad alternative forms of popular theater, street theater and performance activities, which are more difficult to document but ubiquitous throughout the Americas. As our definition of theater has become more expansive, everything from the cabaret theater of Jesusa Rodríguez and Astrid Hadad in Mexico City to the protest activities of the Madres de la Plaza de Mayo in Buenos Aires have become the subject of books and critical articles. A popular theater festival runs opposite the elite festival in Bogotá, for example, as a vehicle of alternative offerings. All five of Latin America's Nobel laureates were involved with theater, but the grassroots manifestations are equally exciting and valid.

Along with the proliferation of authors, directors, plays, and performances throughout Latin America and within the United States has come a corresponding increase in corollary activities. Pioneer theater historians from the 1960s who conceived of and documented a "Latin American theatre" (Carlos Solórzano, José Juan Arrom, Frank Dauster) have been followed by many others. Texts are published, sometimes anthologized in interesting combinations, while periodic journals disseminate texts, as well as critical and performance information about the field (*Apuntes, Conjunto, Diógenes, Tablas, Teatro XXI*, to name only a few). The two best known in the United States are *Gestos* and the *Latin American Theatre Review*. Theater festivals provide venues to see Latin American theater, often within an international context, in Manizales and Bogotá (Colombia), Buenos Aires, Bolivia, Central America, the Dominican Republic, Mexico, and Cádiz (Spain). Within the United States an itinerant academic conference features work on Latin American theater and encourages deeper study in the field, now recognized in academic circles in the United States as an important area of

Hispanic literature and performance culture. The past fifty years have witnessed a remarkable development in this area; the future of Latin American theater looks bright for years to come.

FURTHER READING

Bixler, Jacqueline. *Convention and Transgression: The Theatre of Emilio Carballido.* Lewisburg, Pennsylvania: Bucknell University Press, 1997.

Graham-Jones, Jean. *Exorcising History: Argentine Theatre under Dictatorship.* Lewisburg, Pennsylvania: Bucknell University Press, 2000.

Versenyi, Adam. *Theatre in Latin America: Religion, Politics and Culture from Cortes to the 1980's.* Cambridge University Press, 1993.

Polish Theater

Artur Grabowski

EARLY THEATER IN POLAND

From the Thirteenth to the Sixteenth Centuries

"Quem queritis?" (Who are you looking for?) Jesum Nasarenum (Jesus from Nazareth). With these words, half spoken, half sung, theater in Poland began, according to Zbigniew Raszewski. A dramatic script of the "visitation of the grave," known in all of medieval Europe, "was initially strictly ritual. It appeared once a year, on Easter morning, spoken in Latin with the words of the Gospel. It consituted part of the liturgy; therefore we call it liturgical drama." The contents of those micro-dramas, usually performed by seminarists or monks in churches, consisted basically of one scene: three women, all named Mary, visit Christ's grave and, having found it empty, talk to an Angel guarding it. He explains that the Lord has risen from the dead, so they should hurry back to the disciples to proclaim the completion of the foretold miracle.

The oldest records, found in Cracow, come from the thirteenth century. With time, scripts of the performances retelling individual episodes of Christ's final path evolved into longer passion plays and finally into complete mystery plays. Unfortunately, we do not know much about them; we can only boast of a few fragments preserved in the form of religious lyrics. The rest was destroyed by wars. Therefore, for a historian, medieval drama in Poland "began" at the time when Renaissance was already in full bloom. In 1580 *The Story of the Most Glorious Resurrection of Our Lord* came out in print. It was signed by a certain Michael from Wilkowiecko, but he was not necessarily the work's only author. The drama narrates events after the death of Jesus of Nazareth—beginning with the scene in which Jewish priests, called bishops here, hire guards to watch His grave (Good Friday), through Christ's descent to Hell and leading the sinners out (Easter Saturday) until Resurrection (Easter Sunday). It includes a fragment already known to us as the "visitation of the grave" and finally the appearance of the resurrected Teacher among his disciples at an inn in Emmaus. The whole piece consists of short scenes, alternately tragic, lyric, and comic in which a total of thirty-five characters appear. One has to admit that the author succeeds in creating convincing, deep, and individualized psycho-social portraits. For instance, the apostles themselves, ordinary and imperfect, are much like their audience. The figure of God's son towers above all that human weakness pictured here with forgiving understanding. He is a lonely hero serving his brothers and sisters, who are unable to understand him. But, when he breaks the bread for them at the table, he is among them again as their Earthly guide. The text was created probably in the fifteenth century, as an imitation of an even older original. It is, in fact, a detailed record of a completed performance and, at the same time, appears to be a "director's" version of a potential show. Drama here was clearly born of the stage and the stage was born of liturgy. Liturgy in turn resulted from imitation of history of Man, both real and mythical. In the twentieth century Jerzy Grotowski (1933–99), the famous director, employed that method again.

All through the sixteenth century medieval dramatic forms, the rather uninteresting examples of which would not fit into this broad essay, dominated the already secular city theater. It was almost professional, because it was created often for monetary gain by students and finally by itinerant actors, on temporary street stages. In the mean time, as if on the side, purely literary drama developed —not entirely religious anymore, but not yet entirely humanistic. Mikolaj Rej, an unusually prolific poet, who became the father of Polish literature, because he did not know Latin very well, left behind two brilliant dramatic pieces. In 1549 his *Life of Joseph* came out in print. It is a Protestant parody of the Catholic faith in the form of a grotesque morality play. Four years later he published *The Merchant,* another morality play in the vein of *Everyman,* but as if topsy turvy. The protagonist is an entrepreneur, who does not fall for the papist babble about sins and good deeds, but places all his trust in the Lord, achieves his goals with hard work, which ultimately earns him eternal rest. As with all of Rej's work, these "non-stage dialogues" are also characterized by colorful language, not devoid of peculiar charm, but as for the thoughts expressed in them, tolerance rather than critical analysis is in order.

Finally, the time was ripe for a masterpiece. Jan Kochanowski (1530–84), an erudite humanist, but above all the most eminent poet of the Polish Renaissance, created a tragedy based on a classical foundation, constructed perfectly as a column. The story is the author's reworking of an episode from the Trojan war but it is immediately clear that this is only a costume. The characters speak and act like

Poles through and through and the problems that occupy them stem from the current politics of the Polish-Lithuanian Commonwealth. The situation is as follows: the conceited and hot-headed Trojan prince Paris has abducted Helen, wife of the Greek king Menelaus. Now the emissaries sent by the betrayed husband come to demand the return of the beauty, threatening an armed intervention. Everybody conducts long negotiations, which are the main part of *The Dismissal of the Grecian Envoys,* but in vain. The Trojans refuse, in spite of the wise counsel of Alexander, their most valiant knight. The tragedy ends with an ominous prophecy of the soothsaying princess Cassandra, who predicts war. That ending, as if broken off, with a catastrophe approaching unavoidably but still not realized, suspended above the heads of those who are to decide the fate of the kingdom, is probably the most original idea of this play, which is poetically beautiful but dramatically rather boring. The audience, of course, knows what will follow and it is as if their knowledge is written into the script. The author is not concerned with creating suspense—quite the contrary: he intends to calmly analyze and clearly picture the political and psychological causes of the potential conflict.

That masterful political dialogue in verse, with choir songs and displays of rhetorical prowess in monologues, was staged in 1578 during a wedding celebration at the court of a wealthy aristocrat and influential politician, in the presence of the King himself. The poet clearly took into consideration the anticipated presence of the King and the political elite. It seems at times that (like a hundred years later at he court of Louis XIV) the characters speak directly to the audience, involving them in the discussion. One needs to remember here that the writer lived in the country in which a democratic parliament was the highest power and where kings were elected in universal vote. Therefore the audience would pass judgment in this case and the conclusion would be clear—it is not Fate who decides the fortunes of nations, but (contrary to classical tragedy) decisions resulting from the personal motives of every citizen, responsible to God and history. The nation (that is, the theatrical audience) will have to wait for another public debate of this kind until the eighteenth century.

Kochanowski's political tragedy was apparently so perfect in form and so momentous in its ideas that none of his contemporaries dared to write anything similar. Court theater, supported by rich magnates, developed soon enough, but its repertory consisted of moving images with lyrical couplets rather than serious dramatic works. At the turn of sixteenth century it was probably still difficult to make money in theater, since the only people able to make a living at writing and performing plays were Cracow students (expelled from the Academy) and seminarists (banished from the Seminary). They left behind a series of dialogues for stage, relating a story of a certain Albertus. With time, his name became a designation of a genre—short, grotesque comedies for a small cast, written in a language parodying plebeian-scholarly style and with rhymes like the clickety-clack of an old jade on cobblestone. Their central character is a curious combination of Don Quixote with a braggart soldier hailing back to Plautus. Salty dialogue and unsophisticated jokes make up the plot of those almost cabaret-like scenes. Their sole content is a process of turning a fool into a hero. A large number of those "variations on a theme" were created over several decades. It is this same spirit of play that gave rise to *Peasant into King* by Cezary Baryka. This comedy was performed in 1633 at an aristocratic court, but was clearly aimed at a less sophisticated audience. Bored soldiers find a drunk peasant asleep by the wayside and, having dressed him up in royal robes, ridicule him now with military subtlety. This subject, straight from carnival games, characterizes the dramatic imagination of the time, which still inhabits the space between church ritual and folk customs. The author tells his simple story with surprising realism and bluntness, in spite of the conventional motif, as if he were addressing a "popular" spectator, desiring confirmation of his social position. Baryka gives his audience a weapon that is sharp and easy to handle.

POLISH THEATER IN THE SEVENTEENTH AND EIGHTEENTH CENTURIES

Paradoxically, in spite of the lack of easily accessible theatrical spaces, in the seventeenth century drama became not so much popular as universal. Soon every Pole became a practicing theatergoer. A vast majority of noblemen's sons were educated in colleges run by orders of Jesuits and Piarists. There, Latin and Polish plays were performed as part of a rhetorical and moral model of education. The form and content of those plays were supposed to teach the skills of debating the most serious theological and social questions. They were so successful that this use of drama became second nature to the Polish audiences who, since then, have expected from drama serious ideological debate on stage. On the other hand, popular forms of folk theater connected to church holidays developed from a grassroots level. Among others, a form called *jaselka* (Nativity play) appeared. It was staged at Christmas and told, in fairy tale images, the miraculous circumstances of Jesus's birth. As time passed, the puppet theater version gained the most popularity. This medium, in combination with a serious religious subject, tempted the imagination of authors toward grotesque deformations. The popularity of those plays, usually enriched with digressions referring to current issues of the time, exceeded all expectations. Even today children in every school and kindergarten perform these *szopki*. In the country young people dress in costume and walk from house to house, national TV shows secular (that is, political) versions of the puppet theater with politicians in leading roles. The inherent tendency to theatricalize social life and a puppet theater with a revolving stage returned at the beginning of twentieth century in *The Wedding* by Wyspianski—the play by which the Poles define their identity.

Baroque Style

Baroque was the first "original" literary style in Poland. Therefore, in the eighteenth century it was still present in customs and poetry—but theater responded to change faster. That is because it was created not by landed literati scattered among manors but by a true intellectual elite, by thinkers clustered in the capital and receiving salaries. The professionals counted on applause, which they still described with restraint as "educational mission." That is why they created mostly comedies—not trivial though, but manifestly "activist," meaning not devoid of hope for political scandal. And so Franciszek Bohomolec (1720–84)—a cross between a courtier and a monk—appeared on the literary scene. As a professional writer and an editor of the most influential paper he was a frequent guest at the court of the last Polish king famous for his taste in sophisticated art and ladies of the same kind. Presumably, Bohomolec was able to find there an endless source of examples of the spectacular deterioration of mores. Being a Jesuit and a rhetoric teacher, he was able to transfer those with passion onto the stage in the shape of bitingly satirical comedies. In them, caricature characters once and again trip on moral prejudices and reveal the dirty lining of their fashionable garments under the eyes of an amused public, who obstinately refuse to identify with them. His works, like those of other dramatists of the time, usually owe their basic plot to popular French writers. The rest, though, is thoroughly familiar, so that the national vices pictured in them are, even today, easily recognizable by the Polish audience. It is indeed difficult to decide whether the accuracy and endurance of these comedies should be ascribed to the talents of the author or rather to the persistence of his subjects. A more modest official, but a much better writer, Franciszek Ksawery Zablocki (1754–1821) followed close in Bohomolec's footsteps. He also adapted French comedies to Polish customs. Additionally, he introduced a new type of character, one who is impossible to judge unequivocally. This forces the viewers, both in boxes and up in the gallery, to take a stand and to become aware of the moral standards he is bound by. *Fop-Suitor* (staged in 1781), an excellent comedy performed to this day, depicts a young playboy and flirt who, however, does not posses either the grain of cynicism of a true libertine or the philosophical grandiloquence of Don Juan. On the contrary, the young man, free from existential fears and social ambitions, is as happy in his imperfection as most of the young gentlemen in the rows. Truly, it is hard not to like him. For the first time in the history of the Polish theater, in this graceful farce the author was able to create an "audience's pet"—an ambiguous and extremely vivacious character who speaks the language of everyday conversation and, at the same time, brilliant verse.

In the mean time Polish drama left churches, palaces, and fairs and came out onto the streets buzzing with political debates. In 1765 the first public theater was created in Warsaw. It was a solid private institution, supported by state funds. Before its early demise, this theater was a living example of the privileged place that the theater occupies in Polish life. Plays created for the benefit of such a stage not only served as a mirror to the society, but also turned out to be an efficient tool of political intervention. Therefore, from that time until 1989 political censorship was a constant partner in their creation. The National Theater produced mostly comedies, even though nobody was in the mood for laughter. At that time Poland was slowly disappearing from the map, becoming absorbed into neighboring empires. In 1795 a real tragedy took place—and it did not play out on the stage. The final partition of Poland, which was reversed only in 1918, became the source of long lasting depression for the whole nation, but also an inexhaustible reservoir of tragic feelings. Only at this point would Polish drama prove to be a truly great and deeply original artistic achievement.

FOUR DRAMATISTS OF THE NINETEENTH CENTURY

This achievement happened thanks to four romantic poets. One of them was born in Lithuania, another in Ukraine, and all of them lived and created in Paris. The only theater where they were able to stage their plays was the imagination of their readers.[1] In return, they could count on an audience devoted more than ever before or after. In time, the romantic dramas created a common sphere of ideas as symbols for the Polish nation on a scale never seen before, encompassing all classes of society and lasting practically to this day.

Adam Mickiewicz

The first play in the long string of masterpieces was the most important. It has affected the imagination of Poles with the power comparable only to what *Faust* did to Germans. *Forefathers Eve* by Adam Mickiewicz (1798–1855) is, formally speaking, a three-part dramatic poem. It was written, in fact, as three separate dramas. It consists of over a dozen loosely connected scenes in which dreams and visions intertwine with realistic political debate, and ghosts from pagan rituals are barely distinguishable from allegorical figures from mystery and morality plays. Everything here is in confusion, beginning with numeration and chronology. The part called "the second" was created the earliest, in 1823. It contains a scenario of a proto-Slavic ritual summoning souls of the dead. Those spirits arrive straight from hell, the point being that those sinners (known in the neighborhood when alive) tell about their suffering in the other world and by that impart a moral lesson to the group of peasants gathered at the cemetery chapel at

midnight, on All Saints day. Those simple spells clearly predate the Christianiza-
tion of Lithuania and Byelorussia but the moral message is thoroughly Catholic.
The purpose of the ritual is to present a moral sensitivity still rooted in archaic
imagination, which will become the basis for the subsequent moral choices of
the protagonist, a young poet. His own spiritual adventure from the age of immaturity will play out in the following part, described by the author as "the fourth."
After the conclusion of the ritual, at the darkest hour before dawn, a zombie
appears in the chapel. It is the dead body of a certain Gustaw, with a bleeding
wound in his chest and a soul that comes to confess a grave sin—an excess of
love, unrequited. However, a kitschy romance is not the essence of his three-
hour monologue, but an accusation the intellectual aim at nothing less than literature. With pragmatic calculation it led him to false faith in untainted love.
He can be quite convincing, because this inspired monodrama is truly an explosion of poetic energy. This part, written in 1824, as the next part of recognition of
the mythical scenario which shaped innate Polish sensibility, seems to be in
intentional opposition to the preceding section—like paper drama versus true
(sacral) reality.

Thanks to the errors in his life Gustaw knows now what he needs to avoid. We
watch him in the last part, described as "the third" when he decides to change his
destiny. He is alone in a prison cell. In a dream he sees his Guardian Angel, who
foretells his future—first poetic genius, then martyrdom and, finally, a spiritual
leadership of the nation. After a while a young man, called here the Hermit, wakes
up and immediately writes on the wall these Latin words: "Gustavus obit, hic
natus Conradus" (Gustaw died, Konrad is born) and underneath the date:
November 1st. Only now the real tragedy will take place—his own as well as that
of his generation, his nation, and finally him as a new Adam, for whose immortality devils and angels will duel. In the following scene we meet Konrad's fellow
prisoners—his college friends imprisoned on a suspicion of subversive activities
against the authorities (that is, a local governor of the Russian emperor). While
the student-prisoners, all of them gentlemen from homes of nobility, talk, joke,
drink, and sing, they unwittingly depict for viewers the real political situation
and the social moods prevailing outside the prison walls. What is there? Repres-
sions, torture, exile, executions—in one word: the everyday life of a nation
condemned to death by a decision of cynical politicians of the occupying empire.
At some point (all motivations here are miraculous) Konrad begins to speak like a
possessed. He talks to God, even argues with Him and finally demands from Him
rule of his compatriots' souls. A poet is better suited to the role of a leader than
the Omnipotent, isn't he? Contrary to Him, the new Adam loves humanity with
a true love that is humanely compassionate and, even more, knows better how
to institute happiness on Earth, in place of a blatant massacre of the innocents
allowed by "the one who calls himself Love." Pride elevates the poet to such

heights of inspiration that a spectacular comparison of God to Tsar is at the tip of his tongue...but the Angel takes away his consciousness in time, making the devils, already sure of their prey, furious. Now, apparently smelling sulphur, his friends call an exorcist to the unconscious poet. He is a humble young Franciscan friar named Peter. He will be able to overcome the Evil one and even more, he will be given a competitive vision, flowing from his surrender to God. He will see Poland in an allegorical icon of the Crucified—a nation which will regain for Man his innate moral perfection (the archaic one) thanks to exceptional suffering and, by following in the footsteps of the resurrected Christ, will redeem the sins of demoralized Europe.

The main section of *Forefathers Eve,* the mythical scenario in beautiful verse (which the Poles will use like a looking glass), was created in Dresden, during several sleepless nights. Remorse was tormenting the poet who was stopped by his romances from giving up his life in the national uprising that started in November 1830 and was stomped out after a few months. Mickiewicz joined the insurgents, escaping from Russian persecution, in Paris. There, *Forefathers Eve—Part Three,* published immediately, gained him the rule of Polish souls.

Juliusz Slowacki

This was a rule that even Juliusz Slowacki (1809–49), his most eminent competitor, a much more modern artist and a more prolific playwright, would not be able to wrestle away from him. Slowacki was a precocious scholar and a loner. Initially a dandy, later almost a saint, he began to write plays in response to the work of his rival. In 1834 he published *Kordian,* a story of an indecisive melancholiac who wants to give his heart to somebody, but, since he hasn't come across anybody worthy of his egotistic love, he will give it to the nation. This enables him to overcome a personal crisis of adolescence. Before all this can take place, though, the author manifests a modern technique of psychological and symbolic playwriting. First, he creates a panoramic series of scenes from travels of the young master, and then a brilliant scene of a verbal duel between Tsar Alexander and his brother Constantine. Finally, like Konrad before him, now Kordian will have a vision. This time not in monastery cellars but at the top of Mont Blanc, the highest mountain in Europe. It is there that he receives (without special negotiations with the Lord) a detailed plan of action—which, unfortunately, fails. When at night the young man approaches the door of the Tsar's bedroom to carry out the death sentence, he is overcome by doubts, personified as Fear and Imagination.

The story of the would-be hero who, like Hamlet, was prevented by his own hypersensitivity from fulfilling a moral and political obligation, is merely the beginning of the whole series of magnificent tragedies by this romantic "Shakespeare of the Slavs." Indeed, Slowacki knew Elizabethan drama very well and borrowed from it freely, but, contrary to the opinions of hostile critics, his work was no ordinary imitation. Rather, it was a proof of the independence of the author, who had the courage to measure subjects with the great Englishman. Later, Slowacki would choose Calderón as his master and would learn from him how to create daring tragedies of religious passion, romantically set in baroque style. His extraordinary paraphrase of Calderón's tragedy *The Constant Prince* would become, in the hands of Grotowski, one of the most magnificent achievements in the history of theater. Among his later stage works the dramatic fairy tales seem to be particularly beautiful. They mix Slavic and Celtic mythologies and by that convincingly picture common sources of all of the Western religious imagination. For example, in the monumental characters and chorus songs of *Lilla Weneda* (1840) one can sense the solemnity of the "northern" variety of the classical drama. *Balladyna* (1839) is the opposite—an alluring fairy tale, bloody and lighthearted in its charming naiveté. The essence of both is the unique atmosphere of a land created from literary allusions, which lead the reader deep down to the foundations of a myth about that lost civilization, still lasting in our irresistible archetypes, rather than leave him in the surface of the poem. In 1842 Slowacki experienced a deep religious crisis and began to write feverishly. These works are tragedies of passion, written in baroque style and full of special effects. The plays take their inspiration from historical events at the beginning of eighteenth century, which enable Slowacki to express a mystical message. *Father Marek*, written in that period, takes place on a battlefield, among explosions and flames. It is no wonder that it talks about "apocalypse time," immediately before the final fall of Poland. Every line of that excellent, although hard to bear, drama seems to be shouted, so strong are the passions possessing the "Lucipheric" aristocrat and his demonic lover. They both are miraculously reborn under the influence of the Carmelite father who does not mince words, but is pure as Jesus himself. Similarly, *Salomea's Silver Dream* (1843) is woven around love and war. It has a beautiful female role, dominating the fantastic and dreamily implausible world of mysterious signs and prophecies. Should they be believed or not? The whole play, from the very beginning, is a colorful dream. It does end in an awakening, but within another dream.

The convincing psychology of Slowacki's modern characters makes Mickiewicz's medieval allegories seem to be behind by at least an epoch, in spite of a seeming resemblance. Slowacki, an existentialist well read in philosophy, found his inspiration in banal romances, while hanging out at Parisian theaters. In *Fantazy* (1841), published posthumously, Slowacki performs a synthesis of melodrama and tragedy in the salon of a provincial manor. But maybe I am wrong? Because it is an ironically cruel comedy! Ambivalence of meaning is the dominant feature of this extraordinary masterpiece of the monumental small-audience theater. It foretells the world in parentheses of twentieth century dramaturgy.

What begins as a simple romance and comedy of errors concludes with a ritual of genuine sacrifice of life on the altar of love. The protagonists give up their lives for the cause at one instant and immediately afterwards they ridicule self-sacrifice. Almost nihilistic farce blends with mystical pathos. The lovers use flirtatious dialogue to lead one another to religious ecstasies. One could think that in this drama the great romantic is pulling a rug from under his own feet, trying to deconstruct an era at its peak of development.

Zygmunt Krasinski

The history of Polish playwriting seems to whirl rather than flow. In 1833, on the way from Petersburg to Rome, a twenty-one year old count Zygmunt Krasinski (1812–59) wrote a masterpiece on a world scale—*The Undivine Comedy*. He succeeded only once. This heir of one of the most magnificent aristocratic families of Europe saw a bloody panorama of a social revolution through the reflection of his own frightened face in the coach window. His dramatic vision turned out to be a metaphysical and political autobiography. The play, written in rhythmic prose, falls into two halves and each of those into halves again. This is how one could describe a relationship between the four parts, each of which is preceded by something like an overture, introducing the subject of the following realistic events in a symbolic image. The subject matter is as much domestic as cosmic.

A certain twenty-one year old aristocrat has recently married a maiden from his own sphere. Since he just had a son, his whole family gathered in the cozy palace for the christening of the little boy. And maybe they would live happily ever after, if the head of the household were not an unfulfilled poet, clearly frustrated with the family idyll. The young man succumbs to a beautiful and treacherous temptress— art. The abandoned wife will end in a psychiatric hospital and the child will inherit his father's sensitivity. It will make him unable to see the reality, but instead will lead him to schizophrenic visions. What is one to do? One needs to grab hold of something true, or put an end to one's life. Luckily a real opportunity do die with dignity arises—a revolution, almost a communist one. Its inevitable victory is certain—not because the simple people are morally right, but because the ruling class is none other than our Count Henryk, not a knight, but a long falling decadent nihilist. In part three we see him as a commander of the last troop of the conservative forces, defending the castle of the Holy Trinity. Soon, he will be called to negotiate capitulation with the leader of the progressive forces, named Pankracy. In disguise, he walks among fires, through the enemy encampment, talking to the people, who do not pretend to be anything other than a lustful body of a fallen civilization that has filled its empty skull. The following verbal duel between the two gods of humanity should be counted among the greatest political debates of the nascent modern democracy. In the end both opponents commit suicide (but, it is real?) facing the vision of Christ-Pantocrator: one because he lost his past, which sustained him with illusions, as imagination sustains a poet and the other because he created a future which will be unlivable, like a totalitarian reality of a populist state. Each encountered nothingness face to face. Both find it in themselves, in the very essence of their lonely humanity, lacking the Other. Krasinski says clearly: Europe is headed towards barbarism. I know, because I am the essence of the Western culture.

Soon after, the demise of civilization, and not a national revolt, became a dominant theme of the Polish dramaturgy. In the twentieth century it brought forth an equally singular masterpiece by Stanislawa Przybyszewska, *The Danton Case* (1929), beautifully filmed by Andrzej Wajda.

Cyprian Norwid

The last of the great Polish romantics, maybe even a post-romantic, Cyprian Norwid (1821–83) spent most of his life as an entirely unappreciated poet. He was rediscovered decades after his death and immediately became a patron saint of avant-garde poetry. Norwid, who was a descendant of a royal family on his mother's side, spent his days in utter poverty among the Parisian homeless and evenings in the drawing rooms of cosmopolitan aristocracy. He was invited there probably only to be ridiculed. No wonder then that the oeuvre of this brilliant artist (he was also a draftsman) and thinker is characterized by biting social irony and ability for deep psychological analysis.

As a dramatist, he probably intended more than he was able to accomplish. He left behind two dramatic poems, of great literary beauty, but not very theatrical, in the style of medieval chivalric epics. *Wanda* (1851), called a "mystery," most likely due to the mysterious images of the play, is conceived of as a great outdoor show and *Krakus* (1848), which its author described as "rhapsody," in reality resembles a fairy tale about miracles witnessed by two brother knights lost in the woods. The archaic charm of those legends stems from their genuine depth. Their author was interested in the psychology of heroism and also in something that could be called a spiritual archeology of Christianity. His short salon comedies are more theatrical in form. They are, however, not very funny, just painfully sarcastic. The main character is usually an oversensitive young man, of exceptional moral purity, rare in that era of universal hypocrisy. Norwid's ambition is to show the subtlest nuances of the protagonist's psyche as an honest "actor" in the comedy of good manners. The audience should see stark truth, on the scale of the classical tragedy, taking place "in the wings" of ostensibly conventional conversation, in the words uttered in passing, in small and accidental gestures. This gives us a foretaste of comedic writing in the style of Muset and Eliot. Unfortunately, the poet's sensitivity to language subtleties in his virtuosi dialogue in verse, usually composed of ellipsis and symbolic associations, results in a subjectivity of meaning that makes it difficult to react to the words without conducting an analysis first. It is a rare theatergoer who is able to perform one. Norwid reached the height of his dramatic abilities in *The Ring of a Grand Lady* (1872). It is a three act play, resembling, by its psychological and symbolic aura, Ibsen's dramas. The main character is a poor poet, a resident of a wealthy family. One evening, during a game of a "hidden ring" the jewel is really lost. Who could have stolen it, if not he, the only pauper in this company? The youth is accused. Not directly, but by snide allusions—all this for the entertainment of the soulless members of the high society. The playwright also included in the main text author's commentary, giving detailed descriptions of gestures and even of the internal life of the characters. This enables the audience to know about the characters more than they know about each other. In his numerous theoretical utterances Norwid called that type of drama "white tragedy," where crimes are committed not by use of sharp objects, but words sharp as needles and the victim is not even able to die in peace—he will have to live, humiliated, among his tormentors.

It seems then that what is most important here is consciously silent so that it can more clearly express itself. Norwid's plays are based on his biography, but their edge is aimed at the deeply demoralized elites of the modern plutocratic society, in that early phase of its development, in which it was still unacceptable for "members of society" to admit openly that the only morality they adhered to was the "scientifically" proven biological struggle for survival. But the author, a contemporary of Marx and Darwin, does not succumb to the belief that the individual is determined by uncontrollable forces of nature. He believes that a human being remains metaphysically free and entirely responsible for the deeds he performs in the name of the values he believes in. That is why Norwid's anthropological thinking leads directly from the humanistic tragedy of Kochanowski toward the moralistic prose of Joseph Conrad and the ethics of Karol Wojtyla.

COMEDY IN THE NINETEENTH AND EARLY TWENTIETH CENTURY

The beginning of the nineteenth century is the time immediately after the loss of Polish independence and the birth of a long lasting national depression. One could hardly expect comedic talent to bloom in that era. The only outstanding comedy writer of the time was Count Aleksander Fredro (1793–1876). In his youth he was a swashbuckling officer in the Napoleonic army. After his return he settled near Lvov and began a life of a landed writer. In over a dozen years he created a model and a canon of the genre which would last for over a century. The characters he created became part and parcel of the popular culture and fragments of his brilliant dialogues were assimilated into everyday language.

He began with virtuosi situation comedies. Their fast action, consisting of small episodes and straightforward characters, makes us laugh like modern burlesque. In 1820 he created a "love quadrangle" entitled *Husband and Wife.* The comedy, produced in the Lvov city theater, gained Fredro popularity in the eyes of the bourgeois audience and infamy under the pen of shocked patriot-romanticists, who could not forgive the former officer for such banal subject matter in such tragic times. But the divorce farce in which the "masters" mingle with the servants in purely erotic liaisons ends not with a happy ending, as comedy should, but, "like in real life," in general distaste and a feeling of moral defeat. The comedies of our Count, even though they have you in stitches, are lined with melancholy, sarcasm, and later even misanthropy. Fredro achieved mastery in the portraiture of human types, due to skillful combination of stereotype with realism. This allowed him to surround each individual character with his or her own world of social habits, resulting in a sense that the whole Polish society is on stage, as well as, (as it turned out with time) "society" as such, an essence of human relationships. In *Mr. Jowialski* (1832) a farce about a shrewd man of letters unexpectedly turns into a caricature of that human tendency to build systems, in which the only goal is domination of all over one. The protagonist of *Maiden Vows or Magnetism of the Heart* (1827) is related to *Fop Suitor,* whom we have already met. Here he is enriched with qualities of a romantic lover, a grotesque version of Gustaw from *Forefathers Eve—Part Four.* The wonderfully simple plot of this comedy consists of a subterfuge the protagonist uses to test the true feelings of his beloved. To that end he pretends to be a wounded insurgent and asks her to write a letter from him to his imaginary fiancée. And so the "magnetism of the heart" of the tender maiden draws out tender feelings towards the youth, who takes advantage of the situation with alacrity. The sweet lyricism of this intimate comedy is intermingled with a bitter derision of the feelings which the oversensitive poets from Paris tried to impart to the unfeeling provincial landowners.

But Fredro is not cynical and devoid of patriotic exaltation. He is, however, a sober realist, with a dose of conservative pessimism. In his most famous comedy, *Vengeance* (1834), he built Poland in miniature, based on the old Shakespearean motif of a family feud. Here, two old gentlemen for years have been quarreling about the wall which separates them inseparably. In the characters of those two gentlemen one can most clearly distinguish Fredro's principle of colliding whole worlds. One is a former soldier, pig-headed and thoughtlessly impulsive; the other is a typical nouveau riche, hardened and methodically cruel. When one waives his shotgun around, the other threatens a lawsuit. Both are so cowardly that all they make is wind. Under their wing the youth suffer separation and, tired of their own sentimentality, ridicule the old. Among them we see probably the most delicious character in all of Polish drama—a certain Papkin. He is a figure in part from *commedia dell'arte,* in part from seventeenth century "albertus": a braggart soldier. And maybe there would be nothing unusual in this type of character, if not for the fact that at this point in history it had become a cruel caricature of the Polish heroism. Therefore *Vengeance* soon became not only the most popular comedy, but also a model—a fixed reference point for future comedic works, as Mickiewicz's *Forefathers Eve* was in tragedy.

And there were a lot of opportunities to reflect upon this model, because all through the second half of the nineteenth century almost only comedies were written. In any case, drama in this period was inferior to novels and its main source, which was poetic imagination, almost ran dry under the influence of the enlightened ideas of the pragmatic generation of realists. Theater developed, but in the form of paid entertainment for middle class, when the audience dictates the terms. Plays, mostly comedies of manners, become mass produced, but one would be hard pressed to pick a master in that crowd. There are rather individual successes. For example *Mrs. Dulska's Morality* (1907) by Gabriela Zapolska (1857–1921) remains commonly known until this day. Zapolska was a prolific second-rate writer, who came up with several better plays in the style of social-erotic satire, with a background of naturalistic anthropology, possibly due to her experiences as a professional actress. Her dramatic achievement gained such popularity that "dulszczyzna" (just like Grundyism) entered the Polish language as a term describing moral hypocrisy resulting not so much from cynicism as from ordinary stupidity. To tell the truth, realism has never been a strong point of Polish literature. More so, Jan August Kisielewski (1876–1918), an author who rapidly achieved success to suddenly vanish into oblivion, deserves our attention. Before he became mentally ill, he managed to write two excellent plays: *In the Net* (1897) and *Caricatures* (1898), both successfully produced in 1899. They talk about the troubles of unruly youth. Those long dramas consist almost solely of family quarrels. That allows directors, at least those equipped with scissors, to make multiple uses of the material. One can see clearly that the text was written "for theater," with the author's commentary blown up to the size of narration. What is here more interesting than the anecdote is the "situation" and its emotional and moral consequences. Adolf Nowaczynski (1876–1944) was a much luckier contemporary of Kisielewski. He became initially famous as an aggressive newspaper columnist and a ruthless satirist. His impetuous temperament bore fruit in the form of many excellent, well crafted and not shallow plays, which he delivered for 30 years to the city theater in Cracow. This city's society became the subject of the author's attacks and—by the same token—a source of his inspiration. Cracow, one of the most beautiful cities of Central Europe, the seat of a medieval university and rich in literary traditions, was maintaining that incurably high opinion of itself as the spiritual capital of the country, while a the same time displaying characteristics typical of a parochial small town. In his comedies, such as *New Athens* (1913) or *The Spring of Nations in the Quiet Corner* (1929), the author mercilessly derides the presumptuous professors of the Academy and shreds to pieces the snobbish fellow artists assuming poetic poses. In his fervor he sometimes crosses the line of satire and enters the domain of lampoon but one built on language virtuosity, reminiscent of the ribald humor of Rabelais.

In those times Cracow was where all was happening. The best way to get to know the artistic and at the same time pretentious climate of that Austrian town sitting in the shadow of a Renaissance castle was to visit *The Little Green Balloon* cabaret. In fact, it was a literary café, which played host to a small theater, established in 1905. Local literati performed there, either in person or manipulating puppets. The repertoire of the cabaret consisted of songs as satirical sketches, giving a commentary on current major political events as well as city gossip. Its theatrical form harked back to *szopka* medieval Nativity plays. Those characters were well suited to being adapted to "social roles" and given the features of real and commonly known personages. In this way the grotesque crèche became at the same time mythical and topical.

STANISLAW WYSPIANSKI

In this intellectual atmosphere Stanislaw Wyspianski (1869–1907)—the greatest Polish artist of the stage—grew up. Being a son of a painter he initially followed in his father's footsteps, creating impressive works of visual art: stained glass windows, paintings, applied art objects. After a period of study and travel and several years spent in Paris he came back to his unloved Cracow, where he found an unending source of inspiration. His work opened an epoch of entirely new dramaturgy, which flows from theater itself. Since the beginning of his artistic career Wyspianski was also an active director, stage-designer, theoretician of theater, and a writer possessing not only stage experience, but even more, the imagination of a man who sees theater in everything. He wrote fast, but each play is an original form, simple verse filled with stylized language. In the course of his short life plagued by illness, he created over a dozen great plays, which became turning points in the history of Polish literature. By uniting romantic poetic drama with concepts of "The Great Reform" he planted the seeds of the triumph of the Polish theater in the twentieth century.

He began with plays from the lives of peasants, written in the style of symbolic realism. *The Curse* (1898) and *Judges* (1899) are constructed so perfectly and at the same time so simply that one immediately senses the noble solemnity of a Greek tragedy. Wyspianski's first works are permeated with a pessimistic view of man as overpowered by a force greater that he. Even if that power turns out to be morally valuable, still it does degrade humanity, by depriving it of free will. His two early mythological dramas, *Meleager* (1899) and *Protesilas and Leodamia* (1899) address the same issue. In the latter one he creates an unusual female role.

The heroine does not leave the stage all through the play, so that we watch almost a monodrama. Her monologue is an unceasing lamentation over the absurdity, from her point of view, of her lover's death while, from his point of view, he died for his homeland, with joy and in glory. The subject of the play is not conflicting passions or mutually exclusive values. It is the freedom of an individual limited by the freedom of another. Freedom soon became the problem around which all thoughts of this talented dramatist began to revolve. Wyspianski was able to elevate the question of the political enslavement of his nation to the level of a great existential metaphor. According to this deeply religious Catholic, man is endowed with free will (that is, with creative activity). However, that free will becomes "bound" by our common tendency to spiritual sloth. As a result, the ambitious project of humanity becomes degraded and turns into passive sterility or self-destruction. Some people fabricate then a defensive idea of sacrificing one's life in the name of a beautiful death. Wyspianski recognized this national tendency in himself and began to overcome it. In 1901 he wrote *The Wedding*. Its premiere, a month after the play was finished, has been considered the greatest event in the history of Polish theater.

And it all started by accident. The poet was invited to the wedding of a friend, also a poet. He, like Wyspianski himself, succumbed to the trend of intelligentsia fraternizing with peasants and decided to marry a peasant girl. The wedding took place in a village by Cracow; the invited guests were "masters" from the city, artists, and peasant neighbors. The playwright employed here for the first time his most fruitful creative method—he drew contents out of symbolic treatment of form. In the dancing guests he saw "the whole nation," the house looked a lot like a crèche, which allowed him to connect the Polish "shepherds" with a metaphysical idea of renewal. The first act consists of a few dozen brilliant, short dialogues, very funny because of the clash between the alien spheres. The characters show up and disappear like puppets on a revolving scene. In the second act the innocent bride and the decadent poet, just for fun, invite a scarecrow to come inside. Since this is an enchanted night, their wish is unexpectedly granted. From then on (with all the guests already intoxicated) several of the most important guests begin to see "what's in their soul"—that is, fantastic figures (called *dramatis personae*) from ancient times of imperial Poland reproaching them for their sins, especially the sin of omission. Finally a spirit of Wernyhora appears, like a Slavic Tiresias, who calls that finally united nation to "act." It is about a communal act of liberation, but also about activity of the individual. It turns out that after years of oppression military might is no longer the main threat for the oppressed. Now it is the internal inability to act, attrition of the will to fight, fear of freedom. The final dance in the enchanted circle, to the sounds of monotonous music, is an expressive metaphor of impotence. The wedding of a poet and a peasant girl really took place. It was a big event in the city. At the premiere, the protagonists were watching themselves on stage; they attended, of course. At every performance we, the audience, are also guests at this wedding where the real nation weds its fantastic projection. Not for a moment does the music die down; the dancers do not stop; fantastic images and real life scenes keep rolling in front of our eyes like in a kaleidoscope. Wagneria "Gesamstkunstwerk" and the monumental theater of Gordon Craig has been realized here magnificently and in full; café cabaret joined a temple of art, current commentary met great metaphor. Thus the idea of *teatrum mundi,* recorded in the romantic drama, became fulfilled.

No wonder that in the wake of the success of *The Wedding* the director of the city theater enlisted Wyspianski to direct Mickiewicz's *Forefathers Eve.* It was the first full staging of that text so important to the Poles. The playwright performed his task very well. During his work on *Forefathers Eve* he found inspiration for his next masterpiece, which would be produced several months later. He again derived form from a true event and in that form he recognized a metaphor, the development of which constitutes the plot of the play. *Deliverance* (1902) takes place during rehearsals. That rehearsal, in that theater. Its protagonist cannot be anyone else but the hero of that drama. The actor portraying Konrad is at times himself, at times his character and at times the director and the author (that is, Wyspianski/Mickiewicz). In fact, the process of defining one's own identity seems to constitute the story line of this unusual drama about Every-Pole. When the protagonist struggles with his own ambition and powerlessness, when he leads a dispute with 22 masks trying to take away his face, when he tries to free himself from the fictional world of literature and step out of the artificial space of theater—what is he looking for? Deliverance. The goal of each fight for freedom, the author tells his fellow Poles, is above all liberating one's true self, free of falsehood. This play about creating a work of art tries to separate creative action from creating illusion. A modernist, unlike a romantic, does not wait for an inspiration which will possess him, but searches for a source of authenticity in the super- and subconscious. At this point in his career, Wyspianski was at the height of creative tension. He began work on the most ambitious, in his own estimation, work. *November Night* (1903) relates directly to the 1830 Insurrection, which for Wyspianski's contemporaries was a painful wound but already a myth. The action takes place, as an exception, in Warsaw, in one of its beautiful parks, filled with classicist architecture and white sculptures of Greek gods. The author's imagination immediately saw Greece here and turned the works of art into protagonists of the play. On that November night when the insurrection started, goddess Demeter brings her marble daughter Persephone into the underworld, so that she may, as it happens every year, spend the winter dying in the arms of Hades, who will send her, renewed, back to Earth in the spring. That ritual of initiation, a scenario of an Eleusian myth and a peculiar liturgy of death and resurrection are taking place simultaneously with the earthly plot, consisting of the events of that night "of triumph and death," mainly songs and war cries of the insurgents. Action shifts to the city; the fire of insurrection spreads to various spots in Warsaw that serve as a backdrop and finally returns to the park, where there is a beautiful, intimate theater in the style of a Hellenic temple. That night the future leaders of the uprising are watching from the boxes.

A city and works of art came to life again in his next drama, *Acropolis* (1904). Here, characters from Greek myths and biblical stories come down from tapestries hanging in the cathedral of the royal castle built on a hill (hence Acropolis) overlooking the city of Cracow. They are joined by sculptures from sarcophagi. All this takes place on the night of Resurrection. Paris and Helen cease to be lifeless patterns on a cloth; they love one another passionately and sensuously, because love is the life-giving force. The image of Jacob's dream with angels climbing up the ladder to heaven comes into life by the power of faith. Finally, the first ray of light comes in through a stained glass window, bringing a message of immortality—a shared message from Greece, Jerusalem, and Cracow. More than half a century later director Grotowski saw in it a metaphor of a death camp. In his *Acropolis* prisoners themselves build the hill—this time a Golgotha. The myths of Western civilization will turn into ashes and purify in the crematoria. Wyspianski also wrote a series of dramas based on motifs from medieval chronicles, as if this time he wanted to bring archaeology to life. His final work was a return to a Greek myth. *The Return of Odysseus* (1906) was a portrait of soldier who cannot bear the blood on his hands, rather than of a shrewd hero from Troy. Much later, during the Nazi occupation, Tadeusz Kantor—a painter, scenographer, and director—chose that play to start building his vision of the monumental "theater of death."

Wyspianski's vision of theater has been influential, but at the same time he was too original to have disciples and followers. We see some similarity to Wyspianski's monumental symbolism in the work of Tadeusz Micinski (1873–1918). An esoteric poet and an occultist philosopher, he was fascinated with Russia and believed in mystical renewal of the world through a bloody revolution (which killed him). He left behind several too-long dramatic poems, consisting of a series of too-vast moving images, filled with too many symbols, decoding which requires one to become familiar with his ungraspable quasi-religious system. This probably was the reason there were very few brave ones who decided to dive into that ocean of symbols, in spite of indisputable admiration for Micinski's ambitious imagination, straddling German expressionism and Russian symbolism. Karol Hubert Rostworowski (1877–1938), another count-dramatist, is more interesting theatrically but philosophically less extravagant. He began with symbolic legends in verse, composed with unusual precision, making use of musical forms. The title character of *Juda of Carioth* (1913) is a shopkeeper; blinded with material things he did not quite raise to the level of spiritual mission of Christ's disciple. The psychological realism in the portraiture of a contemporary little man, perfectly balanced with a symbolic image of magnanimous people from an epoch long gone and a masterful orchestration of collective scenes justify a little stiffness of the verse in dialogues. *Caius Cesar Caligula* (1917) was even more technically ambitious. It resulted from the same aristocratic contempt for base feelings. Here, the author gives an almost a virtuosic display of his compositional skills, creates dialogue fugues and tense suspensions of action and recurring motifs. The choir functions like a rhythm section and the monologues resemble concert solos. Further development of the author's parabolic imagination resulted in excessive trust in the expressive power of allegory. The ideologically motivated universality of the message exceeded the limits of human sensitivity. *Surprise* (1928) turned out to be Rostworowski's next success. It grew out of fascination with the peasant tragedies of Wyspianski and is equally classical in spirit. That ascetic story of domestic crime holds one in suspense until the very end. One feels a growing unease, as if a catastrophe has happened in the audience before it takes place on stage.

TWENTIETH CENTURY POLISH DRAMATISTS

At that time the great poetic drama was an established and model form of Polish playwriting. But in the modernist period literature is not isolated anymore in the confines of a single language. Plays by two authors writing both in Polish and German became popular, not only within Polish borders. The first of those writers, Stanislaw Przybyszewski (1868–1927), the author of over a dozen expressionist-symbolic dramas, was first a friend of Strindberg, then his sexual rival. The incomprehensible popularity of his dramas at that time equals the deserved oblivion in which they are now. Their erotic intrigues almost always take place in a bourgeois home, all protagonists have "flames in their eyes" and every word reveals their "naked souls" in equally scantily clothed bodies. Before the unfaithful wife, picturesquely shot by the husband who is madly in love with her, dies in the arms of her remorseful lover, all of them will have enough time to discuss a system of metaphysics based on unassailable foundation of esoteric psychoanalysis. One is better off going to plays by Tadeusz Rittner (1873–1921). He was the author of psychological portraits of rebels (but only verbal) against life in a world devoid of any other material ambitions. In them he was able to create an atmosphere of reflection and an aura of subtle irony with the use of understatement, allusions, and unobtrusive symbols. His family dramas, particularly *In a Little House* (1904), *Silly Jack* (1910), *Summer* (1912), and *Wolves of the Night* (1916) turn into melancholy comedies about a society which successfully gags outstanding individuals, providing them with comfortable spots in the crowd with the use of dialogues, felicitously devoid of expressive tension. The value of those works have been proven in a surprising way—they were a starting point for a creative dissent.

At this point, unnoticed, another genius arrived—Stanislaw Ignacy Witkiewicz (1885–1939). A painter, playwright, novelist, art theoretician, and philosopher, Witkiewicz was one of the most colorful figures in the history of European avant-garde art. The stature of Witkacy (his self-designated name) would eventually be comparable to that of Wyspianski's, but his contemporaries were so successfully able to marginalize the work of this man who during his lifetime was treated like a harmless lunatic, that it was not until twenty years after his death that his dramas found their way onto the stage.[2] But since then, they have been performed every day in one of the theaters of the world.

His dramatic work is an integral part of Witkacy's whole philosophical system. It consists of several basic concepts. The "mystery of existence" reigns above all. It is revealed to a sensitive individual as a "sense of strangeness" of what that "specific being" undergoes and what he desires. It is conscious, but the character does not yet understand the "unity in multiplicity" that is his finite separateness and at the same time coexistence with others. Witkiewicz considered the ability to personally experience the "metaphysical sentiment" as the essential characteristic of humanity. This ability is disappearing in a world headed towards universal unification and mechanization of life. After the loss of religion, philosophy isolating itself from metaphysics, and the exchange of political ambitions into a technique for providing comfort and security, only art still has a chance to bring out humanity in man.

In Witkacy's thinking, theater would be the main tool for this task. Theater has a heritage of religious rite and social ritual but would be acting upon the audience with the "pure form" of aesthetics. That "pure form" dominated Witkacy's thinking about drama. It would have to be devoid of any content that would not result from the sheer composition of stage effects. How to achieve this? Easy. It is enough to pick a human type out of pop culture, infuse it with "strangeness" through caricatural deformation and assign it a task of achieving "metaphysical sentiment." The protagonist starts to strain, tense up, provoke, break the norms, until a strange biography of "individual being," something unique and, at the same time, extremely common, results. The form of such a performance would be precisely necessary as an obsessive conspiracy theory, and the contents absolutely free (that is, psychologically and socially unmotivated). The poetics of the grotesque and the absurd appears to be an obvious choice here.

Most often in his plays a character of a spiritually insatiable intellectual appears as an adventurer in the style of an "artist of life" surrounded by "demonic women." One feature unites them—a degeneration of the social type they represent. As Daniel Gerould, an American scholar, wrote, here everything is past and wasted, the present escapes experience and there will be no future at all. Why? Because only individuals can be "alive" but the world is clearly intent on producing mechanically happy creatures, subject to universal control of "quasi-humans," engineered with a biotechnological faith in the populist rule of the people. That, in short, would be Witkacy's anarchistic-aristocratic worldview. He did not want to wait for the fulfillment of the prophecy and took his own life at the news of the pact between communist and fascist populism, intended to facilitate another partition of Poland, the land of incorrigible individualists.

His last and most "normal" play, *Shoemakers* (1935), is a vivid image of those anxieties, not unlike *The Undivine Comedy*. It presents, in fast forward, the history of revolutionary upheavals affecting Western democracy, afraid of individualism and metaphysics and headed toward a mass society of perfect pragmatists. The shoemakers (that is, "the lowest") assume power in various incarnations: national socialism, people's socialism, and finally as humanoid robots (that is, technocrats devoid of any spiritual needs). They do not have any goals anymore, nor desires. They enjoy the very mechanism of controlling the bestially happy citizens. In his play *The Mother* (1924) Witkiewicz most likely parodies himself as a serious philosopher. Here, a forty year old brilliant young man, who has lived for years at his mom's expense, decides to grow up and build a career for himself in order to spread his noble, Witkacy-like social ideal. However, in the utterly demoralized world, those achieve more who are bigger scoundrels. So then his illustrious career as a spy and drug-addict terminates in a doorless and windowless room (a mother's womb?) into which enter (from where?) executioners (that is, the society of morally healthy idiots) who severely punish him for breaking the noble norms of mediocrity. All in all Witkacy's dramas are very difficult to outline. Their plots are as complicated as they are irrelevant. They are full of surprising and absurd events as if from a dream or a narcotic trance. Politics, eroticism, and art make an appearance in every play, but those are most clearly substitute actions. The sole aim is to intensify experiences up to the level of the desired "strangeness of being." We watch the most fantastic spaces, we travel in time form the Middle Ages to the future, but it is enough to close our eyes and listen to imagine oneself in a literary café, full of passionately philosophizing intellectuals. They are unable to just be, all they are able to do is to act out themselves imagined. They are aware of it, but the very awareness of the pretense blocks the authenticity of their experiences. That is what engenders the atmosphere of grotesque aggression, which will dominate Witkiewicz's most famous plays: *The Madman and the Nun, The New Deliverance, In A Small Country House, The Water Hen, The Belzebub Sonata,* and *The Cuttlefish*. That intentional oddity, ostentatious theatricalization, and the unending grotesque are the reasons why all of the twenty-something preserved plays seem to constitute such "unity in multiplicity," so much so that the protagonists could easily move around between dramas, without particular surprises. They must know one another anyway; they all come from the same milieu of degenerate almost-artists and post-artists, they speak the same language, proclaim the same views, and behave equally perversely. And all of it so they can, with suicidal desperation, discredit the highest values—values in which they are unable to believe any longer but for which they still long, surprisingly genuinely. But, is it not what performers conducting a ritual do? One can shuffle at will individual layers of the whole structure, with varying trust to each one of them. What happens on stage does not attempt to "imitate" anyone. It is the imitating that is happening under the eyes of the audience. Witkiewicz was read and produced as late as in the 1960s, thanks in part to Tadeusz Kantor, the creator of Cricot 2 theater and a direct disciple of the master. But the marginalization of the great lawgiver of the avant-garde was only the case as far as his public presence is concerned. His influence appeared later and with enormous power.

As a matter of fact, he had many admirers among young writers. One of them was Witold Gombrowicz (1904–69), the creator of "metatheatrical dramaturgy," who left behind only three plays, and each of them a masterpiece. He spent his aristocratic and artistic youth in Warsaw coffee houses, his adult years barely getting by in Buenos Aires, and his short old age as a star of European literature in France. By writing solely about himself he was able to create three dramas, four short novels, and a three-volume *Diary*. He hated theater, but his whole vision of the world, artistically and philosophically outlined, was full of theatrical metaphors: mask, role, pretending and authenticity, dialogue, and interpersonal play. He debuted with *Ivone, Princess of Burgundy* (1936), a parody of a court play. Here, a prince decides, purely for provocation, to marry the maiden considered the ugliest and stupidest in the kingdom. The girl is a perfectly passive dummy and hardly ever speaks. That turns out to be dangerous, because it will require everyone to "take a stand" in the face of nothing. This results in a truly amusing tragicomedy about humanity, suffering in a stiff corset of forms, but at the same time unable to exist outside of them, in the space of chaotic naked instincts which lead to crime. Immediately following the great crime of war, at "mid-life" Gombrowicz published a work about a crisis—a personal and European one— *The Marriage* (1946). The drama presents a story of creating a drama out of life, similar to *The Undivine Comedy* or *Deliverance*. It also directly refers to *Forefathers Eve* and indirectly to *Hamlet* and *Faust*. All of this is against the backdrop of a medieval morality play in the style of *Everyman*, based in form on a sacrificial liturgy. Is this a whole history of theater in one play? Or is it rather a big metaphor of theater as "form" (Gombrowicz's favorite philosophical term) of human relationships, but also a relation of the man with himself and maybe even with God, even if he is already dead? For many this represented the highest and at the same time final achievement of playwriting.

The Marriage is a dream of the protagonist, who dreams he has returned home from the war. His home, however, looks like a second class inn, his parents resemble a couple of brutal idiots and his old time fiancée looks like a whore. All that was holy to him is desecrated. But maybe not, since it is just a dream? Therefore the protagonist (a former knight) would like to wake up (but how does he know he is dreaming?). He decides to "test" (like Hamlet) what is really real and what is only a theatrical mystification of the social norms of mutual deceit, a world turned upside down, like in a carnival. He provokes, arranges situations, pretends, and demystifies—he direct life in hopes that in theater he will find (as in Witkiewicz) an experience of mystical certainty of his own existence. While doing it he climbs up the ladder, appoints his father as king, by the same token (by law of pure form) he finds himself a prince. From there it is just a step to a palace coup and then toward Him who anoints with power. By signing a peculiar pact with the powers "outside the human realm" (*Faust*) he demands the power of Creator (Mickiewicz's Konrad) who, by the power of his (Modern Man) individuality will rule the forces of creation flowing from the source of absolute freedom (Wyspianski's Konrad). In the finale, seeing that he is finished in his impotence (Krasinski's Count Henry) he forces his best friend, his innocent alter ego, to commit suicide, to sacrifice a Man (liturgy) on the altar of the impossible Humanity. The protagonist (bearing a universally royal name Henry) is constantly conducting, through Hamletic monologues, an ideological debate with Christianity and humanism, the two allegories of mysterious forces eliciting a confession of his perverse sins from the soul (*Everyman*) of a Western man. Finally Gombrowicz wrote *Operetta* (1965). Its old-fashioned form of musical theater became a metaphor of a ridiculous political-philosophical debate about fashion, about something that never existed—our civilization.

Which has just dramatically come to an end? The war divides the dramaturgy of Jerzy Szaniawski (1886–1970) into two parts. The first part, which was the time of his greatest triumphs, and not only on the Polish stage, contains dramas with realistic plots, with conceptual and somewhat melodramatic conflicts. They have an aura of melancholy and are full of symbolic details, gently introducing the audience to the world of poetic suggestions and subtle humor. Works such as *The Sailor* (1925), *Attorney and Roses* (1929), *Pianoforte* (1931), and *The Bridge* (1932) invite onstage provincial intelligentsia, average, lonely, and shy characters. They are emotionally weak and poorly adjusted to life in the world of pragmatic necessities. They appreciate spiritual beauty above immediate gain. They adhere to "old fashioned" morality, which condemns them to failure in confrontation with the cynical materialism of progressive society. They suffer existential pangs in a nook of a drawing room. This confrontation of "poetic" with "real" will become the subject of Szaniawski's most interesting play. *Two Theatres* (1946), written immediately after the war, depicts, behind a veil of allusive debate about theater, the romantic fiber of the Warsaw Uprising. The sensitive author of "theater of dreams" will have to set the power of his subjective daydreams recorded in poetic vision against the director of "mirror theater" who is interested only in what can be shown.

Soon after this play was staged, that literary concept became reality. Starting in 1949 only one kind of art was officially permitted: "realist in form and socialist in content." The most correct and, surprisingly, quite interesting executor of that postulate was Leon Kruczkowski. Above all, his domestic political tragedy *Germans* (1946), but also his later works, were able to merge political correctness with talent—genuine, even though unfortunately employed. One has to admit that the soc-realistic works were often "well done"—so much so that their authors were able to eliminate all the ambiguities which could have caught their reader's interest. Therefore, with the coming of "the thaw" nonrealistic and non-socialist dramas poured out. The poetic drama, referenced here, had been developing continuously since the beginning of the century, as if insensitive to the historical changes. Eminent poets such as Boleslaw Lesmian and Jozef Czechowicz left behind dramatic texts, even if not ready for the stage. Most often they were based on fairy tale motifs, sometimes in the form of pantomime or puppet theater. They ventured into areas only seemingly marginal for the dramatic art. In reality they were close to folkloric forms, with the background of medieval and baroque traditions. The absurd miniatures of Konstanty Galczynski from the cycle *The Little Theatre of Green Goose* and the cabaret scripts by Jerzy Afanasjew are close to postwar grotesque surrealism. In the 1950s through the 1970s a whole school of dramaturgy emerged that made use of poetic language and the structure of the parable to describe realistic, psychologically touching existential situations. They were created by another excellent poet—Stanislaw Grochowiak (1934–76). He began with realistic, morality plays from the time of the Nazi occupation, such as *Partita for the Wooden Instrument* (1962), composed for the radio. His works slowly evolved into tragic parables of universal enslavement and finally achieved a symbolic emotional tension. Realism turned into the grotesque, and into a poetic parable about dying in the quintet for old men, *Boys* (1964). His brutally true autobiographical play about an alcoholic, *Morning Fears* (1965), is a passionate accusation of human nature, with its tendency to eagerly hurt one's brother for his human weakness. The plays of Jerzy Sito, written in competent verse, as well as successful pastiches of medieval and baroque forms by Jaroslaw Marek Rymkiewicz could also be included in that category.

Miron Bialoszewski's (1922–83) "theater apart" is an entirely separate phenomenon. Bialoszewski, an exceedingly original author of short works based on amusing and original language play created, essentially, variations of the same "text" in different genres. An outstanding achievement of the theatrical mode is his series of miniatures for stage meant to be performed in the family theater at the writer's home, by a group of friends operating puppets, mannequins or dressed in paper costumes. Those *dramatis personae* emerge from the wagon of a medieval theatrical troupe, from a nativity play or *commedia dell'arte* thrown together hastily in a cramped kitchen. In the little poems, loosely related to the aesthetics of the grotesque and Dada, filled with neologisms, dialogue is split into ambiguous monosyllables or even morphemes, which, colliding , create a reality composed, like a collage, of images provoked by language associations and from objects of everyday use recognized as philosophical metaphors.

At that time intimate drama and monumental theater began to drift apart. In Poland, subjected to the dictatorship of the proletariat, the stage seemed to overly expose those views and problems which the writers would rather hide in a quiet corner of a subjective world. For example, radio plays gained popularity. They were an excellent vehicle for the poetic temperament of local playwriting. One of the greatest achievements in that genre is *Lalek* (1961), "a play for voices" by Zbigniew Herbert (1924–98), a world famous poet, who left behind five dramas in all. Radio itself became thematized and metaphorical here, which imparted exceptional vividity to the story. Also some dramas by Ireneusz Iredynski (1939–85), a writer in the type of an "angry young man," were close to the nature of that medium. Iredynski tracked psychological mechanisms of violence, domination, and oppression, hidden behind the models of social behaviors which form states and even civilizations. In dramas such as *Modern Nativity Play* (1962) or *Terrorists* (1982) the author created highly formalized but realistically convincing conflicts and saturated them with an atmosphere of danger, aggression, and cruelty which elevates the plays to the level of a contemporary morality play. Equally cruel, poetic-grotesque sensitivity can be found in the works of Helmut Kajzar (1941–82), an original theater director. All of them are constructed with the use of a method deconstructing recognizable dramatic forms and reducing the plot to self-conscious scenic action. That was why they worked the best when staged by the author. The most interesting one was *Paternoster* (1969), a true theatrical feast, in which grease is dripping from the national kielbasa and the ritual vodka drinking gives spiritual life to the bodies firmly planted on the ground under the table. A whole galaxy of writers referring openly to the religious roots of Polish literature has been moving in the opposite direction. Roman Brandstaetter (1906–87) achieved the most interesting results in his plays based on biblical and classical motifs. His *The Return of a Prodigal Son* (1945) sets the biography of Rembrandt in the parable about suffering as a source of creation. *You Will Not Be Killing* presents a war tragedy of hero-murderers who, treating the Decalogue with deathly seriousness, condemn themselves to existence within a sphere of irresolvable moral choices. Also the static plays of Karol Wojtyla (1920–2005), the future Pope John Paul II, seem intriguing, although more philosophically then artistically. *The Jeweller's Shop* (1950) contemplates the religious essence of marriage. *Our God's Brother* (1960) is a piece about an artist who renounces art and devotes his life to the homeless. Finally, the mystical mono-drama *Radiance of Fatherhood* (1978) is at the same time a poetic "improvisation" and a theological treatise, much indebted to romantic dramaturgy.

The writings of Tadeusz Rozewicz (b. 1921), a famous poet, on the other hand, are demonstratively anti-Catholic and anti-national. It is a manifestation of unequivocal although schematic criticism of Western civilization, discredited definitively after the end of World War II. Now, the barren land of the ambitious project of Modernity has revealed emptiness and false values, which were there from the very beginning and which still support its decaying mock-up that is pop culture. The author, making original use of collage, has composed dramatic situations, most often with discontinuous plots, creating out of ready-made media clichés a picture of the present as a great landfill of European spirituality on the verge of nothingness. A perfect example of such a drama in a Beckettian climate is *The Old Woman Broods* (1968). In it, out of a woeful lamentation of Job emanates a message defending human weakness, from which flows a source of a mysterious faith in biological survival as the highest, because not illusory, value. Anthropological problems, viewed in social-historical and even existential perspective come up in Rozewicz's dramas *The Witnesses* (1969), *On All Fours* (1971), and *Death and Buried* (1972). However, he always declares himself on the side of anti-metaphysics and, in spite of his reference to Christian motifs, of a desacralized view of the world. The greatest popularity was gained by *The Card Index* (1959) in which Rozewicz was able to unusually deftly join formal disintegration of plot continuity with deconstruction of subjective integrity of the protagonist. The main character in this static post-morality play is Hero, at once Nobody and Everyman, by the power of theatrical tradition condemned to action, to "moving the plot forward." In reality he is incapable of anything more than talking about what happened to him in the universally historical drama of his own, even if written by others, biography. In his more traditional, ambiguous erotic comedy *Mariage Blanc* (1973) we can find reflections on the role of the artist in a post-cultural society. *The Trap* is an interesting psychological study of modern ideologies within the framework of Franz Kafka's life.

While Rozewicz was gaining international recognition and the position of the head avant-gardist, a more radical poet and dramatist began to slip into oblivion, in spite of his initial success. Tymoteusz Karpowicz (1921–2005) deserves a position at least equal, if not higher. It behooves the author to admit here that his judgment differs in this case from universally accepted views. Karpowicz's dramas, just like his extremely avant-garde poetry, seem to emerge from the matter of language, as if trying to direct its semantic capabilities. The ostentatiously mediocre characters ostensibly converse with one another, but in reality their attention is focused elsewhere. Not on communication, but on the very utterance. It is as if everyone listens to what the language itself has to say to him. They allow the "revelations" hidden in the language to surprise them, they give in to them, respond to them, and so follow the path of fate they have forged for themselves. But this does not free them from desires, from the sense of freedom and, above all, from their conscience. Morally oversensitive, but at the same time passive, they are only able to experience and understand. In those dramas of everyday life, not unlike those of Norwid, both psychologically true people and allegories of archetypal ethical attitudes perform. All of that usually happens in places so common as to be strange by their rarity in theater—in the courtyard of an old tenement house, in a taxi cab, at a railway station. It is as if the author preferred to spy on people in the city rather than peek through "the fourth wall" of a salon and to find archetypal scenarios in the most common behaviors, like hidden meanings in thoughtless prattle. His plays (mostly written in the 1960s and 70s), often cruel, even brutal, full of Christian symbols, make skillful use of the formal challenges of modern media. *When One will Knock at the Door* is meant for the radio, *His Little Girl* for television and others, like *Wells are Everywhere*, *The Strange Passenger*, *Breake in a Travel*, can be freely adapted to a director's imagination.

It is the director, and not the playwright, who is the most important person in Polish theater. That is why Polish authors rarely have big stage careers. Slawomir Mrozek (b. 1930) is a laudable exception here. "Witkacy came too late, Gombrowicz was apart, but Mrozek we have just at the right time," wrote Jan Kott. He was right: that writer, draftsman, director proved to be their worthy heir. His success came quickly and was well deserved and lasting. He is the most often performed Polish author in the world, the most eminent, next to Fredro, Polish comedy writer, and the most recent of the heirs of the mainstream of Polish playwriting extending from the romantics, through Wyspianski and the avant-garde, to the author of *Tango*.

He began as a satirist, taking the hearts of his fellow Poles by storm. They immediately recognized the essence of Polishness in his characters. But that would not condemn Mrozek to parochialism, because his precise constructions were entirely universal. An initially realistic situation, by the power of the unrelenting work of merciless reason, leads the resulting conclusions to the edge of life decisions. It is here that its absurd un-resolvability is revealed, stuck between the demand of "pure thought" and the expectation of "impure emotions." The unceasing conflict between idealism and pragmatism discredits both extremes, without any hope for the third path. Mrozek writes from a European perspective, but based on experiences of his socialist homeland, where such tragic grotesque was commonplace. In his debut *Police* (1958) the totalitarian state is so efficient that it finds it necessary to support the last rebel, in order to justify the existence of its apparatus of oppression. In *Out at Sea* (1961) two men in a boat will not use violence to eat the third one; they unleash a political debate to convince their companion that he should sacrifice himself for the good of the majority. Mrozek writes about social mechanisms, but he does not look for them outside—instead he looks inside an individual subject to the power of ideology, stereotypes, myths, and finally archetypes. Totalitarianism and anarchy are not systems—they are inborn human deficiencies transposed onto inter-human relations. Situations in those extremely intelligent comedies, witty rather than funny, seem to be demonstratively artificially arranged; the author, without ceremony, imposes a problem requiring final decisions, involving their whole worldview on unprepared and weak characters. By that he achieves their necessary confrontation with the Absolute. This is the case in excellent *Slaughterhouse* (1973)—a discussion of art desiring zeal without faith, ideal without idealism, reality without truth, derived from the spirit of Witkiewicz—and in *On Foot* (1979)—an epic historio-philosophical treatise with Witkacy as a main character. Mrozek delights in juxtaposing opposite types and attitudes, as in *Emigrants* (1974) where a romantic intellectual and sentimental worker de-mystify one another's sanctities in a windowless cellar, so that when they finally see through each other they don't have anything left. In an amusing parable *The Party* (1962) with dialogues written in rhythmic prose of a folk song we see village youths standing in front of the closed door of a local dance club, trying to clear their way to culture with kicks. In *The Tailor* (1964) a half-savage conqueror of Rome gradually loses his brutal nobility among satin comforts of civilization, slipping softly from barbarism straight into decadence. In *Vazlav* (1968), stylized after one of Voltaire's philosophical tales, we see an honest young man from the unspoiled part of the West who, trying to escape oppression and poverty, has to choose between freedom and comfort.

But it is *Tango* (1964) which has proved to be Mrozek's greatest triumph. This comedy, written soon after he left Poland, to which he was to return only thirty years later, poses problems derived from the heart of the Polish dramaturgy in universal perspective. Here again, as in *The Wedding* by Wyspianski and in *The Marriage* by Gombrowicz there is matrimonial drama; here again, like in *The Undivine Comedy* by Krasinski and *Shoemakers* by Witkacy we have revolution. Artur, a young idealist, inspired by the ideas of conservative moral renewal of his demoralized family (read: civilization) decides to become ritually married, so as to rebuild all the traditions in one swoop. In the course of his engagement he begins to dream (he is a descendant of Konrad, after all) about power over souls. In our times, however, reaching for it can only end up in totalitarian dictatorship. This contemporary spiritual leader is an incarnation of the whole class of sophisticated intellectuals and shifty politicians. Finally he too will lose (because he "loved too deeply") against the pure brutality of a simple butler. Where did he come from? No, he did not come from the outside. He lived with his masters, silently waiting his turn since the first scene.

Slawomir Mrozek's wealth of ideas has not yet run out. One of his latest plays, *Love in the Crimea* (1993) gives us a panorama of European spiritual history in a metaphoric image of the twentieth century history of Russia, which is, at the same time, a history of drama (that is, the human ability to dramatize history).

Mrozek wrote it in the country already post-historical, where contemporary "normality" lasts eternally. Poles have stopped seeing themselves as romantic rebels and now, in a panic, they are looking for new masks. Those are being offered by the writers "discovered" thanks to that changed perspective. Two "oddities" of Polish modern playwriting belong to this category. Marian Pankowski (b. 1919), who lives in Belgium and also writes in French, is a former soldier and an inmate of concentration camps. He expressed his experience of history not in parables about Man, but in intimate stories about unique individuals. In his many plays, written in expressive, blunt language with baroque roots, he passionately destroys the high opinion Poles have of themselves as a nation of heroic individualists by drawing their attention to their bellies and below. His opposite is Boguslaw Schaeffer (b. 1929), an excellent avant-garde composer and dizzyingly cold intellectual. Schaeffer composes short, dynamic "scenarios for actors" based on cultural clichés and language play between players posing as actors. Among his forty dramas, most became successful in German-speaking countries.

In 1989, luckily for Poles, their common history ended. What is left is unending present, divided into biographies so different, that it is difficult to recognize their similarity to one model. Have they suddenly found themselves in a Spanish play by Calderón or a French drama by Alfred Jarry, which take place "in Poland, that is, nowhere"? The last but one decade of the past century was marked with an intense expectation of a drama summarizing the epoch. Silence was the answer. On the other side of the Atlantic Janusz Glowacki (b. 1938) began to experience the success of his plays exploiting the plight of an immigrant, in archetypal rather than political context. In his plays *Fortinbras Got Drunk, Hunting Cockroaches,* and *Antigone in New York* he attempted to view the homeland he had lost in the perspective of the other, not yet realized one. Only in the middle of the 1990s did Poland experience an amazing outpouring of new plays. Tamara Trojanowska, a Canadian scholar of Polish modern drama sums it up by pointing out three main themes: social-political topicality, revision of national myths, and psychological exploration of mysteries of personality. She mentions names such as Ewa Lachnit and Marek Prochniewski—authors of dramatic studies of the margins of the new Polish society; Tadeusz Slobodzianek and Piotr Tomaszuk, both with a background of alternative theater, trying in different ways to tell contemporary fairy tales derived from folk lore; and finally Anna Burzynska, the creator of a new variety of post-modern comedy based on brilliant dialogue and journalistically topical subjects. At the end Trojanowska points to the three "loners": Lidia Amejko creatively uses the tradition of the grotesque, by engaging language into inter-textual games playing with the semiotic surface of culture; Jerzy Lukosz continues the line of de-mythologizing symbolic realism, confronting ideology with the power of personality; Artur Grabowski provokes interpersonal rituals in metaphorical dramas of communication.

NOTES

1. The "imaginative" existence of those plays belongs to the certain legend. In fact fragments were "performed" occasionally in the form of public readings. The significant role in popularizing romantic drama in the nineteenth century was played by Helena Modrzejewska (Modjeska), also in America.

2. Some of them were actually produced— "experimentally" and unsuccessfully— during his lifetime.

FURTHER READING

Braun, Kazimierz. *A History of Polish Theater. Spheres of Captivity and Freedom.* Westport, Connecticut: Greenwood Press, 1996.

Filipowicz, Halina. *A Laboratory of Impure Forms. The plays of Tadeusz Rozewicz.* New York-London: Greenwood Press, 1999.

Gerould, Daniel. *Witkacy. Stanislaw Ignacy Witkiewicz as an Imaginative Writer.* Seattle and London: University of Washington Press, 1981.

Gerould, Daniel. *The Witkiewicz Reader.* Edited, translated, and with introduction by Daniel Gerould. Evanston: Northwestern University Press, 1992.

Gerould, Daniel. *The Mrozek Reader.* New York, Grove Press, 2004.

Gombrowicz, Witold. *Three Plays.* Translated by Krystyna Grifith-Jones, Catherine Robins and Luis Iribarne. Introductory essay by Jerzy Peterkiewicz. London-New York: Marion Boyars, 1998.

Grotowski, Jerzy. *Towards a Poor Theatre.* New York: Simon and Schuster, 1969.

Kott, Jan. *Theatre Notebook 1947–67.* Translated by Bolelaw Taborski. Garden City, New York: Doubleday, 1968.

Milosz, Czeslaw. *The History of Polish Literature.* Berkeley: University of California Press, 1983.

Segel, Harold B. *Polish Romantic Drama. Three Plays in English.* Amsterdam: Harwood Academic Publishers, 1997.

Terlecki, Tymon. *Stanislaw Wyspianski.* Twayne's World Authors Series. Boston: Twayne Publishers, 1983.

Trojanowska, Tamara. "New Discourses in Drama." *Contemporary Theatre Review* 15, no. 1 (2005).

ॐ

Russian Drama in the Eighteenth Century

Lurana Donnels O'Malley

Although professional theater companies performed in Western Europe as early as the sixteenth century, professional theater did not develop in Russia until the eighteenth century. Despite the lack of a formal public theater in Russia before the age of Peter the Great, numerous types of theatrical activities took place in various contexts much earlier. For centuries, fairs and festivals featured such popular performance forms as dancing bears, puppet shows, and *skomorokhi* (minstrels). Folk dramas were particularly associated with Shrovetide and Easter celebrations. Liturgical dramas were sometimes associated with the church; for example *The Fiery Furnace* played in Novgorod in the sixteenth century. In the seventeenth century, a school drama emerged, first in Kiev, and later in Moscow at the Slavonic-Greek-Latin Academy. Kievan cleric Simeon Polotsky wrote elaborate school plays on biblical and historical themes. Later, under Peter the Great, the Ukrainian bishop and church reformer Feofan Prokopovich also contributed to school drama repertory.

Tsar Alexei Mikhailovich (r. 1645–76) disliked the popular minstrels and festival performances, and issued a ban on all such forms of entertainment in 1648. But in 1672, Tsar Alexei invited a German minister named Johann Gregory to produce a pageant on the biblical story of Esther (*The Play of Artexerxes*) in the palace theater. Gregory's company performed a mix of biblical stories and adaptations of Elizabethan drama. The theater fell into disuse after Tsar Alexei's death.

Peter the Great (r. 1682–25), as part of his broad effort to westernize Russia, established a short-lived public theater. Peter brought German manager

Johann Kunst (and later Otto Fuerst) to perform Russian adaptations of foreign plays in a theater on Red Square from 1702 to 1707. Other nobility, including Peter's sister Natal'ia Alekseevna, began to give private performances in their homes, for public audiences.

Both Empress Anna (r. 1730–40) and Empress Elizabeth (Elizaveta, r. 1741–62) sponsored foreign companies for elite court performances. Under Anna, three Italian companies visited, performing *commedia dell'arte* as well as opera and ballet. The French ballet master Jean-Baptiste Landé established the ballet troupe that would become the foundations of the Russian Imperial Ballet. The German director and reformer Caroline Neuber also visited. The mainstay of the court stage was French neoclassical drama; as there was as yet no Russian repertory.

THE FIRST PROFESSIONAL THEATER

Empress Elizabeth created the first Russian professional theater by bringing together two key figures: Sumarokov and Volkov. Aleksandr Petrovich Sumarokov (1717–74) had begun to create a new Russian drama, performed by the students at the Cadet Academy in St. Petersburg. Some of his plays were adaptations of other material (such as his 1748 *Hamlet,* a neoclassical version of the Shakespeare play) and others such as *Dmitri the Impostor* (1771) treated Russian historical subjects. In 1755, he also wrote the libretto for the first opera in Russian, *Tsefal and Prokris,* with music by Francesco Araja, an Italian composer from Naples who had come to Russia in 1735 under Empress Anna.

Fedor Volkov (1729–63) is considered the father of professional theater in Russia. Word of his troupe of actors in a barn theater in Iaroslavl reached Empress Elizabeth, and she invited him to St. Petersburg. Sumarokov gave some of the Iaroslavl actors training at the Cadet Academy. In 1756, by Imperial decree, Elizabeth established the Russian State Theatre, with Sumarokov providing the Russian scripts, and Volkov as the leading tragic actor. Ivan Dmitrevskii (1734–1821), originally an actor with Volkov's troupe in Iaroslavl, went on to become a celebrated performer in the new State Theatre, and later a teacher of actors. Tatiana Troepolskaia, an actress from the Moscow University Theatre, specialized in the leading tragic heroines of Sumarokov's plays. Volkov died in 1763 from a cold he caught during the preparations for Catherine the Great's coronation pageant, *The Triumph of Minerva.*

Catherine II (r. 1762–96) saw herself as the inheritor of Peter the Great's mantle, and shared his view of theater as a key element in the desired Westernization of Russia. Under Catherine, an Imperial Theatre School was established in 1779, and there was ample theatrical activity in both St. Petersburg and Moscow, at a variety of public, court, and private theaters. In 1771, Catherine ordered the construction of a public theater in St. Petersburg. Originally known as the Stone Theatre, it was designed by Antonio Rinaldi and seated approximately 2,000 spectators. The building (completed in 1783) became known as the Bolshoi Theatre.

PLAYWRIGHTS

Aleksandr Sumarokov continued to be the most respected writer of Russian tragedy. In 1771, he wrote *Dmitri the Imposter* as a vehicle for the versatile actor Ivan Dmitrevskii. Other playwrights working in this neoclassical vein were Mikhail Lomonosov, who in addition to being a playwright was a scientist and the founder of Moscow University, and Iakov Kniazhnin (Sumarokov's son-in-law).

While Sumarokov is a significant writer who made an enormous contribution to the Russian literary language, his serious plays seem overly formal today. Russian comedies of this era, however, are more lively and accessible. Since they are typically set in their own time, they reveal the language, manners, and concerns of the late eighteenth century—seen through a comic lens.

The acknowledged master of comic playwriting in this period is Denis Fonvizin (1745–92). In his two great comedies, *The Brigadier General* (1769) and *The Minor* (1781), he juxtaposed the exaggerated foibles of his comic characters with the exemplary behavior of wiser and more reasonable ones. The former are far more memorable and theatrically vibrant than the latter. These broadly drawn fools, such as *The Minor*'s foolish young nobleman Mitrofan who rejects both work and education, anticipate the later grotesque characters of Nikolai Gogol.

Russian comic operas added a musical element to the comic genre. As opposed to European comic operas, the Russian versions had a more distinct separation of scenes and songs. Masterpieces in this genre include *Misfortune from a Coach* (1779) by Kniazhnin with music by Vasilii Pashkevich, and *The Miller as Sorceror, Deceiver, and Matchmaker* (1779) by Aleksandr Ablesimov with music by Mikhail Sokolovskii.

In addition to supporting theater as a tool of the Enlightenment, Catherine the Great herself was also a playwright; she authored over two dozen neoclassical comedies, historical plays, fairytale operas, and dramatic proverbs. Her most famous play, *Oh, These Times!* (1772), is a reworking of a play about religious hypocrisy by German playwright Gellert, with a clear nod to Molière. In 1785–86, she composed a trilogy of plays, including *The Siberian Shaman*, which parody Freemasonry, superstition, and shamanism. In some of her historical plays and one comedy, she notes that she is imitating Shakespeare, in violation of the "usual theatrical rules." Most of Catherine's plays were produced and published anonymously.

ACTORS

Others in the nobility were actively involved in running their own private estate theaters. In most cases, a nobleman forced his serfs to perform as actors, often in elaborate private theaters. The most notable of these "serf theaters" are two theaters at the estates of Count Peter Sheremetev: Kuskovo to the east of Moscow and later Ostankino to the north. Sheremetev's son Nikolai was a theater aficionado who fell in love with the serf company's lead actress, Praskovia Kovaleva, whom he had nicknamed Zhemchugova or "the Pearl." He eventually freed Zhemchugova and her family, and secretly married her. Most serf actors did not receive such favors, and many were cruelly treated. Historians have noted the terrible irony of the serf actor's existence, living enslaved but portraying kings onstage.

Mikhail Shchepkin (1788–1863), who was to become the lead actor of the early nineteenth century in Russia, was born a serf, and gained his freedom by proving his acting talent in the provincial theater. He went on to act professionally in Moscow at the Maly Theatre. Shchepkin originated the roles of Famusov in Aleksandr Griboedov's *Woe From Wit* (1823) and the Mayor in Gogol's *Inspector General* (1826), and is considered to be the founder of the realistic acting style that was later explored and expanded by Konstantin Stanislavsky.

For much of her reign Catherine the Great, inspired by the intellectual currents of the Enlightenment, allowed writers great freedoms. But toward the end of her life the events of the French Revolution made her more conservative. In 1793, possibly disturbed by the play's anti-autocratic tone, she banned the publication of a historical drama by the late Iakov Kniazhnin, titled *Vadim of Novgorod*.

Catherine the Great died of a stroke in 1796, and succeeding rulers were more restrictive in their regulation of theater companies and the dramatic repertory. In the nineteenth century, Aleksandr Pushkin (1799–1837) would take Russian drama in a new direction, by rejecting French neoclassical models in favor of a more romantic approach.

FURTHER READING

O'Malley, Lurana Donnels. *The Dramatic World of Catherine the Great: Theatre and Politics in Eighteenth-century Russia.* Aldershot, England: Ashgate Publishing, 2006.
Vickery, Walter N. *Alexander Pushkin, Revisted.* Boston, Massachusetts: Twayne Publishing, 1992.

ॐ

The Russian Drama of Anton Chekhov

Ralph Lindheim

Anton Pavlovich Chekhov was born in January of 1860 in the Ukrainian port city of Tahanrih (or, as it was known at that time, the Russian city of Taganrog). The city, located a thousand kilometers south of Moscow on an inlet of the Sea of Azov, which is itself an inlet of the Black Sea, was at one time a booming trade center in which grains, fruits, and wines were the major products bought, sold, and shipped. Yet the city's fortunes began to wane as Chekhov grew up in the 1860s. It lost its prominence as a trading center as the more vigorous cities in Ukraine, such as Odessa and Rostov on the Don, lured the richer, more successful traders and merchants. And the arrival of the railroad proved disastrous to the teamsters of Chekhov's home town; the local haulers were put out of work and no longer had the money to spend in the shops of the smaller merchants who remained, smaller merchants like Chekhov's father.

Chekhov's family on both sides was rather remarkable. Both his grandfather on his father's side and his maternal great grandfather were born serfs but saved enough money to purchase their freedom. Chekhov's father Pavel became a petty merchant in Tahanrih, but he unfortunately was never successful. When his business failed in the mid-1870s, he had to move most of the family to Moscow. The traumatic loss of a family home was a situation that Chekhov was often to explore in his stories and plays. When the family left, Anton remained behind to finish the last three years of his secondary education and obtain the diploma needed for college entrance. Upon graduation, he rejoined the family bringing with him a scholarship to the University of Moscow as well as a newly generated attitude of independence and self-respect that he had developed in his three years living away from his parents and making his way in the world independently.

He became the head of the household upon his arrival, since his father did not live at home and his elder brothers did not seem to care much about the family. He saw to it that he, his mother, and three younger siblings moved to a better, larger apartment, which they could afford since he had convinced two fellow students from his hometown to board with his family, and then enrolled in the Medical School of the University of Moscow, beginning a long, hard 5-year course of studies. He applied himself so earnestly that he did not get involved in extra-curricular political activities, which were intense until the repression that followed the assassination of Alexander II in 1881. His only diversions from his studies, because of his friendship with some of his elder brothers' bohemian friends, involved visits to pubs and brothels. Yet he had little spare time to devote to carousing, for he soon began moonlighting as a writer for a series of popular comic magazines and newspapers published both in Moscow and St. Petersburg. The material he provided—parodies, comic anecdotes, farcical scenes, amusing advertisements and calendar listings, cartoon captions—was all fairly conventional, as were the few serious tales and one large unwieldy play he wrote in the first stage of his career. Much of what he produced was dashed off, and yet it pleased the reading public and is in fact still popular today. But in the mid-1880s it was his more serious work that attracted the attention of influential or significant writers, who urged him to take his craft more seriously: to devote more time to his writing, and to turn his attention to more complex characters and content.

CHEKHOV'S CAREER

Chekhov was not quick to respond to these urgings, for, as he put it, he considered literature his mistress and medicine his legitimate spouse. Yet though he never gave up his interest in medicine, he never acquired a large private practice, and many of the patients he treated throughout his life, especially his peasant neighbors, were treated free of charge. Gradually he came to spend more time with his mistress, although he soon escorted her to better places. He turned away from the lowbrow periodicals and began to place his writings in more important papers and journals. In 1888 he published a detailed description of a boy's trip across the Ukrainian steppe in a major and respected Russian journal, one of the so-called "thick" journals that played such a prominent role in the development of Russian social thought and cultural life in the nineteenth century. From this date on there was no looking back, except for a series of amusing one-act farces that he dashed off for money and for the audiences, as he put it, "to laugh their buttons off." Most of his work was written more seriously, more carefully, and much more slowly; as one sees when comparing the 129 sketches and stories he produced in 1885 with 112 in 1886, 66 in 1887, and in 1888 only twelve.

Apart from two trips—one extremely dangerous journey across Siberia to the Russian penal colony on the island of Sakhalin and a more pleasant tour of Europe—the next decade of his life was spent in European Russia where he wrote a series of short stories that won him such a reputation that he together with Tolstoy was recognized among the greatest living Russian writers. Yet in the middle of the 1890s the symptoms of tuberculosis, which he had not taken seriously for about ten years, announced themselves undeniably. He had to be hospitalized for a complete checkup, and the examination revealed an advanced case of the disease in both lungs. The need to convalesce slowed him down considerably, and he was ordered not to spend the harsh winters in central Russia. The winter of 1897–98 found him in Nice where he indignantly followed the events surrounding the reopening of the Dreyfus affair. Upon his return to Russia his health deteriorated, and he was forced to settle in the Crimea for most of the year and cut down on the time and effort he devoted to his writing. The decrease in the quantity of his creative output was certainly attributable to the physical toll of his disease, but the quality of his work was little affected, and it may be argued that he produced his finest works in the last years of his life. His death in 1904 at age 44 ended a brilliant but short literary career of only 25 years.

Outside of Russia his dramatic output, at least the four major plays and the earlier *Ivanov,* is perhaps better known than his fiction. In the first twelve years of his writing career Chekhov wrote a few plays of varying quality but he fully blossomed as a playwright in the middle of the 1890s when he wrote *The Seagull* and transformed an earlier unsuccessful play into what we now know as *Uncle Vanya.* The sympathetic and acclaimed productions of these plays in 1898 by the Moscow Art Theatre, a theatrical company formed by the soon to be world famous director Konstantin Stanislavsky and his friend and associate Vladimir Nemorovich-Danchenko, together with a love affair with Olga Knipper, the troupe's leading lady whom Chekhov married in 1901, prompted Chekhov to write his best plays, *The Three Sisters* and *The Cherry Orchard,* for this company and its able corps of actors. Though his relationship with Stanislavsky was far from untroubled, the successes of the Moscow Art Theatre at home and on tour in Europe and America, together with a later series of distinguished productions of Chekhov by major directors such as Jean-Louis Barrault, Giorgio Strehler, and Peter Brook, established Chekhov's reputation as a playwright and contributed to the astounding fact that in the English-speaking world today the plays of Chekhov are performed more often than those of any other playwright except Shakespeare. Even in the percussive, argumentative and highly ideological world of contemporary theater, in Russia as well as outside it, we are surely surprised—though some of us are heartened—that these plays written just over a hundred years ago still cast their spell on theatrical audiences. Not only are they performed in various styles, respectful approaches that may be either traditional or experimental, but also they have given rise recently to many cheeky deconstructions, which at one and the same time pay homage to the pre-eminence of his plays in the world of the theater as they attempt to demolish or undermine their authority and dominance.

WHY CHEKHOV IS IMPORTANT

Actors and Chekhov

One important reason for the attraction of these plays and the continuing desire to stage them is the creative challenge they pose to actors, directors, set designers, and those who devise both the lighting that bathes the sets and the sounds that provide an essential aural background for the action. Ever since Stanislavsky's first successful staging of *The Seagull* in 1898, actors have been drawn to and challenged by the characters of Chekhov, whose complexity and dynamism require of the performers imaginative insight into their inner psychological worlds and demand all their professional skills to project these figures, even those who are secondary, compellingly onstage. The major characters prove more elusive, not just because of the range and depth of their emotions, which more often they conceal than reveal, but also because of their moral mobility. Beginning with *Ivanov*, at least its title character, Chekhov's figures cannot be summed up quickly and neatly. In their responses, audiences must be as dynamic as the characters, evaluating positively their good, strong moments and finding reprehensible their weak, unworthy moments. In *Three Sisters* we can and should respond skeptically at times to the youthful impracticality of Irina, the crude words and actions of Masha, worthy of any hussar in the regiment their father headed, and the maternal watchfulness and boosterism of Olga. And yet the contrasting presence of Natasha, their sister-in-law, who can take to an unpalatable extreme the basic traits of the sisters —the immaturity of Irina becomes Natasha's grating childishness, with particularly nasty and unjustifiable tantrums; the repressed passion of Masha, which holds her back so long from an affair with Vershinin, is refracted in Natasha's wanton adulterousness; and the motherly affection of Olga is transformed into a saccharine, indiscriminate protectiveness for her offspring—makes us wince and appreciate more the sisters. In Chekhov's final play, *The Cherry Orchard*, the main characters have all too often been simplistically censured or lauded, according to the ideological camps to which the critics belong, but essential to the play and the vision of the playwright is an evenhanded appreciation of the charms and decencies of his figures as well as their questionable weaknesses and failings, an understanding not only of what makes them attractive and likable but also of the inflexible foolishness that nevertheless gives them the urge and the strength to survive, to continue living as they had done.

The actors, however, must do more than simply enliven the roles they are playing; they must also establish the world in which the dramatis personae live as well as the world which exits outside of and beyond them and their concerns. The amount of "felt life," to borrow a term from Henry James, in the plays of Chekhov is vast. *Three Sisters*, which traces, after a bright, hopeful beginning, several dismal years for the Prozorov sisters and their brother together with many of the people connected with their family, has an exceptionally large cast involved in a number of unhappy marriages or unions, somewhat reminiscent of the unhappy series of relationships at the heart of *Seagull*. The later play has four large roles for women, the sisters and Natasha, with six major roles for men. And one should not forget both the important minor parts for the nurse Anfisa and the deaf courier Ferapont, with his funny lines in three of the four acts, and the two minor officers Rodé and Fedotik, who have few lines but are present in every act and add body and texture to the ensemble on stage.

Adding to the capaciousness of Chekhov's plays, the sense of a broad spectrum of life beyond the temporal and spatial limits of the stage to which the players are bound, are many important figures who are mentioned but never appear. Their presence is marked: sometimes feared, sometimes lauded, but always significant. To this group belongs Treplev's father in *Seagull,* a talented figure mentioned only once, but whose evident lack of concern for his son seems equivalent to Arkadina's and helps to account, in part, for Konstantin's exhibitionistic urge to attract attention. And Vanya's sister, the first wife of Professor Serebryakov and Sonya's mother, is mentioned in the second and fourth acts of *Uncle Vanya*. Both times Sonya's resemblance to her mother moves Vanya deeply, the second time to give up his notion of suicide. *Three Sisters* offers a greater number of offstage characters who never appear: the parents of the Prozorovs, whose values govern their children's lives, the Director of Schools whom Kuligin imitates and fears, and the most powerful man in Town, Protopopov, who becomes Natasha's lover and is probably the father of Natasha's second child, Sofochka. Stanislavsky, by the way, wanted Protopopov to appear in the last act chasing a ball thrown out of the window by one of the children, but Chekhov insisted the character remain an unseen force. Finally, in *The Cherry Orchard,* Ranevskaya's unseen lover draws her back to Paris in the end while Lopakhin often refers to his dead father, whose savage beatings, which he cannot forget, permanently scar and cripple the son.

The ensemble, to which the actors in a Chekhov play must contribute, is not just a group reflecting the socio-economic realities of the age, in which the plays were written, though such has been the worthy goal of many productions. More important is the group of dramatic figures who share and explore common problems and concerns announced and firmly embedded in the texts of the plays, that is, in the particular clusters of words, images, and motifs that are explored and illuminated in the individual plays. Art and artists are important considerations for the major characters in *Seagull,* but it is unrequited love that so many of the suffering characters experience. And linking the realms of art and love is the ethical motif of integrity, which is unfortunately sacrificed by all the major figures except Nina, the character most identified with the fragile but beautiful bird of the title, to notoriety, to success, to aesthetic commitments that are not fully believed in, to popularity, to routine relationships even with unloved or unloving partners. The fragility of decency and beauty in the face of environmental depredation is later explored in *Uncle Vanya,* with the inevitable decline and self-destructive desperation of people inhabiting a progressively depleted, rural landscape announced in the following lines from the third act lecture on ecological catastrophe given Elena by Doctor Astrov:

> Here we're dealing with decline resulting from a struggle for survival beyond human strength; it's a decline caused by stagnation, ignorance, the most total absence of self-awareness, when a frostbitten, starving, sickly man, to preserve the last vestiges of life, to protect his children, instinctively, unthinkingly grabs hold of whatever can possibly satisfy his hunger, to warm himself he destroys everything with no thought of the morrow . . .[1]

In *The Three Sisters* almost all the characters at some time in the play utter the stock expression *vsë ravno,* applying it to themselves or others. The phrase has a range of synonymous meanings "I"—or one could add a different subject—"don't care," "it's all the same to me"—or another indirect object—"what's the use?" "it makes no difference" But it is the thematic issue of indifference binding all the possible variations of this phrase that lies at the heart of the play. Even the dream of Moscow, the symbol of a useful, fulfilling, purposeful existence elsewhere, shared by the three sisters and their brother, encourages them not to concern themselves with what happens around them in the large provincial city where they live. They, too, succumb to indifference, though the sisters do not fall as deeply as the men and do finally attempt a not necessarily successful or painless escape. And for his last play Chekhov places the idea of change at its heart. The orchard itself stands as a symbol for a change in time or history since so many of the characters talk about and view the orchard as either a means or a hindrance to alterations they want to make in their lives, as a model to be restored, renovated, or renounced.

Directors and Chekhov

Directors, too, are stimulated by the texts of the plays to aid their performers to explore the subtle and not so subtle depths of the characters they portray, to help their actors establish appropriate gestures, to translate psychology into motion or stillness, to generate a shared emotion or mood, and—this is very important in any Chekhov play—to devise choreographic movements and groupings that sculpt the multidimensionality of the Chekhovian stage. One could recall in this context the breathtaking entrance of Ranevskaya and her entourage in the first act défilé, the first of many processions in *The Cherry Orchard*, where the audience is engulfed by a sudden and progressive surge of energy and vitality, beginning with offstage sounds and then sweeping onstage to overwhelm the sleepy, early morning torpidity suggested by the opening of the play. Or consider the tableaus so characteristic of *Three Sisters*. One can never forget the effect in the opening act when, all of a sudden, a photo is taken of the festive crowd celebrating Irina's nameday, and the many merry and lively figures at the table in the back of the stage or on the side freeze and assume the rigid, unnatural to our modern eyes, ceremonial poses characteristic of people sitting for a nineteenth century daguerreotype. But tableaus are at the core of the entire play, with the contrast between the opening scene and the closing suggestive of the movement of the entire play. As the curtain rises on Act I, before a word is spoken, the three sisters are seen in different parts of the room, wearing different colored dresses, posing in different ways that brings out differences in age, emotional and psychological state or condition, and occupation. Yet as soon becomes obvious in the first act, no matter how different they appear, they have so much in common: their tastes and sympathies and values are one. But at the end of the play, where the three of them are huddled together, supporting each other as they face a bitter future and standing as a group in contrast to the men left on stage, their brother, Masha's husband, and the old doctor Chebutykin, we sense that their union is more apparent than real and that each is about to go her separate way.

The controlled though muted and understated integration or orchestration of a spectrum of stage effects—another feature of the Chekhovian theater a director must create—is best illustrated by the concluding scene from *Uncle Vanya*, the darkest of Chekhov's plays. Here a powerful though devastating counterpoint in position, speech, posture and sound between the main characters, Sonya and Vanya, whose body language and voices graphically illustrate the explosion of their hopes and dreams for a new and better life, and the sleepy satisfaction of the secondary figures, Vanya's mother, the parasite Telegin, and the peasant nurse Marina. The latter figures are happy that life is returning to a routine that had been disrupted. And they signal their satisfaction through the background sounds of what are for them normal everyday activities: Telegin strums his guitar, the nurse knits and her needles click against each other, while Vanya's mother does what she has so often done before, and we hear the scratching of her pen as she copies out or comments on some articles from a liberal journal. The sights and sounds of resumed normality clashes jarringly with the hopelessness projected by the slumped figure of Vanya and the exhaustion undercutting Sonya's religious affirmation of an afterlife that will compensate them for their misery in this world. Similarly, the third act of *Three Sisters* focuses on the weariness of the main characters in the early morning, but there is a different spectrum of reactions to both the external fire, destroying much of their city, and a more powerful internal holocaust, devastating old illusions so desperately clung to and, for at least two of them, inspiring new affirmations to be seized, even if for the moment.

Set Designers and Chekhov

The role offered by Chekhov to set designers and other members of the creative team collaborating with the directors and actors and contributing to the impact of a single act or to the contrast between two adjoining acts or to the movement of a whole evening in the theater cannot be underplayed. The magic lake of *The Seagull* must be seen differently in Acts I and II, and its presence must continue to be sensed in the final two acts. Similarly a sharp contrast must be palpable between the outer two acts of light in *Three Sisters*, where Natasha enters late and thus plays a minor part, with the middle two acts of darkness, in which Natasha enters early and her stinginess—she is ever on the watch for candles burning without any purpose—does much to set the tone. She even accentuates the darkness of Act III by wandering across the stage with a candle. Time itself —four years pass between the opening and closing of Three Sisters—is one of the important themes catalogued before our eyes by the sets and costumes and lighting designs. And finally in *The Cherry Orchard,* the march of time is reflected in the second act setting where there are some old tombstones scattered about the set, and the light in this act gradually darkens with the passage of evening into night making palpable time's inexorability. As does the contrast in the settings of the first and last acts, which take place in the same room but is seen in the closing scenes with the walls stripped, the furniture reduced and covered, and suitcases, trunks, and bundles scattered in the back.

Universal Themes in Chekhov

Another reason for the longevity of his plays and for their continued appeal to theater people and their audiences is their retention of familiar and conventional features exploited in nineteenth century melodrama, realistic drama and prose fiction, if not much of the dramatic literature of the Western tradition. A traditional arrival-departure scheme is used or slightly altered in all the major plays to give a skeletal shape to the whole structure, and it should be clear that Chekhov's structures are not as shapeless as those who argue for his modernity insist. Also welcomingly familiar to an audience is the motif of generational conflict that modulates into *The Seagull*'s family explosions and the harsh quarrels between the entrenched aesthetic traditionalists and the combative innovators. Another predictable variant of the central issue of conflict are the class tensions on the surface of both *Three Sisters* and *Cherry Orchard*. As noted earlier, the conventional melodramatic situation of a family facing the loss of the family homestead is a particular obsession of Chekhov; it is threatened in *Uncle Vanya* and actually occurs in the last plays. In *Three Sisters*, Natasha progressively takes control over the Prozorov house room by room, and in the last act she has moved outside and threatens nature itself, promising to cut down the trees and replace them with fragrant annuals. And in *The Cherry Orchard* the family estate is purchased by the merchant who grew up on the property as a serf. But as the last play makes so abundantly clear, the traditional situation is not treated in conventionally melodramatic terms. The rich merchant, Lopakhin, who eventually buys the estate and oversees the departure of the bankrupt owners, turns out to be quite a decent fellow so different from the dark, rapacious figures from the merchant class in the melodramatic plays of Alexander Ostrovsky, the major Russian playwright of the middle of the nineteenth century. As for the heroes who lose their property, Madame Ranevskaya and her brother Gaev are far from saintly passive creatures victimized by external, malevolent forces. Not only does the play subvert certain melodramatic clichés, it downplays much that is conventionally dramatic. Many of the play's exciting events take place off stage, behind the scenes: Ranevskaya's lurid love affairs, Trofimov's political activities leading to his expulsion from university, and the critical auction, at which the estate is sold to Lopakhin, are not shown but are only reported or hinted at. And, as so many critics have pointed out, in this his last play Chekhov finally avoided having a gun fire either onstage or off. So it is this combination of traditional and novel, established and innovational that characterizes Chekhov's special voice and vision as playwright and writer.

Chekhov's Technique

Technically, too, Chekhov was more of a "gentle subversive," as Simon Karlinsky has called him, than a fierce experimentalist. He made use of standard devices that had so long served his fellow playwrights. Telling entrances and exits are exploited in *Three Sisters*. Vershinin declares that if he had his life to live over, he would do it without getting married again—thus speaks a man who has married twice—but it is at this very moment that Kulygin, that most satisfied of married men, makes his entrance. And in the same act Irina's confession that the pessimism reflected by her and her sisters is directly related to the fact that their position of idle privilege blocked them from the healthy necessity of work, a necessity which was despised by her parents. Her words are immediately followed by the entrance of Natasha, whose parents we may assume did not share the prejudice of Irina's parents yet nevertheless spawned a far from elegant creature whose health, energy, and fertility are not put to useful and positive ends. Moreover, Chekhov did not even hesitate to employ the most hoary but useful devices of drama, the soliloquy and the extended monologue, in which a character thinks aloud or announces or explores for himself or others his feelings and attitudes and ideas. In *The Seagull* each act features at least one major monologue— Konstantin's in the first act, Trigorin's in the second, Arkadina's in the third, and Nina's in the last act. Long speeches and shorter soliloquies dot the middle acts of *Uncle Vanya* and, of course, Sonya slowly delivers her famous poetic vision of the future in a tired voice at the end of *Uncle Vanya*. The same devices prove useful in *Three Sisters,* though here Chekhov attempts to justify the device of the monologue by making Doctor Chebutykin drunkenly spill his despair in the third act and having Andrei pour out his secret thoughts and feelings to a deaf comic servant or confess the failure of his life and marriage to an empty stage, from which two of his sisters have just retreated to rest on their beds behind screens. And this allows, once Andrei makes his exit, Chekhov to create a powerful conclusion to this act with the sisters still hidden behind screens giving disembodied voice to their desperation on a stage whose silence and emptiness reverberate almost as much as the words that are heard.

Yet there were revolutionary aspects to Chekhov's dramaturgy, again a "gentle" rather than aggressive modernism that was nevertheless to prove productive and influential for later drama and dramatists. Here at least three closely related features of a Chekhovian playscript are worthy of mention: subtext, fragmentation, and oscillation. Perhaps too much is made of subtext or the feelings and emotions that lie submerged beneath the spoken words. That there is a hidden range of sensations, feelings, attitudes and emotions not communicated by the logical content and flow of a character's word is suggested by the dots in the text that suggest something is left unsaid—one translator remarked that a page from his plays looks like it is suffering from measles. And then there are the many specifically marked pauses, pregnant moments of silence. It is not always clear what lies beneath the surface, and in this way Chekhov's subtext—mobile and at times palpably present but not fully comprehended by the speaker—is different from the psychological subtext built by dramatists before him, who made it clear to speaker and audience alike what was left unsaid.

Also characteristic of Chekhov's dialogue is a constant transition from one topic to another or one feeling to another or one person to another that seems unscripted, undetermined, reminiscent of the formlessness and fragmentation of everyday chatter. But it is not just the dialogue that give this impression; even the monologues are characterized by deviations, deflections, or digressions. Sudden, unexpected emotional outbursts explode in the middle of a conversation, addressed to no one in particular, but they, too, are suddenly and unexpectedly squelched with a return to everyday trivia, a turn from the lyrical to the banal, which, in its turn, is itself incapable of being sustained for more than a moment. Ranevskaya in the first act of *Cherry Orchard* offers the following short monologue that displays her emotion at returning home, both to Russia and to her estate:

> Can really be I sitting here? *Laughs.* I feel like dancing, waving my arms about. *Covers her face with her hands.* But maybe I am dreaming! God knows I love my country, I love it tenderly; I couldn't look out of the window in the train, I kept crying so. *Through tears.* But I must have my coffee. Thank you, Firs, thank you, dear old man. I'm so happy that you're still alive.

The major, extended monologues in the play, Ranevskaya's recounting of her sins in the second act and Lopakhin's announcement that he is the new owner of the estate in the third act fluctuate perceptibly in intonation, pitch, emotional intensity, and subject, thus at one and the same time reinforcing the apparently chaotic structure of the play but also generating a tension between the apparent simplicity and triviality of life's surface and the hidden though not completely camouflaged depths of complex emotion. Lopakhin's monologue is yet another opportunity for an actor to display his flexibility, for he must rapidly pass from triumphant pride to anger at his father to sorrow at the plight of the former owners and then to a deeply felt anguish at the absurd and painful social and historical process of change which all, even he the apparent victor, must endure. But then, with yet one more twist, one more display of inconsistency, Lopakhin leaves the stage proclaiming loudly and crudely, as he almost knocks over a candelabra, "I can pay for everything!" Even if his final words have an ironic coloration, they reveal a basic peasant mentality, with its crude belief in the power of money.

It is this constant alternation between lyric and prosaic that characterizes the texture of Chekhovian dialogue and action. In every play one finds a set of poetic images or lyrical motifs capable of rousing intense emotions or reveries about the past or dreams of the future, but what generates intense heat and light is all too quickly extinguished or deflated by banal talk or inappropriate responses or unexpectedly ungainly words or movements that bring to earth a temporary flight. And in its turn the flat and dull is surprisingly succeeded by a sharp unexpected turn towards the emotional and musical. The first act conclusion of *Three Sisters,* for example offers a constant fluctuation between poetic delights and prosaic banter. The sound of the spinning top reminds Masha once again of two lines from Pushkin, but her recitation is immediately followed by table talk about common superstitions. And when Andrei draws Natasha away to speak of his love for her, his rhythmic emotionally tinged speech is undercut by the self-absorption of his beloved, and his passionate kiss is accompanied by the entrance of two army officers who express comic astonishment at the tender scene they encounter. The third act of *The Cherry Orchard* is a brilliant string of incidents or episodes highlighting in comic fashion the characters' inability or outright failure to maintain control and consistency over their bodies and brains and words and emotions. Varya begins the act dancing tearily with the stationmaster, but a very short moment later, when she enters with Trofimov, she responds to his teasing by angrily shouting, "Mangy master!" And then a second later she ponders, deep in thought, how money will be found to pay the musicians. Next is the sudden transition from composure to panic, when Simeonov-Pishchik realizes that the money he needs for tomorrow has been lost, only to express outrageously joyful relief when he finds it in the lining of his jacket. Even more important transitions from one extreme to another occur in the middle of the act. Ranevskaya's long conversation with Trofimov begins with her plea for understanding and kind words and tokens of pity: "Save me, Petya, tell me something, talk to me." And a few lines later she begs, "Pity me, you good, kind fellow!" But when the response she wants is not forthcoming, she immediately demands the opposite, "don't say anything, don't say..." And a few seconds later she angrily tongue-lashes him: "you're simply a queer fish, a comical freak!" But, of course, she immediately retracts her words and alters her tone when he runs off in indignation, "Petya! Wait! You absurd fellow, I was joking. Petya!" With his fall comes a rapid oscillation in the reactions to it heard offstage: Anya and Varya's shocked cry of horror is immediately followed by their laughter. Whether comic or sad or a combination of the two, the failure to sustain for any length of time a topic of conversation, a tone, an attitude or emotion, even the inability to support without qualifying or altering any of the moods that the individual acts attempt to build, is one of the most important features of a Chekhovian play.

The Heart of Chekhov

A final word about Chekhovian themes is in order, though many of them have already been prefigured in this treatment of Chekhov's texts, his characters, and the vision of the world projected by the plays. To get to the heart of what he explores, the spectators must pay close attention to the words and the images repeated by the characters. Translators, therefore, should not display their ingenuity devising stylistic variants for the same word or phrase used by different characters. All in the audience must be attuned to what the characters share, which even the relationships of primary to secondary characters comment upon. But beyond the specific concerns of the individual plays, it is best to conclude by isolating time as the overriding concern of Chekhov. It may be the changes that do not occur in time that seem to weigh so heavily. In *Seagull*, for example, two years pass between the third and final fourth act. But what is stressed—and I do mean clearly and openly reiterated—until the arrival of Nina near the close of the play, is the lack of any significant change in the characters, in what they feel and what they do. But if there is a change in time in the plays, it is often not substantial and it is definitely not for the better. The desperate situation of the main characters in *Uncle Vanya* is the one that had been building before the arrival of the Professor and his young wife. But after their departure, the heroes are even deeper into a quicksand-like situation from which they realize there is no escape. In *Three Sisters*, however, the final embrace of the sisters comes at a time when each is about to go her separate way, never to enter again into the house that has marked and united them for so long. When Olga voices uncertainties and doubts and lack of knowledge about their future, she repeats four times, "If only we could know." Her line could also mean, "If only it could be known." What a change, then, for them who at the beginning of the play were certain of their future in Moscow and could so easily judge and evaluate the men in their lives and the people in their provincial city. Yet this change need not be interpreted as a disastrous one.

Finally, in *The Cherry Orchard* it is clear that here none of the characters do more than change superficially, but that they remain in this comedy what they were at the beginning, and even before the beginning of the play, seems paradoxically positive. Rather than accommodating themselves to and making their peace with a changing reality that will certainly diminish them, rather than submitting to the frightening pace of time and the overwhelming force of other external powers and processes that clearly demonstrate their continual instability and impotence, they, in effect, refuse to face the facts, refuse to collapse sensibly. To the end and beyond they continue to act foolishly, heeding the absurd call of their illusions. Failure may give them a moment's pause and even momentarily overwhelm them—think here of the final embrace of Gaev and Ranevskaya, when they attempt to subdue their tears, followed by Gaev's collapse. Yet he exits with the help of his sister, bloodied but not broken. Throughout the play they hold on, hoping against hope, expecting a miracle to happen, the estate to be saved, Lopakhin to propose to Varya, Russia to grow and prosper, when the only miraculous things in the play are Sharlotta's parlor tricks. And, when some of these expectations are not realized, they are convinced that all is for the best and that the future will be better. Gaev will undoubtedly fail as a banker, Trofimov will probably be punished more severely for agitating among the students, Lopakhin will rush away to complete another business deal that will guarantee only material improvement ("armwaving" is what Trofimov calls the action of Lopakhin's hands working independently of the heart and mind), and Ranevskaya will return to her leech of a lover in Paris, relieved that the estate has been sold at auction and its burden taken from her shoulders. Their folly, projecting their strengths as well as their weaknesses, is and apparently will continue undiminished. But in this play their foolish inflexibility, their inability to change, contributes to their resiliency.

NOTE

1. This edition may be recommended for those interested in translations that are "play-able," but, as with all translations of Chekhov, Senelick's readings of the lines should be compared with other versions to incorporate the more successful renderings by other translators. One very good translation of *The Cherry Orchard* by Avrahm Yarmolinsky appears in The Portable Chekhov, Penguin Press.

FURTHER READING

Chekhov, Anton. *Anton Chekhov's Selected Plays*. A Norton Critical Edition. Translated and Edited by Laurence Senelick. New York: Norton, 2005.

———. *Anton Chekhov. The Complete Plays*. Translated, Edited and Annotated by Laurence Senelick. New York/London: W.W. Norton & Company, 2006.

———. *The Cherry Orchard*. In *The Portable Chekhov*. Translated by Avrahm Yarmolinsky. New York: Penguin Press, 1977.

Gilman, Richard. *Chekhov's Plays: An Opening into Eternity*. New Haven, Connecticut: Yale University Press, 1995.

Pitcher, Harvey. *The Chekhov Play: A New Interpretation*. London: Chatto and Windus, 1973.

Modern Scandinavian Drama

Katherine Egerton

HENRIK IBSEN AND BJØRNSTJERNE BJØRNSON

The history of Scandinavian drama intertwines artists and companies from Denmark, Norway, and Sweden because of the countries' tight political, social, and linguistic relationships. Christiania Theatre, Norway's first professional playhouse, founded in 1827, had a Swedish-born founder and for many years, was home to a predominately Danish acting company. In its debut season, the theater put on plays that were largely French, Danish, and German, with only two pieces by Norwegian writers out of sixty performed. Early in his career, Henrik Ibsen (1828–1906) was sent to Copenhagen to study theater management at Denmark's Royal Theatre, which had long been considered the preeminent home of drama in the Scandinavian countries. Through the work of Ibsen and his contemporary, Bjørnstjerne Bjørnson, Norway emerged as a theatrical power.

Because of Ibsen and the Swedish playwright August Strindberg (1849–1912), Scandinavian drama remains on the world stage today despite the relative obscurity of the languages. Although Ibsen had a long career in the Norwegian theater before writing the plays which made him famous—and infamous—in Europe and America, it was his psychologically truthful social dramas that became the focal point of a revolution in dramatic art. Starting with *A Doll's House* (1879) and *Ghosts* (1881), Ibsen's mature masterworks changed not only the Scandinavian theater, but also had profound impacts on writers in English such as George Bernard Shaw and James Joyce. Born and raised in the Norwegian town of Skien, Ibsen left Norway in 1864 and would not return until 1891. He spent most of the intervening years, during which he would write his most celebrated plays, living in Italy and Germany. Sven Rossel writes in his *History of Scandinavian Literature:*

1870–1980 that "[w]hen Georg Brandes," the Danish critic and theorist of modernism, "encountered Ibsen at the train station in Dresden, the latter said to him challengingly, "You go home and annoy the Danes; then I will annoy the Norwegians." Annoy them he did, albeit from a comfortable distance.

Modern Norway did not emerge as a separate state until 1905, and the nineteenth century in Norway was a period of emerging nationalism. This fervency affected all kinds of artistic production. After making its impact elsewhere in Europe, literary romanticism, with its predilection for historical subjects and supernatural forces, was embraced by Scandinavian artists and writers beginning in the 1840s. In Norway in particular, writers under the influence of romanticism turned to the medieval Norse sagas for material and also began to work in the spoken language of the people rather than in the Danish that had long been the language of culture and education. The first Norwegian language theater, Det Norske Teater, was founded in Bergen in 1850 by the violinist Ole Bull and others. Ibsen joined this theater as playwright-in-residence on the strength of a very romantic one-act play called *The Warrior's Barrow,* and travelled to both Denmark and Germany to polish his skills in both direction and theater management. Bergen's Norske Teater was soon followed by the Christiania Norske Theatre, which Ibsen managed between 1857 and 1862. Ibsen's early experience emphasized theatrical spectacle, complicated sets, romantic themes, and extravagant costumes, all of which were nearly unknown in his later work, but he learned a great deal during this period about actors and audiences and the day-to-day realities of the theater, which helped him throughout his career.

Ibsen wrote his first full-length play, *Cataline,* a drama set in ancient Rome, in 1850, but this romantic and atmospheric work was rejected by the Danish-run Christiania Theatre. *Cataline* remained offstage until 1881, when it was performed in Stockholm. By that time, the style of the play was well out of fashion, largely because of Ibsen's own later triumphs, but Ibsen thought well of it and was glad to revise it for production and publication. Shortly after he left Norway in 1864, Ibsen wrote two of his best-known early plays, *Brand* (1866) and *Peer Gynt* (1867). Perhaps burned out after many hard years in the theater, during which he was often extremely poor, Ibsen wrote both of these plays for readers, rather than for audiences. Both were eventually successful both on stage and off despite rapid changes in theatrical taste. After writing *Peer Gynt,* a romantic verse drama in five acts with a huge cast of characters and many features difficult to envision, much less stage, Ibsen confronted European literature's move toward naturalism directly. As he wrote to fellow playwright Bjørnstjerne Bjørnson, "If I am no poet, then I shall try my luck as a photographer."

However, it would be Bjørnson, rather than Ibsen, who would first bring the social problem play to the stage. Bjørnstjerne Bjørnson (1832–1910), a prolific writer in many genres, began his career writing poems and folk tales and stories of everyday people. He captured a middle ground between romanticism and deterministic naturalism in his writing, and also pursued a career as a critic and theater manager, following in Ibsen's steps as theater manager. One of his more successful early works, the trilogy *Sigurd Slembe* (1862), was drawn from the Old Norse sagas. In the 1870s, however, Bjørnson shifted his focus away from the romantic stories and folk tales that had filled his career. Instead, writing in Rome in the early 1870s, he produced the "plays that introduced the modern problem drama in Norway," *The Editor* (1875) and *The Bankrupt* (1875). The latter of these two provides an interesting counterweight to Ibsen's *The Pillars of Society*, as both plays stage the conflict between social and individual morality. In Bjørnson's version, it is the immoral man who bows to public morality, whereas in Ibsen's plays, the process almost always works the other way around. These two plays were soon followed by *The New System* (1879), which strongly criticized the church, and *Leonarda* (1879), an even more controversial piece about the rights of a divorced woman that was widely seen as contrary to conventional morality. He also composed the lyrics to Norway's national anthem, and was awarded the Nobel Prize for literature in 1903.

A Doll's House

Thus, when Henrik Ibsen wrote *A Doll's House* in 1879, he was participating in an already vibrant artistic discussion about the conflicts between society and the individual, the waning influence of the church in European society, and the rise of naturalism and social realism in art. Georg Brandes, the influential Danish critic and author of *Main Currents in the Literature of the Nineteenth Century*, declared that "what is alive in modern literature shows in its capacity to submit problems to debate." Following *The Pillars of Society* (1877), one of Ibsen's first attempts at the social problem play, Ibsen showed in *A Doll's House* that the "woman problem" was not going to slink away without triggering massive social upheaval. *A Doll's House* was first performed at the Royal Theatre in Copenhagen in December, 1879, and performances soon followed in Christiania (now Oslo) and Bergen. The problem posed in *A Doll's House* was that of a woman, Nora Helmer, who walks out of her home and marriage, choosing to become an autonomous adult rather than remain as a child. *A Doll's House* ends on the sound of a slamming door which, as the play's fame spread, became known as "the slam heard around the world."

The play opens in the Christmas season, and Nora has been shopping for her family. Her husband, Torvald, a newly-promoted bank manager, scolds her for wasting money and preaches against debt, but he can't bear to be harsh with his darling for long. Ibsen quickly establishes Torvald and Nora's relationship as that of an indulgent master and his pet, and when Nora begs for even more money,

Torvald cannot refuse. Nora's spendthrift ways, a legacy from her father, are part of her charm; Torvald cannot hold her responsible for serious matters while maintaining his cherished illusion that she is his "little lark twittering." Soon, Nora's old friend, Kristine Linde, arrives after a ten-year absence. Mrs. Linde tells of a harsh but expedient marriage to provide for her mother and brother, and years of work after her husband died leaving her poor again. She has come to see if Nora can secure her a job in Torvald's bank. This reunion provides Nora with the chance to describe her own marriage and its history, including the Helmers' early poverty and a dangerous illness of Torvald's that necessitated a year's recovery in a warm climate. Nora says at first that she got the money to pay for this southern sojourn from her father, but later, when Mrs. Linde condescends to Nora, telling her that "you really know so little of life's burdens yourself…you're just a child," Nora reveals that she raised the money—forty-eight hundred crowns—herself. Given that it was illegal at the time for a married woman to borrow money without her husband's consent, Mrs. Linde is dubious, but Nora coyly assures her a resourceful woman can accomplish many things. Torvald never knew the money did not come from her father, and that this is the great secret of their marriage. While Nora has been acting the pretty young thing, begging for treats, she has been scrimping and saving and even secretly earning money to repay this hidden debt. Torvald's promotion, therefore, will give Nora financial freedom far beyond what Torvald can imagine.

Two other characters enter the Helmers' house. Doctor Rank, an old family friend and a regular visitor, occupies Torvald and so when Nils Krogstad arrives, he joins the women. Krogstad is a shifty lawyer who now works as a clerk in Torvald's bank and has "a hand in all kinds of business." Soon, Rank and Krogstad exchange places, and Rank goes off on Krogstad, calling him as a blackmailer. Krogstad, after his conversation with Torvald, leaves the house. Nora has clearly been affected by Krogstad's presence, and soon after she is left alone, he returns. They speak of many things, including how Krogstad lost his reputation, his fears that he will lose his job at the bank in favor of Mrs. Linde, and Nora's loan. Rank's suspicions of Krogstad turn out to be well-founded; Krogstad is Nora's creditor, and he knows that Nora's loan documents show her father's signature, dated three days after his death. Confronted with this information, Nora admits to forgery, protesting that she would have done anything to save Torvald's life, even when his pride would have kept him from borrowing money in the same situation. Krogstad gives Nora an ultimatum: she must secure his job at the bank, or he will tell Torvald about her loan and the forgery. Krogstad assures her that the crime that ruined his career "was nothing more and nothing worse," and "if I get shoved down a second time, you're going to keep me company." The first act ends when Torvald, who saw Krogstad leave, asks Nora if he begged her to plead his case. Nora, working hard to squeeze information out of Torvald while still keeping up her childish banter, must seem unconcerned as Torvald, reveling in righteous-ness, condemns Krogstad. Krogstad's very presence in his own home, Torvald declares, must morally contaminate his children, and Torvald "feel[s] physically revolted when [he's] anywhere near such a person."

Throughout the second act, Nora must manage the unfolding events as best she can. In the gaiety of the Christmas season, the fashionable Helmers are going to a costume party at which Nora will dance the tarantella. Nora's preparations set the stage for the act's new revelations. Torvald's past intimacy with Krogstad, an old childhood friend, complicates the situation even further. Dr. Rank also reveals himself to be ill, but wishes to spare Torvald the sight of his death, and Mrs. Linde begins to suspect that is was Rank who lent Nora the money because he loves her. There is a great deal of drama with passing letters as Torvald sends off Krogstad's dismissal, and Krogstad leaves a letter describing Nora's crimes in the Helmers' locked post box. Nora desperately tries to delay Torvald's reading of the letter by focusing his attention on her dancing as she prepares for the party. Meanwhile, Mrs. Linde has gone after Krogstad in an attempt to make him retract his charges. When Nora discovers that Krogstad, having left town, is beyond reach, she begins to count the hours before her suicide.

The third act sets up two contrasting domestic scenes. The first, between Krogstad and Mrs. Linde, reveals that when she chose to marry for money, it was Krogstad she left behind. Once she explains that she only married before for the sake of her family, she offers to marry him and help raise his children. Remorseful about the letter he sent Torvald, Krogstad offers to retract it, but Mrs. Linde now believes that the lies in the Helmers' marriage must be exposed, whatever the consequences. When Torvald reads the letter in Nora's presence, he explodes, carrying on about how Nora has deceived *him*, about what this information could do to *his* career, how *he* has been betrayed. In the middle of his tirade, another letter from Krogstad arrives, apologizing for his earlier threats. Torvald is elated: "Yes, yes, it's true! I'm saved. Nora, I'm saved!" Having burned the letters, Torvald turns magnanimously to Nora, offering to right all her wrongs and protect her from the cruelties of the world:

> You're safe here; I'll keep you like a hunted dove I've rescued out of a hawk's claws. I'll bring peace to your poor, shuddering heart. Gradually it'll happen, Nora; you'll see. Tomorrow all this will look different to you; then everything will be as it was. I won't have to go on repeating I forgive you; you'll feel it for yourself. How can you imagine I'd ever conceivably want to disown you—or can even blame you in any way? Ah, you don't know a man's heart, Nora. For a man there's something indescribably sweet and satisfying in knowing he's forgiven his wife—and forgiven her out of a full and open heart. It's as if she belongs to him in two ways now: in a sense he's given her fresh into the world again, and she's become his wife and his child as well. From now on that's what you'll be to me—you little, bewildered, helpless thing.

During this speech, Nora has been just offstage, changing out of her dance costume, so the audience does not get to see her reaction to Torvald's new declarations as they are spoken. When she emerges, she is entirely transformed. She insists on confronting him as an equal, an adult, and she questions the whole basis of their marriage. Remembering her father, she tells Torvald that he "used to call me his doll-child, and he played with me the way I played with my dolls." Now she sees that Torvald sees her as nothing but a child, but she understands that this makes her unfit to be either a wife or a mother. First, she must become an adult. Throughout the play, Nora has been waiting for a "miracle," for Torvald to treat her as a woman and an equal rather than as a child and a toy. Once she understands that her miracle is impossible, she declares her intention to leave her home, her marriage, and her children. "I'm a human being, no less than you," she says, "or anyway, I ought to try to become one." Torvald appeals to religion, to morality, and to her affection for her children, but Nora remains steadfast in her determination. She absolves him of any legal responsibility for her welfare, forces an exchange of wedding rings, and gives back her house key. Torvald, now certain that she is serious, begs to be told what "miracle" could keep her at home. "You and I," she tells him, "would both have to transform ourselves to the point that—Oh Torvald, I've stopped believing in miracles." As she leaves the house, the offstage slamming of a door ends the play.

A Doll's House had immense social and psychological impact. The play utterly changed the drama in Europe and America as actors, writers, and audiences struggled to adapt to a newly realistic and socially relevant theater. The role of Nora made Danish actress Betty Hennings an international star, and other ambitious actresses rushed to play the part. In Germany, however, Hedwig Niemann-Raabe refused to play a Nora who would abandon her children. Although he denounced it as a terrible choice and a "barbarous outrage," Ibsen opted to provide an alternate ending, in which Nora sees her sleeping children and cannot bring herself to leave, rather than see another writer change his text. "Oh, I am sinning against myself," she says, "but I cannot leave them." The first professional production in London, starring Janet Achurch, was mounted in 1889, and while critics were generally unimpressed, partially because the still-dominant acting style of the day was incompatible with Ibsen's text, the actress Elizabeth Robins saw in the role a completely new kind of theater for women that she would pursue for the rest of her career. In her essay, "Ibsen and Feminism," Gail Finney traces Ibsen's interest in and sympathy with the feminist movement, noting both his socialist views and his friendship with noted Norwegian writer and feminist Camilla Collett. The play became a rallying point for advocates of socialism and feminism alike, and an amateur reading of the play in England in 1886 included both Eleanor Marx, daughter of Karl Marx, and Bernard Shaw in the cast.

Ghosts

After the spectacular success of *A Doll's House,* Ibsen followed with an even more controversial play. *Ghosts,* published in 1881 and first performed in Chicago (although not in English) in 1882, holds as its theme that children cannot escape the sins of their parents. As in *The Doll's House,* the determining events in *Ghosts* have already occurred by the time the play opens. These are the ghosts of the title. The play follows through on the characters' histories, and the audience is left to gape in horror as the consequences reveal themselves in Sophoclean fashion. The provincial American premiere was only one of many signs of the controversy *Ghosts* generated after its publication. The play was widely considered to be obscene, and J.L. Styan writes, "even well-educated people would not have the book in the house." Oswald Alving, the play's protagonist, is a young painter who has been fatally infected by his father's misdeeds, both by a venereal disease (likely syphilis), causing him to lose his mind, and by the fact that his mother's maid, Regine, whom he loves, is revealed to be his half-sister. Ibsen's target in *Ghosts* is not Oswald or his suffering mother, Helene Alving, but the social codes and mores that forced Mrs. Alving to hides her husband's crimes and remain in his house. "After Nora," Ibsen wrote in 1882, "Mrs. Alving had to come." Mrs. Alving is a Nora who left, but could not stay away.

As the play opens, Mrs. Alving has just used her dead husband's money to build an orphanage. The two other principal roles in the play are that of Engstrand, a dissolute laborer who Regine believes to be her father, and Pastor Manders, Mrs. Alving's friend and spiritual advisor. Manders is at once overbearingly righteous and also a hypocritical buffoon. The audience soon learns that Manders was responsible for Mrs. Alving's return to her degenerate husband. Even now, he berates her for having sent her son away as a child, although Mrs. Alving believes that removing Oswald from his father's baleful influence was the correct thing to do. Horrified to learn that Mrs. Alving is reading free-thinking literature, he convinces her not to insure the newly-built orphanage against fire, as it would reflect badly on her faith in God, and, therefore, on his reputation as a clergyman. Despite the fact that Mrs. Alving's money cannot build two orphanages, and that Engstrand only the day before started a fire in his building-site workshop, she agrees. She is not so pliable, however, when Manders suggests that Regine return to live with Engstrand, who has asked her to preside over a seaman's home (and likely brothel) that he wants to open in the town. Manders may have vague designs on the young woman himself, which will be difficult to fulfill as long as she lives under Mrs. Alving's watch.

When Oswald arrives on the scene, looking like the ghost of his father, he further horrifies Manders as he tells him that many of his artistic friends eschew marriage, and start their families without the blessings of the church. After Oswald

leaves the room, Mrs. Alving tells Manders in a horrifyingly straightforward manner that she returned to a marriage as poisoned as the one she left; her return had
no salutary effect on the Captain's behavior. At the end of the first act, Mrs. Alving
hears Regine cry out from another room, and when she investigates, she discovers
that Oswald has tried to force himself on the maid, behaving toward her just as
Captain Alving had to her mother. "Ghosts," Mrs. Alving calls them, "Those two
from the greenhouse—have come back."

In the second act, Mrs. Alving's feelings about Regine change once she understands that Oswald is pursuing her; she becomes determined to send her away.
Manders and Mrs. Alving continue to discuss the family's sordid history and
Manders' own role in it, but their views on the moral questions involved remain
vastly different. As George Bryan writes, "[Manders] sees his behavior as a victory; [Mrs. Alving] views it as a crime". Once Manders leaves and Oswald rejoins
his mother, he tells her about the illness which is destroying his body and his
mind. A doctor in Paris has diagnosed his disease as inherited, telling Oswald "
[r]ight from your birth, your whole system has been more or less worm-eaten."
Oswald, who had at that point been spared the knowledge of his father's debauch-
eries, had preferred to think that he has brought this fate upon himself. Now back
in his mother's house, he wishes that his illness were his father's, as that would
lessen his self-loathing. Mrs. Alving, distraught, decides to tell her son everything
and give him every chance at happiness—even Regine—but before she can
speak, word comes that the Captain Alving Orphanage is going up in flames.

In the aftermath of this catastrophe, Engstrand blackmails Manders, telling the
pastor that he saw him carelessly throw a just-extinguished candle into some
wood shavings. Mrs. Alving, still determined to be rid of her husband's money,
empowers him to dispose of the rest of it, which Manders then gives to Engstrand's planned seaman's home. Once Regine learns the truth about her parent-
age, she leaves the Alvings' house, resentful that she has been brought up as a
servant. The dying Oswald and his mother are left alone in the house, and
Oswald, fearing his impending dementia, asks his mother to overdose him with
morphine once he begins to lose his mind. She finally agrees, but when the attack
comes, she cannot (perhaps yet) bear to kill her child. The curtain comes down as
Mrs. Alving stands "staring at him in speechless horror" as Oswald, lost to
rational thought, finally sees the sun shining on his father's house.

Hedda Gabler and Other Ibsen Plays

Ibsen followed *Ghosts* with several other plays in which he slowly began to
replace social and psychological realism with a more mystical and symbolic
universe that audiences sometimes found hard to penetrate, much less accept.
An Enemy of the People (1882) and *Hedda Gabler* (1890) are the two later Ibsen

plays most often performed today, and they, together with *A Doll's House* and *Ghosts*, have solidified his enduring reputation as a social realist. Other late plays in the Ibsen canon, including *The Wild Duck* (1884), *Rosmersholm* (1886), and his final play, *When We Dead Awaken* (1899), feature characters who, unable to find emotional fulfillment in this world, gladly leave it. Some interpreters of Ibsen's work, such as Elizabeth Robins, saw his last play in particular as a betrayal of his earlier social ideals, but Ibsen was determined until the end of his career to write what he thought was true regardless of whether it was popular.

AUGUST STRINDBERG

The career of the prolific Swedish playwright August Strindberg (1849–1912) follows some of the same patterns evident in Ibsen's; the early romanticism, a move to realistic drama that brought widespread fame, and a later transformation away from the social problem play toward new forms. In Strindberg's case, this last stage takes its name from his 1902 work, *A Dream Play*. Strindberg, in the Dream plays, moves much farther into expressionism and surrealism than Ibsen had travelled, and today, these late plays form an important part of his legacy. Born in Stockholm to a prosperous merchant and a woman from a lower social class who had been his housekeeper, Strindberg attended the University of Uppsala and worked as a teacher and journalist while trying to establish himself in the theater.

It was a novel that first established him as a literary success. *The Red Room* (1880) was celebrated for social and political insight in the wake of Sweden's economic upheavals of the 1870s. His new fame led to the staging of his earlier play, *Master Olof* (1872), but it was not well received. Perceived even today as something of a misogynist, Strindberg reacted sharply to Ibsen's *A Doll's House*, writing a short story of the same title in which "[o]nly the woman who wants to lead an independent life *outside* the family is censured." In the same collection, entitled *Married* (1884), his novella *The Reward of Virtue* led to his being brought to court in Sweden on charges of blasphemy. While he was acquitted, he found the experience personally devastating, and it was followed by the first of many periods of mental instability. Heavily influenced by Emile Zola's "Naturalism in the Theatre," when he returned to writing plays, he turned to naturalism in *The Father* (1887), *Miss Julie* (1888), and *The Creditors* (1889). In these plays, the protagonists succumb to the cruel forces that surround them. Julie's fate is perhaps the most tragic, as she has triggered her own downfall by allowing herself to be caught in the larger class struggle. An aristocratic young woman who falls for a servant, Jean, while at a party, Julie walks off the stage at the play's end prepared to commit suicide.

After he moved to Berlin in 1892, Strindberg became fascinated with alchemy and theosophy, eventually undergoing a religious crisis he later wrote about in the books *Inferno* (1897) and *Legends* (1898). He also wrote a dramatic version of this story in the three parts of *To Damascus* (1889–1904). The plays he produced after this upheaval fall into two categories: historical dramas in the Shakespearean mode such as *Gustavus Vasa* (1899), *Gustav Adolf* (1900), and *Gustav III* (1903); and experiments in Expressionism, including *The Dance of Death* (1900), *A Dream Play* (1902), and *The Ghost Sonata* (1907). Heavily symbolic, both *To Damascus* and *A Dream Play* required new modes of theatrical production in order to succeed. Strindberg eventually insisted on minimal props and sets, which the Intima Teatern in Stockholm, founded by Strindberg and the actor August Falk in 1907, achieved through both necessity and design. Seating merely 161 people, and with a playing area only twenty feet wide and thirteen feet deep, the Intima Teatern dispensed with painted scenery altogether, allowing the actors to create the spaces they inhabited. In that year, Strindberg wrote to Falk, "[w]ith simple décor, the really important points become evident: the personality, the part itself, the speech, the action and facial expression....Yes, the spoken word is everything....[T]he play can be acted anywhere." Strindberg wrote five plays specifically for this space, known as the Chamber plays: *The Storm*, *The Burned House*, *The Ghost Sonata*, *The Pelican* (all in 1907), and *The Black Glove* (1909), although twenty-four of his plays were performed in the theater during the three years of its existence.

Strindberg's dramatic legacy can be seen in the work of many of the great twentieth century playwrights, including Eugene O'Neill, Luigi Pirandello, Tennessee Williams, Harold Pinter, and Edward Albee. In the speech he sent to be read at the Nobel Prize presentation, O'Neill wrote of Strindberg:

> It was reading his plays when I first started to write back in the winter of 1913–14 that, above all else, first gave me the vision of what modern drama could be, and first inspired me with the urge to write for the theater myself. If there is anything of lasting worth in my work, it is due to that original impulse from him, which has continued as my inspiration down all the years since then—to the ambition I received then to follow in the footsteps of his genius as worthily as my talent might permit, and with the same integrity of purpose.

Compared to the immense influence that both Ibsen and Strindberg have had on the drama, Scandinavian playwrights working later in the twentieth century have had relatively little impact on the world stage. In Sweden, the most important playwrights to follow Strindberg were Hjalmar Bergman (1883–1931) and Nobel laureate Pär Lagerkvist (1891–1974), whose *The Secret of Heaven* (1919) follows on stylistically from *To Damascus*. In Denmark, playwright and pastor Kaj Munk (1889–1944), author of *Herod the King* (1928) and *The Word* (1932), wrote strong religious dramas until his death at the hands of the Gestapo during World War II.

Danish playwright Kjeld Abell (1901–61) carried on the symbolic drama in *The Blue Pekingese* (1954) and *The Cry* (1961). Today, the Norwegian playwrights Jon Fosse (b. 1959), whose plays include *The Name* (1995), *Night Songs* (1998), and *Dream of Autumn* (1999), and Cecilie Løveid (b. 1951), author of *Barock Friise* (1993) and *Austria* (1998), have achieved increasing prominence in many European theaters, and their work has been featured at the Ibsen Festival at Norway's National Theatre in Oslo. In 2006, the centenary of Ibsen's death, his work was celebrated around the world.

FURTHER READING

Bryan, George F. *An Ibsen Companion: A Dictionary-Guide to the Life, Works, and Critical Reception of Henrik Ibsen*. Westport, Connecticut: Greenwood Press, 1984.

Finney, Gail. "Ibsen and Feminism." *The Cambridge Companion to Ibsen*. Edited by James McFarlane. Cambridge: Cambridge University Press, 1994.

Ibsen, Henrick. *A Doll House*. In *Ibsen: Four Major Plays, Volume I*. Translated by Rolf Fjelde. New York: Signet Classic, 1992.

———. *Ghosts*. In *Ibsen: Four Major Plays, Volume II*. Translated by Rolf Fjelde New York: Signet Classic, 1970.

Marker, Frederick and Lise-Lone Marker. *The Scandinavian Theatre: A Short History*. Oxford: Basil Blackwell, 1975.

Rossel, Sven H. *A History of Scandinavian Literature 1870–1980*. Translated by Anne C. Ulmer. Minneapolis: University of Minnesota Press, 1982.

Shafer, Yvonne. *Approaches to Teaching Ibsen's A Doll's House*. New York: The Modern Language Association of America, 1985.

Styan, J. L. *Modern Drama in Theory and Practice*. 3 vols. Cambridge: Cambridge University Press, 1981.

❧

Southern U.S. Drama

Catherine Seltzer

The theater of the American South is intimately connected to American drama in the larger sense, sharing many of its varied thematic and formal trends. However, Southern drama also can be examined as a discrete entity, one that possesses its own unique history and that is marked by a distinct aesthetic. In each of four broadly defined historical periods—the colonial era, the Civil War era, the modern era, and the contemporary era—Southern dramatists were guided by a sense of regional self-consciousness, repeatedly taking as their focus the evolving identity of the South and its relationship to American culture and political life. By examining each of these periods and considering a number of representative works, we can trace the development of Southern theater and the ideological challenges it has faced over the past two hundred and thirty years.

Colonial-era Southern drama was often erratic in its production, and, in fact, much of the early eighteenth century theatrical scene in the South was comprised of European works performed by English troupes. Despite this, however, the theater held an important place in early Southern culture. Whereas Northern colonists often viewed the theater with mistrust, perceiving it as a challenge to Puritan values, Southerners embraced the idea of drama as a public source of entertainment. Moreover, the theater ultimately was incorporated into the Cavalier ideal: to attend the theater, or even to try one's hand at playwriting, was a mark of gentility. This appreciation of theater in the South led to the creation of a number of traveling companies; the establishment of permanent theaters in important colonial centers such as Williamsburg, Richmond, Charleston, and New Orleans; and, eventually, the production of work by native playwrights. Most of these works are not considered to be of exceedingly strong literary merit, but they do provide important insight into the development of the Southern culture.

EARLY SOUTHERN DRAMA

Early Southern playwrights often took regional themes as their focus, but while they frequently rooted their plays in depictions of local color, they also portrayed the South as making important contributions to the emerging identity of the new nation. Virginia playwright Robert Munsford (c. 1737–83) is identified as the first Southern dramatist, and while his plays were not produced in his lifetime, they speak to the importance of local politics and their role in the national ethos. *The Candidates* (c. 1770), a three-act play, chronicles the attempts of an earnest candidate, Mr. Wou'dbe, to be elected to the House of Burgesses. Wou'dbe is opposed by two corrupt candidates, the aptly named Sir John Toddy and Mr. Strutabout, and his fate is determined by voters of seemingly dubious judgment, the comic Mr. Guzzle and Mr. Julip among them. Munsford's play functions most obviously as a satire of Virginia politics and, more specifically, as a condemnation of the pervasive role of alcohol in legislative proceedings, but in its satisfying resolution, in which Wou'dbe is elected, *The Candidates* also asserts the triumph of personal integrity and celebrates the power of democracy. Thus, although he takes aim at the folly of local politics, Munford also underscores what Wou'dbe identifies as "a spirit of independence becoming Virginians."

A second Virginia playwright, George Washington Park Custis (1781–1857), viewed his plays as a platform to remind his audiences of the South's role in the birth of the new nation. The step-grandson of George Washington, Custis's first play, the historical drama *The Indian Prophecy* (1827), predates the story of Washington as statesman, and instead positions him as central to the exploration of the new American land. The prophecy of the title is an Indian chief's declaration that Washington is inextricably linked to the future of the nation. Custis's most popular play, *Pocahontas; or, The Settlers of Virginia, a National Drama* (1830), is similar in its emphasis on Virginians' importance in early American expansion. The work takes as its focus the legends surrounding Pocahontas, recounting her decision to save John Smith by offering to sacrifice herself, as well as her celebrated love affair with John Rolfe. While Pocahontas's narrative was already highly romantic in its basic premise, Custis took a number of liberties with recorded history, highlighting the patriotism and bravery of Rolfe and Smith. The play appealed to audiences already invested in a vision of the South as a chivalric idyll, and *Pocahontas* both underscored the importance of Virginia in the nation's history and linked cavalier values with American imperialism.

In the mid-nineteenth century, however, Southern drama became less concerned with aligning Southern and American values and instead focused on defending the South's position on the issue of slavery. Before the 1850s, issues of race had been relegated to minstrel shows, musical theater in which white actors depicted African American culture, relying heavily on the predominant stereotypes of the day. The minstrel shows, highly troubling in today's context, offered white Southern audiences a voyeuristic glimpse into black life. However, as regional tensions grew in the years before the Civil War, race was not merely an object of fascination for Southern audiences, but was acknowledged as a subject of political importance.

This shift can be credited in part to the popularity of Northern adaptations of Harriet Beecher Stowe's novel *Uncle Tom's Cabin*. Northern productions of the play depicted the human toll of slavery in highly sentimental terms, encouraging audiences to view the North as the morally sound counterpart to the slave-holding South. While Stowe's work was banned throughout much of the South, abolitionists hoped that toned-down versions of the play might convince Southern audiences of the horrors of slavery, and they encouraged Southern stagings of *Uncle Tom's Cabin*. Southern versions of the play often radically altered Stowe's message, however. In one of the most famous among them, Joseph M. Field's (1810–56) *Uncle Tom's Cabin; or Life in the South as It is* (1854), abolitionists are cast as absurdly misguided philanthropists who do not understand slavery but are driven by their knee-jerk mistrust of all things Southern. While Field's depiction of Northerners is highly satirical, his depiction of the South is more sentimental: in his rendering of Stowe's work, the slaves beg to return home to their Southern masters after their emancipation. Field's play was followed by a slew of satiric versions of the novel by Southern playwrights, many of which were greeted by enthusiastic audiences throughout the South.

Other antebellum playwrights moved away from a romanticized treatment of slavery, instead focusing on issues of states' rights and regional identity. For example, the novelist, poet, critic, and playwright William Gilmore Simms (1806–70) saw himself as a spokesperson for secession, and his plays often echo the didactic nature of his essays, including his well-known contribution to the 1852 collection of essays, *The Pro-Slavery Argument*. Simms's 1847 play, *Norman Maurice; or the Man of the People*, for instance, features extended arguments for the sanctioning of slavery in Missouri. The play culminates when Maurice defeats an antislavery candidate in a Senate race, establishing himself as the voice of the people; in this way, even if Maurice cannot guarantee the presence of slavery in Missouri, the fact that he is given a platform in Congress is seen as a triumph in the crusade for the preservation of states' rights.

The sectionalist fervor evident in antebellum theater spilled onto the wartime stage as well. During the Civil War, the theater became even more popular in the South as audiences sought diversions from the war, and many new theaters, acting troupes, and playwrights were born in its cauldron. James Dabney McCabe's (1842–83) immensely popular play *The Guerillas* (1863) was the sort of romantic epic that Southern audiences sought. The play tells the story of the multi-generational Douglas family, each of whom bravely staves off the Northern soldiers who attack their Virginia homestead. *The Guerillas* includes a number of

Southern types—the honorable patriarch, the heroic cavalier, the revered steel magnolia, and the devoted slave—and in doing so, the play functioned to reify the South's image of itself and to assure audiences of the continuity of Southern values.

THE TWENTIETH CENTURY

Yet antebellum theater's insistence on a coherent vision of the South became untenable in the decades following the South's defeat, and drama of the modern era is preoccupied with exploring the South's paradoxes rather than celebrating its mythic stature. Southern drama was not alone in this shift; rather, it was part of the larger cultural movement of the Southern Renascence, a period that produced a "literature conscious of the past in the present," in the words of Allen Tate. This period, generally recognized as existing from 1920 to 1950, spawned many of the South's greatest works of fiction and poetry, and it represents a flowering of Southern drama as well, much of which is credited to the period's three most important playwrights: Paul Green, Lillian Hellman, and Tennessee Williams.

Paul Green (1894–1981), who originally was based in Chapel Hill, North Carolina, wrote a number of plays for performance by the Carolina Playmakers, and later, for Group Theatre troupes in New York. Regardless of where they were staged, however, many of his best plays deal with Southern themes. While he is recognized for his treatment of folk themes, Green's plays avoided sentimentalized depictions of Southern life and instead sought authenticity in their depiction of Southern culture, including the generally taboo subject of race relations. His 1926 play, *In Abraham's Bosom: The Biography of a Negro,* was widely acclaimed and ultimately was awarded the Pulitzer Prize. The play tells the story of Abe McCranie, who is half black and half white, and his attempts to build a school for African American children in a skeptical rural community. He is opposed both by whites, who see his project as threatening, and blacks, who are dismissive of the importance of education or question the effectiveness of Abe's school. Abe grows increasingly frustrated, lashing out at lethargic students and at his half-brother, Lonnie, who leads the charge against the school. The play ends as a tragedy: Abe kills Lonnie and the school is burned down by the Klan; the promise of the improvement of race relations is destroyed along with the school. In the final phase of his career, Green turned his attention to historical drama, the most popular of which was the outdoor drama *The Lost Colony* (1937), a play that still is regularly performed today on Roanoke Island, North Carolina. While the outdoor dramas have not received the critical acclaim of Green's earlier plays, they serve an important function as what Green identified as "a theatre of the people," one that is free of the trappings of urban theater.

Like Green, Lillian Hellman (1905–84) was interested in the role of the socially disenfranchised in Southern society. As the first important woman playwright in the South, she did not embrace the expectations of the genteel "lady writer," but explored once unmentionable subjects, including bigotry, homosexuality, and industrial exploitation. One of her most well-received plays, *The Little Foxes* (1939), is a brutal analysis of the destructive elements of the ideologies of the New South. Set at the turn of the twentieth century, it follows the Hubbard family's attempts to abandon their lower-class origins by entering the ruthless world of cotton manufacturing, an enterprise that preys on the poor whites and blacks of the community, pitting them against one another. The Hubbards' greed is juxtaposed by the fragile Birdie, a once landed aristocrat who has married into the family. Birdie is helpless in the face of the Hubbards' materialism, just as the ideals of the Old South are lost in the exaggerated capitalism of the New South. Hellman revisited the Hubbard family saga in her 1946 play, *Another Part of the Forest*, which traces the family's desire for a higher status a generation earlier. These plays, along with *The Children's Hour* (1934), which addresses lesbianism, and *Watch on the Rhine* (1941), about Nazisim, have cemented Hellman's position as one of the South's most important playwrights.

The central figure of Southern theater, however, is unquestionably Tennessee Williams (1911–83). Just as William Faulkner's novels serve as a touchstone of Southern fiction, Williams, a fellow Mississippian, has had an enormous impact in defining Southern drama, and, in fact, in shaping the notion of "Southernness" itself. Like Green and Hellman, Williams sought to explore the complex terrain of the New South, and his plays depict the simultaneous decadence and emptiness of the Southern ideal in the twentieth century. His first important play, *The Glass Menagerie* (1944), is not set in the South, but, in its depiction of Amanda Wingfield, a single mother who clings to the mannerisms of the Southern belle, Williams depicts the irony inherent in the notion of the Southern lady inhabiting a modern industrial landscape. The play chronicles the disintegration of the Wingfield family, as Amanda's children, Tom and Laura, struggle to meet Amanda's outmoded expectations for them. Much of the play revolves around Amanda's hopes that a "gentleman caller" will come for the disabled and introverted Laura, and when the relationship fails to materialize as Laura had hoped, the painful reality of their situations washes over Laura and Tom. Williams identified the work as a "memory play," and while the term refers in large part to Tom, who narrates the play, and his recollections of Laura's plight, it also can be seen as underscoring the ways in which Amanda is haunted by the memories of her Southern past.

Many of the same themes are explored in Williams's 1947 Pulitzer Prize-winning masterpiece, *A Streetcar Named Desire*, which places at its center Blanche DuBois, perhaps Southern literature's most famous fading belle. Like Amanda,

Blanche desperately clings to the markers of aristocratic standing, and her down-fall is both tragic and fascinating. Blanche arrives at the New Orleans apartment of her sister, Stella, after a series of scandals have forced her to leave Belle Reve, the family plantation. Disdainful of Stella's brutish husband, Stanley Kowalski, and critical of the dilapidated condition of the couple's neighborhood, the ironi-cally named Elysian Fields, Blanche tries to inhabit a world of "magic" rather than to face the realities that surround her. Ultimately, when her past indiscretions are revealed and she is raped by Stanley, she fully retreats into her fantasies and is taken to an insane asylum, left only to rely "on the kindness of strangers." Blanche's breakdown, and Stella's determination to believe Stanley's denial of her sister's rape, speak in part to the impossibility of balancing Southern ideals with the modern condition. Williams returns to the theme of the inherent repres-sion of identity in Southern gender roles in many of his later plays, including many of his most famous: *Summer and Smoke* (1948), *Cat on a Hot Tin Roof* (1955), and *Suddenly Last Summer* (1958). It is his use of sex and violence to explore a range of Southern experiences that have made him among the most famous of American playwrights.

The modern era of Southern drama is also notable for its inclusion of a number of important black playwrights. While not as widely celebrated as Green, Hellman, and Williams, their contribution to Southern letters was undeniable and it gave birth to a new era of African American playwriting in the South. Zora Neale Hurston, the anthropologist and novelist, wrote a number of plays during this period, several of which focus on discriminatory practices within the black community. For example, *Color Struck* (1925) demonstrates how one character, Emma, loses both her partner and her daughter because of her paranoia that she will not be compared favorably to lighter-skinned women. Hurston's 1930 play *Mule Bone,* written with the poet Langston Hughes, is a comedy that depicts black folk life, focusing on the ways in which inhabitants of a small town can argue passionately with one another but still coexist happily. Willis Richardson (1889–1977) was one of the most prolific black playwrights of the modern era, composing more than thirty plays. His play *The Broken Banjo: A Folk Tragedy* (1925), is a one-act play that depicts an argument between Matt Tuner and his brother-in law over a banjo. Their disagreement escalates until Matt is taken to jail and family is fractured. The play serves as a commentary on the fragility of the black commu-nity. These plays not only provide important insight into black life in the twentieth century South, but they represent the inclusion of African American playwrights into the Southern canon, a genre that was most visibly dominated by white, male playwrights in the colonial and antebellum periods.

The contemporary era of Southern theater represents yet another shift in focus. While, like their predecessors, contemporary Southern playwrights often place the region at the center of their imaginative vision, the contemporary South is not as clearly defined as the Old South, certainly, or even the New South. This "No South," as it has been termed, is the result of regional homogenization, or what has been identified as the "McDonald-ization" of the South. Contemporary Southern playwrights, then, are charged not with either justifying or challenging Southern culture, as were their predecessors, but determining if a distinct Southern culture still exists and locating that culture in the national ethos.

One of the most successful recent Southern playwrights is Beth Henley (b. 1952), whose 1981 play *Crimes of the Heart* won the Pulitzer Prize. The play examines the lives of three sisters, each of whom is unconventional in her own right: Meg refuses to be evacuated in a hurricane, Lenny snaps and attacks a neighbor, and Babe shoots her wayward husband. The sisters are traditional Southern eccentrics, those tolerated despite, or even celebrated because of, their dysfunctionality. Yet *Crimes of the Heart* is not merely a contemporary local color tale: instead, the play concerns itself with the sisters' attempts to understand how the past has affected them and to form a genuine community that both acknowledges this past and allows them to move forward. The play ends on an optimistic note, as the women recognize that they share an undeniable and meaningful bond.

Like Henley, Horton Foote (b. 1916) is interested in the role that the fading Southern tradition plays in contemporary life. While he is known primarily for *The Orphans' Home Cycle,* a series of nine plays written between 1994 and 1997 that follow the development of a single character, one of his best plays is *The Trip to Bountiful* (1953), a work that offers a meditation on the power of the Southern home. In it, Carrie Watts travels from the city of Houston to her family's country home, where she finds she is filled with purpose. The Agrarian ideals of the South are blended with a modern world-weariness, and Carrie finds a sense of true belonging among the country people she encounters.

Henley and Foote are not alone, and, indeed, the contemporary South has already produced a slew of successful playwrights, including Marsha Norman, Preston Jones, and Romulus Linney. They join a long tradition of Southern dramatists who have sought to explore the complex and shifting environment of the South, seeking to identify the region's unique qualities while defining it in relation to the American experience.

FURTHER READING

Flora, Joseph M. and Lucinda Mackethan, eds. *The Companion to Southern Literature.* Baton Rouge: Louisiana State University Press, 2002.

Hobson, Fred. *The Southern Writer and the Postmodern World.* Athens, Georgia: University of Georgia Press, 1991.

Rubin, Louis D. *The Faraway Country: Writers of the Modern South.* Seattle: University of Washington Press, 1963.

❧

Spanish Drama

Jeffrey T. Bersett

EARLY SPAIN

As many critics have noted, it is difficult to identify a true "beginning" for Spanish drama, given the extremely complex nature of the development of Spain as a nation and culture. Even in the most superficial of inquiries, one must consider questions of language, ethnicity, religion and politics when attempting to identify theatrical productions that can be considered "Spanish" in some meaningful way. Early Spanish society consisted of various sociopolitical realities that intertwined and evolved in notably convoluted ways until 1492, when something resembling a unified cultural starting point can be identified. Even this date proves somewhat problematic, though. Among other things, it marks the fall of the Islamic kingdom of Granada and thus the final piece of the "reconquest" of Spain by the Christian monarchs, and also the official expulsion of the Jewish faith, which brought with it forced conversions to Catholicism by those who chose to remain in Spain. These steps toward a sort of cultural homogenization led to other problems, such as tensions between those of "pure blood" (who could prove unpolluted Christian family lines) and *conversos* (members of families converted to Christianity who were not treated as citizens with equal rights).

If nothing else, we know that before 1492 (and, indeed, after) Spain offered a complex mixture of societal influences and cultural trends. It is difficult to comprehend the linguistic diversity that existed on the Iberian peninsula, where people used Latin, numerous Romance dialects, Arabic, and Hebrew. The people who spoke these languages represented varied ethnic and cultural heritages that functioned both independently and in tandem—consider, for example, that tensions among Christians, Muslims, and Jews at times reached open warfare, while at others the three groups coexisted and intermingled in a sort of progressive and productive tolerance. Scholars have raised very real questions about what constitutes the earliest Spanish culture, questions which, for the purposes of the present study, we can pose in terms of drama. Is Spanish drama that work which was written somewhere within the confines of the country that we today call Spain? Should we only consider those works that were written in the particular Romance dialect that would come to be called Castilian (the language that most of the rest of the world refers to as Spanish)? Or—an even more difficult proposition—do we attempt to identify some sort of cultural through-line to later works that are universally acknowledged as part of the Spanish dramatic canon? Most critics today proceed under the assumption that the last of these three questions provides the most sensible approach, though they recognize that the complexities of Spanish culture during the Middle Ages, and the lack of surviving textual evidence, do not allow for easy answers.[1]

It is generally accepted that the earliest Spanish dramas were liturgical in nature. Fernando Lázaro Carreter, for one, is of the opinion that the growth of religious dramatic production may have stemmed from boredom on the part of congregations with routine services and rituals. He also notes how the need to reach the people led to the use of the vernacular rather than Latin (although Latin would remain an important component of liturgical drama into the sixteenth century). The earliest surviving example of religious drama, the *Auto de los reyes magos* (*The Play of the Magi*), dates from the twelfth century. This work, and others from the medieval period, indicate that although the most likely celebrations on the religious calendar for theatrical representations were Easter, Christmas, and Epiphany, they were not the only occasions for such activity. Most notably, the feast of the Assumption provided an opportunity for some of the most elaborate early productions—Assumption plays mounted in various regions of Spain (such as Aragón and Valencia) in the fourteenth century involved elaborate staging and machinery to facilitate the illusion of an ascending Virgin Mary.

Secular drama covered a wide range of subject matter and tone. Political satire and propaganda, on one hand, and love and death, on another, were among the many topics featured in pieces that ran the gamut from simple debate to dynamic spectacle. Critics cite a number of important dramas outside the religious vein, among them Francisco de Madrid's *Égloga* (*Eclogue*, 1495)—a political allegory with propagandistic goals—and Rodrigo de Cota's *Diálogo entre el Amor y un viejo* (*Debate Between Love and an Old Man*, c. 1511). Lázaro Carreter notes that some authors, such as Gómez Manrique, wrote works that are difficult to call "theater," as they rely heavily on their poetry for dramatic effect.

Other key figures of the late medieval period include Juan del Encina (1469–c. 1530), Lucas Fernández (1474–1542) and Gil Vicente (1465–c.1540), all of whom wrote both religious and secular works. We should note also that these authors wrote various allegorical plays, which, as Charlotte Stern indicates, would serve as important predecessors to the *autos sacramentales* ("eucharistic plays") of later centuries, an important component in the history of Spanish drama.

One other title deserves mention here, although its status as drama remains somewhat controversial (it is written in the basic format of a play, with only character names and dialogue on the printed page, and is considered by many to be a work of narrative prose). The *Tragicomedia de Calisto y Melibea* (*The Tragicomedy of Calisto and Melibea*, 1500), known also as *Celestina* (the name of the title characters' go-between), by Fernando de Rojas (c.1475–1541), serves as an important bridge between the Middle Ages and what would follow. James Burke calls it "a very medieval work [that] bears within it indications of radically new ways of conceiving lengthy discourses in prose." A similar assessment can be made of its themes, which include doomed love and corruption—the work thus seems more comprehensively "modern" than other works of its time period. Either way, the *Celestina* carried Spanish literature into a new era, when many cultural and dramatic trends developed in the fourteenth and fifteenth centuries would crystallize into a vibrant new artistic tradition.

THE GOLDEN AGE, 1500–1700

The so-called Golden Age of Spanish art and letters is a complex combination of developments spanning roughly the period between 1500 and 1700. Most critics divide this phase of cultural growth at the midpoint of those two centuries, and describe two separate stages with unique philosophical underpinnings, citing the sixteenth century as the Spanish Renaissance, while identifying the main feature of the seventeenth as the development of the Baroque esthetic. These labels, though simplistic, can be applied to drama and the evolution of Spanish theater during the Golden Age, but do not begin to delineate the richness to be found there.

Spain as a nation experienced unprecedented growth as a world power during the early part of its Golden Age, as the ruling Habsburgs amassed one of the largest global empires the world has ever known. Success in its colonization and exploitation of the Americas provided Spain with unimaginable wealth that, inevitably perhaps, was squandered as the weakness of the monarchy grew with each successive generation. Corruption took hold, as also seems to happen in such situations, and the Habsburg dynasty was doomed by the time that Carlos II, the last Habsburg king of Spain, took the throne in 1665. The seventeenth century is, in part, remembered as a time of decadence and decay for Spain, a decline that initiated the development of a darker philosophical stance, one of the primary features of the Spanish Baroque period.

However, a century and a half before this would occur, Spanish reality (and thus Spanish culture), was in an ascendant phase. In all artistic areas Spaniards were experimenting with new and innovative approaches to the world around them. Duncan Moir indicates that the Renaissance, in terms of drama, began in Spain with Juan del Encina, Lúcas Fernández, and Gil Vicente. The patterns established by these authors were continued well into the sixteenth century by playwrights such as Bartolomé de Torres Naharro (c. 1485–c. 1520), who did most of his work while living in Italy, and Diego Sánchez de Badajoz (d. 1550) who, though he is primarily remembered for his religious plays, also wrote allegory and satirical farce. Melveena McKendrick also asserts that it was during the sixteenth century that Spanish drama became theater, and that "There can be no doubt that until the mid-1550s performed drama in Spain was dominated by the Church and its activities."

Several developments during the second half of the sixteenth century guided the further evolution of Spanish theater. Perhaps the most important of these was the decision on the part of Felipe II to name Madrid as the Spanish capital in 1561, one effect of which was, as Margaret Greer comments, that "this new court city became the principal hub of theatrical activity." The first two major theaters were established some two decades later—the Corral de la Cruz and the Corral del Príncipe were outdoor theaters, as was the practice elsewhere in Spain and Europe, and provided an affordable form of entertainment for a public which quickly came to demand large quantities of dramatic offerings. This led to a massive increase in theatrical production that further refined the Spanish dramatic tradition through a process of experimentation. The result—the three-act Spanish *comedia,* one of Spain's most significant contributions to world drama—is a satisfying art-form whose strength, indeed, is to be found in its flexibility, not just for subject matter, but also for verse form: authors could infuse their works with meaning on a rhythmic level, thus allowing for greater impact than had previously been possible.

Perhaps the greatest practitioner of the *comedia* was Lope Félix de Vega Carpio (1562–1635), one of the most prodigious playwrights ever. Some estimates of his literary production put the total number of plays he wrote at 2,500, of which more than 400 have survived to the present day. His dramatic works run the range from comedy to tragedy, from pastoral to epic, from social and political satire to religious sanctity. One of his great works, *Fuente Ovejuna* (c. 1614), offers a story that highlights concepts of nobility and power, and questions whether honor is the sole domain of those in the ruling classes . *El castigo sin venganza (Punishment without Revenge,* 1631), considered by many critics to be Lope de Vega's masterpiece, exposes "the moral squalor which underlies the fine appearances of a great Court," according to Edward Wilson and Duncan Moir. Victor Dixon claims that the play (along with several other works by Lope), "bear[s] comparison with anything written in Europe during [Lope's] time."

The second great dramatist of the seventeenth century in Spain, if only in chronological terms, was Pedro Calderón de la Barca (1600–81). Calderón, in a clearer fashion than does Lope, represents the baroque sense of esthetic and philosophy that typified the growing sense of skepticism in the Spanish national psyche. While, like Lope, Calderón wrote a number of plays that fall under the category of *comedias de capa y espada* (cape and sword comedies—plays of intrigue that focus on themes of love and honor), he is perhaps best remembered for his more profound examinations of the human condition in plays such as *La vida es sueño* (*Life Is a Dream*, 1635). Although this play does not bear the more obvious darkness of other works by Calderón, it does probe our perceptions of reality through the story of a Polish prince, Segismundo, whose worth is tested by his father. One of numerous possible readings of this play is that it demonstrates that our worldly concerns have only an ephemeral importance, and that we must act in an upright fashion no matter how we interpret the reality around us.

Calderón also composed a number of tragedies that question the potential perils of the Spanish system of honor, plays like *El médico de su honra* (*The Surgeon of His Honor*, 1635), in which a jealous husband extracts vengeance from his wife both literally and figuratively, bleeding her to death when he suspects her of having betrayed him with another nobleman. McKendrick asserts that "This tough, uncompromising play commands our admiration but not our affection, for our sense of outrage is never dispelled."

We should note as well Calderón's great skill in another dramatic genre, for he also wrote a number of distinguished *autos sacramentales*. The most famous of these is *El gran teatro del mundo* (*The Great Theater of the World*, c. 1644), in which, through the use of elaborate allegory, Calderón describes the fleeting nature of our existence. It is with this sort of philosophical focus that Calderón's work most aptly demonstrates the more skeptical nature of his time—the world is no longer a place for the certainties demonstrated in earlier, usually religious, drama. A form of despair (which can be seen to have developed in a parallel fashion to the decline of the once seemingly omnipotent Spanish Empire) has overtaken the civilization of which Calderón is a product, and his work frequently reflects these greater concerns on both microcosmic (personal) and macrocosmic (allegorical) levels.

Other authors whose work had a significant impact on Spanish drama in the seventeenth century include Miguel de Cervantes (1547–1616), Tirso de Molina (c. 1584–1648) and Francisco de Rojas Zorrilla (1607–48), a friend and colleague of Calderón who was, as McKendrick notes, "seventeenth-century Spanish theatre's most uncompromising and ablest satirist."

Cervantes, forever remembered for his *Don Quijote* (Part I—1605, Part II—1615), also wrote a number of important dramatic works, the most famous of which is *El cerco de Numancia* (*The Siege of Numancia*, c.1585). This tragedy, profoundly patriotic in its retelling of "Spanish" heroism in the face of overwhelming odds (the play recounts the valiant defense of Numancia against the invasion of Scipio in the second century B.C.), has been revived at numerous times during Spain's history, most notably during the siege of Madrid during the Spanish Civil War (1936–39).

Tirso de Molina (born Gabriel Téllez) was a Mercedarian monk whose masterpiece, *El burlador de Sevilla o El convidado de piedra* (*The Trickster of Seville or The Stone Guest*, c. 1630) contains the earliest version of the don Juan story. This character has become of world literature's most archetypical figures, and his exploits have been reworked by some of the most famous artists in history, including Mozart and Byron (not to mention José Zorrilla, whose work is described later in this chapter).

One final note regarding the Golden Age should be made, given that this period witnessed the crystallization of the dramatic tradition of short pieces, called *loas* and *entremeses*. *Loas* were comic preludes that opened a session of theater, while *entremeses* were performed between the acts of the featured full-length drama. Cervantes wrote a number of memorable *entremeses*, but was hardly the only author who created such works. These pieces would become a staple of the Spanish theatrical experience, and would remain an important dramatic form well into the twentieth century.

THE EIGHTEENTH CENTURY

Habsburg control of Spain ended in 1700 with the death of Carlos II, and after a brief period of conflict over who would take over the Spanish throne, the French Bourbon dynasty stepped in as rulers of what remained of the Spanish empire. The century which followed, in terms of culture, began a pattern in which European influences arrived over the Pyrenees and were made particularly Spanish. The first example of this process came during the Enlightenment, when French ideals of reason and progress took root in Spain.

The artistic descendents of Lope and Calderón still dominated Spanish drama during the first decades of the eighteenth century, but Ignacio de Luzán's *La poética* (*Poetics*, 1737) called for a return to classical forms. The material in this work which dealt with popular theater in Spain (that is, those works in the tradition of Spain's Golden Age playwrights) identified it as unacceptable in terms of the desire to revive classical concepts of drama. Luzán hoped for the restoration of the classical unities (action, time, and place) in dramatic works, so as to bring a more lifelike representation of reality to the stage.

While many authors did not answer Luzán's call, those who did created a new type of drama in Spain that lasted into the nineteenth century. One of the most important playwrights of the eighteenth, Leandro Fernández de Moratín (1760–1828) wrote two plays of special note in the Spanish neoclassical vein. *La comedia nueva o El café* (*The New Comedy, or The Coffee House*, 1792) satirized the excesses of popular theater, while *El sí de las niñas* (*The Girls' Consent*, 1801, premiered 1806) demonstrated a progressive stance toward the practice of arranged marriages of convenience, among other things. These plays, the latter of which has been called Moratín's masterpiece, demonstrate the playwright's full support of Enlightenment ideals, and thus call for the rejection of unhealthy customs and artistic tendencies.

Other writers who shared Moratín's philosophical and artistic goals included Gaspar Melchor Jovellanos (1744–1811), José de Cadalso (1741–82) and Vicente García de la Huerta (1734–87). Jovellanos and Cadalso are better remembered as writers of nondramatic works, but García de la Huerta's lasting fame is as author of *Raquel* (1778), a play many critics recognize as the finest example of neoclassical tragedy. *Raquel,* in typical Enlightenment fashion, seeks to dissect the problems of the present day (in this case, the dangers of absolutist rule), and does so while staunchly observing the neoclassical unities.

One other essential writer from Spain's eighteenth century bears mention. Ramón de la Cruz (1731–94) specialized in shorter theatrical pieces called *sainetes* (comedy sketches, usually one-act farces). Joaquín Álvarez Barrientos notes that "Though [Cruz] began his career writing in the classical style, he slowly shifted his talents to the most widely appreciated genres, notably the *sainete.*" Cruz was not alone in his departure from neoclassical norms—a number of playwrights, such as Nicasio Álvarez de Cienfuegos (1764–1809), approached drama with a more gothic esthetic. Popular theater as such would survive the Enlightenment and evolve into something entirely different during the early decades of the nineteenth century.

SPANISH ROMANTIC DRAMA IN THE NINETEENTH CENTURY

Spanish drama during the first thirty years of the nineteenth century was a hodgepodge of style and tone, varying from works modeled on Golden Age classics to those descended from Enlightenment ideals.[2] One of the most popular genres was the *comedia de magia* (magical comedy) which featured outrageously complicated plots and staging, and frequently included elaborate machinery to produce required special effects. This sort of spectacle was not new to Spanish theater, but reached a certain peak with works like *La pata de cabra* (*The Goat's Foot*, 1829) by Juan de Grimaldi (1789–1872). David Gies notes that this play "became the most popular play performed in Spain during the first half of the century." However, we remember Grimaldi more as the impresario who brought numerous improvements to the Spanish theater, and who staged some of the most important works of the romantic period.

Romanticism arrived late in Spain relative to the rest of Europe, and when it did it evolved in its own peculiarly Spanish way. The romantic dramas that have had the most lasting impact have a desperate, angry quality, and depict a cruel world in which there are few answers. Given the political and social history of early nineteenth century Spain, these characteristics are not surprising—French invasion and control of Spain at the beginning of the century set in motion a series of events that led to profound difficulties on the part of the Spaniards in establishing and maintaining any sort of governmental stability. This pattern would last into the twentieth century, but many of its most harrowing moments occurred during the years preceding the adoption of romantic tenets as a form of artistic expression.

Thus we find that dramas such as *La conjuración de Venecia* (*The Venice Conspiracy*, 1834), by Francisco Martínez de la Rosa, and *Don Álvaro o la fuerza del sino* (*Don Alvaro, or the Force of Fate*, 1835), by the duque de Rivas (1791–1865) are intense, disturbing works that focus on our inability to control the reality around us. In the case of the latter, the title character's quest for love ends in utter disaster, and the world becomes a place where all hope is futile. The play reaches a climax in which don Álvaro, having lost or destroyed everything dear to him and his beloved (despite his sincere efforts to do right by everyone around him), throws himself off a mountain after shouting "¡Infierno, abre tu boca y trágame!" ("Hell, open your mouth and swallow me!").

The obvious existential despair depicted in this and other romantic works would fade with time. In 1844 José Zorrilla (1817–93) would write the work which, for many critics, closed the door on this extreme form of Spanish romanticism (even though plays of notably romantic nature would continue to appear for decades). It also became the most popular play in the history of Spanish theater, performed even today in annual celebrations of All Souls' Day. *Don Juan Tenorio* is a reworking of the story told in Tirso's *El burlador de Sevilla*, only here don Juan finds forgiveness and salvation through his love for doña Inés, rather than the eternal damnation suffered by Tirso's protagonist. The fact that Zorrilla's don Juan achieves what his immediate dramatic predecessors could not is indication enough that Spanish drama had moved beyond the world of don Álvaro, but what remains fascinating about the play is that Zorrilla uses numerous romantic tropes on the way to saving his don Juan—we get a real sense of the despair of our reality, but hope survives in the end. It is little wonder that the play achieved the iconic popularity it did during later decades.

A similar circumstance can be found in *Baltasar* (1858), by Gertrudis Gómez de Avellaneda (1814–73), one of numerous female dramatists to find success during the nineteenth century in Spain. The play contains romantic trappings similar to those found in *Don Juan Tenorio*, but offers a conclusion in which love and faith bring redemption. However, one must not interpret this seeming pattern as the norm for Spanish drama at mid-century—Spanish society had by this point begun moving in a new direction, and various artists would step forward to represent new concerns.

THE LATE NINETEENTH CENTURY: HIGH COMEDY, MELODRAMA, AND SHORT THEATER FORMS

The growing middle class became, collectively, an increasingly important voice in Spanish culture during the middle portion of the nineteenth century, and those topics of import to the bourgeoisie became topics of import for writers and other artists of the day. In terms of drama, this trend took the form of the *alta comedia* (high comedy). Gies asserts that "the *alta comedia* comprises one of the best series of documents we possess about the Spanish middle class, that is, the *upper* middle class, since the plays capture not only the anxieties but also the manners, customs, look, frailties, and strengths of this newly privileged segment of society." One obvious theme in plays such as these is financial security, and this is demonstrated in plays such as *El tanto por ciento* (*The Percentage*, 1861), by Adelardo López de Ayala (1828–79), whose plot deals primarily with an important real estate deal involved in the construction of a canal. The play demonstrates the fact that in Spain at this time dramatic heroes are no longer concerned with achieving eternal salvation (or even the most minimal existential comfort), but rather financial solvency.

The *alta comedia* was one form of theater which laid the groundwork for the development of realist drama. As in the rest of Europe (but again, as with romanticism and other cultural movements, somewhat later than elsewhere), Spain began to see a growing predominance of the realist mode in the last decades of the nineteenth century. A number of authors (some more "realist" than others, to be sure) deserve attention here, especially given the wide variety of offerings available in Spanish theater.

The most recognized figure from this period, and arguably the most important literary figure in Spain during the second half of the nineteenth century, is Benito Pérez Galdós (1843–1920), noted primarily for his prose narrative, and in particular for his stunning novels about contemporary (and historical) Spain. His drama must be acknowledged as well, though, and at its best—as in *Electra* (1901), considered by many to be Galdós's dramatic masterpiece—Galdós's ability to comment metaphorically on the problems of contemporary society still has resonance today. We can see more overtly socialist leanings in works by authors such as Joaquín Dicenta (1863–1917). His *Juan José* (1895) captures, with no small amount of anger, the unfair treatment of the working class by their socioeconomic superiors. The play, and others like it, reveal the tensions that had been building in Spanish society for decades, as the workers began to unite as a political force.

A much different type of drama can be found in the plays of José Echegaray (1832–1916), whose work bore little comparison to that of Galdós and Dicenta. Considered by most as a neo-romantic practitioner of melodrama, Echegaray's plays were extremely popular in his day. The most notable of these is *El gran galeoto* (*The Great Galeoto*, 1881), which uses the hyper-emotional sensibilities of romanticism in combination with a clever framework that creates various levels of dramatic reality to present a number of societal problems, such as a compulsive penchant for gossip. We should note that, of the great writers of the late nineteenth century in Spain, it was Echegaray, not Galdós, who eventually won the Nobel Prize for literature (in 1904)—although most critics today agree that it was Galdós whose work was more inventive and representative of his time, the Nobel Committee praised Echegaray for having tapped into the great traditions of Spanish theater.

Another important development in the last decades of the nineteenth century was the explosion in popularity of short theater forms. In locations that ranged from the major theaters to local coffee houses, short plays were being performed every day and, in some cases, all day. Some establishments admitted customers on a system of *teatro por horas* (theater by the hour), and offered a wide variety of comedic sketches, musical revues, and one-act plays. Of this last type of drama, we see a vast number of works being written in the parodic or satiric mode, taking famous theater pieces and mocking them through the filter of the day's concerns. A frequent target was Zorrilla's *Don Juan Tenorio*, which received treatments in seemingly every register possible—as *comedia alta*, as socialist drama, even as pornography, to name just a few. This trend would continue well into the twentieth century, where we find feminist *Tenorios*, as well as don Juan playing soccer and fighting bulls. One interpretation of the apparent need to appropriate Zorrilla's play is that it demonstrates its continuing popularity—as long as it remained in the collective consciousness of Spanish theatergoers, it would be fodder for other playwrights. Don Juan was not the only target, though, and frequently a serious drama would premiere, only to have its parody appear days later on another stage. This sort of irreverent handling of both theatrical tradition and present day trends served as notice that the pace of change, both socially and artistically, was accelerating. It is a noteworthy precursor of the vast amount of artistic experimentation that would occur in the early decades of the twentieth century.

BEYOND REALISM: THE TWENTIETH CENTURY

The turn of the twentieth century marked a time of profound crisis for Spain. The disastrous Spanish-American War of 1898 had left the country stripped of what little remained of its once massive empire, and Spaniards searched desperately for a new form of national identity. Discussion ranged from a nationalistic level, recalling the lost great days of bygone eras, to one of sheer existential anxiety. Artistically, this quest was best represented by the so-called Generation of 1898, which consisted of intellectuals and authors like Miguel de Unamuno (1875–1939), Antonio Machado (1875–1939) and Ramón María del Valle-Inclán (1869–1936), only the last of whom is remembered as a dramatist.

Valle-Inclán's most important contribution to Spanish drama was the *esperpento,* a type of work that filters reality as if through a funhouse mirror, distorting our world to reveal its grotesque nature. His theory of the *esperpento* is found explicitly communicated in a number of places in his writing, including one of his best plays, *Luces de bohemia* (*Lights of Bohemia,* 1920). His works display the grotesque through a carnivalesque take on life, in which the author (and thus the audience) view the world in a fashion that highlights both the aforementioned distortion, but also with a sense of distance, in an attempt to observe without being directly involved in the pain to be found there. The use of carnival is frequently explicit, as can be seen in plays such as *Martes de carnaval* (*Mardi Gras,* 1930) and *Divinas palabras* (*Divine Words,* 1933), in which the horrific passions and greed of a group of rural circus people become representative of the universal struggle to find answers of any kind.

The experimentation with dramatic form and content in Spanish theater continued during the first three decades of the twentieth century, and produced a number of (sometimes bizarre) avant-garde productions. One great writer who participated in the search for new modes of expression was Federico García Lorca (1898–1936), whose life and literary career are now legendary. A poet and playwright, Lorca held firmly to his rural Andalusian roots while developing sophisticated new poetic sensibilities. Two of his most accomplished works are *Bodas de sangre* (*Blood Wedding,* 1933) and *La casa de Bernarda Alba* (*The House of Bernarda Alba,* 1936, not produced until 1945 in Argentina). The latter play, an exploration of personal repression as represented by a family of women ruled heartlessly by a cruel matriarch, can be seen as symbolic of Lorca's thoughts on the political possibilities in Spain, thoughts which would prove prophetic—the Spanish Civil War, begun in 1936 after Lorca had already completed *Bernarda Alba,* would end with the rise to power of Francisco Franco, the fascist dictator who would rule Spain until his death in 1975. Lorca would not live long enough to see even the Civil War, as he was executed in 1936 by the Spanish Civil Guard, the rural police force that, perhaps not ironically in hindsight, had appeared in a number of his poems as the agents of the very oppression against which he struggled.

Franco's rise to power, and the government that he shaped around himself, brought with it the severe limitation of artistic liberty in Spain until the end of the dictatorship. Not surprisingly, dramatists who wrote works of the "official" theater thrived, with the sponsorship of the government, but these pieces remain little more than historic footnotes due to their propagandistic nature, as do many comedies which can only be called light escapist fare. Some writers, however, managed to work within and around the strict censorship that was a hallmark of the Franco dictatorship. One such author, Antonio Buero Vallejo (1916–2000), had at one point even been condemned to death by the new government. He survived this to go on to become one of Spain's most prolific and creative dramatists of the twentieth century. In works such as *Las meninas* (1960), *El concierto de San Ovidio* (*The Concert at Saint Ovide*, 1962) and *El tragaluz* (*The Basement Window*, 1967), Buero created strategies through which he could symbolically criticize the realities of life under Franco without attracting the attention of the censors. For example, he sets *El concierto de San Ovidio* in eighteenth century France, and tells the story of a blind orchestra organized by a ruthless impresario. The parallels to contemporary Spain (in Buero's opinion a country populated by people who are figuratively blind either out of ignorance or by choice) are obvious, as they are in many of his plays. There were other successful writers of social and political drama during the latter part of the Franco dictatorship, such as Lauro Olmo (1923–94) and Alfonso Sastre (b. 1926). Sastre, like Buero, has taken a violently conflictive reality and tried to apply to it a humanistic vision that allows us to understand the world in which we live and, especially in the case of Buero, give us some hope of a potentially positive future toward which to strive.

With the death of Franco and the end of fascist censorship, Spanish culture experienced a dizzying transition to a new democracy, a transition which for some has not yet ended. The new level of freedom available has been joyously (and excessively, in some cases) embraced, and its effects are staggering. Madrid finds itself no longer the center of the Spanish theatrical universe, as Barcelona and other cities have stepped to the fore as thriving cultural communities. Drama itself has also become de-centered—Sharon Feldman posits that "Since the transition to democracy, the theatre of Spain has evolved into a cacophonous state of aesthetic heterogeneity, cultural diversity, and linguistic plurality that is truly unprecedented in modern times."

In a tentative way, then, we can observe certain similarities between the context in which Spanish drama found its earliest voices and those in which it exists today. Medieval Spain was a multiethnic, multicultural society that lived in conflict within itself, between its constituent parts—in a most basic sense a parallel to today's more complex world. The conflicts faced today have arisen in a fashion which fails to surprise: after three and a half decades of enforced homogeneity (from political and religious beliefs to the very language used in every aspect of everyday life), Spaniards are now citizens of a freer world in which a multitude of options lies before them. Their culture and, consequently, their drama reflect the complexities of this new context.

NOTES

1. The present study is greatly indebted to a number of scholarly works regarding Spanish culture and drama. Those contributions will be noted as appropriate, but to begin we should note the particular usefulness of the recent *Cambridge History of Spanish Literature* (Gies 2004), an essential resource for anyone needing a thorough introduction to Spanish literature.

2. In fact, the entire nineteenth century in terms of drama is so vastly complex that what follows in the present study cannot possibly capture even a fraction of its richness and variety. An argument can be made for this being the true Golden Age of Spanish theater. See *The Theatre in Nineteenth-Century Spain* (Gies 1994).

FURTHER READING

Barrientos, Joaquín Álvarez. "Neoclassical versus popular theatre." In Gies, 2004.

Burke, James. "Medieval Spanish prose." In Gies, 2004.

Dixon, Victor. "Lope Félix de Vega Carpio." In Gies, 2004.

Feldman, Sharon G. "Post-Franco theatre." In Gies, 2004.

Fucilla, Joseph G. Introduction, *Raquel*. by Vicente García de la Huerta. Madrid: Catedra, 1984.

Gies, David T. *The Theatre in Nineteenth-Century Spain*. Cambridge: Cambridge University Press, 1994.

———, ed. *The Cambridge History of Spanish Literature*. Cambridge: Cambridge University Press, 2004.

Greer, Margaret R. "The development of national theatre." In Gies, 2004.

Lázaro Carreter, Fernando, ed. *Teatro medieval*. 2nd ed. Madrid: Editorial Castalia (Odres Nuevos), 1965.

McKendrick, Melveena. *Theatre in Spain, 1490–1700*. Cambridge: Cambridge University Press, 1989.

Menocal, María Rosa. *The Ornament of the World*. New York: Little, Brown, 2000.

Rivas, Duque de. *Don Álvaro o la fuerza del sino*. Edited by Donald L. Shaw. Madrid: Castalia, 1986.

Ruiz Ramón, Francisco. *Historia del teatro español, Siglo XX*. Madrid: Cátedra, 1977.

Santiáñez, Nil. "Great masters of Spanish Modernism." In Gies, 2004.

Stern, Charlotte D. "The medieval theatre: between *scriptura* and *theatrica*." In Gies, 2004.

Wilson, Edward M. and Duncan Moir. *The Golden Age: Drama, 1492–1700*. A Literary History of Spain 3. New York: Barnes & Noble, 1971.